TECHNIQUES IN
GEOMORPHOLOGY

Cuchlaine A. M. King M.A. Ph.D.
Professor of Geography, University of Nottingham

EDWARD ARNOLD

© C. A. M. King 1966
First published 1966 by
Edward Arnold (Publishers) Ltd
41 Maddox Street, London W1R 0AN
Reprinted 1967
Reprinted 1971

SBN: 7131 5238 9

Printed in Great Britain by
ROBERT CUNNINGHAM AND SONS LTD., ALVA

PREFACE

Many books have been written about geomorphology, but nearly all are concerned with the results of geomorphological studies rather than with the methods by which these results have been achieved. The purpose of this book is to illustrate, by means of specific examples, some of the techniques that have been developed to further the aim of the geomorphologist, which is to understand the genesis of landscape. Because of the great variety of landforms the methods of investigating the different features must vary, and this variation has been dealt with by discussing each major geomorphological process separately, the chapters being divided on this basis.

Geomorphology is essentially a field study; the emphasis has, therefore, been placed on field work. However, not all the problems can be solved in the field, partly because of the great complexity of geomorphological processes in nature; other methods of attacking the problems must be considered. The controlled conditions obtainable in models are very useful for studying many processes, and model study can often link the field observations with the basic theoretical research that is essential to a full understanding of the action of the geomorphological processes that create the visible landscape. Like many other branches of learning geomorphology is becoming more quantitative in its methods, and statistical techniques play their part in many stages of study; they provide a sound basis for field sampling, for assessing the significance of the results and for establishing correlations. The laboratory analysis of sediment samples can often provide data that are of considerable geomorphological significance. Empirical relationships can often form a useful preliminary to analytical studies and can be set up both from field observations and by cartographic analysis; but to be of value they must depend on quantitative measurement.

In such a wide field the discussion must clearly be very selective, but in the, examples that have been chosen both the methods and the results are given because by considering the results obtained by the use of any particular technique its potentiality can be more profitably demonstrated. The intention has been to show, in some measure, how far progress in geomorphology has reached and how this is being achieved. Some of the methods described are simple, but others rely on complex equipment beyond the scope of many geomorphologists. No attempt has been made to describe this equipment in detail, but where possible references have been given.

ACKNOWLEDGEMENTS

I would like to acknowledge gratefully the helpful comments made by those who have read parts of the manuscript, and I would like to thank all those authors who have kindly given me permission to use their figures. I am also grateful to the following for permission to publish figures that originally appeared in their publications: The Institution of Civil Engineers for figures 3.1 and 4.2, the Glaciological Society for figures 3.4, 4.12 and 5.13, and the Coastal Engineering Research Center (formerly the Beach Erosion Board) for figures 3.10, 3.14, 3.16, 4.1, 4.6, 4.8, and 4.9.

CONTENTS

1 INTRODUCTION

The aim of geomorphology is to understand the shape of the earth and to elucidate the processes at work on its surface; this goal is far from easy to achieve on account of the complexity of the phenomena and processes involved. However, an ever growing number of increasingly elaborate and delicate techniques are becoming available to achieve this end. Before discussing these techniques it is useful to examine very briefly the origin and development of geomorphology and to consider the type of problem to be solved and the broad methods of approach that are frequently used.

THE DEVELOPMENT OF GEOMORPHOLOGY

Geomorphology has developed from the work of the late eighteenth- and nineteenth-century geologists and hydrologists. Their work and views have been described in detail by Chorley, Dunn and Beckinsale (1964) in their book on the history of the science of geomorphology. The development of geological and geomorphological thought was strongly controlled in Europe by the acceptance of the idea of uniformitarianism, first proposed at the turn of the eighteenth and nineteenth centuries and stressed by Charles Lyell in his *Principles of Geology* first published in 1830. Uniformitarianism is based on the view that the present is the key to the past, that the processes acting at present have acted throughout geological time and that changes in landforms, although slow, can be far-reaching. Given enough time whole landscapes can be created and destroyed again by the operation of slow yet relentless forces. This view was a great advance on the ideas of the 'catastrophic' school of thought; as long as it was held that the world was created suddenly in 4004 B.C. and that all phenomena were due to catastrophic events, such as Noah's flood, progress was impossible. On the other hand, uniformitarianism can be taken too far; it is easy to appreciate that the occasional extreme flood accomplishes more change in a river valley than the intervening years of more normal flow. On a larger scale, glaciation can be shown to have had a world-wide effect, either directly or indirectly, on the landscape of the world at present, though throughout most of geological time there appears to have been no ice on the earth. Again, the landscapes of the earth at any point in time are unique so that, even if the processes acting throughout time were uniform, the resulting landscapes would differ. Although a broad cyclic pattern on a world-wide scale may be identifiable in the processes acting on the earth, their effect on the landscape will be unique as they act on different configurations. The escape from the ideas of extreme catastrophism, nevertheless, opened the way for the development of modern ideas on the genesis of landforms.

James Hutton, who lived from 1726 to 1797, laid the foundations on which modern geomorphology has been constructed. He first studied chemistry and medicine, but later became interested in agriculture, which led him to study the origin of soil and the processes of geology. He was no narrow specialist and had contact with scientists in many fields, for example James Watt, the inventor of the steam engine. It was to the newly organised Royal Society of Edinburgh that in 1785 he read his first important paper entitled 'Theory of the Earth, or an investigation of the laws observable in the composition, dissolution and restoration of land upon the Globe'. This was followed in 1795 by his larger work in two volumes *A theory of the Earth, with proofs and illustrations*. These works show the influence on Hutton of the writing of G. H. Toulmin, whose contribution has been largely forgotten. Toulmin accepted the doctrine of uniformitarianism, believing that slow processes, if they continued long enough, could effect large changes. Like Toulmin, Hutton believed in the orderliness of nature, that its development proceeded along an orderly course, whereby destruction led to construction. Hutton stated that nature was systematic, coherent and reasonable, and that the uniformitarian view of the evolution of landscape was more satisfactory than the catastrophic view. This view is summarised in his words 'no vestige of a beginning, no prospect of an end'. It is likely that Hutton's medical training and his work on the circulation of the blood helped him, by analogy, towards his views concerning the circulation of matter in the growth and decay of landscapes. He does himself use such analogies in his major work published in 1795, towards the end of his life, referring to the physiology of the earth.

It was unfortunate that Hutton's work was written in rather obscure language and did not make the immediate impact that it deserved. However this disadvantage was partially overcome by the great work of John Playfair in making the views of Hutton available in a clear and attractive form. In 1802 Playfair published his *Illustrations of the Huttonian theory of the Earth*, a book which greatly influenced Charles Lyell. Playfair, who was a professor of mathematics and philosophy in Edinburgh, not only clarified Hutton's views, but also added many valuable contributions of his own. Again however, it was some decades before these new views seriously modified geological thought. The mathematical ability of Playfair enabled him to see that by integrating the tiny fraction of time that any one man can experience in his own life-time it is possible to appreciate the long periods of geological time and the events that had taken place within them. Playfair was aware of the power of rivers and glaciers to erode and the part they play in transporting waste material; he stated that 'The Alps are but a vaste ruin'. Playfair was also struck by the balance between the forces forming the soil and those of mass movement, by which means a fairly uniform thickness of soil could be maintained beneath a cover of vegetation. On the origin of valleys Playfair was also far in advance of the views current at this time. Valleys were considered to be independent of the rivers flowing in them. He showed that rivers could develop a graded profile and implied superimposition and antecedence.

It seems strange that such a lucid account of landscape development should not have been accepted more readily. Charles Lyell in his first edition of *The Principles* followed Playfair, but it was not until the last half of the nineteenth century that his views came to be widely accepted. This was partly because Lyell in the later editions of his book turned away from subaerialism and stressed unduly the importance of marine erosion. A good word was put in for Hutton and Playfair by C. G. Greenwood in 1857, when he published a paper entitled 'Rain and rivers: or Hutton and Playfair against Lyell and all comers'. This recognition of the work of subaerial processes led away from the emphasis placed on marine erosion in Britain at this time. Greenwood has been called the father of modern subaerialism, and one of his important contributions was to stress the importance of rainwash relative to the work actually done by the river itself, although he did recognise the importance of rivers as agents of transport. He put forward the idea of the base-level of erosion before Powell in America.

Mention must be made of one of the most important names in the science of geomorphology, William Morris Davis, as it is generally recognised that he did more than any other single man to found the subject, even if his views can no longer be held in their entirety. However, Davis, who lived from 1850 to 1934, built on a strong foundation laid by other American geologists who worked in the latter part of the nineteenth century. J. W. Powell has already been mentioned, but the best known of these workers is G. K. Gilbert, who has been called the first true geomorphologist, and he was also an excellent geologist in other fields.

The work of Gilbert is as valuable for his scientific contribution as for his masterly use of scientific method and his analysis of it. In his investigations he used four essential elements; first he observed the features to be studied and arranged these observations in orderly fashion; next he invented hypotheses to account for the antecedents of the features; thirdly he deduced the consequences expected to follow from his hypotheses; and finally he would test the consequences against new observations. Thus he set the method of geomorphological analysis on a sound and logical base, the fruitful results of which can be seen in his own work.

The best-known is his paper on the geology of the Henry Mountains and his study of the shorelines of Lake Bonneville, the forerunner of the Great Salt Lake, while his work on the action of running water was of a very high standard and is still of value. He stressed the importance of creative imagination, of testing a number of hypotheses, and of analogies in the field of geomorphology. His great influence came not so much from the conclusions presented in his papers, as from the logical reasoning that led to these conclusions, which often carried his arguments beyond their obvious limit, to explain apparently unrelated phenomena. Nevertheless his introduction of the concept of grade was of great importance, and his attempt to arrive at a quantitative study of factors such as river volume, velocity and gradient foreshadowed much more recent developments. C. E. Dutton, 1841-1912, from his work in the Colorado area, made many useful contributions to geomorphology, particularly with regard to the ability of subaerial erosion to produce an extensive plane surface.

It is interesting to note that the American geologists of this time were not troubled by the problems of marine versus subaerial erosion; on the whole they considered only the capacity of the latter processes, because much of this early work was carried out in the centre of a large continental land mass. On the other hand, British geologists, working in a small island group, were much more concerned with the power of the sea, and marine erosion was considered for many years to be more powerful than subaerial erosion in producing large areas of planation.

W. M. Davis was born in America but he travelled very widely; his major work on geomorphology *Die erklärende Beschreibung der Landformen* was written in German in 1912, and he greatly influenced the development of the subject in Britain and elsewhere during his many visits and by his writings; he taught in Cambridge, Oxford, Berlin and Paris, apart from his main centre at Harvard, where he was professor of physical geography. He published a great deal of work on many geomorphological problems ranging from glacial scenery to coral islands and deserts, to all of which he brought his clear analytical mind. According to S. W. Wooldridge, Davis 'towers above predecessors and successors, like a monadnock above one of his own pene-plains'; he has been called the great definer and analyst. It is in this that he has perhaps had most effect on the course of geomorphology, his essential contribution being, according to his own opinion, to systematise the succession of forms in an ideal cycle and to procure a terminology.

The idea of a cycle of erosion was not entirely new, but he systematised the concept and described representative and recognisable forms for each stage. Having evolved a so-called 'normal' or fluvial cycle, he then went on to develop glacial, arid and karstic cycles. To his critics, who complained of over-simplification, he replied that he had deliberately simplified his description, but that complication, such as changes in base-level or climate, could be allowed for under his scheme. It is interesting to note that Davis was keen to show that geomorphology, as treated by him, belonged to the field of geography; his views on this are worth quoting: 'It is important, however, to insist that the geographer needs to know the meaning, the explanation, and the origin of the forms he looks at, simply because of the aid thus received when he attempts to observe and describe them carefully' (*Geographical Essays*, p. 253). Davis points out the difference of view-point between geographers and geologists concerning geomorphology: the geologist examines the past for its own sake, inasmuch as geology is concerned with the history of the earth; the geographer examines the past only in so far as it illumines the present. The geographical cycle, as proposed by Davis in the *Geographical Journal* for 1899, has remained a basic concept of landscape evolution for many years.

Perhaps the most valuable facet of this concept is the emphasis placed on the three factors on which landscape development depends. Landscape, according to Davis, is a function of structure, process and time, the last factor being of the most practical value in geographical description, while structure is the foundation on which the landscape is built. One of the major criticisms of Davis' work is that he ignored the study of process, the second of his three factors, and to a certain extent this criticism is justified; it has been left to modern geomorphologists to concentrate on this aspect.

It is interesting to note that, although Davis was a mathematician, he did not feel the need to express any of his ideas quantitatively, and in no instance does he use mathematical formulae in his work. Davis strongly influenced geomorphological thought in America, although amongst geographers at least there has more recently been a change of approach, and in Europe his influence was rather varied. In England his work was received with interest and good will but it has not taken deep root, while in France it has been stated that Davis is more celebrated than known. In South Africa, Australia and New Zealand his views were accepted readily, at least for a time, but it was in Germany that they were most effectively opposed by alternative ideas.

The generalisations and simplifications made by Davis and more particularly by his followers did not appeal to the Germans, who desire thoroughness; also in Germany the work of von Richthofen was already well established. F. von Richthofen lived from 1833 to 1905 and in 1886 produced his work on the genetic treatment of landforms, in which he supported a marine origin for plains found beneath marine transgressions, these being produced when sea-level is rising slowly. The main critics of Davis' views in Germany were his personal friends, Albrecht and Walther Penck, while in turn Davis' criticisms of their work, and particularly that of the son Walther, have played no small part in its later misunderstanding by most geomorphologists. Walther Penck, unlike Davis, looked at the study of landforms from a geological point of view and the aim of his work was to determine, by studying the present landscape, the nature of the internal forces that had acted and were acting upon it. Penck's major work *Die Morphologische Analyse* which was originally published posthumously by his father in 1922, is incomplete. This fact and the obscure and difficult German in which it is written led to its being either misunderstood or ignored. A translation in English, published in 1953, has revived interest in Penck's views, and although many of these are not tenable, they are of value in that they compel more careful study of concepts taken too easily for granted.

A more recent contribution (Simons, 1962) has drawn attention to some of the more common and important misconceptions concerning Penck's work, which have resulted from his own obscure style and the faulty criticisms of Davis. Some of the misunderstanding arises from Penck's attempt to relate the characteristic slope form to the nature of crustal movement, the centre of his problem. In attempting to arrive at a solution of this problem he divides the forces at work into the exogenetic forces, acting externally on the earth's surface, and the endogenetic forces, acting internally within the earth and represented by movements of the crust. The exogenetic forces cannot begin work until the internal forces have raised up a land mass for them to operate on. Penck's aim is to elucidate the character of the endogenetic forces from the visible effect of the exogenetic forces on the earth's surface which represents a field of reaction between the opposing forces. If the two sets of forces are working at the same intensity a state of equilibrium will be achieved; this does not occur only when both sets of forces are nil. The character of land forms is dependent on the ratio of intensity between the exogenetic and endogenetic processes. According to Penck the three elements that must be studied are the exogenetic processes, the endogenetic processes and the actual morphological features that depend on their interaction.

Penck points out that it is necessary to study both the forms of denudation and the depositional character of the sediments derived from the destruction of the land, to enable correlation of denudation and deposition in any system. This is a point which could well be considered more often in modern geomorphological analyses. Morphological analysis according to Penck is 'the procedure of deducing the course and development of crustal movement from the exogenetic processes and the morphological features' as stated in the translation of his own words. Penck makes an interesting distinction between denudation and erosion. The former term he uses to denote the movement downslope of material first prepared by weathering, a process which acts mainly on valley sides of considerable areal extent and which can never make a slope steeper. It is implied that weathering and preparation must operate at a similar rate to denudation. Erosion is a term reserved for the cutting of solid rock by a moving geomorphological agent, such as a river, glacier or the wind; it operates mainly linearly, particularly where rivers are concerned, and removes unweathered material. Only erosion, by producing a new type of slope, can cause a hill-side to become steeper. The principle of flattening of slopes under the processes of denudation is an important element in Penck's thought.

One of Penck's most valuable contributions was the attention he focused on the development of slopes. Their formation is an important aspect of his interpretation of the internal crustal movements. But it is also in this field that he has been most misunderstood. He is usually thought to have stated that convex slopes are caused by accelerating uplift, although in fact he never did. He thought that convex slopes result from an increasing rate of river erosion, when relative relief is also increasing. An even more serious misinterpretation is the view that Penck thought that slopes retreated parallel to themselves under certain conditions. In fact Penck considered that, although all inclined surfaces retreat parallel to themselves, another surface forms at their foot at a lower gradient, and this grows upwards at the expense of the steeper slope above and, as the steep parts are denuded more rapidly than the flatter, they therefore consume the flatter parts above on an originally convex hill crest. As the development proceeds, however, the lower, gentler slopes extend uphill at the expense of the steeper and the slope flattens with time, provided there is no erosion by the river at the base of the slope. Penck, therefore, was more in favour of slope flattening than parallel retreat, as shown in figure 1.1. This is a corollary of his view that, everything else being equal, the rate of retreat of any part of a slope is proportional to its steepness.

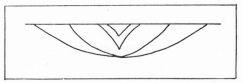

FIGURE 1.1. Diagram to illustrate W. Penck's views on slope development.

Penck's criticism of Davis' supposed instantaneous uplift of his ideal landscape at the beginning of the cycle of erosion is also valid and helpful, although it was clearly only for simplicity that Davis considered the uplift as instantaneous. It is clear that uplift and erosion take place simultaneously, and often the amount of erosion taking place during uplift is very great, owing to the increasing relief; this is often apparent in the nature of the deposits that are associated with this stage of the earth movements. An example of the relationship between earth movements, denudation and erosion and the accompanying deposition can be seen in parts of New Zealand, where earth movements that are geologically very recent have taken place. Although the crustal uplift dates mainly from the Pleistocene and is still operative in some parts, already major mountain chains have been reduced by up to 12,000 feet by erosion. The intensity of erosion is demonstrated by the very coarse nature of some of the associated deposits, for example the Great Marlborough Conglomerate. This deposit attains many hundreds of feet in thickness and its very coarse nature testifies to the intensity of erosion on very steep slopes that must have produced it. Erosion was, therefore, extremely active during the process of crustal upheaval, which took place in some areas along fault lines.

Thus although many of Penck's views may not be tenable, he did a great service to geomorphology in drawing attention to slope forms and the processes operating on them and in pointing out some of the weaknesses in the theories of Davis, whose lucidity and persuasive argument made his views perhaps too readily accepted.

MODERN GEOMORPHOLOGY

The early work in geomorphology led to a variety of different methods of approach, from which developed several schools of thought. There are three major groups; the first arises out of the work of Penck, and may be called the mobilistic view. The second gives priority to the effects of climate in studying the characteristics of the landscape, while the third is based essentially on the idea of correlation by altitude and may be termed the eustatic view.

The extreme mobilistic view has collected relatively few followers since the time of W. Penck, and many of these come from Germany, although less extreme views are held by workers in the school of Grenoble. The latter hold that stability is unlikely to last long enough to enable wide erosion surfaces to form, and they criticise the large number of erosion levels that some geomorphologists postulate. They seek to show that many such flats are the result of glacial action or structural control and that true erosional flats are indeed rare, particularly in young mountains where instability is still apparent. Such workers tend to push back into older periods, such as early Tertiary or pre-Triassic, such surfaces as cannot be explained by other means. World-wide conditions appear to have been more stable during these times than in the recent geological past. This applies particularly to the incontestable erosion surfaces of the more ancient and stable massifs.

The views of Bourcart on continental flexure suggest movement of the land rather than the sea and may, therefore, be included in this category. French and Soviet writers also support these views, as seen in the work of Cailleux and Tricart (1954). This school of thought considers that the most normal type of landscape is one in which the rate of crustal uplift more or less keeps pace with denudation and erosion, thus leading to a landscape of moderate relief. In contrast the areas of very high relief, in extremely unstable crustal conditions on the one hand, and areas of very low relief, indicative of extreme crustal stability on the other hand, are in their view both relatively rare. However, these workers often do not belong to the pure mobilistic school, as they also consider that climate plays an important part in landscape development, while Penck did not consider it of great importance.

A modern school of geomorphologists is growing up and centring its views on the significance of variations of climate in accounting for different types of landscape features. It was long ago realised that extremes of climate such as glacial and desert conditions could produce their own distinctive landscapes, but the much subtler subdivisions that are now proposed and the emphasis now placed on processes operating at different rates under different climatic regimes have carried this point of view much further. The work of Peltier on the periglacial cycle and his division of the earth into morphogenetic regions based on variations in climatic conditions gave prominence to this method of approach. L. C. King (1953) places process first in importance in the list of Davis' three factors. From this it follows that climate is one of the most important elements in determining the landscape type, as process is partially dependent on the character of the climate. Subsequently however, he considered that the differences between the humid-temperate, semi-arid and arid landscapes are only a matter of degree. Nevertheless he holds that the term 'normal' is a misnomer if its use is restricted to the humid-temperate landscape as suggested by Davis; in King's view the semi-arid climate has more claim to normality on the ground that pediplanation is more widespread than peneplanation and occurs even outside the semi-arid environment. It is worth noting in this connection that it is only during the Tertiary period that swards of grass and other covering vegetation have developed, and that in the earlier geological ages the effect of vegetation on slope development must have been very different, and probably more akin to the part it now plays in the semi-arid environment.

Climate plays an important part in the character of slope development and partly through this it affects the development of the river and its valley. Many terrace features can be explained, particularly in the upper reaches of rivers, by changes in the load-water discharge ratio, rather than by changes in base-level. In fact these two factors often operate in the opposite direction, particularly when changes from very cold to milder conditions are taking place. Thus in periglacial phases the upper reaches of a river valley may be undergoing aggradation because, as a result of the cold, reduced vegetation allows more waste to reach the river and a reduction in river flow is caused by freezing, while in the lower reaches rejuvenation may be taking place as a result of glacial lowering of sea-level. The reverse argument applies during the interglacial phases, with aggradation in the lower reaches and erosion in the upper reaches, as the load decreases in proportion to the discharge (figure 1.2).

It is true that nearly all landscapes are polygenetic in nature at the present time, which is so close in time to the colder periods of the Pleistocene. They show the influence of two or more climatic types; thus deserts show evidence of wetter periods, and the temperate areas often show evidence of periglacial or glacial processes having been in operation. This complicates geomorphological analysis because present forms are in many instances not adjusted to the processes now acting on them. This gives weight to the views of the school of thought that emphasises the importance of the climatic element in landscape evolution.

It is generally recognised that the end result of a long period of erosion under relatively stable conditions gives rise to a surface of low relief, called by Davis the peneplain. However, more recently the term 'pediplain' has been proposed to describe the end result of long-continued erosion in an area of semi-arid or similar type climate. Some authorities, for example L. C. King, go so far as to deny the existence anywhere of a peneplain in the Davisian sense. Most geomorphologists would not go to these extremes and they recognise that the end product of long-continued erosion in different climatic types leads to rather different landscapes.

The third point of view in its more rigid form probably has few adherents at the present time. The eustatic theory was fostered by the work of Suess in the early period; in the second volume of his major work *Das Antlitz der Erde* published in 1888 he put forward his 'eustatic theory' in which he expressed his view that most of the continental areas, apart from the orogenic belts, remained stable and that changes of level were due to world-wide fluctuations of sea-level of an eustatic nature. If this premise is accepted then it follows that erosion surfaces may be correlated by altitude over very wide areas. The changes of sea-level were thought to be due to slow filling of the ocean basins by sediments, causing transgressions, followed by basin formation and a more rapid regression. These views were widely held at the beginning of the twentieth century and continued to exert their influence strongly for the first three decades. The optimism of the adherents to these views can be seen by the setting up of an international commission at the

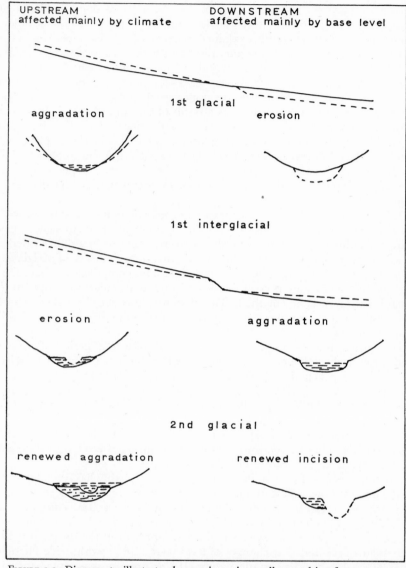

FIGURE 1.2. Diagram to illustrate changes in a river valley resulting from upstream changes of load and discharge ratio and downstream changes of base-level.

International Geographical Congress in 1926 to work out the world-wide correlation of Pliocene and Pleistocene marine and fluvial eustatic levels. One of the most influential workers in this field, H. Baulig, in his work on the Central Plateau of France, which was later incorporated into his more general work on sea-level changes (1933), had a profound effect on the development of British geomorphology. The search for past base-levels by the techniques of denudation chronology became associated with the eustatic theory, and correlation by altitude only is still not entirely abandoned, despite the warning by D. L. Linton (1957). Most geomorphologists are now aware of the dangers of this approach.

GEOMORPHOLOGY IN BRITAIN

British geomorphologists have devoted much work in the last two decades to elucidating the denudation chronology of relatively small areas of the country. The results of this work cannot always be easily linked together, either from the point of view of the number of erosion surfaces suggested or of their mode of origin. Such difficulties are to be expected on account of the nature of the evidence and the character of the land; some probably arise through differences in the interpretation of the evidence. Some workers find evidence for a large number of surfaces at very closely spaced height intervals, thus implying a changing base-level with frequent short periods of stability for surface formation, for example B. W. Sparks' (1949) work on the South Downs. Others find more support for a smaller number of surfaces covering a wider height range, a result often found appropriate to higher inland areas, such as Moseley's work (1961) in the Forest of Bowland. There is also difference of opinion in some instances concerning the origin of the surfaces, whether they are formed by marine or subaerial forces. A marine origin would appear quite reasonable in some situations, for example around the coast, while in the inland areas a subaerial origin is usually favoured and more likely.

The range of geomorphological work in Britain is now becoming much wider, as shown in the Register of Current Research. Emphasis on various aspects of Pleistocene geomorphology, including studies of drift deposits, glacial and periglacial features, is increasing, and other systematic fields are being actively studied, such as slope forms, coastal and submarine geomorphology, stress being laid on the processes operating. Where applicable some of the recent contributions are using mathematical techniques in analysis, and the work as a whole is becoming more quantitative. Details of the methods being used will be considered in the appropriate sections.

THE SCOPE OF GEOMORPHOLOGY

Geomorphology is the study of the form of the earth and its genesis and it can be undertaken on a variety of scales, to solve different problems. On the smallest scale and covering the largest area is **world geomorphology.** This branch of the study must draw rather heavily for its data on other sciences, such as geophysics. In considering the shape of the whole earth such problems as the distribution of land and sea assume great importance, and the geomorphologist is interested in the views on continental drift. Although much of the evidence for and against this must come from other sciences, L. C. King, in his study of world-wide erosion surfaces, has shown how geomorphologists also can add their arguments to the attempts to solve this problem. In his view these surfaces show evidence in favour of continental drift and in this he endorses the growing evidence in favour of the theory.

The form of the earth is greatly affected by the periodic major phases of crustal upheaval which create the major morphological elements of the earth's surface, such as the mountain belts and deep sea troughs on the one hand, and flat plateaux and abyssal plains on the other. The unity of the earth means that it is necessary to view it as a whole and to ignore neither the land nor the ocean areas in attempting to arrive at any conclusion concerning its overall shape. Nor must the surface of the earth, whether it be above or below the sea, be the only aspect to be investigated. In order to understand the surface morphology of the earth it is necessary to probe beneath the visible landscape into the crust and mantle beneath. It is in this field that the geomorphologist is dependent upon the work and techniques of the geophysicists, who have by their studies of seismology, magnetism, both modern and ancient, and by their gravity and heat-flow studies arrived at a working knowledge of the earth's interior character and the operation of processes within it. However, much still remains to be learnt.

One of the most fundamental of their results shows that there is a basic structural difference between the oceans and the continents, as indicated by the thickness and character of the crust beneath each of the major types. The boundary of the structural ocean does not necessarily coincide with the edge of the visible oceans, as there are regions of deep ocean that do not exhibit true oceanic structure. Nevertheless the broad division between oceans and lands is both geographical and structural in character, though their essential unity is becoming apparent in some of the more recent views concerning the movement of continents and oceans under the influence of world-wide convection current systems, the operation of which throughout geological time has probably been responsible for the present distribution and character of the major morphological features of the earth. It is thus in the broad field of world morphology that the cause and character of earth movements must be sought, and the importance of these to a study of geomorphology has already been made apparent.

Next in order of scale is the study of the geomorphology of whole continents or all the land-areas as a unit, which might be termed **continental geomorphology**. This analysis can start from the recognition and study of the broad structural and morphological types found on the continents. Such types would include the orogenic belts, the shield areas, the basins, horsts and rift valleys. An analysis of the world on this basis has been published recently by L. C. King under the title *The Morphology of the Earth*, a study which also includes the oceanic sector of the earth. This work makes it clear that it is necessary to consider both the structural or endogenetic forces as well as the exogenetic processes in attempting to understand the basic nature of the continental lands. The development of these through geological time must also be borne in mind. The orogenic belts, for example, may be distinguished according to the period of their most intensive deformation, when mountains were made from the structural point of view and probably also, at a rather later date, from the morphological point of view. Various major orogenic periods, for example the Caledonian or Alpine earth movements, have been established. Umbgrove has shown how these can be related to one another and to the solid shield cores round which they are often built. Thus in some continents orogenic belts become increasingly recent away from the shield areas against which they are folded, for example in Australia. From a morphological point of view the different orogenic belts may display very different landscapes, because erosion can reduce the mountains to a low elevation in a geologically short period of time, but once the structures are formed they remain more or less unchanged. Even the shield areas, which now and for long past geological ages of more than 600 million years have remained relatively flat morphologically, show evidence of former orogenic activity, sometimes, as in Canada, giving evidence of three quite separate orogenic periods of upheaval. Thus time is of great importance in relating morphology to structure, and true structural relief is rare, being associated with the most recent periods of earth movements in restricted areas, such as Otago in New Zealand and the Basin and Range area of the western U.S.A.

Most of the mountain belts of today are associated with the Alpine earth movements, but the high ground is not the direct result of the structural movements; rather is it an indirect effect, caused by the action of isostasy, the concept of which was proposed by Dutton in 1889. The work of the last few decades on gravity measurements over the earth's surface has shown how close is the relationship between isostasy and structural forces in the formation of high mountain belts.

Elsewhere, in the more stable parts of the world, L. C. King has drawn attention to the importance of cymatogenic arching. The processes giving rise to these broad areas of uparching are related to internal movement of material, whereby gneiss is formed by laminar movement of material along steeply-inclined upward courses. The resulting regions of upwarping may be as much as 5000 feet or more high and more than 250 miles across. If the uplift is considerable, a rift may form in the centre, giving rise to rift valleys such as those of Africa or possibly the Irish Sea. Such rifts are tensional features and may be associated with volcanic activity. According to L. C. King the process of cymatogenic arching has been the characteristic tectonic activity during late Tertiary and Quaternary time. The reason for the distribution of these features must again be sought in the subcrust, where extra heat and volatiles may set off the process; thus again the results of the geophysicists are essential.

According to some geophysical views it is only under the continents, where continental crust is present, that cymatogenic movements and the orogenic cycle can operate; thus in the oceans vertical movements may be lacking although horizontal movements can clearly take place. If this should be found to be correct, then support is given to the mobilistic view-point at the expense of the eustatic concept of continental movement and base-level fluctuations. Thus on a continental scale the aim of geomorphology is to relate the internal forces, as revealed by geophysical methods, to the nature of the surface form, and to provide a genetic classification of the units of continental morphology, such as shield areas, rift valleys and basins and the major orogenic belts, and to study their distribution.

The 70% of the earth's surface beneath the sea must also not be ignored. The **geomorphology of the ocean floor** has received much attention particularly in the last two decades, since new and accurate instruments have become available for its study, and many interesting features have been revealed. Some of the major features fit in well with current ideas on the movement of the main structural units of the earth and the internal forces causing them. The great mid-oceanic ridge system, which is one of the greatest morphological features of the whole earth, is perhaps the best known. This 40,000-mile-long ridge extends right down the Arctic Ocean and the Atlantic Ocean before it turns east into the Indian Ocean, and finally after crossing the South Pacific appears to terminate in the active structural zone of the Gulf of California. Such a large-scale feature must clearly be related to the deep underlying forces within the earth. The plausible theory put forward to explain it, in terms of rising convection currents, also helps to explain other oceanic phenomena, such as the deep sea trenches and the associated island arcs. It is argued that the median rift valleys and volcanic activity characteristic of the mid-oceanic ridge indicate the tension that would be expected to be associated with diverging convection currents. The island arcs and deep sea trenches on the other hand, with their large negative gravity anomalies and distribution marginal to the edge of the structural Pacific Ocean, show evidence of compression. This is further supported by evidence from the neighbouring continental zone where the deep-seated shear zones, on which earthquakes of increasing depth of focus inland are situated, appear to be associated with a continentward-sloping plane. Thus the major morphological forms of the suboceanic features help to explain the nature of the fundamental structural processes, leading in their turn to the main elements of the pattern of land and sea on the earth's surface.

The smaller oceanic forms also give valuable evidence on internal forces and external processes in the ocean, where the latter are very different from their subaerial counterparts. Thus sea-mounts and guyots, as well as their coral-crowned relatives the atolls, give good evidence of the movement of the ocean floor in relation to volcanic activity. Submarine canyons also provide many data concerning processes of sedimentation and submarine erosion, for example the action of turbidity currents. Much of the oceanic environment is a field of sedimentation, and erosion only occurs locally where currents are unusually strong; the situation is the reverse of that on land, where erosion in many areas is dominant over deposition. The study of submarine sediments and their environment can give much information about the nature of submarine water movements and the character of the overlying water in relation to climate. In this way submarine research can aid the work of those who are studying related problems on land.

Turning from a study of whole continents or oceans in their broader structural or morphological units, the geomorphologist may next consider the landscape of **areas of smaller dimensions,** for example one of the size of the British Isles or New Zealand. In an area of the size of Great Britain, although the structural elements may still be of great significance, the landscape can be studied from a rather different point of view and its development can be treated as a whole unit. The aim of such geomorphological work is to understand the genesis of the present landscape by studying the stages through which it has passed to reach its present character. There are two major paths by which this objective can be approached; firstly, the development of the drainage pattern can be investigated, and secondly, the stages of the denudation chronology can be elucidated as far as possible. The difficulty of both these methods of approach is that so little of the evidence on which they must be based is left for study, as each stage of development is normally achieved at the expense of the previous one, so that the remaining clues are necessarily small. Taking the British Isles as an example, the difficulties of drainage reconstruction are apparent if the results of the classic work in this field by W. M. Davis and S. S. Buckman are compared with the more recent reconstruction of D. L. Linton (1951). In the former the streams are shown flowing south-eastwards, more or less at right angles to the dip of the rocks in south-east England, while in the later interpretation the main trunk streams are thought to have flowed east, along the flank of a cymatogenic arch of upwarping, the crest of which has dropped to form the Irish Sea. The streams in the latter case are thought to have been superimposed from a cover of long-since vanished chalk. Still other views have been expressed (Sissons, 1960) in which the drainage is considered to have been initiated on a thin marine covering stratum, spread over a peneplain, which was warped and then submerged, to emerge later in stages. The fact that such diverse views have been put forward indicates the complexity of the problem, which can probably never be solved without some measure of doubt, because so little evidence is left.

The study of denudation chronology of the area will, however, provide some evidence which can be used to check the results of the analysis of the drainage development. S. W. Wooldridge (1950) has summarised much of the data on denudation chronology available at the time he wrote. His conclusions were based to a certain extent on the eustatic view of landscape development, while a study of Wales (E. H. Brown, 1960) is also largely based on the same assumptions.

In studying the denudation chronology of an area the problem of limited evidence again occurs. In some studies only those parts of the landscape that show evidence of having been reduced close to base-level are used. These remnants usually form only very small parts of the whole landscape, all of which should ideally be taken into account. There is also the problem that it is not known how much they have suffered subsequent lowering after their original formation near base-level. These two methods can, however, provide a good deal of evidence concerning the development of the landscape.

In this type of analysis the emphasis is placed on the historical development of the landscape, based on the cyclic concept of Davis, on the assumption that evidence of the past character of the landscape is still apparent in its present form. This assumption is not always justified, particularly in areas where the processes of erosion and change are very rapid, owing either to the unresistant nature of the rocks or to the unusual effectiveness of the agents of erosion. An example of the former type is seen in some soft clay areas, such as the Badlands of Perth Amboy (Schumm, 1956), while in the heavily glaciated areas of parts of the north-western Highlands of Scotland ice erosion has removed all trace of the pre-glacial landscape. In other parts of Britain and the United States, for example, the pre-glacial landscape has been buried beneath glacial deposits, often after an unknown amount of previous glacial erosion. Thus the difficulty of elucidating a correct evolutionary history of the landscape is apparent.

In certain areas, however, there is enough of the older landscape left to allow a satisfactory denudation chronology to be worked out. A good example of this is the work of S. W. Wooldridge and D. L. Linton (1955) in south-east England. In this area there is evidence of subaerial erosion in the relics of the summit peneplain, and of marine erosion in the features formed by the early Pleistocene marine transgression. Evidence of both drainage pattern and relic surfaces was used to elucidate the development of the landscape, and more precise dating than is usually possible could be achieved by studying the relics of the deposits of the marine transgression. This, therefore, is a good example of the next type of geomorphological analysis, based on a more detailed study of a smaller region on a larger scale. This type of investigation has been carried out over many small parts of the British Isles, but somewhat conflicting results have emerged from neighbouring areas, for example the south-west Pennines and the adjacent area of south-west Yorkshire (Johnson and Rice, 1961, and Sissons, 1954). In the former area subaerial erosion is considered to have shaped most of the landscape and to account for the drainage system, while the latter area is considered to bear the marks, albeit much modified, of marine erosion in both the surface relics and the drainage pattern. That two such different results can be obtained by competent geomorphologists in areas so close together suggests that the evidence is probably not sufficient to justify the methods used to evaluate a denudation chronology. Too many disturbing factors have operated in the recent geological past, so that the evidence of the earlier periods of development has become blurred, at times beyond all hope of elucidation. This is particularly true of the glaciated part of the country; but even the area south of the actual limit of the ice sheets has not escaped the effects of periglacial activity, which under suitable conditions can produce very considerable modifications of the landscape, particularly by flattening slopes and altering river characteristics. Nevertheless in suitable areas valuable studies have been made, which give some clue to stages of Tertiary land formation.

Another approach to the problem of the larger-scale morphological analysis is the more quantitative and empirical approach of some American geomorphologists, who have developed various methods of measuring the geometry of the landscape, as a preliminary stage to its full understanding. Such work is usually based on the natural unit, the drainage basin being most frequently used. Relationships that can be established between the variables may be referred to as the laws of morphometry (Chorley, 1957, Horton, 1945). These laws are based on measurable quantities such as stream length, stream order and slope, which can be related to one another quantitatively or dimensionlessly. This more empirical approach to the problem of the comprehension of the nature of the landscape and the processes acting upon it may yield more useful results in some areas where the historical approach is of little value on account of the destruction of the evidence on which a denudation chronology must be based.

An increasing number of geomorphologists are turning to a very different approach to the problems confronting them. This method seeks to study the operation of the **processes** modifying the landscape; it may be termed the **systematic approach** to the study of geomorphology as opposed to the regional one, although it must be applied to the actual landscape regionally. For example, slope processes could be worked out theoretically or experimentally, but no valid conclusions could be arrived at until the hypotheses had been tested in the field on slopes of different types in a variety of contrasting areas.

One of the major problems of this approach is the great complexity of nearly all natural landscape features, which have been formed as the result of the interaction of a very great number of variables. Nevertheless until the operation of the processes that modify the landscape is understood it will not be possible to understand the genesis of landforms. It is in the field of systematic geomorphological studies, which are usually carried out in a very small area in great detail, that the help of specialists in associated disciplines may be required. Thus in dealing with slope forms the work of the pedologist and the structural engineer may be relevant, and the geomorphologist, in turn, looking at the problem from a rather different point of view, may have a contribution of great value to make. Slopes are ubiquitous elements of the landscape that can be studied in a wide variety of environments, where soil and vegetation differ greatly and form in themselves one of the most important variables. In order to keep the variables as far as possible under control, it is also possible to study slopes on one rock type or in one climatic environment.

Another type of systematic approach is to consider the landforms associated with a particular rock type; a good example is the study of karst features. These can be studied either by considering the genesis of the forms, which implies progressive change, or by considering the effect of external factors on the development of the forms. The work done recently on the variation of karst forms in different climatic types is yielding valuable results. Again the work of the geomorphologist can be assisted and supplemented by geological and chemical investigations.

Another important approach is to consider the effect of different processes as agents of landscape formation. The study of the work of moving ice is a good example; this requires work in the field, the laboratory and in theory. In these spheres, but particularly the last two, the work of the glacial physicist on the movement of ice greatly assists the geomorphological analysis and understanding of the methods by which ice produces the characteristic landforms associated with it. The study of the work of the sea on the coast also depends on the findings of other scientists to a certain extent, although many other forms of evidence, such as historical material, may also be used. A good example of the use of historical data is G. de Boer's study of Spurn Point in Holderness.

METHODS OF STUDY

It is worth while considering the various possible methods of approach to geomorphology. There are at least two major points of view from which the problems of geomorphology can be approached. These have recently been reviewed by Chorley (1962). They are based on the general systems theory, and are the closed system framework and the open system framework. J. T. Hack has pointed out that W. M. Davis based his work on the closed system, while G. K. Gilbert's approach was more that of the open system framework. A system may be defined as a set of objects that are considered together by studying their relationship to each other and their individual attributes. Thus Davis' work was based on a study of an assemblage of landscape units, related to one another on both an areal and a time basis.

In a *closed system* the boundaries are precisely defined and neither materials nor energy may cross them. Such a system clearly cannot be an exact model for geomorphological investigation, nevertheless some views of landscape development possess a number of the attributes of a closed system. W. M. Davis' cycle concept illustrates this clearly; he envisaged a system whereby uplift took place before erosion had time to modify the landscape appreciably. The cycle began with maximum potential energy as a result of maximum height created by the initial uplift, but as the cycle ran its course the height and with it the energy was gradually reduced, until at the end of the cycle the available energy was reduced to a minimum. The reduction of relief, as a result of continued down-wearing, caused a reduction of potential energy until it reached a minimum when the Davisian peneplain was fully established at the end of the cycle. Although there may be a temporary increase of energy if rejuvenation takes place, this is only temporary and the final state always consists of a minimum amount of energy. The final state of a closed system is determined by the initial state, while during its evolution the only other significant element is the length of time that the system has been operating. This type of study, therefore, falls well into the Davisian scheme of cyclic landform development. The only true state of equilibrium in a closed system of this type is found at the end of the cycle, when the peneplain has been achieved. However, during the cycle the rivers and slopes become graded; but this type of equilibrium does not fit in well with the closed system model. Neither the closed nor the open system model is ideal for landform study, but it seems likely that the open system model has more advantages.

The closed system has been shown to favour an historical study of the landscape under a cyclic concept of its evolution, but the open system gets away from this approach. An *open system* is one in which the energy is being continually renewed; this is a necessary condition for the functioning of the system from which material must also be removed. Thus the open system has the advantage that a steady state can be achieved, whereby the influx and outflow of energy are equal and the character of the area is adjusted to suit the amount of energy passing through it, this adjustment taking place in the geometry of the area under consideration, for example a drainage basin. G. K. Gilbert, in his work on the Henry Mountains, realised the significance of this principle of the adjustment of the landscape and of the tendency towards equilibrium, this being a dynamic equilibrium whereby the landforms become adjusted to the forces on which their character depends.

The nature of a stream channel can be considered as an example. The stream channel depends on a number of variables, such as the discharge, the character of the load and the bed, and the slope of the latter. Only a few of these can be directly adjusted by the stream itself and the most important and easily adjusted is the character of the bed, which can be altered more easily than the slope of the bed, although this can be modified in time, as can the calibre of the load. Thus the stream bed becomes adjusted to the variables on which it depends and reaches a state of dynamic equilibrium, changing with significant variations in the controlling factors.

The concept of dynamic equilibrium can also be studied on the beach. This also is dependent on many variables, and can adapt itself to changes in these by altering the profile. The amount of variability of the beach can be seen by plotting a large number of profiles of one beach section together as shown on figure 1.3. The state of dynamic equilibrium is seen in the relatively small range within which the profiles vary with time, unless very exceptional conditions occur.

So long as the energy conditions remain the same the form will not change, although this may be modified slowly with time as the material concerned is modified by continuous action. Once a steady state of dynamic equilibrium has been established the influence of the initial conditions is no longer felt and the historical development of the system can no longer be established by studying its form, for the system is now independent of its original character. This is in striking contrast to the closed system model, where the historical development is elucidated from its present form. Whether the historical approach will succeed depends on the rate at which the landscape becomes adjusted to energy flow, itself not a constant factor. Where the rate is rapid the landscape soon loses all trace of its origins and becomes adjusted to the current processes operating upon it. Even so there may be phases when the landscape is out of adjustment, for example where a landslide has temporarily caused a slope steeper than equilibrium to form. This, however, is a transient stage.

The value of the open system model lies in the emphasis that it puts on the adjustment between form and process, which is a very important principle in geomorphology. It is only when forms can be associated with processes that their genesis can be clearly understood, and much modern geomorphological work is directed towards the association of form with process. The

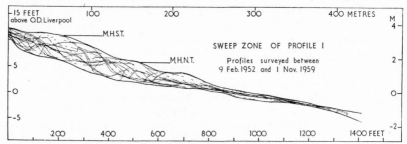

FIGURE 1.3. The sweep zone of a beach profile on a beach in south Lincolnshire, south of Skegness. The profiles of 20 individual surveys are shown covering the period from 1952 to 1959.

open system also stresses the fact that all geomorphological phenomena depend on a large number of variables; this is one of the major difficulties in the analysis of such features. The system also allows a more realistic concept of the influence of time on geomorphological change, which need not be continuous or only in one direction; if a steady state is set up then change will not take place with time. The open system model is also useful in that it allows escape from the historical approach to landscape development, in which facets of earlier stages are recognised but most of the landscape tends to be ignored. These facets are not left out in an open system model, but are treated as parts of the landscape not adjusted to present energy conditions. In the open system way of thinking the whole landscape is considered, and studies on this basis can be carried out in any area, whether there are remnants of earlier stages visible or not.

Research methods

It is valuable to consider a problem from the **theoretical** point of view before attempting to collect data and to formulate hypotheses. By a theoretical approach to a problem is meant the analysis of the factors involved in its solution.

A good example of this approach is the theoretical work of J. F. Nye on the problems of glacier movement. In his analysis of ice flow he assumes that the ice behaves as a perfectly plastic substance and then he determines mathematically the expected movement of the glacier in terms of as many variables as are amenable to treatment without producing a result of undue complexity. The variables he uses are the slope of the glacier bed and of the ice surface, the curvature of the bed and the amount of ablation and accumulation on the glacier surface. These quantities can be measured in the field and the formulae can be worked out for a range of values. Thus it is possible to calculate the expected response of the ice to a variety of different circumstances and values of the factors on which its movement depends. Theoretical work of this type can then be used to predict the result of certain sets of variables acting on the glacier, and field observations can then be planned to test the theoretical results. Theoretical work on glaciers has also been carried out by Nye and other glaciologists to predict the movement of the ice front as a result of certain specific changes in the regime of the glacier, thus enabling a more accurate correlation between climatic change and glacier fluctuations.

Another useful example of theoretical work on ice is the attempt to calculate the effect of the roughness of the bed on the flow of ice. This is relevant to geomorphological study of glacial erosion and produces results that are very difficult to arrive at by any other means, although there is still the problem that the results are just as difficult to check in the field.

Another field in which theoretical work helps to a better understanding of the action of morphological agents and of the forms they produce is wave action on the coast. Such work, like that on the theoretical aspects of glaciology, must be carried out by physicists with considerable mathematical ability, usually beyond the reach of many geomorphologists. R. A. Bagnold (1963) has done some valuable analyses of the movement of particles by waves and wind; the results of these studies have enabled the movement of material on the shore to be based on a surer foundation and have resulted in a better understanding of the processes acting to build up or comb down the beach. Although the very complex and numerous variables involved in such a process must be simplified in theoretical work, it does lead to a much better fundamental understanding of the working of waves, for example.

Still further removed from the resultant landform, but nevertheless of great importance, is the study of the movement of water within the waves, as exemplified by the work of M. S. Longuet-Higgins (1953) on the mass transport in waves. This work in its turn helps to elucidate the movement of the particles and it is their movement that builds up the visible morphological form. Thus in much of the theoretical work preceding or checking other forms of investigation geomorphologists may be dependent on the work of specialists in other fields, such as physicists and mathematicians.

Observation in the field plays a very large part in geomorphological work, whatever the aim of the particular study or whatever the method of approach. Observations can be made to check the results of theoretical work. Going back to the example of glacier flow, certain characteristics of the glacier surface can be predicted from the theory, and values of flow under different conditions are also calculable. The crevasse pattern in different parts of the glacier can be determined from the theoretical results, and these patterns can be checked on the ground or perhaps more easily from aerial photographs if these are available. Observations of glacier flow, longitudinally down the glacier, vertically through it and transversely across it can all be checked with the theoretical results. In some problems of this type a deviation between the theoretical and measured values can then lead to a modification in the theory and a closer approximation to the actual conditions that the theory is representing. J. F. Nye's theoretical flow of glaciers could be tested by specially designed measurements for which the theoretical results were calculated. The fact that the same observations were repeatable in successive years gave further weight to the theory on which they were based. In this way observations and theory can support and confirm each other.

Not all observations can be related to numerical theoretical results; many of the early geomorphologists had to be content with qualitative observation, and it is on this type of field-work that W. M. Davis based his cyclic concept of the development of landscape. Although such observation is still of great value, it is no longer fully satisfying to most geomorphologists, who require greater precision and quantitative information from their field observations. All types of landscape observations are becoming more elaborate; it is no longer sufficient to look at a slope and come to the conclusion that it is steep; its gradient must be measured instrumentally, and if possible the nature of the regolith, the vegetation covering it, the bedrock beneath it and the stream at its foot must all be quantitatively observed and recorded. Not only must it be observed in profile but its areal variation should be recorded, and various elaborate methods by which this information can be recorded on a map will be considered in the next chapter. Thus even the recording of static features in the landscape must be done as far as possible quantitatively and the results expressed cartographically where this is possible. For example relics of erosion surfaces can be mapped and their elevation measured instrumentally.

It is necessary not only to observe the surface form, but to consider the material beneath as well. Many very interesting results have been obtained by a careful study of the superficial deposits, whatever their origin. The finding of undisturbed marine deposits in positions now well above sea-level is by far the best evidence of change of land-level relative to the sea-level, and if they can be dated the value of the evidence is much enhanced; unfortunately it is only rarely possible to date an erosion surface or other feature accurately in this way. A close observation of drift deposits can often give essential clues as to their mode of origin, especially if samples can be collected for laboratory analysis. In this way all available evidence can be gleaned from the field and used for the later interpretation of the results.

Observation should precede interpretation, but further observations may well be found necessary in the light of the interpretation of the preliminary ones, which may suggest certain critical points for closer observation.

Experiment can play an important part in some, though not all, fields of geomorphological enquiry. In some instances the experiments can be carried out on a full-scale basis in the field, in other problems the best results can be obtained from smaller-scale model experiments. In both types the full value of the experiment cannot be obtained unless it is related to natural conditions and used to help solve specific problems.

First considering model experiments, it is clear that not all geomorphological phenomena are capable of being reproduced reasonably accurately on a smaller scale. One of the problems in this connection is the time element, as geomorphological processes operate through very long periods of time, and, even given a considerable scaling down of the time factor, it is difficult to simulate the action of processes over a long period. An example of this type of problem is the experimental work that has been done on the weathering of rocks under different conditions, such as changes of temperature. Even though the changes are speeded up it is very difficult to continue the experiments long enough to give results comparable with natural weathering.

One of the main advantages of model experiments is that the many variables on which the phenomena being studied depend can be controlled. This is particularly true of marine processes, which are among the most amenable to model treatment, because of the relatively quick changes that take place in this environment. There remains, however, the problem of the application of the results to their full-scale counterpart. Nevertheless models of wave action, in particular, have yielded valuable results. The models can be used in two ways, one being to test the result of theoretical calculations, and the other being to simulate natural conditions. An interesting example of the first type is the experimental work done by Russell and Osorio (1958) at the Hydraulic Research Station at Wallingford on the movement of water as a result of mass transport in wave action; their results confirmed satisfactorily the theoretical work of Longuet-Higgins that was mentioned earlier. This work can be carried further in models by studying the movement of sediment as a result of the mass transport of water under wave action near the shore. The model has the advantage that waves of different types can be studied in isolation under controlled conditions, a situation which is not possible in nature. From this study of sediment movement the experiments can be continued to consider the different beach forms that are produced by the action of a variety of wave types. These beach types can then be correlated with their natural counterparts, despite the difficulties of scale in simulating different natural sediments in the model conditions.

Work of this type can be carried out in both two-dimensional and three-dimensional models and still more elaborate models can be built of particular areas. Such models frequently also incorporate a tidal component, which necessitates the introduction of vertical exaggeration in the model, a factor that must be absent from a pure wave model on account of the importance of wave steepness. The tidal models, for example of the Mersey Estuary, are constructed in such a way that they can be made to simulate known past changes in the estuary. When this has been achieved, they can then be used to extrapolate future changes, and the effect of specific improvements to the channel can be tested in the light of the results. Such experiments are now very common as a preliminary stage of important engineering works.

Another type of experimental work that is worth mentioning is the laboratory study of the property of materials, such as the shear strength of different rocks and soils. The work done by J. W. Glen on the flow law of ice under stresses of different magnitude has provided an essential value for one of the variables used in Nye's formulae, which have already been mentioned, and the flow law data have also been tested by field observations.

Full-scale field experiments are concerned with the operation of specific processes in natural conditions. An example of such an experiment is the

TG B

work that has been done on some periglacial features. Polygonal patterns were destroyed in order to ascertain if they were related to current climatic conditions, and if so, the rate at which the features could reform.

One of the more recent methods of approach to geomorphological interpretation is the quantitative **empirical** method. This is often a useful preliminary method in considering problems where the number of variables and their complexity is so great that it is not possible to come to any conclusions until some of the relationships between them have been established. One example of this type of approach is the work that has been done on the factors responsible for the growth of waves in the ocean. A considerable amount of theoretical work has been done in this field, which can be checked against the results of the empirical relationships set up between the main variables involved, the wave dimensions, the wind speed, duration and fetch. The accuracy of the empirical relationships has been increased by the development of wave-recording instruments for use at sea and in shallow water. In this field of enquiry, therefore, all the methods mentioned have been combined to obtain a better understanding of the processes involved in ocean wave formation. This work forms an essential step in the more strictly geomorphological study of the processes dependent on wave action on the coast.

Empirical relationships can be of great value particularly where engineering works are involved, but they should not be an end in themselves. Rather they are a means to an end, the end being the understanding of the operation of the processes involved in the formation of any particular landscape. When the operation of the processes is understood, then the form can be fully appreciated. Empiricism and quantification sometimes go together, but if this method of approach is at the expense of reasoning, then the results obtained will not be wholly satisfactory.

One field in which the empirical approach has been dominant so far is the formulation of morphometric laws, based originally on the work of Horton (1945). This work was associated with the establishment of empirical relationships between certain aspects of drainage basins, such as the law of stream numbers, stated to be 'the numbers of streams of different orders in a given drainage basin tend closely to approximate an inverse geometric series in which the first term is unity and the ratio is the bifurcation ratio'. Other laws of this type are the law of stream lengths and the law of drainage areas. Such laws have been found to apply to several different areas, so that there is clearly some fundamental relationship involved. However, until this can be associated with the relevant processes on which it depends, the results continue to be empirical and not of the highest value as far as genetic geomorphology is concerned, although in descriptive geomorphology they are a great advance on the older, purely descriptive methods. They may well represent a necessary step in the full understanding of landforms.

Methods of analysis

Some of the methods of collecting data have been outlined, but this is only the beginning; the aim is to assemble the data into a coherent whole, whereby they are used to come to some conclusions concerning the nature and genesis of the particular feature being investigated, whether it be a whole continent or one small slope or spit. When the data have been analysed and the conclusions reached then the results must be presented clearly. A useful series of articles by D. Johnson (1938-1941) has set out the various methods that could be used. The important quality of all the methods is that there must be reasoning, by which the data collected can be related together in a logical way.

Mackin (1963) has argued strongly in favour of what he terms the rational approach as opposed to the empirical approach. In the rational approach cause and effect relationships are sought. There is the problem then that one is led back from one effect to the cause that produced it and so on in unending sequence. It is difficult at times to know where to stop the investigation, although the useful stage to which the study can be pushed back is usually apparent either in the nature of the evidence or the competence of the worker.

One of the methods by which it is fruitful to approach a problem is by analogy or association; this is apparent in the work of Hutton, when he associated the circulation of the blood in a person with the circulation of matter in the natural world. Thus geomorphologists have much to gain by experience of a wide field of different phenomena, and hence the great value of field work in as many different environments as possible.

One of the methods used in the development of a geomorphological argument is the **inductive** method. By this means a series of facts is arranged in a logical order so that one leads to another and then to the final conclusion, which follows in a reasonable and acceptable way from the data set forth. In this method the observations are used to draw conclusions as the argument is built up. A classic example of this approach is the paper by A. C. Ramsey 'On the denudation of South Wales', in which he assembled all his observations, each one adding a little more evidence, up to his final conclusion, that the area had been subjected to marine planation. The fact that this hypothesis and some of his other views are now no longer held by all geomorphologists is evidence that the inductive method of reasoning is not infallible and may lead to false conclusions.

The inductive method of reasoning is often not the only one used. But its value is that it is based on observable facts from which inferences may be made and a conclusion finally reached. As a method it is best suited to a fairly simple problem, the solution of which is based on a wide field of observations and relevant data, so that it is not necessary to invoke theoretical reasoning.

Its shortcomings are related to the fact that only one conclusion is stated. This tends subconsciously to the elimination of any facts that are not favourable to the result to which the remaining facts appear to lead, so that in the end a false, or at least questionable, result is arrived at. It is also less easy to criticise this method of approach, particularly if the conclusion is only reached at the end of the argument. Thus it is sometimes helpful to give at least some indication of the final conclusions nearer the beginning of the argument.

The second way in which an argument can be presented is the **deductive** method. This technique is based on the presentation or formulation of a tentative theory to account for a given feature or problem. The consequences that would follow from the theory are then deduced and the actual observations are compared with the deduced ones. The quality of the results will depend on the nature of the deductions and the closeness of the comparisons. When there are many complex or peculiar deductions then there is a better chance that the comparisons will be valid, and the theory will be more strongly supported. The closeness of agreement between the deductions and the comparisons will also determine the value of the final conclusions.

The same weaknesses apply to the deductive method as those mentioned in the inductive method; neither guarantees the correctness of the conclusion reached, and in both types there is no alternative hypothesis explored. Probably the deductive method is the less satisfactory of the two, but the use of both methods together can lead to better results. The deductive method has been used by many of the well known geomorphologists, not least of whom was Davis, whose argument is largely deductive in character. His whole approach to the geographical cycle is largely deductive; he worked out the theoretical sequence of events from an original assumed beginning, and then sought in the landscape examples of the different stages, and features associated with them, with which to justify his deductions. The arguments that have developed since he put forward these compelling ideas indicate that the conclusions of this method are by no means infallible. Another paper of his that has had much influence on subsequent thought is concerned with the sculpture of mountains by valley glaciers. This is largely deductive in approach and has no inductive argument, although it is partly analytical in that two different hypotheses are considered; one is that glaciers can erode and the other is that they cannot. The consequences of each are developed and confronted with the observed data. The fact that the consequences, deduced from the hypothesis that glaciers are effective agents of erosion, can be matched so closely ensured that the theory did a great deal to convince geomorphologists of the capacity of ice to erode. G. K. Gilbert also makes use of the deductive method of argument in some of his work, although he sometimes reverses the normal procedure of making deductions and then comparing them with the observed facts, by describing the features first and then comparing them with the deductions. However, both Gilbert and Davis make use at times of a mixture of the deductive and the analytical approach, the latter in many instances being the best method of dealing with many problems.

The **analytical** method has certain advantages that the two methods already mentioned do not possess, one of the main ones being that more than one possible explanation of the problem is considered. The method has been called in fact the method of the multiple working hypotheses. In it as many hypotheses as possible are put forward in turn, each is confronted with the known facts, and that which agrees with the greatest number of observations is the most likely to be correct. As long, however, as one single fact remains in disagreement with the results deduced from the hypothesis, then it cannot be a full and completely satisfactory theory, although it may only require minor modification. Gilbert was probably the first geomorphologist to use this method deliberately and to discuss it methodologically in 1896.

The paper of T. C. Chamberlin was an important discussion of the methodological value of these different approaches. In his paper he describes and discusses the three possibilities, firstly the method of the ruling hypothesis, secondly, the method of the working hypothesis, and finally, the method of the multiple working hypotheses. The dangers of the first method are those already mentioned in connection with the inductive and deductive methods, that only one theory is considered. This theory may be based on the more obvious and visible features of the landforms being investigated, while more subtle features are not considered. Also there is the danger that, once a certain set of features has been associated with the theory, these only will be observed and other features, conflicting with the theory, will be ignored, probably subconsciously, and as further field work is pursued only those features that fit the theory will be considered. Alternative theories are not considered and the facts tend to become distorted to fit the theory.

The difference between the second and first methods is that in the first the theory has to be established by the observations, while in the second a working hypothesis is established in order to guide the field work and the collection of data. The hypothesis in this instance determines the method of enquiry and there is a danger that it may become the ruling theory. It does not preclude bias in the selection of data and in any case it tends to limit the collection of material and observation.

The third method, therefore, has most to recommend it, as it overcomes the main disadvantages of the other two. The whole process involved in the following through of this method may be long, more suitable to research than publication. Nevertheless it is the best approach. Facts must be observed; the observations must be classified: inductive arguments can then be generalised from the classification: next the hypotheses must be invented; the consequences of the hypotheses must be deduced: the observations must then be checked against the deductions. New facts may be required to decide between two or more of the hypotheses before the final conclusion can be reached.

In the stage of hypothesis-invention both imagination and experience are required, so that use may be made of analogy and association. One of the disadvantages of the analytical method is that many possible avenues of approach must be explored, many of which will prove fruitless. However, in the course of such a search other important relationships may be revealed, and the analytical approach is much the safest and most satisfying method of solving a problem. Some of the advantage of the method results from the use of both inductive and deductive methods of approach and it has the virtue of impartiality in treating the various hypotheses. All the relevant observations are given equal weight, while the hypotheses may well suggest new facets for observation and testing, possibly by experiment.

This method of investigation is best suited to complex and difficult problems, a good example being Gilbert's work on the Henry Mountains, in which he sets up a number of hypotheses on the basis of his observations. The work of Davis on 'The Rivers and Valleys of Pennsylvania' is another good early example of the use of the analytical method to solve a particularly complex problem. The very large number of possible hypotheses put forward by D. W. Johnson to explain the origin of submarine canyons is another example of this method, but in this instance the lack of adequate data made it difficult to demonstrate the impossibility of some of the hypotheses discussed; these could be disproved now on the basis of new evidence. Analytical studies may later prove to be incorrect on account of the failure of the author to put forward the correct hypothesis, which is true of some aspects of Davis' work on the rivers of Pennsylvania. The collection of new data may make it possible to decide between two possible alternative hypotheses.

Another point that it is important to bear in mind when attempting to explain some particular type of geomorphological feature, such as eskers or drumlins, is that two or more theories to account for these features may in fact be correct for different examples of the feature. It has been suggested, for instance, that drumlins can be formed by glacial erosion, shaping into drumlin form an area of till deposited by an earlier advance of the ice in the area. Alternatively, they have been explained as a result of direct deposition from a moving ice sheet, heavily charged with basal till. Both theories may be true of different drumlin fields, so that neither can be pronounced correct at the expense of the other. The problem that arises then is the nomenclature of the feature; if the term 'drumlin' just implies an oval hill formed of drift, with or without a rock core, then it covers both explanations. If, however, a term is required that is genetic rather than descriptive, then different terms should be adopted for the two different types of drumlins, one formed by erosion and the other by deposition, even if the two types of drumlin could only be differentiated as a result of detailed study of the till of which they are composed. Thus it is often found that no one theory can satisfactorily account for all the features that it tries to explain, particularly in the field of systematic geomorphology.

Finally one or two other methods of presenting geomorphological results may be mentioned. Johnson described what he termed the **topical** method, which may also be called the **systematic** method. This is a method that can be used conveniently when a large number of data must be set before the reader. The essence of the method is the classification of the material by some logical system to give clarity. Where possible this should be genetic in character, and there must be a common basis of classification. Simplification is further aided by subdivision of the classification. Such a method usually requires the use of technical terms and these should always be explained before the term is actually introduced, in many cases the citing of examples helps to clarify the explanation of the terms.

The opposite of the topical method is the **regional** method, by which features are classified regionally; but within each region it is possible to classify features topically, so that the two methods are not mutually exclusive. In using the regional method it is necessary to treat the broad characteristics of the area first, and then to fill in the details. A regional geomorphological account can be empirical, merely setting forward the facts, or genetic, in which case the origin of the features is discussed; the latter is the more satisfactory approach and amounts to a study similar to many studies in denudation chronology. This, in a restricted area, may in fact be called the **historical** method. This approach attempts to describe the landscape in terms of its historical development, but unless it is linked to some of the other methods it is unlikely to be of great value. The main essential in all the methods discussed is that observations should be accurate, as far as possible quantitative, and carried out on a systematic basis, while imagination and integrity are required in the development and testing of hypotheses.

REFERENCES

ALBRITTON, C. C. (Editor) 1963. *The Fabric of Geology*. Geol. Soc. Amer.

BAGNOLD, R. A. 1963. Chapter 21 in *The Sea*, edited by M. N. Hill, vol. III, 507-548.

BAULIG, H. 1928. *Le Plateau Central*.

BAULIG, H. 1933. The changing sea-level. *Inst. Brit. Geog. Publ.* 3, 1-46.

BIROT, P. 1955. *Les Méthodes de Morphologie*. Paris.

BIROT, P. 1960. *Le cycle d'érosion sous les différents climats*. Curso de altos estudos geogr., Rio de Janiero, Brazil.

BOURCART, J. 1950. Le théorie de la flexure continentale. *Compte Rendu Inter. Geog. Un.*, Lisbon, 16, 167-190.

BROWN, E. H. 1960. *The relief and drainage of Wales*. Cardiff.

CAILLEUX, A. and TRICART, J. 1954. *Le modèle des chaînes plissées*. C.D.U.

CHAMBERLIN, T. C. 1897. The method of the multiple working hypotheses. *J. Geol.* 5, 837-848.

CHORLEY, R. J. 1960. Geomorphology and general systems theory. *U.S. Geol. Surv. Prof. Paper* 500-B, Washington, B1-B10.

CHORLEY, R. J. 1963. Diastrophic background to twentieth century geomorphology. *Bull. Geol. Soc. Amer.* 74, 953-970.

CHORLEY, R. J., DUNN, A. J. and BECKINSALE, R. P. 1964. *The history of the study of landforms*. Vol. I *Geomorphology before Davis*. Methuen, London.

CHORLEY, R. J. 1957. Illustrating the laws of morphometry. *Geol. Mag.* 94, 140-149.

COTTON, C. A. 1941. *Landscape*, C.U.P.

DAVIS, W. M. 1909. *Geographical Essays*. Edited by D. W. Johnson, Boston.

DAVIS, W. M. 1889. The rivers and valleys of Pennsylvania. *Nat. Geog. Mag.* 1, 183-253.

DAVIS, W. M. 1906. The sculpture of mountains by glaciers. *Scot. Geog. Mag.* 22, 76-89.

DUTTON, C. E. 1889. On some of the greater problems of physical geology. *Bull. Phil. Soc.*, Washington, 11, 51-64.

ENGELN, von, O. D. 1942. *Geomorphology*. New York.

GILBERT, G. K. 1877. *Geology of the Henry Mountains*. Washington.

GILBERT, G. K. 1880-1881. Contributions to the history of Lake Bonneville. U.S. Geol. Surv. 2nd Annual Report 167-200.

GLEN, J. W. 1952. Experiments on the deformation of ice. *Jour. Glaciol.* 2, 111-114.

GREENWOOD, G. G. 1857. *Rain and rivers*. 195 pp. London.

HACK, J. T. 1960. Interpretation of erosional topography in humid temperate regions. *Amer. Jour. Sci.* 258 A, 80-97.

HILL, M. N. (Editor) 1963. *The Sea*. Vol. III *The earth beneath the sea*. New York.

HORTON, R. E. 1945. Erosional development of streams and their drainage basins; hydrophysical approach to quantitative morphology. *Bull. Geol. Soc. Amer.* 56, 275-370.

HUTTON, J. 1795. *The theory of the earth, with proofs and illustrations.* Edinburgh.

JOHNSON, D. 1938-1941. Studies in Scientific method. *Journ. Geomorph.*
    I Introduction. *Journ. Geomorph.* 1, 64-66, 1938.
    II The written presentation. 1, 147-152, 1938.
    III The inductive method of presentation. 2, 366-372, 1939.
    IV The deductive method of presentation. 3, 59-64, 1940.
    V The analytical method of presentation. 3, 156-162, 1940; 3, 256-262, 1940.
    VI The topical method of presentation. 3, 353-355, 1940.
    VII The regional method of presentation. 4, 145-149, 1941.
    VIII The historical method and didactic method, 4, 328-332, 1941.

JOHNSON, R. H. and RICE, R. J. 1961. Denudation chronology of the south-west Pennine Upland. *Proc. Geol. Assoc.* 72, 21-32.

JUDSON, S. 1960. William Morris Davis—an appraisal. *Zeit. f. Geom.* N.F. 4, 193-201.

KING, L. C. 1953. Canons of landscape evolution. *Bull. Geol. Soc. Amer.* 64, 721-752.

KING, L. C. 1950. The study of the World's Plainlands. *Quart. Journ. Geol. Soc.* 106, 101-132.

KING, L. C. 1962. *The Morphology of the Earth.* Edinburgh.

LINTON, D. L. 1957. The everlasting hills. *Adv. of Sci.* 14, 58-67.

LINTON, D. L. 1951. Problems of Scottish scenery. *Scot. Geog. Mag.* 67, 65-85.

LONGUET-HIGGINS, M. S. 1953. Mass transport in water waves. *Phil. Trans. Roy. Soc.* A, 245, 535-581.

MACKIN, J. H. 1963. The Fabric of geology—Rational and empirical methods of investigation. In Albritton (ed.), 135-163.

MOSELEY, F. 1961. Erosion surfaces in the Forest of Bowland. *Proc. Yorks. Geol. Soc.* 33, 173-196.

NYE, J. F. 1952. The mechanics of glacier flow. *Journ. Glaciol.* 2, 82-93.

PELTIER, L. C. 1950. The geographical cycle in periglacial regions. *An. Assoc. Am. Geog.* 40, 214-236.

PLAYFAIR, J. 1802. *Illustrations of the Huttonian theory of the earth.*

POWELL, J. W. 1876. Report on the geology of the eastern portion of the Uinta Mountains. 218 pp. Washington.

RAMSEY, A. C. 1846. On the denudation of South Wales and the adjacent counties of England. *Geol. Surv. Mem. G. B.* I, 297-335.

RUSSELL, R. C. H. and OSORIO, J. D. C. 1958. An experimental investigation of drift profiles in a closed channel. *Proc. 6th Conf. Coastal Eng.* 171-183.

SCHUMM, S. A. 1956. Evolution of drainage systems and slopes in badlands at Perth Amboy, New Jersey. *Bull. Geol. Soc. Amer.* 67, 597-646.

SIMONS, M. 1962. A new review of the work of Walther Penck. *Inst. Brit. Geog.* 31, 1-14.

SISSONS, J. B. 1954. The erosion surfaces and drainage system of south-west Yorkshire. *Proc. Yorks. Geol. Soc.* 29, 305-342.

SISSONS, J. B. 1960. Erosion surfaces, cyclic slopes and drainage systems in southern Scotland and northern England. *Inst. Brit. Geog.* 28, 23-38.

SPARKS, B. W. 1949. The denudation chronology of the Dip slope of the South Downs. *Proc. Geol. Assoc.* 60, 165-215.

STODDART, D. R. 1960. Colonel George Greenwood; the father of modern sub-aerialism. *Scot. Geog. Mag.* 76, 108-110.

UMBGROVE, J. H. F. 1947. *The pulse of the earth.* The Hague.

WOOLDRIDGE, S. W. 1950. The Upland plains of Britain. *Adv. Sci.* 7, 162-175.

WOOLDRIDGE, S. W. 1958. The trend of geomorphology. *Inst. Brit. Geog.* 25, 29-36.

WOOLDRIDGE, S. W. and LINTON, D. L. 1955. *Structure, surface and drainage in south-east England.* London.

2 FIELD TECHNIQUES—OBSERVATION OF FORM AND CHARACTER

Field studies play a vital part in nearly all geomorphological investigations. Observations in the field are essential either to formulate or to test hypotheses and theoretical calculations, and they must also accompany model work. The methods used to study the landscape depend on the nature of the problem to be solved and can be divided into two broad fields of study: either the relatively static landscape forms or the processes at work modifying the landscape. The first aspect, which deals with the visible landscape at any one time, will be considered in this chapter and the second in the following one.

When the landscape is studied as a whole it is often convenient and reasonable to consider it as a static form, although of course it is clearly slowly changing with time. This applies to most studies of denudation chronology. On the other hand major changes of landscape may take place within the life-time of one person; for example some coastal features change measurably from year to year, and also the area adjacent to a rapidly retreating ice sheet may be quite unrecognisable from one year to the next. Features of this type are, however, included in this chapter because at any one time they are static and observable as landscape forms; they can be mapped and their characteristics recorded in a variety of ways that will be considered.

I. GEOMORPHOLOGICAL FIELD-SURVEYING

Published maps at a suitable scale for detailed field work are not always available, and frequently, if they are, they do not show the details that are required. It is, therefore, worth considering some of the survey techniques that can be particularly adapted for the purposes of geomorphological research. One type of study for which suitable maps are rarely available is that of recording the character of glacial retreat and the nature of the area revealed by the retreating glacier. Such an area frequently contains moraine-dammed lakes, morainic ridges or eskers and other features of geomorphological interest. The best method of surveying an area of this type in the field is by plane-tabling, although aerial photography in some instances may be a useful alternative technique. If the survey is done by plane-tabling either a suitable stretch must be found to set up a long enough base line, or it may be possible to plot surveyed points on to the plane-table, to act as a framework.

The latter has certain advantages in that it enables the map to be keyed to the wider area for which cartographic information is available, and is particularly useful in establishing the amount of glacial retreat since any available map was surveyed.

The survey can proceed from point to point by a system of countersection, whereby a ray is taken from one fixed point to the one to be occupied. The table is then moved to the new point and orientated on the point from which the surveyor has moved. The position can then be fixed and checked by drawing back-rays from two other fixed points visible from the new station. This method avoids the necessity of resection and is very suitable for following round an arcuate terminal moraine.

In order to reveal the characteristics of such an area it is necessary to add heights to the map, and this can often be done by the use of an Indian clinometer or telescopic alidade. The height must be carried forward by use of a staff in connection with the telescopic alidade, which can also be used for levelling. This instrument is very suitable for fixing the position and height of any object that is required to be plotted on the map. The height can be read as an angle of elevation or depression, while the distance can be recorded tacheometrically if a staff is used, so that not all points of detail need be intersected. The use of a staff in conjunction with a telescopic alidade fixes the point at one reading and avoids the necessity of using a large number of markers for the points sighted. It is usually necessary to use some form of marker for fixed points in such an environment, as one boulder looks very different from different view-points, and often there is little else to use on the ground. The plane-table is a very versatile instrument for this type of survey and the scale can be adjusted to the size of the area to be mapped. From this point of view it is important to note the plottable error so that time is not wasted in surveying detail that cannot adequately be shown on the scale. Any fixed point from which glacier recession could be measured in future years should be incorporated into the map. Measurements of this type are undertaken on a large number of glaciers by measuring from the fixed point in a given line to the glacier snout. This method does not take into account the form of the glacier snout and can at times be misleading, so that a plane-table record of the glacier snout gives a much more useful starting point for future comparison.

The plane-table survey need not stop at the glacier snout, and there are many features of interest that can best be recorded by this method of survey, for example the pattern of superficial drainage, the position of moraines and ogives. The latter also provide interesting evidence of the annual movement of the glacier, as on most glaciers on which they occur they are spaced at annual distances of glacier flow. Such glaciers have ice-falls and these may cause problems in surveying; many of the points must now be fixed by intersection from known points that are accessible with the plane-table on the sides or flatter parts of the glacier, and heights must be obtained by angular measurements from several positions, as reciprocal observations are frequently not possible. Any fixed point on the ice itself will move, so that

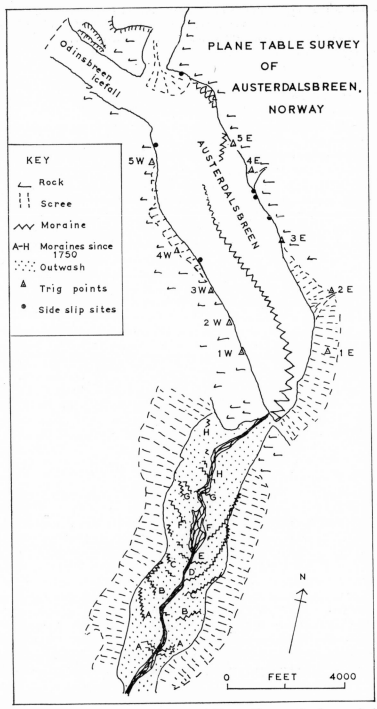

FIGURE 2.1. Plane-table survey of Austerdalsbreen, Norway, showing terminal moraines and certain features on the glacier surface.

any points that are required for comparison on future occasions must be located on solid ground. An example of a glacier survey of this type is shown in figure 2.1. Other methods of glacier surveying will be considered in connection with the observations on the characteristics of glacier flow and glacial processes. For many glaciological problems photogrammetric surveying has been used successfully (Case, 1958).

Another environment in which geomorphological change is rapid enough to cause official surveys to be inadequate for geomorphological analysis is the coastal one. In some areas features change sufficiently rapidly to make frequent periodic surveys of great value. This is particularly true of some features of coastal deposition, whose development can be measured and analysed by repeated surveys. The spit at Gibraltar Point in Lincolnshire may be taken as an example; although it is only a small feature, the same surveying methods could be used on similar landforms. This spit is situated at the northern corner of the Wash, where the coast turns abruptly inland. It has been surveyed annually by plane-tabling for over a decade (Barnes and King, 1957). The annual surveys may be correlated by means of fixed markers the position of which is plotted on each survey sheet before mapping starts (see figure 2.2). One of the objects of the surveys is to calculate the amount of material being added to or removed from the spit, and its

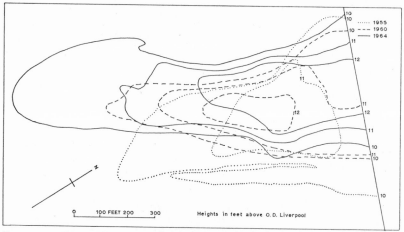

FIGURE 2.2. Plane-table contour surveys of the spit at Gibraltar Point, Lincolnshire, to illustrate the method of measuring movement over a number of years.

movement must also be traced. In order to fulfil the first requirement it is necessary to calculate the volume of material in the spit above a datum plane, and this needs a knowledge of the form of the feature. This can be achieved by surveying contours, but because of the character of the spit the interval must be small. Thus contours were surveyed at 1 foot intervals, using a level and staff graduated to 0·01 ft. The points on the contours were plotted on to the plane-table by first locating the point at the desired height from the known height of instrument of the level, and calculating the distance from the level by tacheometry. The direction can be obtained by alidade from the plane-table. The distance can be corrected for the short space between the level and plane-table which are set up close together. This operation can be done by using both plane-table and levelling equipment, but could be done more easily by using a telescopic alidade, which has stadia wires for direct tacheometric reading and a levelling device, so that it can be used as a level.

The volume of material above the relevant base contour can then be calculated by formula. If the feature is fairly flat-topped the formula for the volume of a truncated cone can be used, this is

$$\text{volume} = \frac{D}{6}(A_t + 4A_m + A_b),$$

where D is the difference in height between the top and bottom sections, A_t is the area within the top contour, A_m the area of the centre section, and A_b the area of the bottom contour. If the top is not very flat the area above the top contour can be added to increase the accuracy, using the formula for the volume of a cone,

$$\text{volume} = \tfrac{1}{3}(\pi R^2\, h),$$

where R is the radius and h the height. This latter figure can be obtained if the highest point on the feature is mapped as a spot height.

The movement of the feature can be measured by the displacement of the contours from year to year. It is important that the height of such features should be known accurately; thus the datum point must be levelled from a bench mark or other fixed point of known height, and the heights can be related to the tide heights by using the equivalent values given in the Admiralty Tide Tables. If a known height is not available the level can be directly related to sea-level by noting the height of one of the fixed points relative to the water-level at a known time or state of the tide. It is useful to add other detail, for example plants, by using the level to obtain their position and height, because this latter factor is significant in relation to tide levels.

A spit is usually a fairly low feature, and this greatly facilitates surveying by the method suggested, which is not very suitable for areas of considerable relief on account of the great number of times the instruments must be moved to read the level. If time does not permit a field survey then useful information can be obtained from aerial photographs, although it is not so easy to do accurate large-scale work by this means.

Not only must methods of investigation include the visible external form of the landscape features, but of great importance are the materials of which the features are made, whether these be solid rocks or superficial deposits. The latter often play a vital part in the interpretation of the development of the features and of the processes that bring about this development.

2. DENUDATION CHRONOLOGY

The aim of a study in denudation chronology is to elucidate the stages by which the landscape reached its present character. Often it is assumed that the development has been the result of a generally falling base-level, usually accompanied by a series of relative still-stands. During the period of still-stand denudation is thought to produce recognisable landscape elements that can be identified by specific criteria. From what has been said earlier it will be clear that not all landscapes can be analysed in this way, because at times landscape adjustment to processes is so rapid that all trace of earlier stages is lost. However, over large stretches of country there is evidence of past phases of landscape development related to base-levels well above the present sea-level. The problem of denudation chronology is to recognise those elements of the landscape that were adjusted to the base-level at the time of their formation, to discover by what processes they were fashioned, to fix their elevation relative to the base level and to date them if possible. The task is made more difficult by the continued action of other processes, which continually modify the landscape. Thus in a study of this type special emphasis is placed on certain parts of the landscape which are often of small dimensions. These must be recognised and mapped in the field before they can be interpreted and they should be considered in relation to the whole landscape as well.

The mapping of erosion remnants in the field presupposes that the remnants can be differentiated from the rest of the landscape, and this is usually done on the basis of their low gradient, assuming that owing to their proximity to base-level they have been flattened. The exact mechanism by which this is achieved is not often mentioned, although this aspect is clearly of great importance and will be considered in connection with their interpretation. The low gradient elements of the landscape can occur on the hill tops as summit surfaces, on interfluves as spur flats, or in valleys as valley benches, for example.

If the peneplain or pediplain is extensive and the landscape belongs to one cycle, then the whole land surface must be considered. However, where polycyclic development is conspicuous only small fragments of partial peneplains will probably be available.

Clearly the mapping of the relic surfaces will be facilitated if a good base map is available to plot them on. In Britain the 1:25,000 Ordnance Survey maps are very suitable for the purpose if the area is not too large. E. H. Brown's work, covering the whole of Wales, was done on the 1 inch to 1 mile scale (Brown, 1960), but normally areas chosen for this type of study are not so large. The advantage of the 1:25,000 or the 6 in. to 1 mile (1:10,560) maps for this purpose is that identification of position is facilitated by the field-boundaries that are marked on the map.

It is important that the surface be viewed if possible from a number of different points, as perspective can mislead in the field unless care is taken; it is essential to plot the information as objectively as possible on the map. From this point of view it is better to undertake any cartographic analysis after field work, so that no preconceived ideas are taken into the field; it is all too easy to see what is being looked for and not what is actually there. E. H. Brown recommends that each erosion surface should be mapped separately by following from one remnant to the next, so that the whole of one surface may be reconstructed from remnants, each viewed from the one on either side. It is best to start such work on the lowest levels, which are likely to be the best preserved.

Surfaces may be identifiable by breaks of slope at their lower and upper edges, and one of the best ways of delimiting the remnants is to plot the breaks of slope bounding them; the character of the breaks of slope should also be indicated by the methods to be suggested in connection with slope mapping. It is important to note the direction and amount of slope of the remnants and the abruptness of the bounding breaks of slope. Field sketches also prove valuable, as they ensure that the landscape is really studied in detail, and their execution entails a preliminary analysis of the view.

The methods suggested are suitable for examining the type of complex polycyclic landforms found in Britain, but in many areas it is neither possible nor necessary to work on such large-scale maps. Where large-scale maps are not yet available aerial photographs may prove a useful substitute, specially where field checking can be carried out. The interpretation can be done from the photograph, or alternatively it can be used as an alternative to a base map. In some areas, such as parts of Africa, where surfaces are very extensive, detailed mapping on a large scale is not necessary. The work of J. A. Mabbutt (1961) illustrates a study of this type in western Australia. He is dealing with an area consisting of two plateaux of different age separated by an escarpment 25 to 75 feet high. The upper surface is covered with laterite. In studying the retreat of the scarp between the plateaux it is necessary to note and map the state and depth of weathering and weathered material, as the preparation of the material by weathering is an essential preliminary to scarp retreat. Detailed examination of the scarp form, showing its overhanging nature in parts and the associated scree slope, supports this view. The difference in level between the two scarps is also significant as it is independent of sea-level, although the initiation of the new surface may result from rejuvenation. It is an example of an erosion surface formed by the stripping off of the weathered mantle, and its level is determined by the weathering front, which is the depth to which weathering extends on the old, upper plateau. This type of study illustrates the importance of examining the state of rock as well as the character of the surface configuration and the danger of associating level surfaces too closely with base-level.

The absolute elevation of the features mapped is nevertheless often of great importance. Contoured maps can give an approximate altitude of the features recorded. However, there are not always conveniently placed spot heights or bench marks, or maps with accurate contours may not be available. It may, therefore, be necessary to add surveyed heights to the map to establish the height of important landscape elements. A useful instrument for this purpose is the surveying aneroid barometer. These can be obtained in a variety of sizes, but for accurate work the 5-inch-diameter one, that can be read to the nearest foot, is very suitable. In this type of work extreme accuracy is not called for, and a height correct to 5 or 10 feet is quite adequate for most purposes. The main problem in using the aneroid barometer is that, unless many corrections are applied, it only gives relative height. It is nevertheless very valuable for short traverses between known heights, which can be used to adjust the value of readings made at points whose height is required. The barometer depends for its readings on variations of pressure and is, therefore, very dependent on weather conditions. It can be used with reasonable accuracy in the tropics, where changes in pressure are regular and diurnal in character, but in the more unsettled middle latitudes the weather plays an important part in the accuracy of the heights read with the barometer. If an accurate reading is required the work should be carried out in anti-cyclonic weather if possible. This is not always feasible, however, and reasonably reliable results can be obtained if a barograph trace is available for the time and place of survey. Then it is necessary to note the time of observations and corrections can be made by reference to the barograph trace. This correction is very necessary when it is realised that pressure changes in advance of or behind a front can amount to an equivalent varia-tion of 100 feet in the barometer reading over a period of between $2\frac{1}{2}$ and 6 hours (Sparks, 1953). In unstable weather conditions short-term pressure fluctuations of height equivalent to more than 20 feet can easily take place over periods of less than one hour. If a barograph is not available it is necessary to take height readings at the beginning and the end of the traverse between known heights, and the best adjustment that can be made in these circumstances is to assume that the pressure change has been uniform throughout the period. Again the weather should be considered, because if a front has passed through during the survey the pressure change may have reversed.

Another point to bear in mind when using the aneroid barometer is the effect of the wind; if this exceeds force 3 and if the barometer is held about 3 feet from the ground the wind can have a considerable effect on the read-ings, which are higher with a wind from behind and lower with a facing wind. With a gale of force 8, the difference can be up to 45 to 50 feet, and even with a force 5 wind it may be 10 to 15 feet. The difficulty of allowing for this factor is that the wind changes with the exposure of the site, and eddies cause local variations that cannot be allowed for by always facing into or away from the wind. Despite these difficulties, under suitable conditions the aneroid barometer is a very useful instrument for obtaining spot-heights in this type of work, and an error of only 5 feet should be possible if the traverse is com-pleted in one hour and is adjusted. Suitable conditions probably occur for about half the time in England according to Sparks.

Once the extent, height and character of the surfaces have been mapped in the field, it is necessary to examine the rocks into which they are cut. This information may be available in the form of geological maps, but it is not enough to know only the age and type of rock; it is also necessary to know its dip, its lithological character, and the pattern of joints or bedding planes. This is of importance in establishing whether a flat surface remnant is the result of structural control or is a true erosional feature.

Good examples of the two possibilities can be seen in the north of England. On the west side of the Dent fault in the Howgill Fells well developed spur flats and summit surfaces occur on the steeply dipping and contorted Silurian rocks (see figure 2.3). These rocks can clearly not control the relief

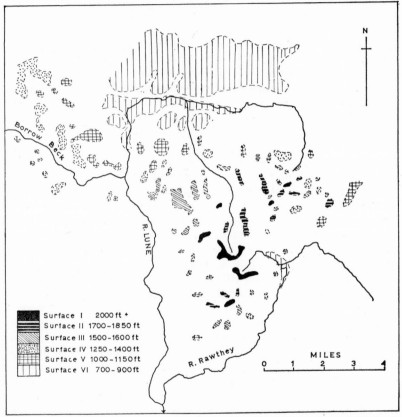

FIGURE 2.3. Erosion surface remnants of the Howgill Fells, north-west England.
(after McConnell)

directly as their structures, visible in exposures in cliff faces, and their lithological character is such that they react as a homogeneous mass to the agents of erosion; thus any low gradient landscape facets in this area must be true erosion surfaces. On the east side of the Dent fault, however, Carboniferous rocks outcrop. These lie almost horizontally a small distance away from the fault. The strata consist of alternating shale, sandstone and limestone of very different lithological character and resistance to erosion. Again flat surfaces are found in this area, but when they are studied in relation to the rock type they can be directly correlated with the outcrops of the harder rocks, the limestone and harder sandstones. Thus in two adjacent areas the rock type plays a fundamental part in the nature of the relief and in the character and origin of the flattish surfaces. Structural control is absent in the west and dominant in the east in this example.

The nature of the rock also plays an important part in the preservation of the surfaces once they are formed. Where the rock is permeable in character, a fall of base-level will be accompanied by a lowering of the water table as rejuvenation works back into the higher ground and this will result in the drying out of the surface drainage and the deceleration of subaerial lowering of the landscape. This is especially true of limestone and chalk areas; in these rocks, therefore, remnants of erosion surfaces will be likely to be preserved better than in less permeable rocks. It is in these rock types that it is particularly important to differentiate between structural control and preservation. It may be necessary to study the character of the rocks in detail to obtain the necessary evidence. For example B. W. Sparks was able to show that the erosion surfaces on the South Downs were cut into various different horizons of the chalk. This required detailed palaeontological examination of the rock to differentiate different horizons of the chalk, but the results showed that the surfaces were true erosion surfaces and not directly due to structural control. M. M. Sweeting (1950) also demonstrated that an erosion surface in the Craven district of northern England, largely found on limestone, could also be traced on to other types of rocks. The upland plain of the Derbyshire Dome is also mainly cut across limestone but can be traced on to Millstone Grit. Thus structure, in the broad sense of the term, in calcareous rocks is important as it helps to preserve erosion surfaces.

M. M. Sweeting has gone further in the study of erosion in the limestone areas to show that not only are the surface forms relevant to the establishment of a denudation chronology in such a region, but that there is also important evidence hidden underground in the cave systems of these areas. In order to make use of this type of information in work on denudation chronology it is necessary to study the character of the caves. In the Craven district the rocks are lying almost horizontally and therefore the cave passages are mainly horizontal and the pitches are nearly vertical, because solution takes place most readily along the joints and bedding planes, the former being nearly vertical and the latter horizontal. This distinction would not apply necessarily to other limestone areas in which the limestone dips steeply, for example in the Mendips, where the cave formation is partly determined by thin shale bands within the limestone.

A first essential is to obtain plans and sections of the cave system, as it is necessary to know the three-dimensional pattern of the caves (A. L. Butcher). The instruments used for cave surveying consist of a prismatic compass, a steel tape for measuring horizontal distances and the rungs of steel-wire rope-ladder for vertical measurements. Traversing is usually the only practicable survey method, using the compass and tape: gradients can be measured with an Abney level, the bubble of which must be illuminated. Offsets can be taken at intervals by using the tape to establish typical cross sections.

It is important to note the nature of the cave roof and floor, as this gives very valuable evidence concerning the origin of the cave. Large-scale scalloping, for example, is associated with paraphreatic cave formation, under the influence of water flowing rapidly under hydrostatic pressure just below the water table, while the character of caves formed in the vadose zone above the water table is different, so that the two types can be distinguished; the amount of cave decoration can be an important factor in deciding the age of the cave relative to the movement of the water table. This latter factor can sometimes be related to the movement of base-level and thus the cave character can give evidence of stages in denudation.

In the Craven district Sweeting has suggested that cave passages can be related to still-stands and cave pitches to phases of rejuvenation, and the altitude of the passages is associated with the height of the base-level at the time of their formation, assuming that they formed near the water table.

Another very important factor that must be examined in relation to the rock type is the degree and nature of weathering that it has undergone. D. L. Linton (1955) has drawn attention to the importance of weathering in the formation of some tors. Weathering can operate to produce landform features by a two-stage process; firstly the rock is prepared by deep weathering and secondly the weathered material is removed, revealing the remnants of unweathered rock, sometimes in the form of tors. Thus both current weathering and past activity of this type must be taken into account. The significance of weathering in some areas in scarp retreat has already been commented upon.

R. S. Waters (1957) has given some interesting views on the importance of examining the state of weathering on Dartmoor. The adaptation to structure of the landscape in this area is much more subtle than that associated, for example, with the cuestas of south-east England. In Dartmoor there are elements of upstanding relief, the tors, and elements of negative relief, the swampy basins that occur between gorge stretches of the valleys. These features are controlled in some way by the joint pattern. The joints may be more significant than change of outcrop, and information on this must be obtained in the field. The pattern is, however, only the first step in the process, and evidence of chemical weathering must also be sought in the field, wherever exposures are available. The depth of weathering, and in Dartmoor the formation of growan, is a very significant factor in establishing both the nature of the process forming the broad basins and their age. The fact that weathering of this type is not occurring on exposed granite outcrops now can be checked in the field, and suggests that the basins date from an earlier and warmer climate before the Pleistocene or during interglacial periods. This type of field evidence may help to solve the problem of how very small streams can make wide mature basins in their upper reaches, where remnants of erosion surfaces are often located. Thus the rock and its state of weathering must be fully examined in the field, as these may supply vital clues.

It is not only the solid rock that must be examined, but evidence of any later deposits may also be of great significance. The finding of undisturbed marine shells or fossils on surfaces well above sea-level is the best evidence of the surface formation by the sea. The marine deposits found at about 450 to 600 feet on the North Downs, at Lenham, contain fossils that enable them to be dated to the Red Crag at the beginning of the Pleistocene; thus not only the character of the erosional agent but also the date of deposition of the sediment on it can be established. At even higher elevations evidence of marine action has been recorded by Waters (1960) on high ground in south-west England, for example on Staple Hill at 970 to 1035 feet; lying on a flattish surface a number of rounded flint pebbles, cherts and quartzites were found. The flints showed characteristic beach erosion features, such as chatter marks, and were very well rounded, although many of them have been subsequently broken by frost action. The cementation of similar deposits further east suggests that they may date from the early Tertiary. The sloping character of the surface on which the deposits rest also supports this view. The slope appears to be due to crustal warping. West of this, however, the superficial deposits are all angular and very different, suggesting only subaerial formative processes, while the surface on which they rest is much flatter, indicating a later origin and less subsequent crustal warping. Thus by a careful analysis of the superficial deposits, the origin and age of these two surfaces may be differentiated much more convincingly.

Another interesting example of the study of deposits on an erosion surface is that made by P. E. Kent (1957). These deposits occur in large pot-holes in the Upland Plain cut across the limestone outcrop in the Derbyshire Dome. They contain Triassic material and a certain amount of glacial drift. They give evidence of a former Triassic cover over the limestone outcrop, and Kent has shown how they can be associated with a mid-Tertiary age of the upland plain. Evidence of deposits on erosion surfaces must usually be a lucky exception; normally the surfaces must be identified by rather less reliable means especially in those parts of the world where glaciation has greatly modified the landscape and removed the original superficial deposits.

Certain criteria can be identified which have diagnostic value concerning the nature of origin of erosion surfaces. One problem is to distinguish between subaerial and marine-formed surfaces, and the various possible types of subaerial surfaces must also be considered. The differences between a peneplain and a pediplain are important, although difficult to define precisely and not unanimously accepted by all geomorphologists. However, in pediplanation fundamental features appear to be the scarp separating flat plains and scarp retreat, while under peneplanation the emphasis is placed on down wearing of the landscape, giving a more undulating final form. L. C. King (1962) has suggested that the relative relief is a significant factor in determining whether landscape development should be essentially by scarp retreat and pediplanation, which he considered takes place when the relief exceeds a critical value, or by lowering to form largely convex slopes, giving the appearance of a peneplain, when the relief is lower than the critical value. The critical height depends on the maintenance of a scarp face, which in turn depends partly on the type of bedrock and its resistance to shear. This is dependent on the cohesion, the stress and a constant determined by the type of material. In clay the critical height is 20 feet, but in hard rock it may be hundreds or even thousands of feet. In the process of pediplanation the landscape evolves across the land area. This complicates the problem of dating a pediplain, which gets progressively younger towards the retreating scarp, the difference of age of parts of the one surface being many millions of years in some instances. The initiation of the new surface is probably the most valid and useful date for correlation with other surfaces elsewhere. The peneplain, on the other hand, is all of one age. There are also other possible methods of forming plane surfaces, such as by prolonged glacial, periglacial or arid processes.

Relating especially to areas such as the British Isles, J. B. Sissons (1954), from his work in south-west Yorkshire, has enumerated ten factors that he considers should be associated with marine-formed surfaces. The first point is that the break of slope at the back of the erosion remnant is fairly sharp and the slope behind fairly steep; this represents the degraded remains of an old cliff line. That such degradation can be quite rapid is seen in the character of the old cliff line on the seaward side of the Lincolnshire marshland. This slope is the modified upper part of a line of chalk cliffs, which formed the coast in the last interglacial. The lower part of the cliff is buried beneath a deposit of till. The ice and associated periglacial conditions may have played an important part in causing the rapid degradation of the old cliff.

The second point is that the break of slope at the back of the surface is at a constant height over a considerable distance. If this condition is fulfilled over a wide stretch of country, it supports the conclusion that the surface was formed by marine erosion and that there has been no subsequent deformation of the surface by warping along the line of the break of slope. However, there might have been warping perpendicular to the old coastline, and this would not be apparent. This is an important point if continental flexure is being considered as a possible cause of base-level changes, as this would be expected to operate at right angles to the coastline, producing a slope at right angles and not parallel to the old coast. Lack of warping can be definitely established if horizontality of raised marine levels can be identified in two directions at right angles, such as has been demonstrated by P. Temple (1964) on the shores of Lake Victoria in Africa. The shorelines from a level of 60 feet above the lake downwards are horizontal on both the western and northern shores. The shorelines in this instance are very recent, dating from between 30,000 and 3,240 years ago and may be due to climatic change or cutting down of the lake outlet as knickpoints retreat upstream into it.

The third factor concerns the close spacing of the surfaces and their arrangement as steps of constant height and limited width. This point is associated with the nature of marine planation as opposed to subaerial erosion. It is often assumed uncritically that marine planation must be the work of the waves only, and if this is true then the width of a wave-cut platform, eroded with a stable sea-level, can probably only reach an extent of about $\frac{1}{2}$ to $\frac{3}{4}$ mile

(King, 1963); this is because waves cannot erode solid rock effectively in depths over 40 feet and the normal slope of a wave-cut platform is about 1 in 100. However, it seems very likely that erosion by tidal currents in suitable environments can be effective to much greater depths, helping to produce such very flat submarine surfaces as underlie the English Channel, although other processes may also have operated here. Thus this criterion is not necessarily valid, especially in those areas, such as the coastal zones of Britain, where tides are of great importance, and this factor should always be considered.

The fourth factor is of considerably greater importance as a diagnostic factor, at least until more is known about submarine abrasion. This is the direction of consequent streams. So far drainage has not been mentioned, but it is an important element in the analysis of the landscape. However it is often necessary to study the pattern on a map rather than in the field. It is also necessary to relate the drainage to the structure and this can best be done in the field. If the consequent streams flow down the slope of the erosion surface and disregard the structure, it may be suggested that they were initiated on a thin cover of marine sediments overlying the emerging surface. If, however, the streams are controlled by the structures, then they are likely to be subsequent in type and developed under subaerial conditions.

S. W. Wooldridge and D. L. Linton (1955) have shown the importance of this very clearly in their observations of the landscape of south-east England, where the area above the level of the early Pleistocene transgression shows drainage adjusted to structure, while in the area covered by the early Pleistocene sea the drainage is consequent upon the marine trimmed surface and is unrelated to the structures.

The fifth and sixth points deal respectively with the straightness and spacing of the consequent streams. Relatively newly initiated streams are thought to be both straight and closely spaced, because there has been little time for the integration of drainage. The seventh point is the feeble development of obsequent streams, which in turn suggests the lack of subsequent streams depending on structure. This is thought to be typical of drainage developed on the exposed marine surfaces. The final three points are concerned with arguments and evidence for river capture.

In attempting to differentiate erosion surfaces formed by marine and subaerial processes in the field, it is necessary to consider the area in relation to its wider setting, and with reference to the submarine surface into which the sea would retreat as baselevel falls. It is also necessary to take into account the subsequent modification of the features since they were abandoned by the sea or lost contact with the downcutting and widening processes in the river valley and came under the influence of the processes of mass movement and slope formation. B. J. Sissons (1960) has worked out deductively the features that might be expected to follow as the result of modification of a marine platform backed by a cliff, when it is abandoned by a fall of sea-level. He indicates the gradual dissection of the platform as consequent streams initiated on it cut down to the new base level; such streams will also widen their valleys at the expense of the cliff. Further falls of sea-level and continued modification will eventually remove all evidence of the former marine erosion surface and old cliff, their place being taken by valley in valley forms. The last remnants of the marine surfaces would survive on the spurs. Thus valley-side benches finally would form the only evidence of the former marine surfaces in the upper reaches of the valleys. Field work could be directed towards the establishment of the correctness of this hypothetical type of development in an area known to have been affected by marine erosion.

This idea presupposes that the sea can retreat progressively downslope to reveal further marine trimmed surfaces; it is at this point that the wider area and offshore relief must be taken into account. Such a development could not take place on the flanks of a large valley unless the valley had been formed before the submergence of the area; this hypothesis leads to obvious problems in many inland areas.

In attempting to establish a denudation chronology from work done in the field, it is necessary to bear in mind a considerable number of factors that influence the results of various forms of erosion, such as climate and vegetation in relation to types and intensity of subaerial erosion. It is advisable to consider the operation of a variety of processes, as most landscapes are polygenetic as well as polycyclic. Subsequent modification must also be taken into account; this can be modification both by the exogenetic processes and by endogenetic forces, in the form of faulting or warping of the crust. It is important to consider the possibility of warping when field work is being undertaken, and the landscape results of warping will be considered under endogenetic processes in the next chapter, pp. 172-175, as these effects are a reflection of the internal forces that are visible in the landscape.

The logical conclusion of denudation chronology is the study of the landform evidence of sea-level changes as available in raised shoreline features and submerged land formation. These features usually belong to the latest geological periods, mostly to the Pleistocene and Holocene times.

A study of coastal forms can give very useful evidence of changes of sea-level, both positive and negative. Evidence of lower sea-levels is very clearly displayed on many coasts in the form of submerged forests and peat beds. Studies of these deposits can be carried out on the foreshore, where they are exposed at low water; for example the work of H. H. Swinnerton (1931) on the coast of Lincolnshire shows how a detailed study of the foreshore exposures of peat and clays enabled a post-glacial chronology to be worked out. The boulder-clay at the base of the succession could be recognised by its erratic content, while the layer of tree stumps and peat overlying could be dated by the artifacts found within it, or by more recent methods. Above this lay a marsh-clay, whose character was again revealed by a study of the flora and fauna it contained and the overlying upper peat could be dated to the Iron Age. Finally there was an upper clay, which revealed again, by close study of its contained flora and fauna, that it was a salt marsh deposit. Thus stages of rising sea-level, with one or two breaks for peat formation, were established. In other areas useful evidence of buried peats is found in dock excavations.

3. RAISED BEACHES AND OTHER SHORELINE FEATURES

Field work on raised shorelines has even more scope, as the features are more accessible and more variable. The interpretation of these features is complicated by the nature of sea-level change relative to that of the land, because in many areas both eustatic and isostatic factors are involved.

The study of certain boulder fields in the Åland Islands off south-west Finland revealed features that could only be reconciled with a marine origin of the landforms, although they lay about 100 m above sea-level; they contained large ridges, typical of shingle beaches at modern sea-level, and the gradation of the stones resembled that of shingle beaches. The fact that the area lay close to the maximum isostatic uplift of Scandinavia indicates that this interpretation could well be justified, as the whole island must have been beneath the sea about 7000 B.C.

In considering the characteristics and interpretation of raised shoreline features a number of considerations must be taken into account. The distribution and height relationships of the features must first be established, then any evidence of their age must be sought, and then suggestions considering their interpretation can be put forward. The features indicative of former higher sea-levels are nearly as varied as those of the modern shore. There are features of erosion and deposition, the latter in many ways providing the best evidence as there is more chance that they can be dated.

Sometimes precise levelling can reveal subtle changes of level of a sequence of coastal features. The work of W. V. Lewis and W. G. V. Balchin (1940) illustrates the use of precise levelling to reveal small changes in level of the long series of shingle beach ridges on Dungeness. In interpreting these results the processes operating to form the ridges must be taken into account, as these may cause irregular variations unrelated to fluctuations of sea-level. However, if the sequence is long enough these irregularities do not obscure the long-term trend in the changes of ridge height, which provide useful evidence of sea-level variations.

A more recent example of the application of this method of establishing sea-level fluctuations from landforms is the work of J. L. Davies (1961) in Tasmania. It is interesting to note that most of his results were obtained by surveying the elevation of sand ridges, rather than shingle ridges as in the earlier study of Lewis and Balchin. Although sand and shingle ridges are formed by different types of waves, they are both related to the sea-level at the time of their formation. The changing elevation of the Tasmanian sand ridges also agrees with that of a local shingle beach. All except one of the sand ridge systems show a very convincing slope down to the present coast, indicating that sea-level must have been falling slowly. The fact that one set of results shows the opposite trend indicates that a considerable amount of evidence of this type is required before it can be relied on, as there are a number of variables involved, such as the range of the tide, which can vary around a coast and change with the changing configuration of the coast as sea-level changes. Differences of exposure will also help to account for variations of height of wave-formed features in different parts of a coastline. There is not normally available such a long and continuous record as in the two areas mentioned, and information regarding raised shorelines must be studied as it becomes available.

The types of feature that are available for study vary according to the nature of the coastline. In the north of Scotland, for example, the features indicative of a former higher sea-level could be divided into four types. First there are the rock shelves or platforms, backed by cliffs in various states of degradation. These platforms are usually bare of beach material, as they frequently are when they are being actively cut at sea-level, because they can only be effectively cut in the absence of any large amount of beach material. These remnants are usually related to a former high tide level, as the notch at the back of the platform was cut at about the high tide level at the period when it was formed.

The second type of feature is the rocky skerries, flattened to a certain extent by wave action, but not backed by cliffs. These are common on the modern shore and similar features are found on what appears to have been an earlier shoreline.

The third type of feature is found in the more sheltered areas where deposits can accumulate; these are remains of depositional features, such as beaches or spits. As indicated by their covering of vegetation and their height, it is clear that some of these are raised above the action of present waves. Both the second and third features are formed at the limit of wave action and are therefore related to the then high tide level and not to the former mean sea-level.

The fourth type of feature is only found in certain areas, where glaciers previously reached close to sea-level. It consists of deposits of glacial or fluvio-glacial sediments, modified by and adjusted to the sea. This type of feature is particularly useful as it may enable former sea-levels to be related to specific phases of the glacial retreat, although, as it requires special conditions, features of this type cannot be expected to occur very widely.

At times, as shown by Stephens (1957), dating can be aided by the occurrence of till overlying an old platform; alternatively the platform may be cut in till. The first possibility applies to many of the known occurrences of raised beach platforms and deposits in the southern part of the British Isles. The site at Sewerby in East Yorkshire is a good example. Here the field evidence for the age of the cliff is found in the succession of deposits, resting on the old wave-cut notch at the base of the cliff. The succession consists of old beach deposits, overlain by blown sand, hill-wash, solifluction head, a layer of till and finally, forming the upper part of the present cliff, a thick layer of fluvio-glacial outwash gravels. These deposits tell of the abandonment of the beach by the sea and the deterioration of the climate to periglacial from one milder than the present; the advance and retreat of an ice sheet were the final events. The remains of *Hippopotamus* in the beach deposits and hill wash provide data for correlation with other deposits elsewhere. This fossil in the north of England is a good indication that the deposit belongs to the last interglacial. Thus clear evidence of the age of the beach is available.

Where the features are entirely erosional dating is more difficult, but even then some clues can be seen in the field at times. The striations that have been recorded on a raised beach platform in County Donegal, indicating that the feature must have been formed earlier than the last ice advance, are an example. Another point that must be borne in mind is that the platform may date from a period long prior to any deposit that may rest upon it. Thus the seaward part of the platform in front of the buried cliff at Sewerby can be shown to be covered by a layer of till dated to the equivalent of the Saale glaciation. The platform, therefore, must have been cut in the great interglacial, and extended slightly further inland in the last interglacial to form the buried cliff. All that can usually be said with certainty is that the deposit is younger than the platform on which it rests. Hence there is a danger in correlating erosional and depositional elements of raised shorelines, but on the other hand one must expect that features formed along any coastline will include both erosional and depositional elements at the same time, according to the nature of the coast, so that if the height ranges are close, it is likely that both erosional and depositional features belong to the same period of coastal formation.

One of the main problems is to establish the height of the raised features relative to sea-level at the time of their formation and to present sea-level. This may be done with a surveying aneroid, but the difficulty is often to find fixed heights to which the readings can be related. Donner (1959) has pointed out some of the difficulties involved, such as variations of tide height both along the present coast and under the different tidal conditions prevailing at the time the features were formed. There are variations of height caused by difference of exposure, and the fact that the height to which depositional features are built by the waves depends partly on the size of the material. This can be seen very readily in the variation of the height of Chesil Beach above sea-level along its crest, which increases from 23 feet above high water at Abbotsbury, where the pebbles are about $\frac{1}{2}$ inch diameter, to 43 feet at Portland, where the shingle is 2 to 3 inches in diameter. Sand features, being built up by long constructive swells rather than storm waves, will not be built so high above high tide level, and rock notches will form only a little above high tide level. Another factor is the blurring of the feature by subsequent subaerial modification since its elevation above the sea.

The height that is normally measured is that of the back of the raised beach or wave-cut platform, at the base of the cliff. The height of this point must then be related to Ordnance Datum and hence to the mean sea-level in relation to the tide. Owing to the rarity of bench marks, Donner fixed the elevation of raised features by measuring their height above a well defined barnacle zone on the shore. He found a fairly sharp upper boundary of the common barnacle, *Balanus balanoides*, and he checked this line in relation to sea-level by levelling to bench marks, showing that the variation in height above O.D. was less than 1 m varying from 0·4 to 1·2 m, increasing up the sea lochs. Another method of fixing the height of raised shoreline features is to measure the difference of height between the features and the water-level. Such a measurement normally only requires a very short traverse, which can be done by levelling or by surveying aneroid. The time of the observation must be noted, then the height of the water-level at this time can be calculated from the tide tables to the nearest foot. Under normal weather conditions, and where the tidal range is not very great, the results should be fairly accurate. Sissons considers that all heights of raised shoreline features should be levelled instrumentally, and this is certainly desirable. In some instances, however, where the height of the feature is not clearly defined, such precision may give a false impression of accuracy. Having established the height of the feature above the present sea-level, it is necessary to make allowance for the other variables that have already been mentioned.

Once the height of the feature has been established, there is the problem of interpretation. This becomes very complex when both isostatic and eustatic changes of level are involved. Isostatic recovery may well not be simple or uniform, and tilting of the features must be expected, so that a beach of any one age need not all be at the same height, and relics at the same height are not necessarily of the same age. A useful method of estimating the tilt of raised shoreline, used by J. T. Andrews for analysing the raised beaches of part of western Baffin Island, is to establish three points in a triangle on the same shoreline. The highest and lowest points are joined by a line, and on this line a point is fixed of height equal to the third point and proportional in distance from the two joined points according to the height of the third point. This last point is then joined to the third point, which is at the same height, and the tilt of the shoreline must be at right-angles to this line, down in the direction of the lowest point. This method can clearly only be used when it is known for certain that all the points are on the same shoreline and at the same height above the former sea-level.

In an area which has undergone considerable isostatic uplift, this can best be shown by means of isobases drawn on a map, indicating the amount of uplift. Alternatively, a shoreline diagram can be constructed along a specific direction. A useful point to plot on such diagrams is the marine limit, indicating the highest former sea-level, as this can frequently be noted in the field. Evidence for the marine limit may be in the form of pushed blocks, sand and shingle beach ridges, deltaic deposits, a wave-planed surface, particularly if the sea has transgressed on to soft drift country, or a nick in the drift or solid rock at the limit of wave action. Shoreline diagrams are frequently drawn by joining up the greatest concentration of points, but this method may lead to errors, especially if the line is drawn straight, when in fact the rate of uplift is such that the marine limit lies on a curved line.

A still more complicated set of circumstances must be borne in mind when the shoreline evidence is tied to that of retreating ice sheets. The type of

shoreline evidence that should result from constant isostatic uplift during a
period of ice retreat has been worked out by N. Stephens, and can be illustrated diagrammatically (figure 2.4). At position 1 an ice marginal outwash
delta is laid down at about sea-level, then as the ice retreats further, subsequent deltas are laid down at 2 and 3; but before deltas 2 and 3 are
deposited delta 1 has started to rise isostatically, thus delta 1 is higher than
2, and 2 than 3. Thus a metachronous shoreline is formed, which at first
tilts down towards the centre of glaciation, but as isostatic recovery continues
the younger deltas are carried up until they are at the same height as the

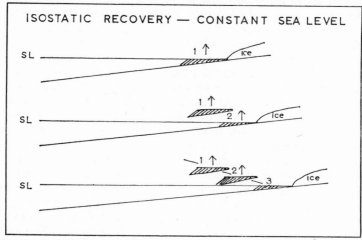

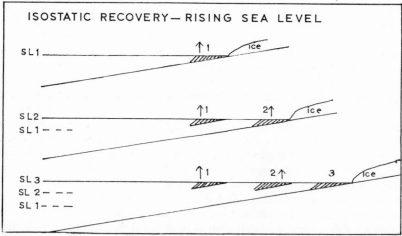

FIGURE 2.4. Diagram to illustrate raised shoreline features associated with glacier
retreat and isostatic recovery. Above, a metachronous shoreline is indicated sloping down
inland as isostatic recovery remains constant in time and space. Below, a similar metachronous shoreline appears horizontal because eustatic rise of sea-level balances isostatic
recovery.

older ones. The final result is what appears to be separate remnants of one horizontal shoreline, but what is in reality a metachronous feature, being of different age along its length.

An even more complex result ensues if eustatic change is taking place at the same time. If the rate of eustatic rise of sea-level is the same as the rate of rise of the land isostatically, then the developing deltas do not pitch inwards towards the centre of uplift. If the eustatic rise of sea-level continues after the delta formation ceases and exceeds a uniform isostatic recovery in the area, then the horizontal metachronous deltas will be drowned, and will lie parallel to a synchronous upper marine limit formed at the limit of the final eustatic sea-level. If, however, isostatic recovery accelerates or continues longer in the direction of ice retreat, then the eventual shoreline remnants will slope downwards from the centre of maximum isostatic recovery. Thus many factors, related both to isostatic and eustatic movements, have to be taken into account in an attempt to analyse glacial raised shorelines.

A necessary preliminary to the establishment of sea-level variation in the more complex areas, affected by isostatic movements, is to arrive at a clear knowledge of the eustatic movements of sea-level, which have had a world-wide effect. The post-glacial eustatic change of sea-level has been on the whole positive, causing a rising sea-level, so that different methods must be used to establish this change. Much of the evidence is now below sea-level, and must be sought in studies of bore-hole data, wherever it is available. It is necessary to date any significant evidence as accurately as possible, and from this point of view the coastal peat beds, and deltaic deposits, such as those of the Mississippi, provide valuable evidence. The deposits were laid down near sea-level and thus have value from this point of view, and they can be dated by radio carbon methods. However, some further precautions are required; many deltaic areas, where the evidence is so abundant, are areas of subsidence, and compaction of the sediments must also be allowed for. Thus the Mississippi is not very suitable to establish eustatic sea-level curves. The Gulf coast of the U.S.A., Holland and other relatively stable areas have provided data that F. P. Shepard (1963) has used to construct an eustatic curve for the last 35,000 years, although reasonable accuracy only applies to the last 16,000 years. The results show a rapid rise of about 25 feet/century from a level of about − 270 feet in 17,000 B.P. to about − 10 to − 20 feet about 6000 B.P. Since this date sea-level does not appear to have been much higher than the present. R. W. Fairbridge, however, (1961) has suggested that there have been fluctuations both above and below the present level by up to + 12 feet in the last 5000 years.

4. SLOPE FORM

a) *Slope profile*. Nearly all the land surface slopes in one direction or another, and slopes are the fundamental type of landscape feature. They therefore merit careful study. The work can be carried out in various ways; the nature of the visible slope profile may be surveyed, the character of the regolith in relation to the slope profile and underlying rock may be considered, and thirdly, the areal distribution of slope types may be studied and mapped.

Some of the major differences of opinion amongst the early geomorphologists, such as W. M. Davis and W. Penck, were their views of slope development; however, these were not accompanied by sufficiently detailed and quantitative observations to make a decision between the opponents possible. One very important problem was whether slopes developed by flattening, replacement or parallel retreat. Observations in the field are essential before some of these problems can be resolved.

The survey of the visible slope form can be carried out most conveniently with an Abney level, which can be read to 10' of arc, a 100-ft tape and ranging rods. The angles are measured both up and down the slope to provide a check, and the profile is measured along the steepest slope. The distances are measured along the ground between ranging rods fixed at breaks of slope. Where there is a continuous curvature they must be placed at uniform distances apart, dependent on the radius of curvature, and where the slope is uniform the ranging rods can be placed the full length of the tape apart.

The survey results can then be converted into vertical and horizontal distances by multiplying the measured distance by the sine and cosine of the slope angle respectively; for convenient plotting these distances should be added cumulatively. The accuracy of the Abney level is such that slope angles should be correct to the nearest half degree, and they should be reduced to this figure, while distances to be of commensurate accuracy should be measured to the nearest half foot.

Some useful preliminary work of slope measurement and interpretation has been done by R. A. G. Savigear (1952), and more recently a rather more detailed scheme of slope description, resulting from field surveys, has been put forward by A. Young (1963, 1964). He divides the slope profile into a variety of subdivisions as illustrated in figure 2.5. The smallest feature is the slope unit, consisting of either a slope element or slope segment; the former is a curved portion of the slope profile, characterised by its curvature or rate of change of angle with distance; the latter is a rectilinear portion of the slope defined by its angle. A maximum slope segment is one which is steeper than the slope units above or below it. The term can also be applied to a segment at the base of the slope, if it is followed upslope by a flatter unit. A minimum slope unit is one which is flatter in gradient than the units above or below it, and this term too can be applied to the lowest unit, if the one above is steeper. A crest segment is that one which is bounded on either side by downward slopes in opposite directions. A convex slope element increases in angle continuously downslope, and the opposite is true of a concave slope element. The term slope sector refers to that part of a slope element on which the curvature remains constant. The term convexity is used to describe that part of a slope profile where there is no decrease in angle downslope, although maximum, minimum and crest segments are excluded. A concavity includes all those parts of the slope where there is no increase of angle downslope, also excluding maximum, minimum and crest segments. Finally, a slope sequence includes that part of the slope consisting successively of a convexity, a maximum slope segment and a concavity.

By using this terminology it is possible to describe the measured slope form accurately and to record the data in tabular form. The maximum and minimum segments should be identified first, by noting points of inflexion. The angle of these can be obtained graphically if the measured figures show some variation. The crest segment is next delimited, which may require the establishment of a specific angle, such as 2 degrees. One difficulty is to obtain the

SLOPE UNIT	crest segment	convex element		segment	convex element	max segment	segment	concave element		min segment	convex element	max segment	concave element	min segment
SLOPE PROFILE														
SECTOR		sector	sector					sector	sector					
ANGLE	0±2°			15°		30°	25°				5°	12°		2°
CURVATURE		2	10	15				5	13		5		8	
		convexity				concavity					convexity	concavity		
SEQUENCE		sequence I									sequence II			

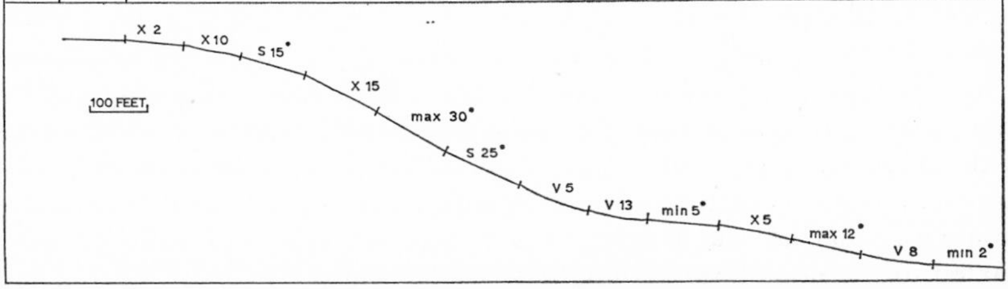

FIGURE 2.5. Slope terminology. (after Young)

curvature of concave and convex elements; this is done by measuring the ground length, and dividing this into the difference in angle between the bounding segments. Thus if a concave element decreases from 12 degrees to 3 degrees in a distance of 300 feet, the curvature is 9/300 × 100, or 3 degrees/100 feet, the values being rounded off to the nearest whole degree if the result is not exact. A rectilinear segment is recognised by the fact that it exhibits no systematic change of angle, although not all the measured angles need be identical, the angle of the segment being the mean angle of all the measurements. Concave or convex elements can be divided into sectors, according to the rate at which the slope changes, the division being fixed in the centre of the measured length on which the change of curvature occurs.

Detailed study of the nature of the slope profile enables critical angles and parts of the slope to be identified, and the number of phases involved in the slope development can be established. It provides a basis for the testing of hypotheses of theoretical slope development. Savigear's work in South Wales for example, shows that slopes of 32 degrees are significant in the modification of initially steeper cliffs. His results also show the great importance of the processes operating at the base of the slope; different developments are indicated where the removal of waste from the base of the slope is unimpeded and where it is impeded. In the examples where the removal was unimpeded the evidence suggested that 32 degrees was maintained and this was attributed to the parallel retreat of the slope. Where the removal was impeded the surveyed profiles indicated that the slope became gentler with time. A similar relationship was also noted for scree profiles measured in Iceland; the one from which material could be removed showed a rectilinear profile, while the other was much more concave (see figure 3.7).

The rather more detailed results of Young's work, carried out in a number of different areas, showed a grouping of the steeper maximum segments around 24 to 26 degrees. There was a tendency for the steeper slopes to have longer maximum segments. The general conclusion reached as a result of the detailed study of slopes measured in the field suggested that the main element of slope modification is a combination of parallel retreat and decline of slope angle, with the maximum segment retreating partially by parallel retreat, especially in the early stages. However, the dominant process of slope modification was one of slope decline. This follows the views of W. M. Davis, although W. Penck also probably intended to imply that slope replacement and decline could take place, had his views been correctly interpreted, as already mentioned on p. 6. Thus detailed field work on slope form is the most reliable and satisfactory method of studying slope formation.

b) *The regolith.* The superficial covering of weathered rock and soil, which forms the regolith, is an important aspect of the slope character. A discussion of the methods of examining this aspect of the slope should logically be included in section 8, dealing with the analysis of sediment, but it is considered here with other aspects of field study of slopes instead, as it is so intimately related to the slope form. Young has pointed out one very important point concerning the nature of the regolith; it is a very thin deposit compared with the dimensions of the slope as a whole, particularly in temperate areas where the relief is considerable. The regolith rarely exceeds $3\frac{1}{2}$ feet in thickness and is usually less than 2 feet, except when its thickness is increased by special processes, such as frost action producing congeliturbate. It is, therefore, permissible to take the plotted profile of a slope as surveyed in the field as being the solid rock slope in most instances unless the scale of the plot is very large. The nature of the regolith is nevertheless of considerable importance in considering the processes operating in the field and it can only be studied by field observations.

In the warm, moist tropics the regolith can reach thicknesses of over 100 feet where conditions are favourable. Where the weathered zone is of great thickness it is of considerable significance in landscape studies. Soil character is of great importance, as it influences the vegetation, which in turn can affect the action of slope processes. A study of the soil can give valuable evidence of both past and present slope-forming processes and of the age of the surface on which they rest. Laterite, for example, is a residual soil characteristic of old, flat surfaces under specific climatic influences. Its formation indicates, therefore, prolonged static conditions where it is well developed (L. C. King, 1963).

Studies of the regolith in the field are made difficult by the paucity of sections, a problem that can usually be overcome only by the laborious method of digging pits. Some useful information could be obtained by auguring, but it does not provide so clear a view of the character of the regolith. As has been indicated, Young's work on slopes also involved a study of the regolith, and one of the points he investigated in particular was the thickness of the deposit. The boundary between bedrock and regolith can be defined as the depth at which the fine material forms 25% of the total. Another important factor is the orientation of the rock particles in the regolith, and the base of the regolith may be taken as the depth at which some indication of outcrop curvature first takes place. The categories used by Young to differentiate zones within the regolith were, first, mainly soil with few or no fragments, second, mainly soil with many fragments, third, mainly fragments with some soil, and finally rock or almost entirely fragments. A second point that was noted was the orientation of the flatter fragments in relation to the slope and the dip of the rocks. As regards the thickness of the regolith the results were rather variable, and depended probably on differences in the lithology of the bedrock. The degree of reduction of the material was studied by analysis of samples weighing 1500 grams. A broad division between soil and rock fragments was made on the basis of separating the fine fraction, under 2 mm, from the coarse. This coarse fraction was further subdivided by sieving into four categories.

It is worth noting that observations of regolith thickness over the whole hill-side showed that even the concavity at the base of the slope was mainly a rock-cut feature, on account of the thinness of the regolith in comparision with the radius of curvature of the concavity, and the scale of the hill-side compared with soil thickness.

Another example of the field study of regolith is the work of J. Tivy (1962) in the Southern Uplands of Scotland. This study was based on the analysis of a series of pits dug in the hill-side. The choice of site for the pits was related to the form of the slope, and designed to give an idea of the character of the regolith from the top of the slope to its base. The slopes in this area usually have a convex element at the top, with a long rectilinear slope below, and often a still steeper, undercut portion at the base. The surveys of the regolith were accompanied by detailed survey of the slope, using levelling and tacheometry. Surface relief and vegetation were also noted in the vicinity of the pits. The information noted in connection with a study of the regolith included the soil horizons, the depth of the regolith, the nature of its constituent material, the colour, the amount of organic matter, the root penetration, texture of the soil, degree of stoniness and size and orientation of the stones. The Scottish Soil Survey system of description was used for noting the character of the soil revealed in the pits. The slope deposits on the whole suggested fairly recent formation under periglacial conditions, and there was no evidence of deep weathered material belonging to an earlier warmer phase. Again, however, considering the total relief of the area, the layer of material overlying the bedrock was relatively thin, except in isolated localities.

The description of the slope deposits that have been mentioned indicates the type of measurement that it is valuable to make in the field, and the type of information that can be obtained from them. Thus the analysis of the processes operating on a slope can be greatly facilitated if detailed information is available about the nature of the material overlying the solid bedrock.

c) *Slope mapping.* A slope profile and its regolith can be surveyed relatively easily, although considerable labour is involved in the latter operation. The results of the survey can be plotted to give a visual interpretation of the field observations; although it is not possible as a rule to draw the regolith to scale, its character can be indicated by symbols according to the data measured in the field. The representation of changing slope form over an area, however, is not nearly so easily or objectively recorded in the field, although this areal distribution of slope form is a very important aspect of slope study. Much thought has been given to this problem lately by a small group of British geomorphologists, including R. A. G. Savigear and R. S. Waters (1958) and several others.

The first step is to define the characteristics of slope form that must be shown on the map, then the most suitable symbols must be devised, and finally the mapping must be carried out in the field. The resulting survey is called a morphological map; this term implies that the map is designed purely to show the form of the ground in a way more suited to geomorphological analysis than the normal use of contours. Thus a morphological map must be distinguished from a geomorphological map; the latter type of map attempts to show the areal distribution of certain geomorphological features that can be plotted by symbols, and implies an analysis of the landforms on a genetic basis, while no such analysis is needed to produce a morphological map, although it can be used as a basis for a genetic approach to the study of the landscape mapped. The morphological map is theoretically objective, while the geomorphological map is subjective and depends on the worker's own interpretation of the landscape.

A morphological map attempts to delimit all the different facets of the landscape in terms of their slope characteristics. Thus breaks of slope and changes of slope are the essential elements that must be shown. One great advantage of the method of mapping is that it ensures that the character of the country being mapped is thoroughly examined, and features that had previously escaped notice are frequently revealed. The aim of the survey is to delimit the extent of each facet of the landscape by mapping its boundaries, where there is a change of slope.

Experiments have been made with a preliminary method of morphological mapping and various suggested improvements have been debated amongst members of the British Geomorphological Research Group, and the results of these meetings have been summarised in the reports of the group (1959-1962). These discussions led to the formulation of rather more complex symbols than the original ones and substitution of the term change of slope for the term inflexion as used in the earlier scheme. New terms were also introduced, which must be defined. A slope is a surface inclined at a gradient less than 40 degrees. A cliff is a surface inclined at more than 40 degrees. A facet is a plane, or almost plane, horizontal or inclined area, differing from the surrounding areas. An element is a smoothly curved or almost smoothly curved concave or convex surface area. An irregular facet or element is one whose surface shows irregularities that are too small to indicate to scale. A break of slope is an angular discontinuity of the ground surface. A change of slope is a smoothly curved concave or convex area whose true ground horizontal equivalent is greater than the width of a line on the field map, but too narrow to allow two boundaries to be shown. An inflexion is the line of maximum slope between two adjacent concave and convex elements.

The basic symbols are a full line to indicate a break of slope and a dashed line to show a change of slope. Tags are placed on the line to indicate the direction in which the slope becomes steeper. The tags or Vs on the lines are always placed on the steepest side of the change or break of slope, pointing in the downslope direction. The true direction and amount of slope can be indicated by an arrow and figure in degrees, a cross being added on the arrow if the slope element is convex and a bar if it is a concave. Inflexions are shown by simple dashed lines.

The symbol for a change or break of slope should cover $\frac{1}{8}$ inch on the map, while the line depicting an inflexion is $\frac{1}{50}$ of an inch. When the inflexion widens out to become a feature with two breaks of slope at either side, separated by a distance of which the horizontal equivalent exceeds the distance required for the plotting of the symbol to scale, it can be shown as a microfacet. This is indicated by a dashed line with straight ticks on the downslope side. If the microfacet becomes wide enough to cover sufficient ground for its upper and lower limits to be indicated separately, that is if its horizontal equivalent exceeds $\frac{1}{8}$ of an inch, then it is shown by symbols at the top and base, according to the character of the change or break of slope at either side. Examples of the symbols are shown in figure 2.6.

A problem arises over cliff facets, because the horizontal equivalent of a very steep or vertical cliff is small and therefore it would not be possible to show it under the rules enumerated above, in which no slope facet is shown if the horizontal equivalent is less than $\frac{1}{50}$ in. A cliff is therefore recorded by a square block symbol if its horizontal equivalent is less than $\frac{1}{8}$ in., but if it is wider, both the top and the bottom can be indicated by the appropriate symbols. Cliff symbols can be combined with the appropriate slope symbol to indicate changes and breaks of slope at the limit of cliffed sections of the hill-side.

A series of symbols has been evolved to indicate various types of micro-slope facets, incorporating both slope and cliff forms; these can best be explained diagrammatically (see figure 2.6), and it will be apparent that the symbols can become very complex. These symbols are an attempt to devise means of showing features of small dimensions relative to the map scale. If a 1/10,560 map (6 inches to 1 mile) is used, it is not possible to show clearly important elements in the landscape the horizontal equivalent of which is less than 100 feet.

A further type of information may be added to the map by shading the ground within certain ranges of gradient. An example is to differentiate between ground sloping at less than 5 degrees, ground between 5 and 40 degrees, and that sloping at over 40 degrees. The flattest ground can be left blank and the steepest shaded most heavily. The lowest category, in this scale, delimits the areas that appear to be practically flat and may be associated with the processes operating near to base-level, which in some

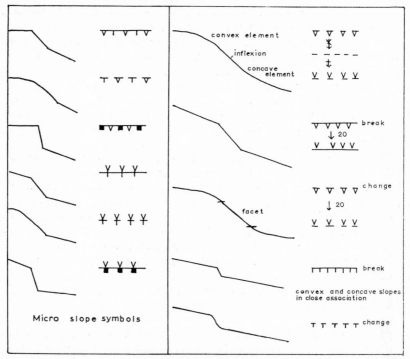

FIGURE 2.6. Slope map symbols. On the left micro-facet symbols are shown and on the right symbols suitable for general slope mapping, to produce a morphological map. (after British Geomorphological Research Group)

instances has diagnostic value as far as denudation chronology is concerned. The slopes greater than 40 degrees are those that normally consist of outcrops of bare rock, and thus these areas are differentiated from those covered by soil and vegetation. This is only one possibility, and other categories of shading may be desirable for specific purposes.

One of the problems associated with the use of this method of morphological mapping, or even the rather simplified system omitting the microfacets, is the relationship between the amount of detail that can be shown and the scale, and the time taken to cover a fairly large area. There is also the problem of the field mapping. Some features are very distinct and all surveyors would place them identically, but the more subtle changes of slope could be mapped differently by different observers.

An experiment was carried out by the geomorphologists of the Bristol Department of Geography to test these points. The test was carried out on an area 5 km. by 2 km. on the Cotswold scarp using, firstly, direct mapping on the 1 in. to 1 mile scale, secondly, 1/25,000, reduced to 1 in., and, thirdly, 6 inches to 1 mile, the result being reduced progressively to 1/25,000 and the 1 in. scales. Both linear and tagged symbols, such as those described, were used. It is interesting to note that, although all the surveyors were skilled geomorphologists, the results did not compare very closely. 75% of the detail was placed in perceptibly different places, and one-third was significantly different in position and some even in type, although many of these differences were probably due to the reduction to a smaller scale. The differences were most marked, as might be expected, on the less steeply sloping areas, where changes are more subtle. The conclusion must be reached that in some areas the type of terrain is such that there is too much genuine room for uncertainty for the results to be truly objective or reliable. The problem of showing crest lines on flat interfluves was responsible for considerable variation of interpretation. It is interesting that an experiment made by mapping the area entirely from the 1/25,000 map, without any field observations at all, produced a valueless result, with very many misinterpretations of the relief, omission of distinct breaks visible in the field and inclusion of others that were non-existent in the field. Even the interpretation of stereo pairs of aerial photographs of the area produced rather disappointing results, except where the relief was strong. The general conclusion from these tests is that the method can be used with advantage in areas of clear-cut relief, but that it is not very suitable for use in areas of gentle relief and long smooth curves.

The scale of mapping must vary with the purpose of the study, the type of country and the available base maps. In some types of terrain aerial photographs provide suitable base maps and can be used to map the major landscape features if field checks are used. Such methods can be applied to semi-arid or tropical landscapes or very mountainous country, where the landscape has fairly sharp breaks of slope and the scale is small. The scale must also be related to the amount of detail to be shown. Morphological maps of areas such as the great plainlands of Africa can be carried out on a very small scale; as vast areas of flat country terminate in scarps or at valley floors; these are features that can be readily mapped. L. C. King (1962) has produced a small-scale map of the whole of Africa; this morphological map shows four major cyclic land surfaces, including both denudational and aggradational surfaces. Morphological maps have also been published of France, Belgium and the U.S.S.R., as well as parts of Africa, and elsewhere.

The method of detailed morphological mapping is no more than a means to an end; in the same way as a contour map can be used to aid analysis of relief, or a geological map to locate rock types, so a morphological map can be used as an instrument of geomorphological research. It does not attempt to do more than record the relief forms and slope types by a method that can yield much information to the experienced worker. One of the main advantages of the technique is that it ensures close and accurate observation of the landscape in the field and provides a basis for its analysis.

Theoretically anyone should be able to produce a morphological map who can locate positions on a map and has an eye for country. A geomorphological map on the other hand demands a knowledge of the genetic origin of landforms and the ability to recognise specific features in the field; as features can be shown symbolically it is more suited to maps of larger areas on a smaller scale than the morphological mapping. The symbols that can be used on a geomorphological map depend on the nature of the country being mapped and the scale of the map. A useful technique to adopt for this purpose is the method of using different coloured symbols for features produced by different processes; the key to the geomorphological mapping of the British Isles, the original sheets of which were drawn on a scale of $\frac{1}{4}$ in. to 1 mile, provides a good example of this method of differentiating landscape-forming processes.

The landforms are divided into six categories: A, shown in shades of red and brown, indicates features related to structural and subaerial denudation processes, such as cuestas and mountain regions. The second group, B, shown in green, indicates fluvial features, both erosional, such as gorges, and depositional, such as deltas. Group C, in cobalt blue, shows features of glacial erosion, for example corries and meltwater channels. Group D, in violet, shows features of glacial deposition, including moraines, drumlins and fluvio-glacial features. Group E, if in black, indicates features of marine erosion, or if in red, features of marine deposition. The final group F is used for miscellaneous features, which are shown in black; this group includes such features as blown sand, tors, boulder fields and karstic forms.

A geomorphological map is a very useful method of summing up a geomorphological interpretation of a piece of country that has been studied, and different symbols and features can be shown as required. For example many studies in denudation chronology sum up the field evidence of erosion surfaces by plotting them on a map and distinguishing the different surfaces, located in the field, by different symbols. Many countries in America and Europe have produced or are producing geomorphological and morphological maps. The geomorphological map of Hungary is one of the most detailed; over 300 separate features are to be shown on maps of a scale of 1:25,000. Denmark and Poland have also produced useful geomorphological maps that can be cited as examples, while the glacial map of Canada, on a scale of 60 miles to 1 inch, concentrates on features of glacial significance. Areas under ice at present, areas that were unglaciated and those under lake or sea water at one time are shaded, and many minor features are shown. Much of the data has been obtained from aerial photographs, but field work has been used to check the data where possible. In such a large, and in parts little known, area the map is more in the nature of a reconnaissance survey, but is nevertheless of considerable interest and value.

5. RIVERS

Although slopes occupy by far the greater part of the landscape, the rivers at their base must not be ignored, as these play a vital part in the evacuation of material brought down the slope by processes of mass-movement. The rivers also, by their capacity to cut downwards under some conditions, provide the relief that enables the slope above to develop.

Certain essential data concerning the nature of river valleys must be collected in the field. The features that are especially important include the gradient of the river bed, the width and depth of the river, the character of the river bed and of the banks of the river, and the nature of the surrounding hill slopes. The study by geomorphologists of rivers and their valleys can be aimed at the solution of a variety of problems, and the approach to the study and methods used will vary with the purpose of the project. Rivers may be studied in order to give information about the denudation chronology of their valleys. Secondly, rivers may be studied to throw light on past climatic oscillation and variations in the other factors that control their character. Thirdly, rivers may be investigated from the point of view of their hydrological regime, to obtain information relevant to their control and use by man, for example to prevent flooding or to supply water by damming. The latter type of work is more often undertaken by the engineer or hydrologist than by the geomorphologist, although each scientist has much to learn from the others. These three approaches to the problem of field work in river valleys will be considered by reference to specific examples.

a) *Denudation chronology.* The recent study of the river Exe by C. Kidson (1962) is a good example of the detailed field study of a river, designed to assist in the elucidation of the denudation chronology. One of the most useful features of a river valley is that its long profile records previous variations of base-level. Thus a detailed study of the river's longitudinal profile provides valuable evidence concerning the stages of evolution of the valley. Kidson has shown that the long profile of the river must be surveyed in detail in the field if it is to be of any value; a profile drawn from even a large-scale map does not give sufficient height control to allow the minor stages to be detected. In order to provide a reliable long profile the river must be accurately levelled, using a level and staff. The most suitable instruments for this purpose are a Dumpy level and Sopwith staff, these being fairly light and also reasonably accurate, as the staff can be read to the nearest 0·01 ft. Kidson achieved an accuracy of ±0·5 feet. The distances can best be measured by tacheometry as the surveying proceeds, and the heights can be checked against all available bench marks. When levelling to this accuracy it is necessary to work to a standard position in the river. For this purpose the water-level is the best height to use, making allowance for changes in water-level during the time taken to complete the survey.

Such a surveyed long profile can then be used for mathematical analysis, as discussed later on p. 255, but owing to the difficulties of such analysis it is of great value to provide a means of checking the mathematical analysis by further field survey. It is, therefore, useful to survey a long tributary that as far as possible has had the same denudational history as the major stream; in the example cited Kidson surveyed the Barle as well as the Exe.

Apart from the profile along the river bed, it is necessary to consider the nature of the valley sides, to survey cross profiles in critical places and to map the distribution of valley benches. These features can provide essential support for the later analysis of the profile. In a fairly narrow and deeply cut valley such as that of the Exe the remnants of valley side benches are very small and may extend some distance above the river; thus instrumental levelling is not a very practicable means of mapping them. Instead it is often found useful to do short traverses with a surveying aneroid which can be read to the nearest foot. This should provide heights that are within the necessary order of accuracy, considering the subsequent downcutting that many of the benches may have undergone. Where the steep valley sides are heavily wooded, an aneroid barometer is the only instrument that can be used for this purpose. The benches can then be related to the knick-points located on the river profile by the levelling.

In analysing the profile and locating knick-points it is necessary to consider other possible causes for breaks in the profile, and to make this possible the nature of the rocks along the river bank should be noted as the profile is surveyed. Other interruptions must also be borne in mind, such as glacial interference; this can produce a sharp break of river gradient and water-falls that have nothing to do with rejuvenation.

The problem of the elucidation of the development of a river valley that has been influenced by both a rising and a falling base-level is considerably more complex and requires further field information. A river such as the lower Thames provides both a wealth of problems and a wide variety of material that can be collected in the field to help solve the problems. The evidence is found not only in remnants of erosional benches, but also in deposition of gravels of different types, the age of which can be established by studying their contained artifacts and flora and fauna. Data are thus provided that enable the date and character of the conditions under which the deposits were laid down to be established. Such material cannot be obtained at the surface and evidence must be sought in any available exposures or by auguring at critical places. The deposits that a river lays down on its bed can give very useful information about the character of its basin, and such materials should always be studied in dealing with the geomorphology of the river valley, because the nature of the river bed depends on the load brought down to it from the valley sides. The alluvial beds of most lowland British rivers can be compared with the gravel beds of some New Zealand rivers for example. The former are normally meandering and flow in one channel, while the latter often follow a braided course.

L. B. Leopold, M. G. Wolman and J. P. Miller (1964) have pointed out how the character of the river channel is reflected in the slope of the water surface. This slope is steeper where the channel is confined by rocks or vegetation and at bends, and is least in the smooth, straight reaches of the river. The presence of riffles or bars in the river bed also causes slight increase of gradient, and this is intensified where the channel divides round an island. Such factors can be demonstrated by detailed field survey, such as that carried out in the Rio Grande del Ranchos in New Mexico. The character of the river bed and banks, the river gradient and the type of bed load can be related by detailed field survey.

b) *Climatic change.* The nature of the bed load is determined to a certain extent by the climate, because this influences the vegetation and the nature of the processes operating on the slopes. The climate, particularly the precipitation, influences the run-off, and this in turn affects the nature of the river valley and bed. G. H. Dury (1954, 1958) has drawn attention to the value of field study of river valleys in an attempt to reconstruct past conditions in relation to the present character of the river valley.

Field evidence, obtained by auguring in the wide valley bends of a number of north Cotswold valleys, has revealed the character of what appear to have been very much larger streams dating from a former period of much higher discharge. The present stream meanders within the large valley bends, the ratio of wave length of the large bends to the present meanders being about 10:1. Auguring through more recent deposits has revealed the true character of the older, larger meandering valleys by establishing the nature of their solid bed. Both the larger and the smaller valleys must have reached equilibrium with the climatic conditions prevailing at the time of their formation. Thus by studying the nature of the valleys it is possible to obtain information both about the former conditions and about the relationship between the various factors that determine the character of the river bed in a graded or equilibrium condition.

c) *Human interference.* In considering the effect of man's activity on river valleys, it is possible to examine the changes that certain river valleys have undergone as a result of interference with the natural regime of the river. The example Mackin (1948) gives of the effects of hydraulic mining in the Sierra Nevada from 1855 to 1884 is useful in this respect. Field observations in the Great Valley of California showed that the large amount of material added to the river valley during this period, resulted in deposition over a distance of 20 miles, and a change in gradient from 5 ft/mile originally to $2\frac{1}{2}$ ft/mile at the mouth, 10 ft/mile in the middle to 20 ft/mile in the upper zone.

The operation of the reverse process, a reduction in load, could be studied in the Colorado River, as a result of building of the Hoover dam. Observations showed that the river cut down 9 feet in two years in attempting to adjust its bed to the new conditions. Upstream of the dam the effect on the river is that of a rise of base-level. The sediment is deposited behind the dam and observation of small dams shows that the sediment forms a wedge extending only a short distance upstream. Many surveys of dammed streams have been carried out by Kaetz and Rich in 1939 and repeated in 1961. They show that the slope of the newly deposited material was 30 to 60% of the original slope. After 22 years the surveys showed that the wedge of sediment had extended only a short distance upstream at a decelerating rate. The decrease of gradient is probably accompanied by changes in the channel, so that conditions are readjusted to the character of the load (Leopold, Wolman and Miller, 1964). Other matters concerning the nature of river valleys can be dealt with more suitably in the following chapter under the heading of fluvial processes.

6. COASTAL LANDFORMS

A series of surveys of the type described at the beginning of the chapter can give valuable information concerning the growth and development of coastal accretion forms, and if these can be compared with old maps the development can be extended back in time. The work of W. E. Yasso (1964) on a small portion of Sandy Hook illustrates how detailed and precise surveys of a small coastal feature can be used to test various geometrical properties of such features. The maps used were surveyed by plane-table and precise levelling was done to obtain a detailed record of the position of contours and details of surface form relative to a number of fixed points, which had been surveyed by theodolite triangulation. Both transverse and longitudinal profiles were surveyed periodically. Observations on transverse profiles were made every 5 or 3 feet according to the detail required, the profiles being plotted on a scale of 1:120 horizontally and 1:12 vertically. This was a very detailed study of a small area, affected only by small waves generated within a short fetch, but it gave useful results that may help to explain larger and more complex features. The shape of the recurved spit that was surveyed in this way was studied, and a computer analysis showed that it conformed closely to a logarithmic spiral law. This form can then be related to wave refraction and other significant factors. This is only one example of the type of information that may be obtained by careful survey of beach forms.

Field work is also required in other coastal problems, for example in the study of coast erosion and erosional features. An assessment of the rate of coastal erosion can be made by measuring at convenient time intervals to the top of a cliff from a fixed point, but more significant are observations that enable the cause of erosion to be studied. The nature of the cliff and the beach at its foot must be examined, and the cliff profile and the material of which it is formed studied. It is also necessary to consider wave action and coastal currents, and the wider setting of the area and the alignment of the coast are also relevant variables. In some circumstances it is possible to show that erosion is cyclic; thus marine undercutting causes slumping, which protects the cliff foot for a time until marine erosion again causes instability by slowly removing the slumped material. A study of the material forming the cliff and the nature of the cliff profile can help to account for this type of erosion.

Cliff profiles on harder rocks sometimes reveal evidence of earlier developmental episodes. Their study gives information that assists in the elucidation of the stages of their formation in relation to sea-level changes. Studies of this type are rare, but that of A. R. Orme (1962) might be given as an example of the type of information that can be gained by a study of cliff profiles. He is concerned chiefly with the character of abandoned cliffs, which he classifies

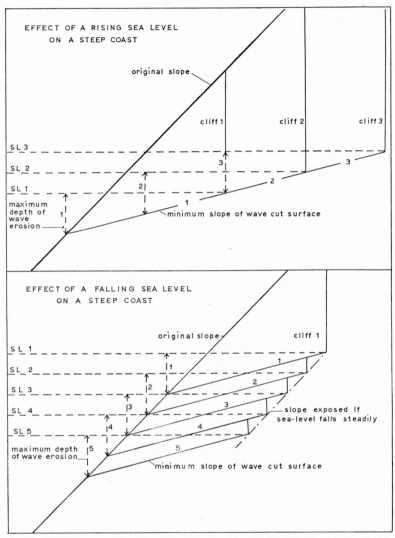

FIGURE 2.7. Diagram to show that only a slowly rising sea-level can be associated with a wide gently sloping wave-cut platform. Three basic assumptions are made: 1. The original coast, both above and below water-level, is steeper than the final wave-cut surface. 2. There is a maximum depth to which wave erosion can be effective and below which no erosion can take place. 3. There is a minimum slope below which waves cannot flatten the wave-abrasion surface, but to which they will reduce it. With a rising sea-level stillstands will not cause any recognisable effect, provided the steady rise is slow enough to allow planation to reach its lowest possible gradient. With a falling sea-level, if the fall is steady a slope parallel to the original one will replace it. Only wave action is considered.

into three groups: those that are abandoned by marine progradation, those raised above the action of waves by isostatic recovery and those abandoned by eustatic lowering of sea-level. He also describes the significance of bevelled cliffs that are so common around the coast of parts of Britain. The interest and value of field work investigations into the problem of cliffs are shown in the symposium on coastal cliffs (Steers, 1962), where a number of different approaches to the subject are demonstrated. The importance of the structure and rock type in accounting for various types of coastal landslips is stressed by W. H. Ward, while A. Wood (1959) has studied the form of the cliff profile, where this is cut in relatively uniform, hard rock. He has shown that the coastal bevel, which can be recognised by field observations of the cliff profile, indicates that the cliffs of the area he studied near Aberystwyth are extremely old and stable. The coastal bevel, in his opinion, marks the position of older cliff lines, now modified by subaerial erosion. It indicates that the sea has not cut into the land to any extent for a long period of time. A. R. Orme goes further in his analysis of the cliffs of Devon to relate the cliff formation to different phases of the Pleistocene; the cliff was probably cut originally in Cromerian or earlier times, and was influenced by marine erosion during the subsequent periods of high interglacial sea-level and then modified during the low glacial sea-levels by subaerial processes and at times by glacial ones. These conclusions are reached by studying the evidence of notches at different heights in relation to the superficial deposits of head or sometimes till.

Another coastal problem associated with cliff forms is the development of wave-cut platforms. These features are sometimes invoked in studies of denudation chronology, without adequate knowledge of how they form in the field, as mentioned on pp. 43, 44, and some points in this connection are illustrated in figure 2.7. Studies of wave-cut platforms in the field must be carried out by observation and measurement. Surveyed profiles of these features at low water can give useful information concerning their character, but in order to understand their formation observations should if possible continue below water level, by sounding or diving.

Other coastal landforms will be treated in the next chapter dealing with the action of marine processes, as their form so closely reflects the forces at work on them.

7. SUBMARINE FEATURES

The significance of submarine morphology in the study of a number of problems has come to be realised recently. The nature of the submarine relief is very important in hypotheses concerned with the marine origin of erosion surfaces and the effects of a falling base-level. It is also realised that to understand fully the operation of marine processes on the shore demands a knowledge of the character of the offshore region and of the processes at work within it.

The general character of the offshore zone can be appreciated from the study of the largest-scale Admiralty Chart available, which gives soundings and information relating to the character of the bottom sediments, and a comparison of a number of such charts for different dates can give valuable evidence of offshore changes. Rarely, however, is the chart on a sufficiently large scale to give adequate information on any one small area, so that this information must be supplemented with field observations.

The techniques of offshore survey are rather different from those of land survey, and different instruments must be used. Sometimes accurate values of water depth are required for only a short distance offshore, for example in the study of profile changes in the immediate offshore zone, when small differences must be detected over short time intervals. This type of work may conveniently be carried out by a modified type of levelling, using a specially designed long staff, marked in 10 cm. divisions and no figures, so that it can easily be read at a considerable distance by means of a system of coloured bands. The staff can be held upright with the help of a lead shoe, from a small boat, and the distance can be measured by intersection on a plane-table set up at a fixed distance from the level on a base line normal to the survey line, which is marked out by two flags that can be kept in line by the surveyor in the boat. The distance must be recorded at the same time as the leveller is taking a reading of the height. The collimation of the level must be carefully checked before operations start, as the sights cannot be equalled.

Sometimes it is of value to obtain measurements of changing beach-level under special wave conditions, when it would not be possible to carry out observations from a small boat. Such work was done at Chesil beach, where the steep gradient meant that the distance to be covered was small. Measurements of beach changes under surf waves were made by using long posts, which were fixed in the beach and to which markers were attached; the markers had a wide base to prevent their sinking into the shingle. They could be operated from the shore by means of an attached string which allowed them to fall to the level of the beach at the time of observation, and a pointer attached to the marker could be used to read off a figure painted on the post. Such equipment will clearly only be useful on a steep beach where it can be operated from the shore. Some valuable measurements have been made by observing the changing profile beneath a long pier, such as the Scripps Institution of Oceanography pier in California. A system for measurement of changes in the offshore zone has also been developed in the U.S.S.R. and has been used in the Black Sea. It enables changes to be noted even under storm conditions, by use of a system of measurements taken from a moving platform on a rail.

More often surveys must be carried out further offshore than is suitable for the methods already mentioned, and other techniques must be adopted. The difficulty of offshore survey is much reduced now that small and accurate echo-sounders are available. The necessity to fix the position of the sounding line in direction and distance still remains. The direction can conveniently be maintained by keeping two markers on the shore in line, and the distance can be obtained by observing horizontal angles with a sextant, between two fixed points on land at right angles to the line of survey (see

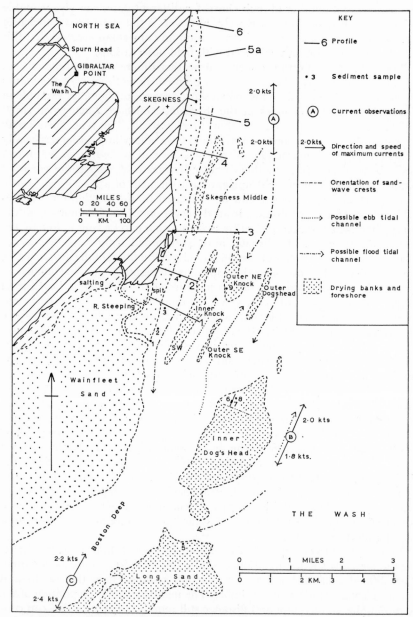

FIGURE 2.8a. Offshore survey off south Lincolnshire, showing the characteristics of the offshore tidal banks.

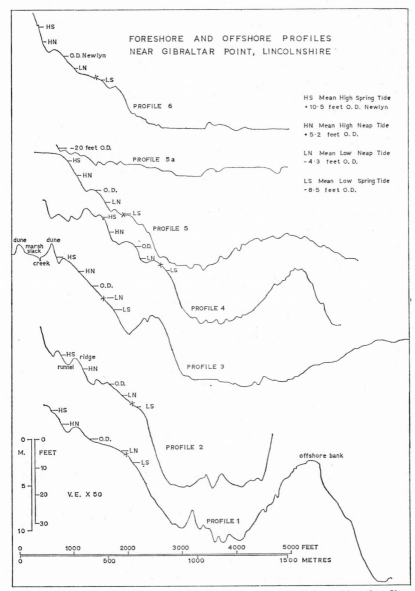

FORESHORE AND OFFSHORE PROFILES
NEAR GIBRALTAR POINT, LINCOLNSHIRE

HS Mean High Spring Tide
+10·5 feet O.D. Newlyn

HN Mean High Neap Tide
+5·2 feet O. D.

LN Mean Low Neap Tide
−4·3 feet O. D.

LS Mean Low Spring Tide
−8·5 feet O.D.

FIGURE 2,8b. Offshore profiles off South Lincolnshire, see figure 2,8a for position of profiles.

figure 2.8). With suitable markers such surveys can be continued for a mile or more offshore, and the recording echo-sounders are accurate to about 3 inches in shallow water. Repeated surveys of this type are very valuable in revealing changes of bottom configuration, and enable the movement of offshore features, such as tidal sand banks, to be studied (Cloet, 1954).

The use of echo-sounders specially designed for work in shallow water has greatly increased the knowledge of the offshore region, but much interesting information must be missed, so that the development of the aqualung for shallow water diving has opened up new possibilities of underwater geomorphological observations. Tests with this type of equipment have been carried out by C. Kidson and others (1962) in the seas around Britain. The test sea-bed survey carried out with the aid of aqualung diving equipment was made in the neighbourhood of Scolt Head Island in Norfolk. The dives gave a much clearer picture of the sea-bed than that obtained by surface methods. The nature of the bottom deposits could be readily appreciated without the need to use a grab to take samples. Particularly valuable were observations on the nature of the microrelief of the sea floor: sand waves were observed and accurately measured, whereas an echo-sounder could not have given such good results and the three-dimensional view is missing in the normal echo-sounding trace. It was interesting to note that shingle in depths of 30 to 40 feet and $\frac{1}{2}$ to $\frac{3}{4}$ mile offshore was covered with delicate marine growths, indicating that no movement of coarse material took place at this depth. This observation could not have been made by surface methods and one dive provided better evidence than most of the more elaborate methods of tracing the movement of material offshore that are discussed in the next chapter. One of the major problems associated with this method of offshore observation, apart from the necessity for a boat and the diving equipment, is the difficulty of poor visibility. The best visibility encountered in the tests was 5 to 15 feet in depths up to 40 feet, but with onshore winds, in particular, the visibility was reduced to almost nil. As soon as conditions began to be choppy it became impossible to locate marked pebbles; to obtain good results calm weather was needed. When working in conditions of strong tidal and other currents a life line was essential and this was attached to the boat or marker buoy.

One problem is to plot position under water; this can be done by positioning the boat above the diver's exhaust bubbles, and fixing this point by horizontal sextant angles to fixed positions onshore; or the diver may fix positions relative to the marker buoy by use of a marked line and compass orientations. This method can provide a very valuable supplement to other techniques. The waters around the British Isles are relatively poor for visibility compared with other coastal areas, where underwater surveys can be carried out to much greater depths.

Off California, at La Jolla, observations made by divers have given much valuable information; surveys of change in offshore configuration and sand-level have been carried out by measuring at various intervals of time the exposed length of posts fixed in the sea floor, thus obtaining a measure accurate to the nearest millimetre of the amount of cut and fill. Another instrument has been devised to measure the size of ripples on the sea bed up to depths of 170 feet; it consists of a metal bar with brass prongs fitted at right angles to form a large comb. The prongs were coated with grease and the instrument was then pressed into the sand and levelled. The sand adhering to the prongs outlined the form of the ripples, which were found to range from 0·14 to over 4 feet in length. Sand samples and underwater photographs could also be taken readily (Inman, 1957, and Inman and Rusnak, 1956).

The new instruments available for exploring the layers immediately beneath the sea floor should also be mentioned. These are modified types of echo-sounders that can penetrate below the surface sediment to obtain echoes of the solid rocks or more consolidated sediments beneath. These instruments are somewhat similar to those used for geophysical prospecting into the deeper layers of the crust and mantle. Another advance is the development of the asdic method of echo-sounding (Chesterman *et al.*, 1958). This method uses an echo-sounder with its beam set at an angle to the sea surface and sweeping a path parallel to that travelled by the ship and up to 500 yards wide. This instrument partly overcomes the disadvantage of the more normal type of echo-sounder, which gives only two-dimensional records. It is also not dependent on the clarity of the water. The best results are obtained when the ship is moving slowly, and the record reveals very useful information concerning the character of the sea-bed, such as the pattern of ripples, evidence of marine organisms and outcrops of rock. The method is relatively rapid, as 5 square miles of sea floor could be covered in 20 hours' survey time, the recording being carried out in strips 500 yards wide. The different types of bottom sediment can be differentiated by the shading on the record, and small features such as sand waves are readily identifiable. Outcrops of rock can be easily traced, but samples should also be taken as the coarse fraction of the deposits tends to be overemphasised. The use of seismic refraction studies to analyse geomorphological features is well illustrated in the work o Stride (1959) who discusses the origin of the Dogger Bank. He shows that there are about 3000 feet of superficial deposits beneath the bank surface; these data support his view of its morainic origin. Such equipment is expensive and requires the use of a ship and geophysical knowledge beyond the scope of most geomorphologists, although the results obtained by these techniques have a direct bearing on many geomorphological problems.

8. THE CHARACTER OF SEDIMENTS AND SAMPLING TECHNIQUES

The field examination of superficial sedimentary deposits can give very valuable evidence concerning the action of geomorphological processes and the genesis of landforms. Drift-mapping plays a very important part in many studies, and a field study of certain aspects of the drift can give significant results. Drift is a term used to cover a wide variety of deposits, so that for clarity the discussion will be based on the depositing agent as far as possible.

The following categories can be enumerated:

a) *Residual deposits*	**g**) *Fluvio-glacial deposits*
b) *Organic deposits*	**h**) *Fluvial deposits*
c) *Wind-blown deposits*	**i**) *Estuarine and deltaic deposits*
d) *Deposition by mass movement*	**j**) *Marine coastal deposits*
e) *Periglacial and nival deposits*	**k**) *Submarine offshore deposits*
f) *Glacial deposits*	

a) Residual deposits consist of the remains of solution and weathering in rocks consisting of materials of different durability or solubility. A good example is clay-with-flints, the residual of the solution of chalk. This deposit consists of flints that are mechanically unworn set in a clayey matrix, and its presence indicates a prolonged period of subaerial weathering. It is, therefore, diagnostic of the nature of the agent of denudation on the area where it is found. In the British Isles it is found only in areas that have not been glaciated, for example the North Downs and the chalk areas of Dorset. Flint, however, is very susceptible to frost action and many areas of clay-with-flints have undergone a period of periglacial conditions, with the result that many of the flints in the deposit are now shattered into angular fragments.

b) Organic deposits can cover considerable parts of the country under suitable conditions, the best example being the upland and lowland peats, known respectively as ombrogenous and topogenous deposits. An examination of these deposits can reveal changes of climate in the former type and of sea-level in the latter, because the ombrogenous peat depends for its growth on a wet climate and occurs on the wet, poorly-drained uplands, while the topogenous type depends on the poor drainage associated with a low-lying situation, such as the Fenlands. The great value of peat for the purpose of study of climatic and sea-level fluctuations is its great preservative quality, by which it retains pollen from the surrounding vegetation in recognisable form; this can be used to build up a picture of the changing vegetation and for dating with associated articles. The peat itself can be used for carbon-14 dating, owing to its organic nature. The present state of moorland peats gives some record of the recent climatic change, as many of them indicate recent erosion, although various other biological processes must also be taken into account, such as over-grazing and fire, with consequent change of vegetation.

c) Currently developing wind-blown deposits in Britain are found mainly along the coast, in the form of coastal sand dunes; but in drier climates true desert dunes occur. In inland areas of Britain blown sand is found in some places, such as alongside part of the Trent valley, where it probably originated during a cold phase of periglacial climate when the vegetation cover was inadequate; it thus has a value as diagnostic of past conditions. Samples of wind-blown sand can often be distinguished from other types of sand deposit by a careful study of the sediment size distribution as discussed in chapter 6, so that it is useful to collect samples, if the origin of the deposit is in doubt.

The process of deposition of wind-blown sand can be differentiated in desert areas in the field by its bearing quality; if the sand is firm it is an accretion deposit, but if it is loose it is a slipface encroachment deposit. The nature of the stratification of a desert dune can be revealed if a little water, not more than one pint, is allowed to seep slowly into the sand. The water seeps more rapidly into the layers in which fine sand is more plentiful and, if the dry sand is gently scooped away from the advancing wetted front, these stand out beyond the coarser layers and the structure of the sand deposit is clearly revealed (Bagnold, 1954).

A study of the dip of ancient dune-bedded sands can give useful information concerning the direction of the wind at the time of their deposition. This may give valuable clues concerning past climates. W. J. Arkell (1943) has shown that east winds were prevalent during some phases of the Pleistocene in south-west England.

d) Deposits laid down by mass movement are very important in the consideration of slope formation, and we have already referred to the identification and description of the type of deposit on slopes that are not subject to the more violent types of mass movement. Another form of deposit associated with mass movement is scree deposit, which fringes many rock outcrops. In analysing scree profiles and the different factors on which they depend, the nature of the blocks forming the scree is of great importance. This is probably the controlling variable as far as the gradient is concerned, although the form of the profile depends more upon the nature of removal at the scree foot. Observations on scree material should include measurements of size, shape and degree of rounding of the debris. Landslip and rotational slump deposits can be recognised by their morphological form, and their material hardly merits the term 'drift' as it consists of solid material moved only a relatively short distance. Deposits of normal mass-movement, such as creep and rainwash, grade into the periglacial deposits and it is not always easy to draw the line between them, although there are some types of deposits that can be definitely ascribed to periglacial action.

e) The periglacial deposits can be recognised by the features resulting from frost action or the growth of ice, but they vary greatly in character. Periglacial action may be identified at times by the formation of an indurated soil horizon, as described by Fitzpatrick (1956). The indurated soil layer, known as 'fragipan' in the United States, is a useful indication of former periglacial conditions, if it can be recognised in the field. The hard layer that occurs at a depth of 16 to 24 inches varies much in thickness, but the upper surface is sharp; it has a platy structure in the upper part, but may become massive below. Three characteristics suggest that it is related to freezing of a wet mass, the platy structure, discontinuous spherical or vesicular pores, and a sheathing of fine material around the particles larger than 2 mm.

Under periglacial conditions superficial deposits may develop the characteristic involutions and fossil ice-wedge structures by which the former presence of severe climatic conditions can be established. There are many other features diagnostic of a periglacial climate, such as polygonal patterns and sorting of material both in section and on the surface, which will be considered in chapter 3. Less obvious on the surface, but more important, and worthy of close field study, are the deposits of head that were formed in many areas adjacent to the ice during the Pleistocene. Head is a deposit derived from the local rocks, broken into small angular pieces by frost action and moved down the slope by solifluction to form thick deposits on the gentler slopes and valley floors. Its recognition is very important as its character and formation have caused a considerable modification of the general landsdape features; it is partly responsible for the subdued landscape found in many parts of Britain and similar temperate areas.

An interesting recent example of the way in which periglacial deposits may be differentiated from glacial till in the field has been discussed by E. A. Watson. The deposits of the coast near Aberystwyth have been previously described as Newer Drift till, but a study of the orientation of the elongated pebbles in the deposits showed that a very high percentage of the pebbles were orientated at right angles to the cliff, and consisted of angular fragments of local rocks. They also dipped consistently downslope. Thus it may at times be difficult to differentiate between solifluction and true glacial deposits, unless detailed field study of the character, orientation and dip of the longer particles is carried out.

Some features formed by snow action are even more difficult to distinguish from true glacial deposits; these snow deposits may be included amongst the periglacial deposits. Morphologically features of this type resemble moraine deposits of small glaciers (Rowell and Turner, 1952), but are probably in many instances deposited by sliding of debris over snow beds from high ground above. Similar features have been ascribed by E. Watson to nivation in connection with snow patches in Wales. The material forming the pro-talus rampart consists of head, and this shows stratification of a rude type, dipping downstream, such as would be expected in a deposit accumulating at the foot of a snow slope. According to Tricart and Cailleux (1962) nival or snow patch deposits may be differentiated from true moraines by the character of the deposit; the former consist only of coarse material, the finer material characteristic of moraines being lacking, and the blocks are generally more angular although the topographic form may be similar.

f) True glacial deposits are worthy of close field study, as their detailed examination can throw much light on glacier activity. Their general character can generally indicate whether they were deposited at the base of the ice or as ablation moraine, according to the degree of compactness and the amount of fine material. A study of the erratic content of the till gives information concerning the movement of the ice depositing it, and the state of weathering of the till indicates its age, a method of analysis that has been used a great deal in America, although some of the results of these studies are now being questioned. Many gumbotils, for example, have been re-interpreted as accretion gleys (Allen, 1962).

A more detailed analysis of the till can indicate the direction of movement of the ice depositing it and this method has been used to provide a means of differentiating between two different tills. The work of R. G. West and J. J. Donner (1956) exemplifies this method analysis of till in the East Midlands and East Anglia. The method used was based on a study of the orientation of the pebbles in the till. Sites for investigation were chosen on level ground to avoid topographic influence on the ice movement as far as possible. The till section was opened up until there was no longer danger of disturbance by cryoturbation and soil formation, and the dip and orientation of 100 elongated pebbles at least 1 cm long were measured with a pocket combined compass and clinometer while the stone was in situ. This can be done more rapidly by measuring the orientation with a protractor fitted with a movable rule; the readings are taken to right or left of a piece of string laid across the exposure. Then only the bearing of the string need be measured by compass. Experiments have shown that 50 stones is usually enough to give a valid preferred orientation. However, measurements of several sets of stones within one till exposure separated by only a few yards show that the pattern can change quite considerably over a short distance. Much more basic work is required before the analysis of the results can be made with certainty.

The results of the observations can be plotted on rose diagrams, showing both dip and orientation, and the preferred orientation can be readily appreciated. It is generally assumed that the preferred orientation of the long axis of the pebbles in the till reflects the direction of movement of the ice sheet depositing the till; thus if two superimposed tills show different preferred orientation of the long axis of the pebbles it may be inferred that the ice depositing them came from different directions. At times, however, the orientation is not parallel to the ice flow; for example, the orientation measurements of stones in a drumlin dissected in half by a stream showed a preferred orientation at considerable angles to the elongation of the drumlin, which lay in a valley and must have been deposited by ice moving down the valley parallel to the long axis.

Not all tills contain stones and sometimes they are difficult to recognise on this account. For example where the till is made up almost entirely of the rock on which it is lying, it can sometimes only be recognised as such by the occurrence of glacial gravels below it. This applies to the till composed mainly of Keuper Marl in the Midlands. One of the essential properties by which till may be differentiated from fluvio-glacial or nival drift is its generally unstratified character, although it may at times show some rude indication of having been laid down in layers, especially where ablation till overlies ground till, and some morainic deposits show faint signs of stratification.

g) Fluvio-glacial drifts can generally be differentiated from true till by the stratified nature of the former, although fluvio-glacial deposits can be about as varied as true till. They can range from glacial lake deposits, showing the characteristic varved bedding, to the very coarse outwash deposits characteristic of the margins of some glaciated areas, such as the Canterbury Plains of New Zealand. Varve clays repay close study, as the counting of their annual layers provides a very valuable method of dating glacial fluctuations, if the varve clays can be related to morainic deposits. In Sweden de Geer has been able to provide a varve chronology covering over 10,000 years by correlating varves from adjacent lakes by the pattern of their thickness.

One of the difficulties of studying glacial and fluvio-glacial deposits is the necessity for obtaining sections through them, so that the succession may be appreciated and observations made. This entails the use of bore-hole data or auguring in specially selected points. The work of F. W. Shotton (1963) illustrates very clearly the necessity for auguring in drift deposits of this type, which included glacial lake sediments, outwash gravels and sand and till. He used 91 holes to obtain enough evidence to elucidate the formation and final over-running by ice of Lake Harrison, events leading to the initiation of the Warwickshire Avon.

It is sometimes assumed that if stratified drifts are found beneath till, then there must have been a retreat followed by a renewed advance. However, R. G. arruthers (1953) has shown that this need not necessarily be so. He has suggested that the stratified deposits beneath the till in northern England may have originated from the undermelting and decay of a stagnant ice sheet. The deposits formed under these circumstances include shear clays; these show very fine striping and equal flow round small particles. Some of the structures show crumpling, but there is no trace of organic matter. There are sand layers whose base lies on an eroded clay surface. The deposits can be clearly differentiated from lake clays. In the silt and sand zones, which generally overlie the clay, there are suspension structures, due to melting of material out of the overlying ice. These flame-like structures become incorporated in the rapidly growing accumulation of sand. These deposits indicate that very complex structures can originate as a stagnant ice sheet melts and they fully repay careful study.

h) Fluvial deposits can also give much useful evidence of the conditions under which they were laid down. Rivers are susceptible to changes of base-level, particularly in their lower reaches, and to changes in climate, reflected in changes of discharge and load, in their upper courses. These changes are indicated in the fluviatile deposits often as river terraces. A study of these deposits can elucidate the nature of the river processes and the development of the valley. The study of the Thames terraces (King and Oakley, 1936) already mentioned shows the type of information to be gleaned from a study of the drift deposits in a valley. The deposits laid down by the river itself often contain remains of the life that inhabited its banks, both plant and animal, and these can help to determine climate and date. Artifacts also are useful for dating.

In considering the study of processes building up a flood plain it is useful to analyse the sediments and differentiate those of lateral accretion, which can be recognised by their relatively coarse nature as they are remnants of old point bars, from those of vertical accretion. The latter are fine grained sediments deposited by flood waters. Sediments of lateral accretion consist of sand and gravel deposited as the result of the movement of the meander system.

i) Deltaic sediments form a link between true fluviatile ones and true marine ones, and being deposited near sea-level are of value in assessing changes of base-level; the deltaic strata often contain some organic material, and much work has been done on the sediments of the Mississippi delta for example, in dating various levels and hence in evaluating the changes of sea-level. Deltaic sediments can often be identified by their characteristic cross or current bedding.

j) Coastal sediments can give very useful information concerning the processes operating in their respective environments, especially when they have been analysed in the laboratory, as will be discussed in chapter 6. In order to obtain good results, however, the sediment samples should be collected in a systematic way in the field. Krumbein and Slack (1956) have experimented on the best method of obtaining sediment samples from different coastal environments, such as the dune belt, the backshore, the foreshore and the nearshore bottom. The object of beach sampling is to obtain data that can be compared with other areas and related to the processes operating at the locality studied. There can also be practical applications, such as the specification of beach fill for artificial replenishment of a beach.

In order to obtain a reliable value of the mean sediment size on any beach area it is desirable to collect samples from each different beach zone, including backshore and offshore zones as far as 30 feet depth. The results can be weighted by reference to the width of each zone sampled, and this can be achieved by taking samples in proportion to the width of the zone. Or more samples may be taken from the more variable zones, but it is not often known which they are until the samples are analysed. It is generally found desirable to take samples from two or more profiles across each zone, and at least one sample should be taken from each zone on each profile. To give some idea of the accuracy of sampling, if six profiles were used, each with five samples, this set would probably provide an estimate of the population mean with a relative error of about 10% at the 95% confidence level. To halve the error, four samples would have to be taken from each point.

Most of the useful analysis of beach sediments must be carried out in the laboratory, as has been shown, but field observations are required to collect the samples from the most suitable areas and to provide data with which the sediment samples can be correlated. Thus if the relationship between beach gradient and material size is being studied, beaches of different grades of material must be surveyed at the time when samples are collected, and these must come from some comparable point, for example the mid-tide point as advocated by Bascom (1951).

k) The study of sediment in the offshore zone can be done either by divers, observing the bottom directly and collecting samples for further analysis as required, or by less direct means. Much work can be done by underwater television and photography, but no direct contact is possible by this means. However, if this can be combined with the use of instruments to collect samples, then the results can be of great value. Perhaps the most rewarding method of studying the deeper water sediments is by obtaining long cores.

The problems involved in this work are very great, but modern equipment can obtain cores that in favourable areas include sediment going back right through the Tertiary period. However, the extraction of such cores and their analysis is only possible for large and well equipped oceanographical organisations and is beyond the scope of most geomorphologists. Nevertheless the results of such work are of great interest in relation to geomorphological processes operating in the ocean and to climatic change and dating, so that it is useful to know something of the difficulties and limitations of the techniques now used in this operation. These are clearly set out in the work done by Heezen, Tharp and Ewing and by Ericsson and others (1961) in the Atlantic Ocean.

In dealing with superficial drift deposits it is often useful to determine their thickness. If borehole data are not available, it can be done by the rather laborious method of auguring on land. This provides samples of the material from different depths and gives a good idea of the drift succession and allows dating and other methods of analysis to be carried out with the sediment. However, various geophysical techniques have been developed that can be used to establish the thickness and other properties of superficial deposits. The main methods used are the resistivity and the refraction ones. The success of the former method depends on the values of the resistivity of the sediments being measured. These must be sufficiently different to be readily distinguishable in the records. Dry sand has a high resistivity, while wet sand has a low value, so that this method can also be used to assess the depth of the water table in sand dunes. Easily portable equipment is now available to measure the thickness of superficial layers by the refraction method. The impulse can be made by hitting a steel plate with a hammer or, where the interference noise is great, a shot may be used. In some instances the velocities recorded are diagnostic of the material traversed by the waves. The lower limit of a deposit can only be found if it overlies a layer in which the waves travel faster, but care must be used in interpreting the results. For example, waves travel slowly in shingle above the water table, but in shingle below the water table they move at the same rate as in clay. For suitable problems, such as to establish the thickness of sand over rock, the method is quick and accurate. However, with both methods it is desirable to check the results against those obtained by auguring or borehole data.

REFERENCES

ALLEN, V. T. 1962. Gumbotil, gley and accretion gley. *Journ. Geol.* 70, 342-347.
ARKELL, W. J. 1943. The Pleistocene rocks at Trebetherick Point, North Cornwall: their interpretation and correlation. *Proc. Geol. Assoc.* 54, 141-170.
BARNES, F. A. and KING, C. A. M. 1957. The spit at Gibraltar Point, Lincolnshire. *East. Mid. Geog.* no. 8, 22-31.
BASCOM, W. N. 1951. The relationship between sand size and beach-face slope. *Trans. Amer. Geoph. Un.* 32, 866-874.
British Geomorphological Research Group Reports: No. 1, July 1959, No. 2, May 1960, No. 3, Dec. 1960. No. 4, Mar. 1961, No. 5, Dec. 1962, unpublished.

BROWN, E. H. 1960. *The relief and drainage of Wales.* Cardiff.

BUTCHER, A. L. 1953, *British Caving.* Chapter 17, 509-535.

CARRUTHERS, R. G. 1953. *Glacial drifts and the undermelt theory.* Newcastle.

CASE, J. B. 1958. Mapping glaciers in Alaska. *Photogramm. Eng.* 24, 815-821.

CHESTERMAN, W. D., CLYNICK, P. R. and STRIDE, A. H. 1958. An acoustic aid to sea bed survey. *Acustica* 8, 285-290.

CLOET, R. L. 1954. Hydrographic analysis of the Goodwin Sands and Brake Bank. *Geog. Journ.* 120, 203-215.

DAVIES, J. L. 1961. Tasmanian beach ridge systems in relation to sea level changes. *Pap. & Proc. Roy. Soc. Tasmania* 95, 35-40.

DONNER, J. J. 1959. The late- and post-glacial raised beaches in Scotland. *Ann. Acad. Sci. Fenniae* A III Geol. Geog. 53, 5-25.

DURY, G. H. 1954. Contribution to a general theory of meandering valleys. *Amer. Journ. Sci.* 252, 193-224.

DURY, G. H. 1958. Tests of a general theory of misfit streams. *Inst. Brit. Geog.* 25, 105-118.

ERICSSON, D. B., EWING, M., WOLLIN, G. and HEEZEN, B. C. 1961. Atlantic deep sea sediment cores. *Bull. Geol. Soc. Amer.* 72, 193-286.

FAIRBRIDGE, R. W. 1961. Eustatic changes in sea level. From *Physics and Chemistry of the Earth* vol. 4, 99-185, Pergamon Press.

FITZPATRICK, E. A. 1956. An indurated soil horizon formed by permafrost. *Journ. Soil Sci.* 7, 248-254.

FRYE, J. C. *et al.* 1960. Accretion-gley and the gumbotil dilemma. *Amer. Journ. Sci.* 258, 185-196.

HARE, F. K. 1947. The geomorphology of part of the Middle Thames. *Proc. Geol. Assoc.* 58, 294-339.

INMAN, D. L. 1957. Wave generated ripples in nearshore sands. *Tech. Memo.* B.E.B. 100, 42 pp. Washington.

INMAN, D. L. and RUSNAK, G. A. 1956. Changes in sand level on the beach and shelf at La Jolla, California. *Tech. Memo.* B.E.B. 82, 30 pp. Washington.

KENT, P. E. 1957. Triassic relics and the 1000-ft surface in the Southern Pennines. *East. Mid. Geog.* no. 8, 3-10.

KIDSON, C. 1962. The denudation chronology of the River Exe, *Inst. Brit. Geog.* 31, 43-66.

KIDSON, C., STEERS, J. A. and FLEMING, N. C. 1962. A trial of the potential value of aqualung diving to coastal physiography on British coasts. *Geog. Journ.* 128, 49-53

KING, L. C. 1962. *The Morphology of the Earth.* Edinburgh.

KING, W. B. R. 1950. Some periglacial problems. *Proc. Yorks. Geol. Soc.* 28, 43-50.

KING, W. B. R. and OAKLEY, K. P. 1936. The Pleistocene succession in the lower parts of the Thames valley. *Proc. Prehist. Soc.* 2, 52-76.

KING, C. A. M. 1963. Some problems concerning marine planation and the formation of erosion surfaces. *Inst. Brit. Geog.* 33, 29-43.

KRUMBEIN, W. C. and SLACK, H. A. 1956. Relative efficiency of beach sampling methods. *Tech. Memo.* B.E.B. 90, 43 pp. Washington.

LATTMANN, L. H. 1960. Cross section of a floodplain in a moist region of moderate relief. *Journ. Sed. Petrol.* 30, 275-282.

LEWIS, W. V. and BALCHIN, W. G. V. 1940. Past sea-levels at Dungeness. *Geog. Journ.* 96, 258-285.

LINTON, D. L. 1955. The problem of Tors. *Geog. Journ.* 121, 470-487.

MABBUTT, J. A. 1961. A stripped land surface in Western Australia. *Inst. Brit. Geog.* 29, 101-114.

MACKIN, J. H. 1948. Concept of the graded stream. *Bull. Geol. Soc. Amer.* 59, 463-512.

ORME, A. R. 1962. Abandoned and composite sea cliffs in Britain and Ireland. *Irish Geog.* 4, 279-291.

ROWELL, A. J. and TURNER, J. S. 1952. Glaciation in the Upper Eden valley, Westmorland. *Liv. and Manch. Geol. Journ.* 1, 200-207.

SAVIGEAR, R. A. G. 1952. Some observations on slope development in South Wales. *Inst. Brit. Geog.* 18, 31-51.

SHEPARD, F. P. 1963. Thirty five thousand years of sea-level. From *Essays in Marine Geology in honour of K. O. Emery.* 10 pp.

SHOTTON, F. W. 1953. The Pleistocene deposits of the area between Coventry, Rugby and Leamington and their bearing upon the topographic development of the Midlands. *Phil. Trans. Roy. Soc.* B 237, 209-260.

SISSONS, J. B. 1954. The erosion surfaces and drainage system of south-west Yorkshire. *Proc. Yorks. Geol. Soc.* 29, 305-342.

SISSONS, J. B. 1960. Erosion surfaces, cyclic slopes and drainage systems in southern Scotland and northern England. *Inst. Brit. Geog.* 28, 23-38.

SISSONS, J. B. 1962. A reinterpretation of the literature on late glacial shorelines in Scotland with particular reference to the Forth Area. *Trans. Edin. Geol. Soc.* 19, 83-99.

SPARKS, B. W. 1949. The denudation chronology of the dip slope of the South Downs. *Proc. Geol. Assoc.* 60, 165-215.

SPARKS, B. W. 1953. Effects of weather on the determination of heights by aneroid barometer. *Geog. Journ.* 119, 73-80.

STEERS, J. A. 1962. Coastal cliffs: Report of a symposium. *Geog. Journ.* 128, 303-320.

STEPHENS, N. 1957. Some observations on the 'Interglacial' platform and the early post-glacial raised beach on the east coast of Ireland. *Proc. Roy. Irish. Acad.* 58 B, 129-149.

STRAW, A. 1961. The erosion surfaces of east Lincolnshire. *Proc. Yorks. Geol. Soc.* 33, 149-172.

STRIDE, A. H. 1959. On the origin of the Dogger Bank. *Geol. Mag.* 96, 33-44.

SWEETING, M. M. 1950. Erosion cycles and limestone caves in the Ingleborough district. *Geog. Journ.* 115, 63-78.

SWINNERTON, H. H. 1931. The post-glacial deposits of the Lincolnshire coast. *Quart. Journ. Geol. Soc.* 87, 360-375.

TEMPLE, P. 1964. Evidence of lake level changes from the northern shoreline of Lake Victoria, Uganda. From *Geographers and the Tropics*, Liverpool Essays, edited by R. W. Steel and R. M. Prothero, 31-56.

TIVY, J. 1962. An investigation of certain slope deposits in the Lowther Hills, Southern Uplands of Scotland. *Inst. Brit. Geog.* 30, 59-73.

TRICART, J. and CAILLEUX, A. 1962. *Le modèle glaciaire et nival.* 226 pp.

TROTTER, F. M. 1929. The Tertiary uplift and resultant drainage of the Alston Block. *Proc. Yorks. Geol. Soc.* 21, 161-180.

WATERS, R. S. 1957. Differential weathering and erosion on oldlands. *Geog. Journ.* 123, 503-509.

WATERS, R. S. 1958. Morphological mapping. *Geog.* 43, 10-17.

WATERS, R. S. 1960. The bearing of superficial deposits on the age and origin of the upland plain of east Devon, west Dorset and south Somerset. *Inst. Brit. Geog.* 28, 89-97.

WEST, R. G. and DONNER, J. J. 1956. The glaciation of East Anglia and the East Midlands: a differentiation based on stone-orientation measurements of the tills. *Quart. Journ. Geol. Soc.* 112, 69-91.

WOOD, A. 1959. The erosional history of the cliffs around Aberystwyth. *Liv. and Manch. Geol. Journ.* 2, 271-287.

WOOLDRIDGE, S. W. and LINTON, D. L. 1955. *Structure, surface and drainage in south-east England.* London.

YASSO, W. E. 1964. Geometry and development of spit-bar shorelines at Horse Shoe Cove, Sandy Hook, New Jersey. Off. Naval Res. Geog. Branch. *Tech. Report* 5.

YOUNG, A. 1963. Some field observations of slope form and regolith, and their relation to slope development. *Inst. Brit. Geog.* 32, 1-29.

YOUNG, A. 1964. Slope profile analysis. *Zeitschr. für Geomorph.* Supp. Band 5, 17-27.

3 FIELD TECHNIQUES–OBSERVATION OF PROCESSES IN ACTION

Landscape is a dynamic entity, continually undergoing change as a result of the action of geomorphological processes, and much geomorphological research is directed towards a better understanding of the processes at work by recording them in action in the field. The most readily observable processes are those connected with the operation of subaerial erosion and depositional agents, but processes at work at the edge of and beneath the sea are also important. The endogenetic forces, acting within the earth, should not be ignored; although their study is more properly the field of the geophysicist, nevertheless the geomorphologist may also read in the landscape the evidence of such internal movements. The processes of subaerial denudation will be considered first, then the processes of marine and submarine action, and finally a brief mention will be made of some of the ways in which geomorphological observations can give information concerning internal forces and their action.

I. FLUVIAL PROCESSES

a) *River flow*. The study of the work of a river depends on a sound knowledge of the characteristics of the water flow within it, and the way in which the river adapts its bed to the flow. The first necessity in a study of river behaviour is to measure accurately the discharge of the river; this should be done at several points along the course and the recording at each place should be continuous. The discharge can best be measured at a weir, or at some position where the cross section can be accurately surveyed to obtain the cross-sectional area. The discharge is then found by measuring the velocity with a current meter to obtain the mean velocity of flow. This value multiplied by the area of the cross section gives the discharge, which may be expressed in cusecs (the number of cubic feet of water passing in each second). Relatively few rivers are gauged regularly in the British Isles, although the number of records is increasing. The information that is available is published in the *Surface Water Year Book*, giving the monthly river flow and the extreme maximum and minimum for each month. Information is also given concerning the precipitation and run-off. The hydrology of a number of small basins is being studied by many river boards at present. In the United States there is a very dense network of gauging stations and data on flow are available from more than 7300 stations.

If no official figures are available the discharge of the river may be determined by first surveying the cross section by recording the depths at intervals, then measuring the velocity with a current meter at intervals across the river and at different depths. In assessing the mean velocity of a stream, the speed at a position 0·6 of the distance from the surface to the bed approximates to the mean velocity, which falls off downwards on a logarithmic curve. Another method of obtaining a good value for the mean velocity is to take the mean between the velocites at 0·2 and 0·8 of the depth from the surface. Velocity can also be estimated from the channel characteristics using an empirical formula, set up with the aid of field observations and laboratory studies. This is $V = C\sqrt{Rs}$, where V is the velocity, C is the Chezy co-efficient, R is the hydraulic radius, almost equal to the depth in a wide shallow channel, and s is the slope. It can be expressed also as

$$V = 1{\cdot}49 \frac{R^{2/3}\, s^{1/2}}{n},$$

where n is found by experiment, values for rough natural streams often approaching 0·06 (Leopold, Wolman and Miller, 1964). If it is only possible to measure the surface velocity, the mean velocity can be found by multiplying the surface value by 0·8. The results for average rivers vary from about 6 to 10 ft/sec when they are in flood, with an absolute maximum of 30 ft/sec. The velocity values are used at a gauging station to form a rating curve, so that the height of water at the gauge can be directly converted into discharge.

A useful method of measuring the discharge of turbulent streams has been described by G. Østrem (1964). It is known as the relative salt dilution measurement and its accuracy increases with turbulence. The brine added to the river is diluted in proportion to the water discharge and the salt content can be measured by electrical conductivity on the assumption that this increases as the salinity increases. A concentrated salt brine is injected into the river and the conductivity is measured at two points downstream. If the time between the passage of the salt wave at the two points is noted, this gives the velocity of the stream and, if the cross-sectional area is known, the discharge can be computed. This method can also be used to study turbulence. It is important that the brine be completely mixed with the water, so that narrow streams with falls or bends are preferable. Observations over a reach of 100 to 500 m should be satisfactory. The salt solution should contain 0·5 kg/m³/sec discharge or about 3 to 5 kg of salt in 50 litres of water for a medium stream. Calibration is necessary before observations can begin and then the salt solution is placed in the middle of the stream and observations are made every 5 seconds as the salt wave passes. One source of error is the effect of temperature changes, and allowance must be made for these variations. The results are as accurate as those made with a current meter if care is exercised and the method can be used in glacial meltwater streams; successful observations have been made in the meltwater stream from the Lewis Glacier in Baffin Island.

Where long records of river flow are available it is possible to calculate the expected frequency of any particular discharge. This is particularly useful where flood frequency is concerned. Analysis of many American stream discharge curves show that the mean annual flood has a recurrence interval of 2·33 years. The mean annual flood is the mean of the highest values recorded each year for the number of years available. A discharge twice the mean annual flood would be expected to occur once every 18 years. The really catastrophic floods would occur only once in 100 years or so. However, the less excessive but more frequent events may be geomorphologically more effective. The bankfull discharge has a recurrence interval of about $1\frac{1}{2}$ years according to the eastern United States data and is smaller than the mean annual flood. The average annual flow will fill the channel about $\frac{1}{3}$ full, while the flood with a recurrence interval of 10 years has about $2\frac{1}{4}$ times the bankfull discharge and one with a 50-year interval $4\frac{1}{4}$ times the bankfull discharge.

Many hydrologists consider that the bankfull stage of a river is of major significance to an understanding of its character and the processes operating on its bed. Thus it is worth considering the work that has been done to establish the nature of this stage and the frequency with which it occurs. There is first the problem of defining the bankfull stage; this depends on the nature of the river channel, which itself depends on the sediment load and the discharge. Definition of the bankfull stage has been made by Dury (1961). He points out that it is not easy to determine the bankfull stage in a natural river, as nearly all the gauging stations are associated with artificial conditions and built-up banks. The important point is to recognise the state in which the river first overflows its banks: this is not always easy as not all rivers have banks they overflow, while braided streams also do not overtop their banks in the same way as other types of rivers. Natural bankfull stage can be considered to be the level equal to the height of the flood-plain, when this is level and there are no banks. Even where there are natural levees, Wolman and Leopold suggest that the bankfull stage is about the level of the flood-plain. Nixon (1959) states that the bankfull flood is the highest one that can be contained within the incised channel of the river and does not cause spilling on to the flood-plain. This does not mean that small pockets of water cannot overflow where the bank is abnormally low, or that the water must overflow everywhere when the bankfull stage is exceeded.

b) *Bed characteristics.* The importance of the bankfull stage is that the characteristics of the river channel appear to be adapted to about this stage. Thus observations of the frequency of this stage in a river and its relation to the width, depth and velocity of the river can give valuable information concerning the processes at work in the river. Definite relationships between these different variables and the bankfull stage of the river have been established. These equations apply to many rivers and are said to define the regime state of the river. By collecting a large number of measurements from many different rivers, it has been possible to formulate some of the relationships empirically. This illustrates the type of results that may be expected from field observations of river flow in correlating them with the characteristics of the river bed. The relationships provide data on which to base an understanding of the action of the processes, and they are important in connection with engineering problems related to the maintenance of river channels and the prevention of flooding.

Nevertheless the study of such relationships is still in its infancy, and there is much to be learnt about the way in which a river alters its bed and the discharge that is most competent to influence the river's character. The importance of the bankfull stage had been recognised by many workers, but there are those who consider that this stage occurs so rarely that it cannot be the main formative agent in the river, while others point out the difficulty of defining and measuring the bankfull stage at various places along the river.

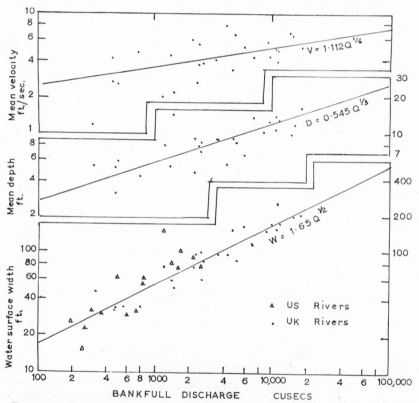

FIGURE 3.1. Graph relating the bankfull discharge of rivers in the United Kingdom and United States with the mean velocity, the mean depth and the mean surface width. (after Nixon)

With these uncertainties in mind, the values given by Nixon (1959) (see figure 3.1) and Leopold, Wolman and Miller (1964) are worth considering as working values and as a standard against which to assess new observations.

The following values are given by Nixon:

$$W = 1 \cdot 65 \; Q_b^{1/2}, \; d = 0 \cdot 545 \; Q_b^{1/3}, \; V = 1 \cdot 112 \; Q_b^{1/6}, \; A = 0 \cdot 9 \; Q_b^{5/8},$$

where W is the water surface width, d is the average depth, V is the mean velocity, A is the cross-sectional area and Q_b is the bankfull discharge. These values apply to a self-formed channel that will remain stable or in regime. The frequency with which the bankfull discharge occurs is given by Nixon as 0·6% of the time, which is about twice a year, instead of once in $1\frac{1}{2}$ years as given by the U.S.A. data. Leopold, Wolman and Miller give the following values for the constants and exponents:

$$W = a \; Q^b, \; d = c \; Q^f, \; V = k \; Q^m \text{ where } b + f + m = 1, \; a + c + k = 1.$$

Exponent values for at-a-station relations vary between these limits:
b: 0·26, 0·04, 0·29, 0·12, 0·13; f: 0·40, 0·41, 0·36, 0·45, 0·41; m: 0·34, 0·55, 0·34, 0·43, 0·43. The values for average downstream relations with bankfull or mean annual flow are as follows:
b: 0·5, 0·42, 0·5, 0·55; f: 0·40, 0·45, 0·30, 0·36; m: 0·1, 0·05, 0·2, 0·09. The value of the exponent b tends to vary with climate and also depends on tha bank material. The values given by Nixon can be applied to natural rivers in England and Wales.

Another possible parameter that could be used in place of the bankfull discharge, which may not be available, is the mean annual discharge. This value can be more easily assessed as it depends on the mean annual precipitation, and can be found by subtracting the annual evaporation, as given by Penman for example, from the mean annual precipitation. Prus-Chacinski has argued that this value is more likely to be the dominant discharge, in that it is responsible for the shape of the channel, because it occurs for a greater proportion of the time, perhaps 20 to 25%; but Leopold, Wolman and Miller consider that the dominant discharge is nearer to the bankfull stage. The mean annual discharge can be more easily obtained as the rainfall figures are usually available and evaporation is much less variable. There is a reasonably close correlation between the bankfull width and the mean annual discharge, so that the bankfull discharge could be obtained indirectly from these data.

There is in nearly all rivers a continuous increase of width, depth and velocity with increasing discharge in a downstream direction. Wolman and Miller (1960) came to the conclusion that the flows that occur with a frequency of once in one or two years are capable of doing more work in moving bed material than the rare very large flows or the smaller mean annual discharge. It is important to bear in mind differences between at-a-station variations in the parameters and those taking place in a downstream direction. Sediment load, for example, increases much more at a station with increasing discharge than it does downstream at any one time; this is also true of velocity, but not of width. Most of these relationships can be represented by straight lines on log-log paper.

In order to provide some basis for comparison it is useful to consider the regime figures given by Blench (1957) for canals of various sizes, on the assumption that they only carry a small load:

Canal type	Discharge Q cusecs	Breadth b ft	$\dfrac{\text{Slope}}{1000}$	Depth d ft	Velocity V ft/sec	b/d
Main line	10,000	225	0·09	12·5	3·55	18·0
Branch	1,000	71	0·13	5·8	2·43	12·2
Distributary	100	22·5	0·19	2·7	1·64	8·4
Distributary	10	7·1	0·28	1·25	1·25	5·7

In natural streams conditions are more variable, and detailed field studies of the Rio Grande del Ranchos in New Mexico (Leopold *et al.*, 1964) have revealed the relationship between the character of the river bed and the slope of the water surface. Thus a river has a steeper water slope and greater kinetic energy, given by $V^2/2g$, when the bed is restricted by vegetation or rock outcrops; straight reaches have the lowest slopes, except where gravel bars or riffles (underwater gravel bars) occur, the highest slopes being where the river divides into two round an island. In order to establish these relationships detailed field observations of reaches with different characteristics are required.

The figures given by Blench reveal interesting relationships between the variables. The greater the discharge and the straighter the channel the flatter the slope will be. A good example of the adjustment of a natural river whose regime condition was upset is described by Nixon, from his work on the Trent at Fiskerton. A wall of steel piles was driven in to protect a road alongside the river; they were fixed in the river 14 feet from the bank, where the river was originally 195 feet wide at the bankfull stage. After the piles were fixed erosion took place on the opposite bank, until the river width had increased to 198 feet after only two winters. The process of adjustment can also work the other way, as illustrated by observations on the River Tame at Hams Hall. To reduce flooding in Birmingham, the river was widened from 40 to 70 feet, but it immediately began to adjust its bed to regime conditions again by the formation of shoals, which reduced the width to 50 feet.

c) *Sediment movement.* It is clear that the river can only adjust its bed to reach its regime or equilibrium conditions by moving the material of its bed and sides, so that a study of the characteristics and movement of its bed material is the most important aspect of field study of rivers. The load of a river is carried in three main ways: bed load, suspension load and solution load. The separation of bed load and suspended load is somewhat arbitrary, and Bagnold defines the bed load as that whose immersed weight is carried by the solid bed; the suspended load is carried by the intersticial fluid. Various empirical equations are available for relating sediment transport to other fluvial parameters and a close correlation exists between transport and mean velocity. The modified Einstein technique as applied to the Rio Grande in New Mexico (Colby, 1961) indicates an increase in load from 6 tons/day/ft width for a velocity of 2 ft/sec to 100 tons for a velocity of 5 ft/sec. These formulae may, however, yield very inaccurate results in some natural streams, so that direct observations are of great value.

Suspended load is usually measured with a sampling 'fish' with a nozzle about 0·3 in. in diameter, and free access to the air is maintained so that the water enters the nozzle with the same velocity as the surrounding water. Such an instrument only works for material finer than coarse sand. There is as yet no satisfactory method of measuring gravel and boulder transport, although traps have been used to catch gravel and sand; but the validity of the results is not known. Hubbell (1963) is not encouraging about methods of measuring bed load, although good methods would have very valuable results. One method that has been tried is to provide artificial conditions, such as small baffles, that have the effect of raising the bed load into suspension, when it can be sampled with the normal type of sampler, but this will not work in all streams. The method currently adopted to measure suspended load is to lower the sampler slowly throughout the depth of water to the bottom to obtain an integrated value. This method provides a value for the discharge-weighted concentration of sediment. The concentration of suspended sediment is usually given in parts per million and from this the weight of sediment can be obtained.

Many rivers appear muddy and have a high suspension load, but have coarse sand or fine gravel beds. The Mississippi is an example of this. The character of the bed material can be assessed by mechanical analysis of samples for sizes up to fine gravel; for large material boulder measurements with a minimum of 60 boulders are satisfactory. Where beds are coarse and bouldery pools and riffles are characteristic forms, and field observations can be made to show that the riffles and bars often contain larger stones than the pools. A method of observing the relationship between the bars and the boulders composing them was carried out in Seneca Creek, Maryland (Leopold, Wolman and Miller, 1964); all the stones on a gravel bar surface were painted, and after a period of high flow they had all moved, some to the next riffle downstream, but the bar had the same dimensions and position. The stones were moved by a discharge filling the channel ¾ full, with a recurrence period of one year. By detailed survey of the same river reach over a period of years it can be shown that on the whole the bars maintain their position. They tend to be spaced 5 to 7 widths apart, and may only move slowly if at all. Evidence of the process leading to bar formation may be obtained by studying the movement of the painted stones on the bars. Where larger pebbles are close together they interact with one another and their movement slows up so that their concentration increases, which has a cumulative effect and helps to account for bar and riffle formation; this helps to increase the velocity gradient near the bed and so a state of equilibrium is set up.

Field observations on bed load have been made by Einstein (1944), and these and other deductions suggest that the bed load is only of the order of 1 or 2 parts per hundred thousand by weight, reaching up to 50 for heavily

TG D

loaded rivers. This, however, with a discharge of 10,000 cusecs and a bed load of 2 parts per 100,000 would provide a yearly load of 160,000 cu.yd, which is a very much smaller load than that carried in suspension by most rivers. To compare the suspension load of a river with the bed load it is worth noting that a large charge of suspended material is about 1%, which is about 1000 times the bed load. Examples of rivers with this size of load include the undammed Colorado in America and the Sutlej in India, whose loads consist of clay, silt and fine sand. Suspension load can increase to 70% in some desert canyons, as a flood wave moves downstream. British rivers on the whole, however, carry a small load in suspension, as a few figures will demonstrate. Values given in parts per 100,000 have been recorded as follows: Thames at Teddington, 1·9 normal flow, 5·6 bankfull: Trent at Nottingham, 2·0 normal flow, 27·2 bankfull: Rio Grande, San Marcial, U.S.A., 2260: Damodar, Rhondia, India, 285: Yangtze at Chikian, 97; Yellow River at Shensien, mean 4400, maximum 46,140: and the Irrawaddy at Prome, 57. These figures are useful in that they express the great range of values of suspended sediment and this helps to account for the different character of the various rivers. It is necessary to know the values of sediment carried in order to arrive at a correct value for use in the formulae relating to the character of the bed, as these must be modified when the sediment charge is high. The effect of the silt factor on the bed characteristic is to increase the width if the sediment charge is high. A channel with fine bed material would have a low velocity and be deep, but for a coarse bed of gravel or boulders the channel would be shallow and have a high velocity. Taking into account the character of the bed reduces the scatter of points calculated only on the discharge at bankfull stage in the formulae already cited.

The nature of the bed material and sediment load must enter into any field observations on river mechanism. However, there is another type of sediment load that can fairly easily be measured, and is very important if the river load is used to estimate the total amount of denudation in the drainage basin. This is the load in solution. It can be measured by taking samples of water of known volume and analysing the water chemically to ascertain the amount of dissolved solids in the water. Samples should be taken at various characteristic discharges as the proportion of solids in solution varies with the discharge. Much of the work of carrying solution load is achieved during mean flow, as the concentration tends to be lowered during flood periods. The amount of load in solution depends to a considerable extent on the nature of the rocks in the drainage basin, but it can be a very substantial part of the whole. In the Salief river in Kansas the solution load is 13%, in the Colorado at Grand Canyon it is 6%, and in the Gunnison River near Grand Junction, Colorado, it increases to 45%, or a total of 341,000 tons per year. The River Fyris in Sweden carries 5500 tons of sediment but 62,000 tons of matter in solution. This type of load is sometimes difficult to measure owing to pollution, but it should never be disregarded in assessing the total load of the river. It is probably only in very insoluble drainage areas that solution is of little importance.

d) *Meanders*. Other relationships that have been suggested as a result of field work on river channels are connected with the sinuosity of streams on wide alluvial plains (Schumm, 1963). Observations have shown a connection 'between the sinuosity of streams and the ratio of suspension load to bed load. The more sinuous streams of the Great Plains have relatively narrow and deep channels and a high percentage of silt and clay on the perimeter of the channel; they also have a gentler gradient for the same discharge than the straighter channels. Thus the sinuosity is another factor of the river character that should be measured in the field. A wide shallow channel is associated with bed load greater than normal quantity, while a narrow deep channel is associated with a higher proportion of suspension load. It is suggested that meandering may be due to a change in the ratio of bed load to suspension load, caused by a lowering of the relief. The following relationships are put forward; $P = 3 \cdot 5 F^{0 \cdot 27}$, where P is the sinuosity, and F is the width-to-depth ratio, P being low for a straight stream; $P = 0 \cdot 94 M^{0 \cdot 25}$, where M is the percentage of silt and clay. Thus the nature of the bed plays a part in explaining the form of the stream in plan, as well as its slope, although the two factors are, of course, related, in that meandering is one of the ways in which the river adjusts its gradient to its discharge and bed character. This illustrates again that observations should be three-dimensional where possible.

Inglis has put forward formulae relating the size of meanders to the discharge, for example $L = 28 \, Q_{\max}^{1/2}$, where L is the meander wave length and $Q_{\max}$ is the maximum discharge or peak river flood, and $B = 84 \cdot 7 \, Q^{1/2}$, where B is the meander belt width. This relationship, which connects meander size to discharge, has been used by G. H. Dury (1958) to relate the present meanders of some rivers to the wider valley bends in which the modern meanders occur, both of which can be measured in the field, and to compare the present discharge with the former discharge that must have made the larger valley bends. A fairly close correlation has also been found between the width of the stream and the breadth of its meander belt, but it should be noted that the factors that enter into the equations are not capable of very accurate measurement, either on the ground or on maps; the maximum discharge especially will vary with different observers, as, even if the river is gauged, the variation may be 20%, while in ungauged rivers the deviation factor may be from $\frac{1}{2}$ to 2. The meander length and breadth are also difficult to measure accurately. The index $\frac{1}{2}$ that enters into the meander equation seems to be accurate within about 5%, and the relationships seem to reflect genuine physical connections. Other empirical relations that are worthy of mention are $L = 6 \cdot 6 \, w^{0 \cdot 99}$ (Inglis), $L = 10 \cdot 9 \, w^{1 \cdot 01}$ (Leopold and Wolman), $A = 18 \cdot 6 \, w^{0 \cdot 99}$ (Inglis), $A = 10 \cdot 9 \, w^{1 \cdot 04}$ (Inglis), and $A = 2 \cdot 7 \, w^{1 \cdot 1}$ (Leopold and Wolman), where A is the amplitude of the meander belt, L is the meander length and w is the channel width. Field experience suggests some of the factors that influence these relationships, although the precise cause of meandering is still not fully understood. The square root of the discharge seems fairly well established as the factor on which the relationships depend in the first set of formulae, but the multiplying factor probably varies with bed conditions, amount of sediment, seasonal distribution of discharge and the nature of the banks. In the second set of formulae (relating L and A to w) the relationship is approxiamtely linear.

e) *Field observations on river processes.* The empirical relationships have been obtained by observation of actual rivers and irrigation canals in the field, and this empirical method is a necessary preliminary to a full understanding of the processes in action, as it provides a basis against which new values may be checked. The relationships can then be made more accurate by the addition of new variables, for example, terms relating to the character of the sediments. The classic work of Hjulstrøm (1935) on the River Fyris in Sweden should be noted in this connection, as he was able to provide useful tables relating the velocity of flow to the movement of sediment, differentiating the velocity at which sediment is first picked up from the bed (the velocity of erosion) from the velocity at which sediment is deposited. He showed that with a uniform bed material the sediment that could most easily be picked up from the bed had a median diameter between 0·1 and 0·5 mm; this required a velocity of 20 cm/sec. The velocity required to pick up both finer and coarser sediment increases rapidly; a velocity of 100 cm/sec is required for material of 0·005 mm size and for about 7 mm size. The velocity of deposition on the other hand falls progressively to very low values for the fine sediment, thus accounting for the large amount of suspension load in most rivers.

Ephemeral streams provide useful experimental sites for measuring cut and fill in stream beds. A method of measuring this is described by Leopold, Wolman and Miller from observations carried out in the Rio Grande del Ranchos, near Talpa, New Mexico. Chains were placed vertically in holes dug in the channel and fixed at the base. When in flood the bed scours, the upper part of the chain is bent downstream and fill is subsequently deposited on top. After the flood has subsided the chain can be relocated and the maximum amount of scour and subsequent fill can be measured. Chains can be fixed along and across the bed to study the change in long profile and cross profile. The results show that temporary flood scour is mostly replaced as the water-level falls subsequently.

Field studies of the actual measurement of river action are relatively rare, so that it is useful to describe the work done by Wolman (1959) in a small drainage basin. The Watts Branch drainage area is only 4 square miles and the channel has a width of 20 feet, crossing grassland. Erosion was measured on the concave banks of the meandering channel downstream from the point of maximum curvature of the bend. The cross-sectional observations were established in 1953 and rapid erosion occurred between then and 1955. More detailed observations were begun in 1955 and continued for 5 years. The banks consisted of very fine sand and poorly sorted silt. The method used to study the processes of erosion was to establish a base line parallel to the left bank at each of two positions where erosion was serious. The two base lines were 65 and 70 feet long and measurements were made from them to the bank at 5 feet intervals. The recordings were made according to changes in weather, following rain, hot or cold periods, but it would also have been useful to take measurements at fixed intervals. One problem encountered was the difficulty of measuring from the base line to the bank owing to the overhanging character of the turf edge. To overcome these difficulties the base line was replaced by the pin method. Pins one foot long were driven horizontally into the bank one foot below the flood-plain level so that 0·05 feet protruded from the bank, the width of the pin being ¼ inch. The erosion could be measured by noting the amount of pin protruding. After each measurement the pin had to be pushed in again so that the original amount protruded. The factors on which the erosion depended were measured as far as possible. These included the discharge, and the level of ground water in the flood plain. The water-level was measured in three shallow wells in a line perpendicular to the bank and spaced 7 feet apart; at all times the water table sloped towards the stream.

During a four-year period 6 feet of material were removed, but not at an equal rate; indeed little erosion occurred during the summers of 1956 and 1957, most of it taking place during the winter. It is interesting to note that the highest flood, which occurred in summer and was 2 feet above bankfull stage, produced negligible erosion. It is possible that the angle of attack plays a part in the effectiveness of erosion, although clearly the winter conditions are more conductive to erosion, the higher precipitation probably being the main factor. Maximum erosion took place when high flow attacked well wetted banks; in summer, high flow does not usually have time to wet the banks thoroughly. Frost action may also accelerate erosion by loosening the sediment by frost expansion; this then renders it more readily erodible at the next high flow, or it may cause undermining of the upper part of the bank at lower flow. Frost action by itself can cause some erosion by pushing particles out on needle ice; when this melts the particle drops into the stream. The details of this study indicate some of the observations that can give information concerning the processes by which a stream can modify its valley. It is best to start with a relatively simple stream, when so many factors still remain to be evaluated.

Opportunity for field observations is sometimes made possible by artificial modifications to natural channels. A good example of this is the work done on the Willow Drainage Ditch (Daniels, 1960). This ditch was originally cut in 1919-1920 to relieve flooding in the Missouri valley. The adjustment of the ditch to a channel more in regime with the prevailing discharge gives good evidence of fluvial processes in action. The ditch as a whole has tended to fill where it was cut in the Missouri flood plain, but in the Willow River valley it has deepened. The original Willow River was a meandering stream with a length of 26·3 miles in a valley only 20·2 miles long. Its gradient was variable, changing at the entry of each tributary; upstream of one tributary it sloped at 6·4 feet/mile, flattening downstream to slope at only 1·7 feet/mile. The river flows mainly on silt and the flattening may be due to increase of load below the tributary entry causing temporary aggradation. When the ditch was originally cut in 1919 it had a bottom width of 12 feet and sides sloping at 45 degrees. Its gradient was 7·66 feet/mile and its length in the area under discussion 10·2 miles. Upstream the sides also sloped at 45 degrees but the width decreased to 8 feet, with a gradient of 12·14 to 8·45 feet/mile. The lowest part of the ditch was 6·6 miles long and had a fall of 2·04 feet/mile. This part has always been subject to filling and has required cleaning twice. This silting is thought to be due to Missouri floods backing up the channel and depositing silt in it.

However, in the two upper sections of the ditch the major modification has been incision. This process started as soon as the ditch was used, early measurements indicating in one place a cut of 6 feet in 5 years. In the process of lowering its bed the channel has changed shape; this was possible because the bed was formed almost entirely of compact silt. Observations of the way in which the ditch has lowered its bed gives valuable evidence of fluvial processes in action. The width at one point increased from 30 feet in 1920 to 110 feet in 1958, while the depth increased from 11 feet to 42 feet in the same period. The deepening of the ditch has tended to reduce the overall gradient; in the reach constructed at 7·66 feet/mile the gradient was flattened to between 4·7 and 6·7 feet/mile. The method by which the incision has been achieved is largely by the recession of knick-points. In 1953 a knick-point was observed moving upstream and increasing in height as it did so from 1½ feet in July 1957 to 3 feet in April 1958. During this period it was moving upstream relatively slowly, covering nearly 90 feet. In contrast from 27 April to 1 May 1958 the knick-point moved 600 feet upstream, then remained stationary till 1 July 1958, but between this date and 15 August 1958 it moved 1400 feet upstream. The periods of rapid movement were associated with high water in the ditch. When slow retreat was taking place the knick-point had a vertical wall, which retreated by undercutting and shearing of the unsupported sediments above, re-establishing the vertical face. The undercutting was assisted by wave action developed in the plunge-pool. The widening of the channel was produced by slumping, which formed rotational slump blocks, with a back-slope facing towards the channel side, as the knick-point retreated upstream. Channel scour occurred below the knick-point during periods of high flow also. Thus deepening has occurred by the upstream migration of an eroding portion of the channel bed. The cause of these changes was probably the increased velocity of flow due to the increase of gradient and straightening of the channel. These observations are of value as they show how modifications of the channel have led to adjustments in its character to suit the new conditions. These two examples have been cited in detail in order to show how field observations of river processes in action can be used to check the empirical relationships that were mentioned in the earlier part of the section.

2. GLACIAL PROCESSES

The aims of glaciological research are varied and as a result the techniques that have been developed are also numerous. The purpose for which research may be carried out includes pure geomorphological research into the nature and origin of glaciated landforms, and glaciological research into the nature of ice movement and glacier budgets. Studies of the latter type can have a more practical application, specially where glaciers provide water for hydro-electric power stations and other purposes (Østrem, 1963). The study of glaciers as indicators of climatic change both past and present can yield information of great interest and value in many fields of study.

For small parties visiting little-known glacier areas some very useful information has been assembled in the form of a Technical Note No. 1 by the Glaciological Research Sub-committee of the Glaciological Society. This note includes methods of survey necessary to define the outline of the glacier and the character of its margins, which were mentioned in the previous chapter, but it also includes measurements that should be made to examine the nature of the glacier budget and its flow characteristics and type.

The observations that will be considered in this chapter include firstly the method of assessing the glacier mass budget or regime. Next will come temperature measurement of the ice, by which temperate and polar ice masses can be differentiated; this distinction is very important when the effect of the glacier as a geomorphological agent is considered. Then methods of measuring glacier thickness will be referred to, as this is an essential element in assessing volume of ice. Finally, observations on glacier flow will be considered; the surface glacier flow, flow at depth and on the bed and at the side of a glacier must all be taken into account to determine the way in which glaciers move and erode their beds, to produce the characteristics of glaciated landscape. Glacial deposition must also not be ignored.

a) *Glacier mass budget.* Before considering the methods of establishing the mass budget of a glacier it is necessary to define the terms used in this connection. The term 'mass budget' is used to define the balance between loss and gain of solid material in the form of snow and ice on a glacier. The budget is positive when more snow and ice are gained than are lost during the budget year. The budget year can be taken to begin when the glacier volume is at a minimum; this will normally occur at the end of the summer season before the first substantial winter snowfall, when the surface area undergoing loss of ice will be at a maximum.

The positive side of the glacier budget is termed the accumulation. The term may be used to cover all processes by which solid ice (including snow) is added to the glacier. The addition of ice may occur by refreezing of melt water at the surface, within or beneath the glacier, as well as by snowfall on the surface. The term 'gross annual accumulation' is used to refer to the total volume of water equivalent added to the glacier by all forms of precipitation and by drifting snow during the budget year. In the lower part of the glacier the gross accumulation is temporary and melts away before the end of the budget year. The term 'net annual accumulation' is used to refer to the amount of material left on the glacier at the end of the budget year. This material is found in the upper part of the glacier in the 'accumulation area'.

The loss of material from a glacier, or the negative side of the glacier budget, is termed 'ablation'. This ablation can be the result of melting, evaporation, wind erosion, or calving if the glacier reaches into a lake or the sea. Most ablation takes place during the summer melting season, although some melting may go on at the lowest elevations throughout the year in some temperate glaciers. The summer melting season is consequently called the ablation season. Most ablation takes place at the surface of the glacier, except in the Antarctic, where calving is the major form of glacier reduction.

The term 'gross annual ablation' is used for the total amount of water equivalent of the snow and ice consumed during the budget year by melting and the other processes mentioned above. However, not all the gross annual ablation remains lost to the glacier, owing to processes such as refreezing of melt water within the glacier. The amount of water equivalent which is lost by the glacier during the budget year and not regained is termed 'the net annual ablation'. Gross annual ablation, then, includes the loss of material which is later regained. It also includes the loss of temporary accumulation, the snow which falls during the ablation season and then melts again almost immediately. Net annual ablation does not include the material lost and then regained nor does it include the material temporarily gained and then lost, as neither of these amounts affects the actual loss from the glacier from one budget year to the next.

The line on the glacier below which more ice and snow melt than accumulate is called the 'equilibrium line'; it separates the area with a net ablation from the accumulation area above it. The equilibrium line must not be confused with the firn line. The latter is the highest line on the glacier to which the winter snow recedes during the ablation season, and is more conspicuous than the equilibrium line on the glacier surface. Dense ice, due to refreezing, may occur between the firn line and the equilibrium line.

The annual budget of the glacier can be ascertained in two ways; it is equal to the gross annual accumulation on the surface of the whole glacier during the budget year less the total net ablation for the whole glacier during the same period. Alternatively, the mass budget can be determined by measuring the net annual accumulation which is added in the accumulation area at the end of the budget year, less the net ablation of dense ice in the ablation area from the level of the surface exposed at the end of the previous budget year. The second method is normally the easier to apply, particularly in temperate glaciers.

Accumulation can be readily measured in the ablation area by taking soundings with a long metal rod through the new snow to the ice surface beneath. This snow will melt away during the budget year and these measurements will only be required if gross accumulation is to be measured. In measuring the net accumulation, observations must be made in the accumulation area. It is necessary to find the level of the previous summer surface, marking the beginning of the current budget year. This can sometimes be located by sounding, if the level is marked by a harder frozen firn layer. Normally, however, pits have to be dug to recognise the summer layer, and frequently the observations can be extended back through several seasons in any one pit. The previous summer surface can sometimes be recognised by dirt layers, but these are not always a reliable guide and the texture of the ice often gives a better indication of the summer surfaces. Where summer melting takes place a hard bed of summer firn often marks the limit of summer melting. The advantage of pits is that they afford an opportunity of obtaining samples of snow and firn from different levels. The density of the samples can then be found by weighing a known volume, and from these figures the water equivalent of the net accumulation at the position of the pit can be calculated. A thin-walled tube should be used to obtain the sample, and care must be taken that the snow is not compressed more than necessary as the tube is pushed into the wall of the pit. Where there are ice layers these cannot be sampled in this way, and allowance must be made for them by measuring their thickness. Saw-edged cutting tubes may overcome the problem of ice layers. A check on the observations may be made by cutting a rectanglular block of fixed size from the wall of the pit very carefully, as this method, though slow, disturbs the snow least.

Ablation can be measured on stakes drilled into the ice before the winter snow has melted. The stakes should be sunk through the snow into the ice beneath and the level of the ice surface can be ascertained when the stake is drilled in. It will often be found that, owing to deposition of refrozen melt water above the old surface, the ice-level is higher than it was originally. Having established the original level of the ice surface the amount lost during the ablation season can be readily ascertained by periodic measurements. The stakes will probably require redrilling during the course of the ablation season, and allowance must be made for this. The density of the ice can be measured to allow the ablation of solid ice to be converted into water equivalent.

Early work on the measurement of glacier mass budgets in different environments around the north Atlantic is that carried out by Ahlmann (1948). He has shown not only that careful studies of the glacier budget provide data of value in assessing climatic change, but also that the changing volume of ice affects the changes of sea-level and the morphological activity of the glacier.

A detailed study of the balance of Nigardsbreen by Østrem (1963) illustrates the number of observations that are required to obtain an accurate mass budget of this and similar glaciers, which drain part of the Jostedalsbreen ice cap in Norway. The nature of the observations that must be taken throughout the year can also be seen. He shows how the ablation and accumulation vary with height on the glacier; accumulation takes place throughout the year above about 1500 m elevation and amounted to about 4 m in the upper part of the ice cap, while ablation increases rapidly with decreasing altitude. It is about 9 m during May to September at the snout of the glacier, at about 300 m. By finding the difference between the accumulation and ablation for every altitude a specific net budget can be obtained (Meier, 1962), but to obtain the actual budget it is necessary to take into account the area of the glacier at different altitudes. For this purpose an accurate map of the glacier outline is required and contours must be included. In this particular example the maximum area lies at about 1600 to 1700 m in the accumulation zone, so that the zone of maximum accumulation coincides partially with the maximum area. In the year under study this caused the budget to be strongly positive, the surplus accumulation being $+94.9$ million cu.m of water equivalent for the budget year 1961-2. However in the following year the budget was negative. The positive value is an unusual state of glacier budget for this particular area, where glacier retreat has been very rapid during the last few decades. (See figure 3.2.)

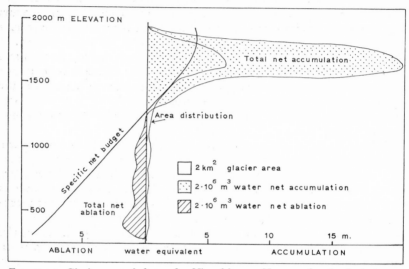

FIGURE 3.2. Glacier mass balance for Nigardsbreen, Norway, for the budget year 1961-62, when the surplus accumulation was 94·9 million cu.m. water equivalent. (after Østrem)

It takes several years of positive budget for the glacier snout to respond. The relationship between the changes in budget and the response of the glacier at its snout has been recently discussed by J. F. Nye (1963), on the basis of the passage of kinematic waves through the glacier. The variables on which his analysis is based, and which must be observed to test the theory are the following: Q, the discharge of the glacier, or volume of ice passing per unit time through a cross section; B, the breadth of the glacier at the surface; h, the height of the surface above an arbitrary datum line; a, the rate of accumulation or ablation averaged along a transverse line; and α, the slope of the upper surface. The normal response time for typical valley glaciers is about 3 to 30 years, but for large ice masses, such as the Antarctic or Greenland ice-sheets, it may be up to about 5000 years.

b) *Glacier temperature.* The importance of the difference between polar and temperate glaciers has already been mentioned, so that measurement of temperature is seen to be important. It is not easy to measure temperature deep in an ice mass unless elaborate drilling equipment is available, but a light portable drill will enable measurements to be made to a depth of 30 to 40 feet. Indirect observation, such as the behaviour of melt-water streams, can give useful indication of the temperature. If melt water comes from the base of the glacier it may be assumed to be a temperate glacier, at the pressure melting point temperature; if, however, the melt water runs mainly on the surface, it indicates that the lower part of the ice, at least, is well below freezing point.

To measure temperature, holes 1 to $1\frac{1}{2}$ inches in diameter should be bored at various heights near to the sites at which accumulation and ablation are being measured. A lagged thermometer is then inserted at intervals of about 5 feet to the bottom of the hole, and left 15 minutes at each depth, to reach a steady state, and then hauled up and read quickly; this should produce a result accurate to $\frac{1}{8}°C$. Paraffin wax or kerosene forms suitable lagging material round an ordinary glass thermometer. Thermistors can be used to record seasonal changes in temperature, but care must be taken to ensure that melt water does not enter the bored hole, which should be filled with water and allowed to freeze, or else packed with snow if it is in the accumulation area.

A knowledge of the temperature characteristics of an ice mass is important, as this is one of the factors on which the strain rate of glacier movement depends; thus cold glaciers, whose ice is always below the melting point, will tend to move more slowly than the temperate type, while the presence of melt water at the base of the latter is an important factor in explaining some of the geomorphological features associated with them.

Other observations concerning temperature in relation to glacier erosion are those carried out by W. R. B. Battle (1960) in bergschrunds. His observations were carried out with an 8-day recording thermograph; one thermograph had two leads and could be used to record temperature inside and outside the bergschrund simultaneously. Experiments were also carried out with an instrument to measure fluctuations of temperature. This was specially designed to register changes over a small range of temperature near the freezing point. Three other instruments were used to record the number of times the temperature passed through the freezing point at $0°C$, and temperatures below freezing point of $-1°C$ and $-2\cdot2°C$, respectively. The instruments were sited in bergschrunds, the thermograph being placed so that its bulb was about 5 cm from the rock wall at the base, and the other instruments near it.

The results of these observations are of value in that they provide precise information concerning the hypothesis that freezing and thawing are important factors in the breaking up of rocks in a bergschrund. The results show that temperature changes are very much damped down in a bergschrund compared with fluctuations outside, values only changing slowly and fairly infrequently through the freezing point. These experiments, therefore, do not support the hypothesis of frost shattering in bergschrunds.

c) *Ice thickness*. In order to measure the volume of ice in any glacier system it is necessary to know the thickness of the ice, but such measurements cannot be undertaken without elaborate equipment. The thickness can be measured by boring a hole through the ice to the bedrock beneath; in a temperate glacier this can be done with a thermal drill, which melts its way to the bottom of the glacier; the main difficulty is to supply the heat that is needed to melt the ice. On a polar glacier the hole may be drilled with a mechanical boring tool. A recently developed instrument, described by Shreve and Kamb (1964), has the merit of being portable and also of extracting cores of ice from different depths. This is valuable as it allows the glacier structure to be studied in three dimensions and samples may be obtained for analysis by other methods, such as oxygen-isotope ratios. The instrument is heated electrically and obtains from depths up to 300 m correctly orientated samples of ice $2\frac{1}{2}$ cm in diameter and 120 cm in length. The thermal element is mounted at the end of the core barrel, which has to be lined to prevent melting of the core. The drill, weighing 20 kg, is attached to a 300-m long wire cable and is raised and lowered by a hand-cranked winch, mounted on a wooden tripod. The power is provided by a petrol engine.

Such an instrument provides very valuable data concerning the nature and thickness of ice in a vertical hole, but this is just one spot depth in the glacier basin, and the instrument is also limited in depth penetration. There are simpler types of thermal boring equipment that can penetrate both further and more rapidly into the ice. However all suffer from the disadvantage that only one hole can be bored at a time and it is difficult to get adequate coverage to obtain a valid picture of the glacier bed.

This difficulty can be overcome by the use of geophysical means. On a smooth ice-cap away from mountain masses the best method of measuring ice thickness is to use a Worden type gravity meter. Results obtained must be correlated with gravity surveys of the surrounding rocks. The other method of obtaining ice thickness can be used either on ice-sheets or glaciers with rocky walls. It consists of seismic observations of the speed of travel of waves, which pass through the ice and are reflected from the ice-rock interface back to the surface recorder. Seismic methods are suitable for estimating the thickness of the Antarctic ice-sheet, and most of the observations have been made by reflection shooting. The results are difficult to analyse on account of the large number of waves travelling through the ice; both P and S waves are transmitted through the ice, unlike echo-sounding in water when the S waves are missing. Changing density of the snow also makes the results difficult to assess, and necessitates a knowledge of the increase of density downwards. This can be obtained from drilled holes. In areas such as the Antarctic it is necessary to drill holes 30 to 60 m deep before the seismic shot can be fired, on account of disturbance from other sources; this slows down the operation.

Another problem was encountered in Greenland, when depth recording proceeded quite satisfactorily up to a definite line beyond which no records could be obtained. This was probably due to the nature of the surface beneath the ice; at the point where waves no longer reach the recording instrument there appears to have been a non-reflecting bottom material, possibly moraine.

Nevertheless many valuable data have been obtained and a fairly accurate estimate of the total volume of ice on the earth can now be made. This is significant in estimating possible future changes in sea-level due to melting ice. Results of seismic surveys suggest that the mean thickness of the Antarctic ice is more than 2000 m and possibly as much as 2500 m, with an area of 11·5 million sq. km. If all this ice were to melt without isostatic adjustment, sea level would rise by about 60 m, or about 40 m if isostatic adjustment is allowed for.

d) *Glacier flow.* The fact that glaciers move down their beds has been known for a long time, but there is still much to be learnt concerning glacier flow, both from the theoretical and observational points of view. The easiest place to measure glacier flow is along a transverse line in the ablation area of a fairly gently sloping, smooth glacier. This may be done by drilling in a line of markers that can be set up and aligned by using a theodolite set up on one of the side walls of the glacier. The position of the line can be fixed by marking a transit point on the opposite wall of the valley. To measure the movement the theodolite is set up at the same point again after the required lapse of time and aligned in the same direction by sighting the opposite point. The movement of the markers in the ice is measured by offsets between the new marker position and the original positions obtained by the theodolite line. This method requires a good signalling system and cannot be used for wide glaciers. If the glacier is wide the position of the markers can be fixed by theodolite intersection.

It is not always possible to set up a theodolite off the glacier; in this situation the survey can be carried out from the ice. The co-ordinates of conspicuous points off the ice can be fixed by theodolite triangulation, and the markers in the ice can then be resurveyed at intervals by resection on the fixed points with the theodolite; both horizontal and vertical angles should be measured.

The problem of fixing markers in the ice is not great in the ablation area, although care must be taken to see that they do not melt out and that allowance is made for change of elevation when they have been redrilled owing to melting. Good hand-boring tools, described by Ward (1958), are available to drill holes up to about 30 feet in temperate glaciers; these holes can conveniently be $1\frac{1}{4}$ inches in diameter and a 1-in. square stake of Ramin wood should be driven into each hole with a maul; 10-feet long stakes are convenient for movement studies.

It is not so easy to measure movement in the accumulation area, partly because the stakes do not stay so firmly in the snow and get buried in the winter and partly because snow melts round them in the summer. White painted aluminium alloy tubes 2 to 3 inches in diameter and 20 to 30 feet long have been found fairly satisfactory. Other difficult areas for good surface velocity studies are large ice-sheets where there are no visible marks of reference. In this case astronomical fixes with a theodolite are the best that can be achieved, but the relative inaccuracy and difficulty of this method means that a fairly long time interval, of the order of years, should elapse between measurements unless the flow is fast.

Where glaciers are very inaccessible it is sometimes possible to obtain evidence of flow rates by using photogrammetric techniques. The success of this method depends on there being recognisable rock nunataks as well as recognisable features on the glacier surface, such as crevasse patterns or melt-water channels. Long time lapses between successive photographs should not be allowed, so that the method only applies for fairly fast moving ice, 15 in./day, for example. Mellor (1958) used an interval of 120 days in Antarctica using the radial line method of plotting the position of the same points on two successive photographic runs.

A photographic method can also be used to measure the flow of ice in an ice-fall, as was done for example in the measurement of the velocity of the ice-fall of Odinsbreen by J. F. Nye (1958). Two photographs, taken seven days apart, were superimposed and the distance between two recognisable points in the ice-fall was measured under a microscope. The photographs were taken daily from the same point head-on to the ice-fall. Assuming that displacements on the negatives represented motion of ice along a line parallel to the average slope of the ice-fall, the displacement on the negative (0·56 mm) was converted into displacement of the ice (47 m). The results gave rates of up to 2000 m/year in the centre of the ice-fall. Errors of movement measured by this method could be up to 20%, but the results are better than no observations at all.

Most measurement studies in the past have been made on lines transverse to the flow. These observations show clearly some important aspects of glacier flow, and allow normal flow to be differentiated from block-schollen flow, in which most of the differential movement between the centre and the side walls takes place very near to the side walls. On the other hand there has been some neglect of observations longitudinally down a glacier from the accumulation zone to the snout. Such measurements can be made by the same methods that have already been mentioned, and the analysis of the results gives useful information of the longitudinal strain rates, indicating whether the ice is accelerating or decelerating down-glacier. This information is of value in testing theories of glacier flow, such as that of Nye (1958) concerning the formation of waves in glaciers below ice-falls.

In testing specific theoretical points, measurements may be specially designed to produce the required information. For example it was thought that the ice waves could have been produced by pressure at the base of the ice-fall. In order to test the theory a system of stakes was set up in a square, with one stake at the centre; by taping the distance of the stakes relative to one another and by measuring their change of elevation by levelling, accurate values of the strain-rate tensors (Nye, 1959a) could be obtained. This information could then be related to the stress required to produce the measured strain rates. These strain rates could then in turn be related to the crevasse pattern on the glacier surface. It was found that the position of maximum compression did not coincide with the crests of the waves, nor were the wave crests rising relative to their surroundings. The conclusion was reached that the waves were not connected with the measured compression and were not being formed by this process. The deformation of the ice could be shown to be independent of the waves, and to be related instead to the curvature of the glacier bed, the widening of the glacier at the foot of the ice-fall and the annual ablation. It is interesting to note that the repetition of the observations in the following summer showed that the deformation was almost the same at the same positions in the two years, which further supported the view that the glacier bed was one of the major factors determining the repeatable pattern of compression and extension at the foot of the ice-fall. Thus detailed measurements of glacier flow can indirectly give information concerning the bed of the glacier. The waves at the foot of the ice-fall could be adequately explained by the measured compression in the ice-fall and the measured rate of change of ablation between the top and base of the ice-fall, the firn line running across the glacier near the top of the ice-fall.

The observations that have just been mentioned indicate that the bed exerts an important influence on the glacier movement at the surface. It is also necessary to obtain information concerning the nature of flow within and at the base of the glacier. This is important as far as geomorphological interpretation of ice movement is concerned. Glacier movement at depth can be measured by inserting a pipe into the glacier vertically, and measuring its deformation by using an inclinometer.

One of the earliest attempts to measure the velocity in a vertical section through a glacier was carried out in the Jungfraufirn area. The borehole was sunk in an area in which it was thought that extrusion flow might occur. This should have shown an increase of velocity with depth, as the ice under higher pressure was supposed to be squeezed out beneath the more rigid surface ice. The results of measuring the movement in the borehole, however, showed a decrease of velocity with depth, falling off to small values near the rock bed, which was encountered at a depth of 137 m. The result was interpreted as due to laminar flow in the ice. However, movement of two stakes on the surface relative to each other showed that the surface was undergoing tensile stress as the distance between the stakes increased from 27·3 to 31·4 m in 368 days. This in itself would cause a tilt of the pipe that must be taken into account. However, the measured tilt of the pipe could be explained if the longitudinal change of strain rate with depth is taken into account, and this is related to the tensile stress that often occurs in the accumulation zone of glaciers.

Results of borehole inclination studies on the Taku glacier (Miller, 1958) show that movement is not only down-glacier at depth, but that there is at times also a transverse movement that must be measured. Movement in the firn was found to be much more complex than the movement of the lower part of the pipe in the ice beneath. Although the pipe only penetrated the upper one-quarter of the depth of the ice, the results could be extrapolated downwards to give some information concerning the proportion of bottom flow. The differential movement through the glacier could be shown to be small; using the field measurements and certain assumptions from other work, such as the flow law of ice derived by Glen, Miller suggests that $\frac{2}{3}$ of the total movement on the surface is transmitted to the bed, only $\frac{1}{3}$ being differential movement through the ice. These results apply where the surface slope of the glacier was 1 degree; as the surface slope increased so the proportion of the basal flow increased.

These examples show that lined boreholes, down which inclinometers can be inserted, provide very useful evidence of englacial flow rates, which are essential to a full survey of glacier movement and for testing various theories of flow. Nevertheless the results of these methods are not always easy to interpret and observational difficulties are considerable, but it is only by using these rather elaborate techniques that glaciology will progress.

Another even more laborious, but more valuable, method of investigating the internal structure and flow of a glacier is to dig a tunnel through it to the back wall. Clearly the tunnel cannot be vertical, so that boreholes remain essential to obtain evidence of the vertical velocity profile. A number of tunnels have been excavated, some for hydrological purposes, such as the Mont Collon glacier tunnel, others for pure research purposes, for example the Vesl-Skautbreen and Austerdalsbreen tunnels in Norway.

The small cirque glacier Vesl-Skautbreen, in the Jotunheim area, has been studied very intensively (Lewis ed., 1960), and the methods used in this survey provide a very good example of the type of observations and the results that can be obtained from them. The glacier surveyed was very small and moved very slowly, so that extremely accurate surveying was essential. Two tunnels were dug through the glacier, one reaching the back wall at the point where the ice reached its maximum thickness of about 50 m, and the other near the top of the glacier. A series of stations was set up on the glacier surface and marked by stakes, while other marks were fixed in the tunnel at points vertically below the surface stakes. Survey of the three-dimensional movement of both sets of stakes was carried out by precise theodolite observations; in nearly all instances the movement was less than 1 cm/day. (See figure 3.3.)

The surface values showed a rapid deceleration near the firn line, with the highest pegs moving down into the firn, while at the firn line the flow was parallel with the surface, but at the lower end it had an upward component. In the tunnel the flow was also upwards near the entrance, horizontally towards the snout in the centre, but slightly downwards along the bed at the inner end of the tunnel against the back wall. The movement against the back wall showed that basal flow made up 90% of the total movement of the glacier in this position of maximum ice thickness, only 10% being accounted for by differential movement within the ice. It is worth noting that the movement of the ice mass as a whole was partially rotational, the whole mass moving along a circular arc of radius about 240 m. This was not the only form of movement, however, as this does not account for the upward movement at the snout. There must have been some deformation of the ice as it moved, superimposed on its rotational movement.

The structure of the glacier surface suggested that movement of the ice took place along discrete thrust-planes in the ice, and observations were made to test this hypothesis, but no movement along discrete thrust planes could be established. Other observations, rather than measurement, of great interest were concerned with the nature of the ice-rock contact at the inner end of the tunnels. There was a very significant difference between the two tunnels from this point of view. The lower tunnel, beneath thick ice, showed that the ice was in general in close contact with the bed; any gaps that there were

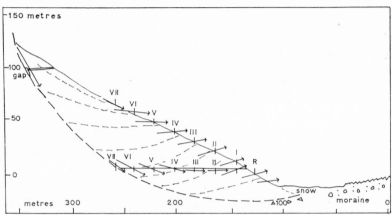

FIGURE 3.3. Diagram to show the direction and rate of movement in the cirque glacier Vesl-Skautbreen, Jotunheim, Norway. The arrows indicate the direction and rate of movement, and the position of the tunnels is shown. The dashed lines show the deformation of the layers within the glacier. (after McCall)

occurred in the lee of obstructions. Between the rock and clean ice a sole 30 cm thick intervened; this layer contained ice of a different type from the glacier ice above and a large amount of rock debris ranging from fine material to boulders. The ice in the sole must have frozen from the melt water trickling under the glacier ice, and incorporating the material in it as it froze. This suggests that scouring may be an effective agent under moving ice, in such a position as this. At the inner end of the upper tunnel, on the other hand, there were large head-wall gaps, and on the rock at the back a layer of clear ice was found. The gap is caused by the fact that the back wall slopes at a steeper angle than the direction of movement of the ice, forming a roof to the cave. Observations showed that the gap was a long-lived feature, because grooves on the roof-ice, made against irregularities in the rock as the ice moved over, were 50 m long, where the flow was only 3 m/year.

It is worth noting that in other glacier caves gaps show that the ice, passing over an irregular floor, adapts its form to that of the surface over which it is flowing. Carol has shown that local increase of pressure as ice passes over an obstruction can cause it to change its speed of flow and its consistency, becoming much more plastic where the pressure is increased,

One of the advantages of digging a research tunnel in a glacier such as Vesl-Skautbreen is that the ice is moving slowly and closure of the tunnel and its movement are not so great that difficulties in surveying and digging are aggravated. These problems can be quite considerable if the glacier is a more active one, such as Austerdalsbreen. A tunnel was dug at the foot of the ice-fall of Odinsbreen, where waves on the glacier surface are very conspicuous (Glen, 1956). The ice in this part of the glacier was moving very actively and one difficulty experienced in digging the tunnel illustrates this; although it was originally dug with a slight uphill gradient towards the inner end, the downward rotation of the inner part of the tunnel was so great that it became flooded. Also the very high ablation rate caused the loss of the outermost 10 m of tunnel during the digging period. The back of the tunnel did not reach to bedrock, although its length was 46 m (150 feet). The surface form of the glacier above the tunnel was surveyed by tacheometry, the slope being between 30 and 40 degrees.

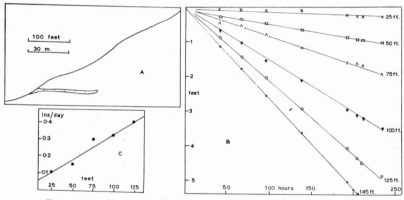

FIGURE 3.4. Observations in the tunnel on Austerdalsbreen, Norway.
A shows a vertical section through the ice-fall and the position of the tunnel.
B shows the rate of fall of the pegs in the wall of the tunnel relative to the peg at 10 feet against time.
C shows the rate of approach of pegs in the opposite walls of the tunnel plotted against distance along the tunnel. (after Glen)

The observations made within the tunnel indicate the type of survey operations that are suitable for such problems. Bamboo pegs were inserted in the walls at 25-feet intervals, in pairs on opposite walls. In order to measure the rotation of the tunnel a level was used, either from the entrance or the inner end of the tunnel, and the height of each peg relative to the level line could be measured by offsets to each one in turn. Other measurements made were to tape the distance between successive pegs on the same side of the tunnel and to measure the distance between pairs of pegs on opposite sides of the tunnel. These results, shown in figure 3.4, gave the rate of longitudinal compression along the tunnel and the rate of closure respectively.

The results showed that the back of the tunnel was falling relative to the front at 14′ of arc each day. The measurements of horizontal distance showed that the tunnel was undergoing rapid compressive strain, particularly near its mouth, the strain rate being 0·5/year here. The rate of closure, found from the measurement of opposite pegs, also shows very rapid movement compared with other tunnels, and was highest near the inner end; the tunnel width decreased at 0·4 inches/day at a position 125 feet from the entrance. This rate of closure is more than would be expected to occur under hydrostatic pressure alone so that compression at the base of the ice-fall is probably an important component. Tunnelling in such active glaciers has both advantages and disadvantages, but much useful information can be obtained.

It is difficult to measure the actual rate of flow of ice over its bed, although some information concerning this can be gleaned from pipe and tunnel observations. The same difficulties do not apply to the measurement of side slip of a glacier past its rock walls and useful observations were made by two different methods. Firstly, one stake was drilled into the ice vertically about 1 m from the edge and two marks were painted on the rock walls on either side; the distances between the stake and the rock marks were measured daily, and from these figures the movement of the stake relative to the rock wall could be calculated. The second method consists of drilling a stake as nearly horizontally as possible through the ice at the glacier margin so that the end of the stake rested against the rock wall in a marginal gap. The point at which the stake rested could be marked and the subsequent movement of the stake could be measured relative to the initial point. Difficulties arose due to ablation loosening the stake, and reboring was necessary at rather frequent intervals. The main advantage of the second method was that it enabled movement closer to the rock-wall to be recorded and both horizontal and vertical components could be measured directly. The main disadvantage was the loosening of the stake by ablation, which made the result somewhat doubtful at times.

Nevertheless both methods can give very useful information, the first showing more uniform movement than the second, possibly because some of the irregular movements, due to boulders on the glacier margin, were damped out at only 1 m away from the margin. Nearly all the stations observed showed appreciable side slip past the rock wall; this was particularly fast at the highest station near the foot of the Odinsbreen ice-fall, where the daily rate was 19·6 cm, but the rate fell off to between 1·5 and 4·3 cm/day downslope, where the glacier was much flatter and where the flow in the centre was about 13 cm/day. The side slip was, therefore, about 10 to 20% of the central movement on the main part of the glacier trunk. These observations have important implications when the processes of glacial erosion are considered, and the heavily striated gneiss sides of Austerdalsbreen testified to the effectiveness of the side scour in an active glacier of this type (Glen and Lewis, 1959).

Interesting theoretical work on glacier movement over a rock bed has been published recently by Weertman (1964) and his results have been tested in the field and laboratory by Kamb and LaChapelle (1964). The field work was carried out in a tunnel cut through the Blue Glacier, Washington. The tunnel reached bedrock at 50 m from the surface under 26 m of ice. The measurements of bed slip were made with a precise dial micrometer, which allowed the ice movement to be recorded relative to the bedrock immediately below. A stake was anchored in the ice 10 cm above the bedrock and this showed an average movement of 1·6 cm/day parallel to the bed. Another stake 150 cm above the bedrock moved 12% faster, and a vertical profile derived from observations of stakes at 10 cm intervals showed that most of the difference occurred in the lowest 50 cm. All the motion of 1·6 cm/day took place as slip at the bedrock-ice interface. Surface movement above the tunnel was 1·8 cm/day or equal to that at 150 cm above the bedrock. The observations showed that the flow rate was irregular over time intervals of seconds and could vary 10% from day to day. The structure and texture of the ice was also examined and showed that under pressure a thin layer of water existed between the ice and rock, but when the pressure was reduced by excavating a layer of overlying ice, then the ice immediately froze to the rock surface. A regelation layer up to 2·9 cm thick of different ice was found. The laboratory experiments confirmed that regelation took place as the ice moved over the irregularities in the bedrock and the thickness of the regelation layer could be related to the wave length of the bedrock irregularities.

e) *The age of ice.* In considering the mass budget of a glacier it is useful to have some means of estimating tha age of the ice. This can be done for a number of years by measuring the annual layers revealed in a pit, or exposed on the surface of a glacier after rotation, as in the small cirque glaciers of Jotunheim (Grove, in Lewis, 1960). Where accumulation is great, as in Iceland, only a few annual layers can be observed in a pit of reasonable depth, but in the Antarctic, where accumulation is very slow, a considerable number of annual layers may be obtained from one pit or core; the absence of dirt in Antarctica means that the layers must be differentiated according to the character of the ice, its density, hardness and crystal character. If the stratification has disappeared in the lower layers, the winter and summer ice can be differentiated according to the proportion of the isotopes oxygen-18 to that of oxygen-16. A study of these isotopes allows measurement of seasonal variations and climatic change over the past 1000 years or more. The age of the ice can also be measured by using the carbon-14 technique, but a very large amount of ice is required for each analysis. As the methods are improved it should be possible by deep drilling to obtain cores adding up to 2500 m in length from the Antarctic; this would push back the age of recorded ice to thousands or ten thousands of years.

f) *Glacial deposition.* It is not often possible to study by direct methods the deposition of material by ice, although at times marginal features, such as eskers, may be observed in the process of formation. An example of this is the study made by W. V. Lewis (1949) of an esker in the process of formation at the snout of Boverdalsbreen. It is also possible at times to observe the deposition of lateral or terminal moraines; for example a small marginal moraine about 2 to 3 feet high formed between 1958 and 1959 along the snout of Austerdalsbreen. More often, however, glacial till must be studied after the ice depositing it has retreated or melted. Relatively few detailed studies have been made of the way in which till is deposited and how the characteristic landforms are shaped. Such studies must rely on indirect methods of observation and inference. The analysis of till fabric has already been mentioned briefly (pp. 74, 75) and this method probably offers one of the best means of studying the way in which ice deposits its load. An analysis of this type should also be associated with a study of other relevant factors, such as the form of the drift surface, unless this has been modified by subsequent erosion, and its relation to other features.

The study of cross-valley moraines in north central Baffin Island by J. T. Andrews (1963) shows how a very detailed, quantitative study of the till fabric helps to choose between various possible hypotheses of moraine formation. Other observations are also relevant to the final conclusion that the moraines were probably formed by the squeezing of saturated till into basal crevasses. The other relevant data include a study of the associated kames, and the relation of the spacing of the moraines to the effective stress at the base of the glacier, which ended in a glacial lake. Thus the evidence for the former presence of the lake is also very important, and this was found to be an essential condition in the formation of this type of moraine. These particular moraines can then be compared with other rather similar forms, such as those known as de Geer or Washboard moraines. However, not all moraines even of this type, have necessarily been formed by precisely the same mechanism, as a study of ice temperatures and pressures revealed.

The work of G. Østrem (1961) on the end moraines of some Scandinavian glaciers illustrates another method of obtaining useful information concerning the character and dating of moraines. Seismic sounding was used to reveal ice cores in moraines, and the thickness of the moraine cover could be found by earth resistivity methods; it was found to be about 1 to 3 m in the moraines under study. A drill and explosives were used to obtain ice samples, which were analysed crystallographically, showing that the ice had originated as snow in situ, probably originally having been deposited in front of a steep glacier and becoming buried beneath moraine from the ice above. Organic particles in the ice were concentrated by melting 200 kg of ice, and this material was dated by carbon-14 methods. The results indicated that the ice was 2600 ± 100 years old. This disproved the supposition that the moraine ridge dated from the known eighteenth-century ice advance.

These two examples serve to show how new and detailed methods of investigation can help to elucidate the character and mechanism of glacial deposition. They show that forms, which are sometimes too much taken for granted, can yield useful information if they are studied carefully. It also demonstrates that a term like 'moraine' can cover features formed in a great variety of ways.

The techniques used in glaciological study are becoming more elaborate and complex; nevertheless simpler methods can also produce useful results if they are carefully analysed. Field studies are particularly valuable when they are used to test theoretical work, as for example the studies made by J. F. Nye and J. W. Glen on Austerdalsbreen; it may frequently be found that from the preliminary observations new theories emerge and require testing in the field in their turn. This is true of the observations made in the tunnel on Austerdalsbreen; these were originally thought to show wave formation, whereas in fact, taking a larger area into consideration, they show that the glacier is unbending and that the waves are produced by a completely different process related to variations in ablation with the seasons. The original glacier boreholes did not show extrusion flow as some had expected, but nevertheless the information they did provide has allowed further advances in theory, and the checking of other theoretical conclusions.

3. PERIGLACIAL PROCESSES

Adjacent to moving ice masses, or in climates that are cold but too dry to accumulate glaciers and ice-sheets, there is often a wide zone in which processes associated with the action of frost and snow play a significant part in shaping the landscape. The recognition and study of these periglacial features in the field must be based on a knowledge of their characteristics, so that it is relevant to describe these briefly, before methods of field study are mentioned. It is not always possible to record the processes in action, as in many areas where periglacial features are found they are fossil or relict features, not being actively formed under present conditions. Nevertheless their recognition and study helps to elucidate the processes that have acted in the past and whose action can still be appreciated in the present landscape. This is true of most periglacial features in Britain, where a wide variety of forms has been recognised.

a) *Snow processes.* The effect of snow activity on the landscape does not often receive attention, but some interesting features can be produced by snow. These forms can be both erosional and depositional, and an example of each type will be considered. Snow patch erosion has been studied in Iceland by W. V. Lewis (1939). The work was carried out on the flanks of Snaefell, which had the advantage that snow patches in different stages of melting could be studied by ascending the volcanic cone. The snow patches could be divided into three types; some were transverse to the hill-side, others were elongated downslope, while the third group consisted of much larger more circular snow patches that were probably embryo cirque glaciers. The transverse snow patches had a steepened back-slope, with boulders and stones set in clay, leading up to a gentler grass slope above, while below the melting snow patch a flattened area of stones, in a muddy matrix, lay in a hollow below the surrounding area of grass. The profile of the snow patch (see figure 3.5) was levelled and the operation of snow erosion was studied by digging pits through the snow and the ground below it. These revealed a frozen subsoil beneath the snow and a melted area in front of it. The snow showed no signs of movement and melt water provided the means of transport for the soil and rock fragments. Frost action must have been effective in breaking up

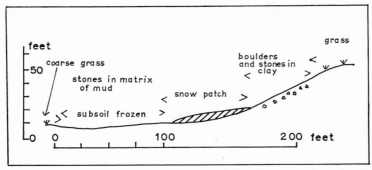

FIGURE 3.5. Profile to illustrate the characteristics of snow patch erosion in Iceland. (after Lewis)

the material at the lower end of the sodden ground. In the longitudinal snow patches, which were the most numerous, it was difficult to differentiate between snow erosion and gully action. The circular snow patches were much larger and formed typically rounded hollows, quite unlike the forms produced by water erosion. The examination of the back of the snow patch after considerable melting had taken place revealed an abrupt fall of ground at the top edge of the patch. Only a small part of this steep wall was being directly affected by the melt-water stream, so that evidence could be seen to show that the snow patch, and the associated process of freezing and thawing, were responsible for the visible forms. The presence of a large amount of melt water was an important point, because where the ground was damped continually, frost action could be much more effective in breaking up the soil. The snow patch appeared to be incising itself into the hill-side where its edges were examined, a process by which it was self-generating. As the hollow got deeper, so the winter snow-fall would become thicker each year, taking longer to melt and thus prolonging the erosional effect of nivation.

That annual snow patches can move stones and boulders and abrade rocks has been demonstrated experimentally by A. B. Costin and others (1964) in the Snowy Mountains of Australia. The position of painted stones was marked before the winter and after the snow had melted in the spring the stones were re-examined and their movement measured. The results showed that movement was generally downslope, but that it could be locally upslope. Striation and abrasion of the rock surface were noted and these observations and measurements confirm that annual snow patches can move and erode the ground.

The erosional features just mentioned were formed by snow patches which were either stationary or moving only slowly; the features described by A. Rapp (1959) on the other hand are the result of fast moving snow, in the form of avalanches. The rapid movement of large masses of snow can have considerable erosional effects, producing long straight gullies that are characteristic of steep slopes in areas subject to heavy snow-fall. The material eroded by this process must be deposited nearby as the moving snow comes to rest, and the resulting morphological forms have been called avalanche boulder tongues. They can be distinguished from somewhat similar deposition features by their characteristics. They are often regular in form, having markedly concave slope profiles. The distal part of the tongue extends far out on to the flat ground, in comparison with alluvial talus cones; at times the tongue can extend a little way up the opposite valley side. The top surface of the deposit is usually fairly flat.

Two types of tongue can be distinguished. The first is called a road-bank tongue, on account of its upraised and flat-topped nature; the second is called a fan tongue and usually consists of a thinner, longer layer of debris, extending further out over the valley bottom. The profiles in transverse section are often asymmetrical. Observations of the rock debris showed it to be largely angular, and sometimes there was some tendency to size sorting, with the largest boulders occurring along the side and the front of the tongue. Where boulders are not numerous, they are at times restricted to the margin of the tongue, with finer debris in the centre. The features occur most commonly on slopes where there is plenty of rock debris and are normally found above the tree-line.

Examples of avalanche boulder tongues have been studied in the field in the Kebnekaise mountain area of Swedish Lappland. The conditions here are suitable for the development of the boulder tongues as the tree-line is at only 700 m and the ground above this is bare and consists of block-fields and rock walls, and frost shattering is active. Field survey of the tongues included the measurement of the gradient of the tongue and a study of the size of its material. One of the boulder tongues was found to be 330 m long and 70-80 m broad throughout. Its thickness was a maximum of 5 m, while the adjacent one had a thickness of 8 m and a breadth of 100-120 m. The material consisted of angular blocks from gravel to boulders up to 2 m in size. The eastern margin was very steep and unstable and showed signs of fall-sorting of the boulders. The slope was about 10-15 degrees near the base, increasing to 28 to 30 near the rock-wall at the top. The lower part in particular was very smooth, the inclination having been measured at every 5th metre. A study of the long axes of the boulders showed that many of them were orientated with their long axes in a downslope direction. The cross profile of the tongue was increasingly flattened towards the distal end and became very asymmetrical, having a steep east slope. Small avalanche debris tails were other interesting minor features; these occurred in the lee of large boulders, and were small, straight ridges of debris about 5 to 10 m long, the other dimensions depending on the size of the boulders in whose shelter the tail had accumulated. The material was loosely heaped and elongated in the direction of the tongue. The asymmetry of some of the tongues was thought to be due to the action of the wind in banking up snow drifts on the lee side of the accumulating shutes of debris, which collapsed as the snow melted to form the steep, unstable lee slopes.

An example of the second, fan tongue, type of feature was examined by Rapp at Abisko; it consisted of three sections; firstly, an alluvial cone with a vertical height of 40 m, secondly, a broad erosion track on both sides of the cone, indicating the greater width of avalanches than streams, and finally, the real avalanche boulder tongue below, reaching far out into the valley, 300 m beyond the end of the alluvial cone, with a slope of only 5 to ½ degree. Avalanche debris tails occurred on it, and its limiting bluff was only half a metre high, but was quite distinct. These features must be formed by large far-travelling avalanches, some of the material being supplied by streams. The feature was not the result of any one avalanche, but had been built up by the superimposition of many, the limits of each being identifiable as lines of boulders.

A. Rapp (1960) has carried his study further by making a quantitative estimate of the amount of material moved by snow avalanches. The method he used for this purpose was to estimate the amount of debris brought down by avalanches that came to rest on a previous snow cover. Large boulders were measured in three dimensions and marked with paint, and the area covered by finer debris was measured and its thickness estimated. Boulders smaller than 50 cm were counted and a factor, based on earlier more detailed observations, was used to assess their volume. The results are regarded as accurate to ± 20%. An example of one avalanche gave a total volume moved of 10·3 cu.m, the average being 5 to 10 cu.m in the area of Kärkevagge, where the experiments were carried out in northern Sweden. It should be noted that slush avalanches were found to be even more powerful and moved ten times the amount moved by snow avalanches in the same period, the volume being measured in the same way.

b) *Permafrost.* One of the most characteristic features of the periglacial environment is the presence of permafrost. With the economic exploitation in arctic regions the effects of permafrost are becoming better known. A good example of the importance of permafrost to economic activity is the development of iron mining in central Labrador, where permafrost is a problem in mining. The economic significance has the advantage that further details concerning the extent and depth of permafrost in this area have become available, and a study of permafrost has been undertaken to assist the development of mining techniques suitable for permanently frozen ground. One of the factors that is relevant is the amount of ice in the rock, as this affects the efficiency of blasting (Ives, 1962).

Study of permafrost and the geomorphological features associated with it has been carried out by a number of methods, but again close observation of the features is indispensable for verifying one or more of the many hypotheses put forward to account for their characteristics. Observations of the extent and depth of permafrost depend on measurements made in boreholes or quarries. Much of the work done up to 1943 has been summarised by Taber (1943). He has shown that the depth of permafrost is greatest in areas not previously glaciated, such as parts of Siberia and the Yukon territory. Measurements in Canada show that permafrost penetrates to a depth of 200 to 300 feet, where the minimum temperature of 26°F was recorded at a depth of 40 feet; the sites of this type were all exposed and had little winter snow cover, while the areas sheltered beneath a deep snow cover developed no permafrost, the minimum temperature of 32·8°F being recorded at 30 feet depth. The two environments could be differentiated by their vegetation, the former having only a lichen-heath plant cover and much bare rock.

One of the superficial effects of ice development during the winter is frost-heave, and a technique to measure this has been devised and useful results obtained. The equipment consisted of six metal posts set in a concrete base fixed on the bedrock. A levelled frame 3·18 m square was fixed to the posts. Cross-pieces were attached to the frame, with holes at intervals for copper rods of 5 mm diameter to pass through, each rod resting on a 1-in. square base plate. There were 64 rods, each free to slide up and down in its support, the changes in level being recorded to ± 1 mm. The measurements could be made beneath a thick snow cover by means of a cat-walk erected over the apparatus. The experiments were made where the soil depth was 33 to 52 cm thick and thermistor readings of temperature were taken near the site. The results showed an initial period of heave in early October, followed by a rapid heave of up to 60 mm in late October, when the temperature fell below freezing in a cold spell. The ground level did not change during January to May, but the ground collapsed very quickly as a result of the spring thaw in May. The apparatus covered patterned ground, and in general the bare areas were heaved up more than the vegetated ones. The accuracy of the method is great and controlled field analysis of the effect of frost heave can be achieved with it (Andrews, 1963).

Other recent methods of measuring mass wasting in Greenland include a study using theodolite observations by Washburn (1962), while Everett has used linear motion potentiometers with a sensitivity of 0·03 mm. They were attached to pipes anchored to bedrock or in permafrost. An aluminium plate buried in the slope was then fixed to the shaft of the potentiometer, so that when the soil moved the potentiometer was moved through a recorded distance. The results showed that maximum movements occurred during the freeze-up and amounted to distances between 0·25 and 33 mm and diurnal movements occurred during the thaw. It is interesting to note that the soil movements recorded in the periglacial climate of Alaska were ten times those recorded in Ohio.

Another method was adopted by Poulin (1962) to measure frost heave. He fixed a scaffold over the area to be studied and took photographs from 3 to 6 m above the ground, and, using aerial photography methods of analysis he could measure the ground movement to an accuracy of 2 to 3 mm. He produced a map on a scale of 1 to 4, with a contour interval of 6 mm.

c) *Periglacial sorting—patterned ground phenomena.* Patterned ground is one of the best forms of evidence for the action of periglacial processes; the variety of forms is very great and features characteristic of a moderately cold climate must be differentiated from those found in areas of permafrost. Small-scale polygons and patterned ground can be produced by frost sorting in areas where there is no permafrost, but true large-scale tundra polygons or ice-wedge polygons are restricted to permafrost areas. T. L. Péwé (1963) has distinguished between active ice-wedge polygons, which form where the mean annual temperature is −6 to −8°C or colder, in Alaska, and the mean annual degree C days of freezing range from 2800 to 5400, and inactive ice wedges, where the mean annual temperature is between about −2°C and −6°C and the degree days of freezing range from 1700 to 4000. The former type have actively forming ice wedges 1 to 2 m wide at the top, while in the latter the ice does not increase and permafrost may not be continuous. Finally there are fossil ice wedges where the ice has melted and been replaced by sediment that can be distinguished from the surrounding material. It is generally agreed now that this type of periglacial feature is formed as a result of contraction due to intense cold, with the crack so formed filling with ice when thawing and refreezing take place in summer. Other terms that have been used to describe fossil ice wedges are ice-wedge pseudomorphs, ice-wedge fill, ice-wedge cast and frost wedge, and sometimes, wrongly, ice wedge. Fossil ice wedges provide valuable evidence of former more severe climatic conditions.

The very comprehensive account of patterned ground features by Washburn (1956) gives details of most of the features and of the hypotheses put forward to account for them. The features that are included in this study are those described as circles, nets, polygons, steps and stripes. Each geometrical shape can be found in either a sorted or a non-sorted form. Steps and stripes are associated with steeper slopes than the more circular patterns. The non-sorted type of feature can usually be recognised by the character of the vegetation or relief, while the sorted type depends on the availability of a variety of sizes of material, either in the original sediment or as a result of selective comminution.

Small features are not restricted to permafrost conditions, but form in the British Isles at present, where examples have been described from the Tinto Hills in south Scotland. The features included sorted stone stripes and sorted polygons. The stripes have been investigated in detail, showing that they occurred down to 1900 feet on the south side and 1300 feet on the north side of the hills. The material ranged from fine debris to blocks 6 inches in diameter. The sorting did not extend below 4 to 6 inches in depth. The stripes were 8 to 14 inches wide, the coarse material lying in 3-inch-deep furrows, the finest material on the narrow ridges. The stripes crossed the contours at right-angles and occurred on slopes of 20 degrees. Experiments done in the area showed that the features were growing under present conditions; they were dug over to a depth of 1 foot but after two years they had reformed (Miller *et al.*, 1954).

Corte (1962, 1963) has carried out laboratory experiments and related these to field work in an attempt to study the sorting of material under periglacial conditions. He subjected a saturated sandy gravel to freezing and thawing. The results showed a vertical sorting of the mixed material, with fine particles moving down and coarse upwards, while the volume of the mixture increased. When the freezing occurred from the side, the fine particles moved away from the freezing point in a parabolic path while the coarser particles moved in a similar way but covered less distance; thus sorting took place. Freezing from the bottom caused upward migration of particles against gravity, the smaller again moving further. The field observations included a correlation of pattern with grain size and ground ice structure and distribution. Differential melting of ice was observed to cause sorting patterns after one season.

It is valuable to obtain data concerning present permafrost features so that fossil forms can be correctly interpreted and the climate at the time of their formation rightly interpreted. The measurement of movement of painted stones in patterned ground is a useful and relatively easy method of assessing the present activity of processes forming these features. Measurements of the rate of movement of various periglacial features have been noted by A. Pissart (1964a) in the Chambeyron district. He used paint marks to measure the downslope transfer of debris on striped ground and in rock screes, allowing the movement to be measured to the nearest centimetre. On the scree a line 200 m long was marked out perpendicular to the slope. Sixty-five blocks were marked with letters to allow their recognition; 60 were found subsequently and of these 12 had either remained still or moved less than 5 cm and 49 had moved between 5 and 600 cm, the mean value being 64 cm. It was shown that size played an important part in accounting for the distance moved.

Sections dug through periglacial features can yield valuable information; for example the study of Fitzpatrick (1960) showed that under mud polygons the soil thawed to a considerably greater depth below the mud than beneath the intervening patches of vegetation; beneath the vegetation the soil had scarcely thawed at all, whereas beneath the bare mud the depth of thawing was up to about 2 feet.

Quantitative methods have been used by J. Smith (1960) in South Georgia; he buried stakes of three sizes vertically in the ground, to 50 cm, 25 cm, and 10 cm, all projected 3 cm above the ground. The mean movement of the longest stake was nil, of the middle size 3 cm/year and of the shortest 5 cm/year; the ground slope at the observation site was 21 degrees. There was no vegetation with the exception of some lichen. Desiccation polygons were found in the area and the water table was at least 2 m down. Stones were also placed on the surface and their movement measured; they moved at a maximum rate of 71 cm/year and a minimum rate of 25 cm/year, the mean rate being 47 cm/year. Observations of temperature were also recorded at 5, 10, 25, 50, 100 and 200 cm depths, and the amount of ice in the soil was measured in November, taking samples from different depths.

Fossil ice wedges are normally associated with polygonal features which may be revealed at times by a study of the vegetation; they often show up conspicuously on aerial photographs. For example the features recorded by Shotton (1960) show that permafrost must have existed in the Midlands of England during the Irish Sea glaciation, while fossil ice wedges have been recorded by Patterson (1940) and Williams (1964) near Cambridge. Fossil ice wedges have been recorded by observations of sections revealed in gravel

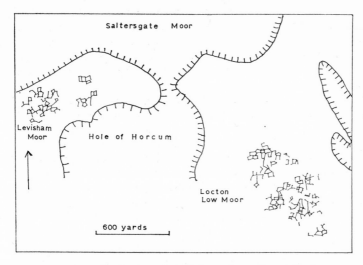

FIGURE 3.6. The distribution of fossil ice-wedge polygons is shown on Locton Low Moor and Levisham Moor on the North Yorkshire Moors, and the detailed structure of one fossil ice wedge is shown in section. (after Dimbleby)

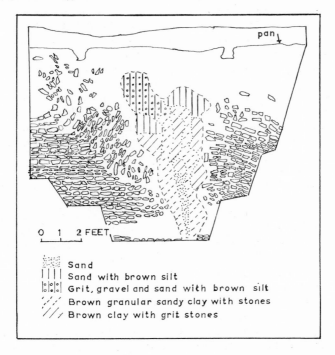

pits, and these features appear to have been similar to features studied round Baffin Bay: thus analogy is essential in identifying features far from conditions in which they could now be generated. These cracks reach a depth of 12 feet and show by the characteristic arrangement of the sediment within them that they have probably been formed in the following way: initial cracks formed during extreme cold, when volume decreased, and then during the summer melt period expansion took place, the edge of the ice filling the crack melted and sediment seeped down between the ice and the the walls of the crack, until as the rest of the ice finally melted, the crack was lined with stratified debris, with the final central part filled with mixed, unsorted material. Similar features, described by Dimbleby (1952) have been found on the Yorkshire Moors and are illustrated in figure 3.6. The contraction theory for the formation of these polygonal cracks was first put forward by Leffingwell in 1915 to explain the ice wedge polygons in Siberia.

Experiments carried out by Pissart (1964b) have thrown light of the process; he used wet mud in a tray 50 cm squaie. The wet mud was allowed to freeze slowly. The formation of ice in the upper part of the mud caused the lower part to dry out, and cracks occurred. The size of the polygons so formed varied with the thickness of the mud.

Ice wedges, formed by contraction in extreme cold, should not be confused with the type of ice vein that forms during the development of ground ice, as freezing gradually extends downwards and water is drawn up into the ground, forming ice veins and layers. In Antarctica, field observations have shown without doubt that contraction can cause polygonal patterns, as reported by T. L. Péwé (1962). These polygons had elevated ridges along their length, and instead of a fill of ice, owing to the extreme aridity, the cracks were filled with sand, to form sand wedges. The increase of size of the wedge with time is indicated by the upturning of the sediments in the bounding walls of the wedge. Where the wedges can be seen to taper downwards and disappear there is clear evidence that they must have formed by contraction. Observations of this type are needed in greater number and over a wide variety of situations, in order to provide data that will enable the processes in operation to be clearly and quantitatively understood.

d) *Frost shattering*. Not all features resulting from periglacial conditions show patterning; for example the cambers described by Kellaway and Taylor in the East Midlands (1953) show none. The importance of periglacial processes has at times been exaggerated and Andrews (1961) has shown that these processes are not always as active as would be expected, considering the climate. Nevertheless, widespread activity by freezing and thawing can produce distinctive features, and this process is probably the most effective form of mechanical disintegration of rocks. The occurrence of boulder-fields and mountain-top detritus can be used as useful evidence for the extent of former glaciation and illustrates the importance of frost shattering in producing distinctive landscape features. Terms which are used to describe such surface deposits are 'Felsenmeer', 'Blockmeer' or 'block fields'.

They are formed as a result of the action of frost shattering and are indicative of periglacial conditions, and more important in some contexts, the absence of glaciation. The character of the deposit depends on the nature of the bedrock. The material is not always angular, as would be expected, as weathering in some gneisses causes the rock to break into subangular fragments with rounded gravel. Also in assessing the time required for the formation of block fields, the rock type is very important; well bedded rocks, or closely jointed granites, can break up very rapidly.

The recognition of the action of periglacial processes may be of great assistance in the analysis of a landscape, and such features as boulder-fields or mountain-top detritus may be especially helpful. Less obvious, but equally useful, are the features produced by cryoturbation, such as involutions and patterned ground.

4. MASS MOVEMENT

Mass movement of material can take place in many different ways, some of which are closely associated with a periglacial climate in that they occur most effectively under these conditions, for example scree formation, boulder runs and boulder-fields and some solifluction phenomena. Other processes less dependent on periglacial conditions are mud flows, common in semi-arid conditions, soil creep and slumping.

a) *Screes.* Scree slopes are features that have not been studied in as much detail as they deserve. Field observations on the form of the scree can be made easily, by surveying the profile with an Abney level and tape. The nature of the surface at the base of the scree is also significant. The form of the slope appears to depend to a certain extent on whether the material coming down the scree is evacuated from its base. Screes can be subdivided into gully screes, having a convex profile in the horizontal direction, and sheet screes, which lack this feature. The similarity of scree slopes in different areas, including the Lake District in England, and central Quebec-Labrador, shows

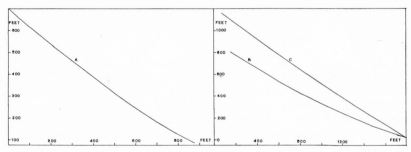

FIGURE 3.7. Examples of scree profiles in Iceland and north-west England.
A Scree on Yarlside, Howgill Fells, north-west England.
B Scree on Stori Blanukur, south-east Iceland, with impeded removal
C Scree in Kjos, south-east Iceland, with unimpeded basal removal.

that despite great contrasts of climate the angles are much the same; the records for both areas cluster round 35 degrees (Andrews, 1961). It is important to note any evidence of vegetation in scree formation, as the slightly

lower angles of unvegetated screes in Iceland and Canada compared with
rather better vegetated examples in north-west England can probably be
explained by the capacity of vegetation to bind the stones and hold the scree
at a higher angle, although the difference in angle is not great. Figure 3.7
illustrates some of these points. Experiments on the nature of movement of
the scree suggest that the scree moves by shearing parallel to the slope and
not by the slow creep of individual blocks. The scree will shear when the internal friction between the blocks is overcome by the force of gravity, so that
the angle is determined by the nature of the blocks and their degree of
packing. Water is not an important agent, as the scree is coarse and permeable. The scree angle does not depend on the length of the slope.

Most screes probably rest at angles below the maximum that the material
of which they are formed is capable of standing. The packing of angular
fragments is usually more stable than that of platy fragments, so that the
angular debris screes can stand at higher angles. Some screes formed of elongated fragments can stand very steeply, at 38 to 40 degrees, if the fragments
are so arranged that the upper ones rest under the lower at their bottom
edge; if the reverse applies the screes are unstable. When the scree moves by
shearing the front face is steepened as the upper material over-rides the lower,
while the slope above is flattened, the larger particles moving to the steepened front. Thus it is clear that a study of the material of which the scree is
formed and its arrangement can give useful information concerning the
formation of the feature.

Screes are largely built up by the accumulation of coarser debris from oversteepened bare rock faces, so that rock falls are an important method of scree
accumulation. A. Rapp (1960) has discussed methods of measuring rock-falls
and their significance in slope development. Where the rock-falls are a long
way from high walls, the talus slope tends to be concave and stable, fringed
with boulders, but where the rock wall is low, so that rocks only fall a short
distance, the scree or talus slope tends to be steep and unstable. As the rock
wall becomes lower so the large blocks rest near the top of the scree. As the
scree develops so the rock wall above retreats, and sometimes overhangs
occur; these then tend to fall, so continuing the process. Where the scars
from which rocks fall are distributed all over the rock wall, it must be retreating by backwearing and not downwearing. By correlating rock-falls
with weather conditions the factors on which they depend can be assessed.
It was found that rockfalls were most numerous when the temperature rose
after a period of frost, occurring mainly in the spring from May to June.
Thus frost bursting is indicated as being an important process.

Methods of measuring the retreat of rock walls can vary with the circumstances. One method is to compare photographs taken after a time lapse of
many years, a second method is to measure the volume of medial moraine
supplied by rock falls on a glacier; such moraines are normally superficial
features. A third method is to calculate the volume of scree cones compared
with the area of rock wall from which they were derived; this involves field
survey and probing of the scree, which is normally a difficult process. A

fourth method is to measure the annual increment of new material as it falls on snow or vegetation. This cannot be done where there is bare talus, but records can be made by spreading netting or sacking on the scree. The pebbles or rocks falling on it could easily be measured and used as a sample to estimate the total addition of material. Rapp spread netting down the slope over a distance of 20 m and found that the annual increment was 2 to 3 cm thickness, mostly accumulating near the top of the scree.

Apart from rock-falls, screes are modified by talus creep. Methods of assessing the significance of this slow but important process are of great value in establishing the rate of denudation. Rapp in his analysis of Kärkevagge used three methods to measure the rate and volume of talus creep; he marked stones and boulders with paint, he buried wooden stakes 40 to 50 cm in the ground and also buried short stakes 15 to 20 cm in the ground. The stakes were arranged in lines down the slope with short transverse lines of painted stones. The distances to the stakes were measured from a fixed point on the rock wall, recording the distance to the base of the stake, as the stakes became tilted downslope. The measurements were made 30 to 40 cm above the ground with a plumb-bob for centering to avoid the difficulty of measuring over a boulder-strewn surface, and are accurate to ± 0·5 cm. On a scree 65 m high and with a gradient of 37 degrees above and 38 degrees below, formed of schist pebbles 2 to 10 cm in length at the top and 2 to 25 cm near the base, the results showed an average movement of 10 cm/year at the top falling to zero at the base. Individual boulders moved further. Observations of orientation and dip of the particles showed that these were arranged to dip downslope at an angle less than that of the scree. This scree moved faster than the others in the vicinity, so that it is necessary to sample with care if extrapolation is to be carried out over a wide area.

b) *Boulder-fields and rock-glaciers.* The accumulation of large masses of boulders in an area of relatively low relief is not very common, but the features produced are interesting. Examples of boulder-fields were studied in the Åland Islands off Finland, where there is a variety of features of this type (King and Hirst, 1964). The interpretation of the boulder-fields was based on observations of their characteristics; surveys were made to determine their size and shape, by plane-tabling and compass traversing. The elevation of the boulder-fields was determined by aneroid altimeter traverses to fixed trigonometrical points, and their surface slope was measured by levelling, revealing marked ridges on some of them. Particular attention was paid to the character of the boulders; their origin was first noted, the presence of erratics being of special significance. Next their shape was determined by observation; a fixed number of boulders was divided into three classes: angular, subangular and rounded. Their size was determined by measuring the longest axis of 100 boulders from each site, these being selected according to the relief of the field, some samples being taken from ridge crests and others from troughs. The result shows a strong contrast in size, the larger boulders being found on the ridge crests. Observations were also made of the layers beneath the surface by excavating in the boulder-field. The nature of

TG E

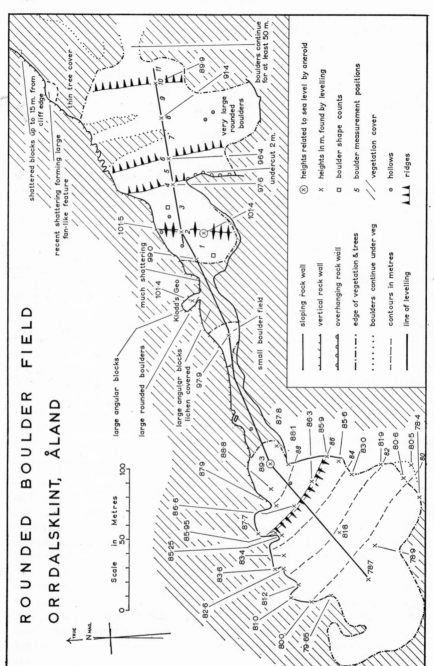

FIGURE 3.8. *a* Map of the rounded boulder-field, Åland Islands, Finland.

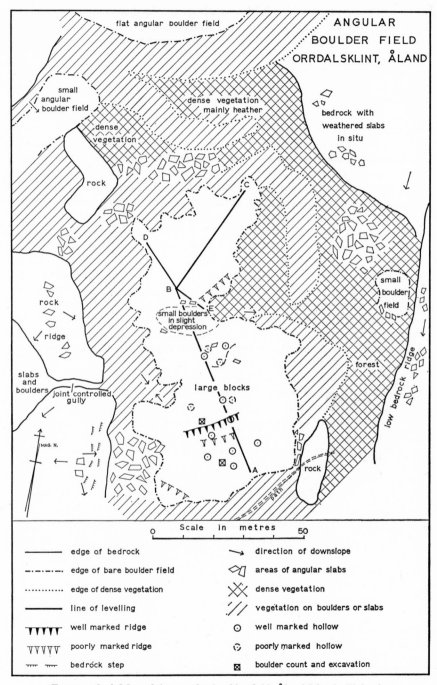

FIGURE 3.8. *b* Map of the angular boulder-field, Åland Islands, Finland.

the margin of the boulder-field was also examined and mapped, as the margin provided valuable information concerning the origin of the features.

As a result of these observations it became clear that there were two distinct types of boulder-field, one dominated by very well rounded boulders and the other by angular boulders. The former type had ridges and hollows, and their aspect, margins and slope suggested that they were formed mainly by marine action. This is not unlikely, because, although they occurred up to 100 m above sea-level, the area is situated in the zone of rapid and great post-glacial isostatic uplift.

The angular boulder-fields, on the other hand, had none of the characteristics of marine-formed features, and in seeking a cause for their formation, processes of weathering and mass-movement had to be considered. The effectiveness of frost action has sometimes been doubted, but it is probably only negligible when there are no cracks into which water could penetrate and freeze. In Åland, however, horizontal cracks and vertical joints were numerous, and the former were probably formed by pressure release due to the melting of the great weight of ice formally covering the area. The angular boulder-fields showed much evidence of having been produced by frost shattering and by slow mass movement caused by rock creep. Again the nature of the margins provided an important clue, as various stages from newly cracked rocks, newly broken rocks, not yet moved, to true angular boulder-field could be observed. The gentle gradient could be explained by this process, and the absence of erratics on the surface pointed to a local origin of the boulders, while on the rounded boulder-fields erratics were common on the surface (see figure 3.8).

These various points are mentioned to illustrate the necessity for considering not only the actual features themselves in as much detail as possible, but also the surroundings and past events. Thus the situation of the area with respect to the centre of the large Scandinavian Ice-Sheet is of significance, as it accounts for the changes of sea-level required to explain the rounded boulder-fields, and the operation of pressure release helps to explain the ready shattering by frost action of the granite to form the angular boulder-fields.

Other boulder-fields have been described by H. T. U. Smith (1950); the Hickory Run boulder-field that he studied is thought to have originated as a result of accelerated frost activity during the Wisconsin glaciation, and to be a relict feature under present conditions. The boulder-runs of the Falkland Islands (Joyce, 1950) also appear to be the result of periglacial conditions; in this area the structure seems to be an important influence on the distribution of the features.

A. Rapp has drawn attention to relevant features that suggest slow movement of many block-fields. The best indication of their stability is the presence of small lakes within them; these would have filled up if movement were at all rapid. The thick cover of lichen on many of the boulders also suggests stability.

c) *Solifluction*. Solifluction takes place most effectively in a periglacial climate, although its action is also possible in other conditions, when much water is available. The results of solifluction can be recognised widely, but the actual operation of the process is more difficult to study.

P. J. Williams (1957a and b) has developed an improved method of assessing the movement quantitatively and examining the factors on which it depends. The instrument he devised gives a record of the velocity profile of movement in a vertical section in the soil. The instrument consists of probes that record the amount of bending they undergo in the soil. The probes are 1 to 2 m long and 2 cm wide. They are 1 mm thick, and the movement is recorded by electric resistance gauges attached to the probe. The gauges record the amount of strain in the strip where they are attached, and several can be fixed to each metre length of the probe. The disadvantage of the instrument is that it cannot record shearing in a thin layer. A very high degree of accuracy is not possible under field conditions because the probe may resist very small soil movements. The probes need to be carefully insulated from dampness; this can be done by sheathing them in a special plastic. Before use the probe must be calibrated, the thickness of the probe being an important factor in determining its sensitivity. It seems likely that only on the flattest ground and in the weakest soils will the probe have any effect on the movement of the soil. It does not seem likely that the soil will flow round the probe instead of bending it.

Where the soil is moving actively under solifluction, hourly readings will reveal considerable movement, but in stable soils daily readings are sufficient. Experiments with the probe were carried out in Dovrefjell, Norway, on a slope beneath a melting snow patch. Ten strain gauges were used on probes of 1 to 2 m in length; temperature observations were taken at various depths and in the air, and piezometric tubes were used to measure pore-water pressures. The probes were inserted into the soil when it was in a frozen state, and as observations continued the thawed layer gradually extended downwards. Two of the probes showed active solifluction movements, three showed only small movements, and two, on stable ground, showed no movement. Thus the local occurrence of solifluction movement was verified, and the results showed that movement can take place to a depth of 75 cm, while points on the surface moved downslope as much as 20 cm. The movement appeared to take place slowly and continuously, and there were no diurnal or other rhythmic movements recorded. There was some evidence that the soil moved fastest nearest to the still frozen ground.

The nature of the movement, and the susceptibility of the soil to movement, was found to depend on the distribution of grain size within the soil; frost-susceptible soils can be differentiated from frost-stable soils by their size characteristics. Thus it is necessary to analyse samples of the material under study. The frost-susceptible soils are those fine enough to allow water to move up into them by capillary action as freezing takes place, yet not too fine, as some clays are not frost-susceptible. Where the median diameter of the soil is greater than 0·5 mm the soil will not be frost-susceptible. Another important factor is the availability of water, as solifluction will not take place unless water is abundant. Slow freezing will also increase the proportion of ice in the soil. Thus factors that must be taken into account in investigating solifluction include the frost-susceptibility of the soil, the availability of water, the rate of freezing and the depth of frost penetration. Where all these conditions are at the optimum values, frost heaving will be considerable, and when thawing takes place the downslope component will be correspondingly great. Saturation due to melting ice and snow is not thought to be sufficient alone to produce solifluction on gentle slopes, where frost heave is the more effective force. On steeper slopes, however, solifluction can take place even in non-susceptible soils where water is available in sufficient quantity, for example beneath melting snow patches, where the melting takes place partly from the underside, increasing the amount of soil water. The theoretical reasons for this can be calculated quantitatively by using the formulae of soil mechanics and calculating the shearing strength, which depends on the cohesion of the soil, the intergranular pressure and the angle of friction. It can be shown that with the addition of water the soil becomes very much more liable to shear. There are, however, difficulties in working out the shearing strength of morainic soils, which are usually very poorly sorted.

A. Rapp (1960b) has recorded solifluction by the same methods that he used to measure talus creep. The results showed a maximum movement of 25 to 30 cm/year on slopes of 15 to 25 degrees, but the results varied greatly from year to year. Movement was facilitated by an abundance of silt, especially when it consisted of small flakes of mica. The movement increased downslope, resulting in the development of the typical lobate form. Movement was restricted to periods of freeze and thaw, thus confirming that solifluction is essentially a periglacial process. Heavy rain did not cause movement of the lobes. Rudberg has developed another method of measuring movement in depth; it consists of a test pillar buried in the soil to a depth at which no movement takes place. By re-excavation the movement of the pillar may be noted and its form reflects the vertical velocity profile of soil movement. In the same area on the lobate front of a solifluction flow the upper part of the pillar moved 15 cm but movement did not extend below 50 cm. The mean movement in Kärkevagge is suggested to be 2 cm/year through a thickness of 25 cm, this agrees well with other observations in periglacial areas such as Spitzbergen and South Georgia.

The detailed measurement of solifluction has been described, but the large-scale operation of the process and its modifying effect on the landscape should also be considered, as it can cause major changes. Solifluction is mainly responsible for the development of head deposits that occur so widely outside glaciated areas. Methods of recognising this type of material by analysis of the sediment have already been mentioned.

Stevens (1957) has drawn attention to the large-scale features formed by solifluction deposits in New Zealand, where whole gullies have been filled by such material, the long axes of the pebbles lying parallel to the direction of movement. It is interesting to note that the movement of solifluction material over the bedrock appears to have had an erosional effect, producing shaved bedrock surfaces beneath the solifluction deposits. This occurs mainly where the sheet of moving material was fairly thin, stripping off all the weathered rock from the solid surface beneath. The great activity of solifluction in the area around Wellington is partly due to the character of the bedrock, which is an easily broken up greywacke. Cotton and Le Punga (1955) have also drawn attention to the capacity of solifluction to produce features of erosion, and they explain the rounded dells at the head of some valleys as the result of subcutaneous processes of corrasion under a moving mass of solifluction material, producing the characteristic shaved bedrock surface. The symmetry of the transverse profile of the dell is a strong point in favour of the suggested origin by solifluctional corrasion. Thus in estimating the modifications due to solifluction, usually under periglacial conditions, note must be made of both depositional features and the effects of possible erosion.

d) *Soil creep*. The measurement of soil creep can be made by the same technique described to measure solifluction, using probes. It is a slower and more widespread type of movement than solifluction, and measurements show that in stiff fissured clay it can take place on slopes of 10 degrees at a rate of about ¼ in. per year.

One method that has been suggested for recording soil creep is to note the curvature of tree trunks. It has been argued theoretically that trees should become bent to form a concave downward curve as soil creep takes place. Parizek and Woodruff (1957) have analysed this effect, and found that the theoretical curve is normally not found in a wood, although many of the trees show haphazard curvature. They point out that the assumptions made are not supported by botanical evidence.

Better evidence of soil creep is found in some exposures in quarries, where the thickness of soil can be seen to increase on the upper side of hedges. Another method of observing the importance of soil creep is to study the outcrop curvature of suitable geological strata. The extent of this distortion of the dip gives good evidence of the extent of soil creep.

A quantitative method of measuring creep has been developed. The experiment was carried out on a forested slope of 33 degrees with a thick regolith of 20 to 40 feet depth. The rainfall in the area was 40 inches/year. Iron pins ½ in. in diameter and 0·7 ft long were fixed vertically in the soil. Twenty pins were placed 5 feet apart with reference to two fixed points in a straight line at right angles to the slope. After four years the movement of the pins varied between 0·23 in. uphill and 0·01 in. down and after six years all the pins moved slightly uphill, although the movement was not much greater than the accuracy of the survey. It is possible that the pins were rotating, due to greater movement at the base; but such movement is very small, and extremely accurate measurements are required to reveal it in such a static environment. On a 45-degree slope in a semi-arid environment movement was measurable, varying from 0·03 to 0·67 in./year. The line in this instance was on the slope of a small gully (Leopold, Wolman and Miller, 1964).

Methods of measuring soil creep and slope wash in the field have been devised by A. Young (1960). In the first method pegs were placed vertically in the soil and their downslope movement was measured from three marks made on a rock outcrop above. On a 30-degree slope after $3\frac{1}{2}$ years the downslope movement was only 1 mm. Tilting of the pegs caused exaggerated movement if the surface moved faster than the subsurface. Another method of measuring soil movement in depth was, therefore, devised; a pit was dug to bedrock and 6 pegs were driven into the bedrock and thin rods 2 mm × 10 cm were driven into the undisturbed soil on one side of the pit in a line perpendicular to the surface and the pit filled in. Their movement relative to the pegs was measured 6 to 12 months later. Another method was used to measure the movement of the pegs, by measuring their distance from a plumb-bob held so it touched the lowest peg, which it was assumed had not moved. On a slope with grass of 20 to 30 degrees the downslope movement was of the order of 0·25 mm/year in the upper 10 cm. Volumetric results gave 0·6 cm³/cm/yr. These results indicate the volume moved by soil creep, a process dependent mainly on wetting and drying of the soil. Another indirect method of measuring soil creep, therefore, was attempted. The moisture content of the soil was measured monthly at three depths on slopes with gradients of 26, 18 and 7 degrees for two years. The soil moisture change was related to expansion and contraction of the soil by experiment and soil movement deduced from these measurements. The results were as follows:

	26-degree	18-degree	7-degree slope
0-5 cm	0·86	0·58	0·61 cm/year movement
5-10 cm	0·41	0·33	0·63
20-30 cm	0·08	0·08	0·05

It is interesting to note that the rate fell off rapidly with depth but not with slope, on account of the finer material on the gentler slope. To measure slope wash tins were inserted in the soil with a lip on the upper side placed just under the *Ao* lower boundary. The soil was washed into the tin below, and an average of 5·1 grams/year was recorded in 49 tins, giving a volume transport of 0·08 cm³/cm/year. Thus on well vegetated slopes, slope wash is much less efficient than soil creep in moving material downslope.

e) *Mud-flows.* Mud-flows are a much more conspicuous and easily recognised phenomenon than soil creep, although they are not very common. They can occur in a variety of conditions, but are probably best developed in the semi-arid environment, where occasional rains are very heavy and waste material abundant, although they also occur in the periglacial environment. It is useful to be able to recognise the forms, although it is rarely that observation of their actual formation is possible, on account of their infrequent occurrence.

The material forming a mud-flow acts as a viscous fluid. A good account of a mud-flow in the southern part of the San Joaquin Valley in California indicates some of its essential features. The mud-flow issued from a canyon, carrying with it whole trees, and stirring up dust clouds as it came into contact with the previously dry soil. The first flow stopped about ½ mile from the mouth of the canyon, but was soon followed by another wave, larger and moving faster than the first; this wave carried large masses of rock, some of the rocks weighing several tons. They were carried along on the surface of the flow. The second wave extended about ½ mile beyond the first. There were subsequent waves following each other at intervals of a few minutes, each getting thinner and travelling faster than the one before, until after about ½ hour the mud-flow had become very muddy water, which washed out a channel for itself in the soft mud. The power of the mud-flow to transport material is very great; one rock carried for at least 7 miles was 8 feet by 16 feet by 25 feet in size. The edge of the flow was strongly marked as a rounded lobate margin resting on the undisturbed ground.

In some instances deposits that have been laid down by mud-flows have been confused with alluvial fans, but the two deposits can be differentiated by the unsorted nature of the mud-flow deposits, their lobate bouldery fronts, 1 to 4 feet high, and the presence of very large boulders. The material is also unstratified, unlike alluvial fan deposits, which show some crude stratification. The lobate tongues, characteristic of mud-flows, can be seen in areas where such features could no longer form, and which are now completely stabilised by vegetation cover. Conditions favouring the formation of mud-flows include unconsolidated material that becomes slippery when wet, slopes that are steep enough to induce flowage in viscous material, and abundant water, which is essential; finally, the ground must not be protected by forest or other stabilising vegetation.

In mountainous districts mud-flows are often closely associated with gullying and occur after exceptionally heavy rain or with snow melt, but are usually smaller than that described in a semi-arid area. Care must be used to distinguish the lobate fronts of mud-flows from those formed by solifluction. Past mud-flows can usually be recognised by the levees that form around the main channel. Particles in mud-flow deposits were found by Rapp to be orientated transverse to the movement in the lobes of both mud-flow and solifluction deposits. Mud-flows are clearly related to heavy rainfall and Rapp suggests that a minimum of 50 mm (2 in.) rain in 24 hours is required to start a mud-flow in mountainous districts with steep slopes.

f) *Rotational slumping.* Another conspicuous form of mass-movement is rotational slumping. This suffers from the same disadvantages in study as mud-flow activity, in that it only occurs rarely and hence is difficult to observe in action. On the other hand, this process produces features that are readily identifiable. Shear slipping can occur under natural conditions wherever the slope consists of weak cohesive strata, such as silt or clay, especially where these rocks are overlain by some permeable material, for example chalk, and where the slope becomes oversteepened. This may occur through undercutting by river or sea erosion. The features can be recognised by their back-slopes and the upheaved ground at the toe of the slope.

TG E 2

According to the work of W. H. Ward (1945) this type of movement is the most common form of slope failure in Britain, and is fundamental in cohesive strata. A study of these slips has been carried out by engineers, in attempting to stabilise banks that are liable to this type of failure. For example the work of the Great Ouse Catchment Board in the stabilisation of the banks of a new cut between Denver and St. Germans may be cited. The immediate cause of slipping in this area was the undercutting of the bank by the river, while silt was deposited further up at high tide level, both processes steepening the bank. When a critical point was reached the bank failed, and rotational slipping took place.

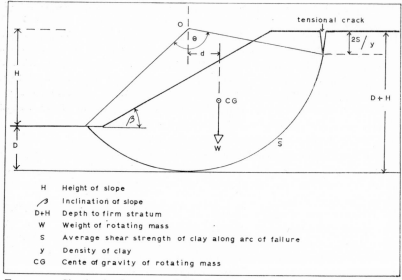

H	Height of slope
β	Inclination of slope
D+H	Depth to firm stratum
W	Weight of rotating mass
S	Average shear strength of clay along arc of failure
y	Density of clay
CG	Cente of gravity of rotating mass

FIGURE 3.9. Simple circular arc method of estimating the stability of a clay slope. (after Ward)

In order to analyse the stability of the strata in relation to rotational shear-slipping the shear strength of the strata must be found by testing of undisturbed samples. A section of the bank slope is then drawn out to natural scale and the strata plotted in. Trial slip arcs are then considered and the moments of weight and shear resistance of the material within each circular arc are equated, and the minimum factor of safety found (see figure 3.9). Where the slope angle is more than 50 degrees the slip circle passes through the toe of the slope and the limiting depth of the weak strata is not critical. If the slope is less than 50 degrees the slip circle passes below the toe of the slope, and when the depth of the underlying firm stratum is large the slope is not critical until it is less than 15 degrees. The height of the slope is the critical factor in the stability of slopes in cohesive strata, unlike granular strata, whose stability is independent of height.

The actual form of the rotational slip is dependent on the strata, and the ideal circular form may not occur, particularly if the weak band is fairly narrow, or if weakening penetrates slowly into the slope parallel to its surface. Softening in clay, which is particularly liable to this form of slipping, may take place very slowly, but it nevertheless plays an important part in the process.

The quantitative methods of observation of various processes at work denuding the slopes of Karkevagge give very interesting evidence of the relative importance of different processes in this periglacial mountain climate. The table gives the essential data, but it is worth stressing the great importance of dissolved salts in accounting for the total volume of denudation. The chemical erosion would amount to a reduction of 0·01 mm/year or 70 mm in the post-glacial period. It should be noted that chemical activity is continuous, while the high value under earth-slides was mainly due to one very heavy storm, of an intensity only likely to occur once a century. Talus creep and solifluction move the smallest volume of material. Only by making quantitative observations is it possible to assess the relative importance of these various forms of mass movement. Similar studies in different climatic and relief areas would help to resolve the uncertainty concerning the importance of climate to geomorphological process and form.

Process	Volume cu.m	Tons/sq. km	Average movement m	Average gradient degrees	Tons/m vertical
Rock falls	50	8·7	90-225	45	19,565
Avalanches	88	15·5	100-200	30	21,850
Earthslides etc.	580	69·4	0·5-600	30	96,375
Talus creep	300,000	—	0·01	30	2,700
Solifluction	550,000	—	0·02	15	5,300
Running water dissolved salts	150	26	700	30	136,500

After Rapp (1960)

General rates of erosion can be assessed by various methods. These include the measuring of river load, both in solution and in solid form, in relation to the drainage area, and the estimation of fluvial deposition. In soluble rocks, such as limestone and dolomite, a study of the concentration of calcium carbonate and magnesium carbonate can give a value of total rock removal in solution. The discharge of the river must be known and the density of the rock, then the net limestone loss is given by the discharge times the hardness divided by the rock density. Alternatively, if the discharge figures are not available, an estimate may be made by using the formula of P. W. Williams,

$$X = \frac{ETn}{10\ D},$$

where X is the value of limestone removed in mm/1000 years, E is the mean annual water surplus in decimetres, T is the mean total hardness in p.p.m., D is the density of the limestone, and $1/n$ is the fraction of the basin occupied by limestone. For the Fergus Basin in west Ireland the results were

$$\frac{8 \cdot 5 \times 140 \times 10}{10 \times 2 \cdot 7 \times 8} = 55 \cdot 1 \text{ mm}/1000 \text{ years.}$$

Observation of calcium carbonate content of spring waters in limestone regions have shown that the character of the rock plays an important part in determining the calcium carbonate p.p.m. value for different areas. Thus solution depends both on the annual run-off and the calcium carbonate content, so that both climate and rock character effect the total amount of solution.

Another interesting method of assessing the rate of weathering and erosion is the study of the modification of archaeological remains. Weathering of rocks in buildings and other structures of known date can give valuable evidence of the rate and extent of weathering, for example Arkell's work on the buildings of Oxford from this point of view. Evidence of erosion and slope modification can be found in the changes occurring in ditches dug at a known date and of known shape. The lower part of the ditch fills in rapidly and is preserved, while the upper part may weather back. Results suggest that slope modification in relatively soft rocks such as chalk may be quite rapid. Observations of chalk levels beneath protective barrows and elsewhere show that the surface may be lowered 15 to 20 inches in 4000 years. This is a rapid rate and should be borne in mind when considering the levels of chalk erosion surfaces.

5. WIND ACTION

The environments in which wind plays an important part are coastal areas where sand dunes sometimes contribute to the coastal scenery, and the arid landscapes where wind plays the dominant role in dune formation, although in other features of the desert landscape wind is probably not the dominant element at any time.

a) *Wind measurement.* Naturally in studying the features dependent on aeolian processes it is essential to measure the velocity and direction of the wind. This can be done at an official meteorological station by means of an anemograph, giving a continuous record of the wind, or alternatively it may be required to establish details of the wind close to the ground in the survey area. This can be done conveniently with a small hand anemometer held at varying heights above the ground to give the variation of the wind with height, or in varying exposures.

When the orientation of wind-formed features is being studied it is useful to obtain information concerning the prevailing wind regime; this can be most easily done by drawing a vector diagram, which will give the resultant wind direction. If sand movement is being studied it is useful to use the third power of the wind speed, as dune-building winds must be given due weight.

Landsberg (1956) has suggested a formula that gives good correlation between wind resultant and the orientation of dunes of a certain type. The wind resultant is worked out using for each individual vector (b) the formula

$$b = s \sum_{j=3}^{12} n_j \, (V_j - V_t)^3,$$

j is the Beaufort number, s is 10^{-3}, V_t is 10 m.p.h. and n the frequency of occurrence. The cube of the wind speed is used, agreeing with the theoretical results of Bagnold's work that the volume of sand moved depends on the third power of the wind speed. Jennings (1957) has suggested that the direction of sand source should also be taken into account; this can be done if only the onshore winds or winds from the source area are used in the construction of the vector diagrams.

b) *Measuring sand movement*—i *Traps*. The problem of measuring the movement of sand by the wind depends on the development of a satisfactory sand trap. The instrument must be such that it can catch, and if possible differentiate between, the various forms of sand movement. Some sand moves along the surface by creep, but the bulk moves by saltation above the surface, advancing in a series of hops; thus the trap must either be high enough to catch the highest saltating grains, or long enough to catch the longest hop of the grains. Sand traps have been devised to collect sand moved both by creep and by saltation; the latter is probably the easier to collect and certainly the most important as far as quantity is concerned.

Horikawa and Shen (1960) have tested two types of horizontal trap and five types of vertical traps in order to evaluate their efficiency (see figure 3.10). The difficulty is to differentiate between surface creep and saltation; this was done by using a horizontal trap divided into several sections perpendicular to the wind direction. It was assumed that all the creep fell into the first trap, and the amount of saltation sand falling into the other traps could be found, and this amount was subtracted from the total amount, leaving the assumed amount of creep only. It was found that this amount was about 20% of the total moved and the percentage did not vary with the wind speed. The advantage of the horizontal type of trap is that it does not disturb the flow of the wind, but it is difficult to select a suitable length, and it cannot give information concerning the height at which movement is taking place.

The vertical traps have the disadvantage that they do disturb the flow of the wind, and this requires careful designing to restrict the disturbance to the minimum. An early trap, devised by Bagnold, attempted to get over this difficulty by making the width of the trap against which the wind was blowing very small. The back pressure on the movement in the vicinity of the trap is another problem, but it is not so acute in air, where the grains have a higher momentum, as in water. There is also the problem of scour around the base of the trap. The vertical traps could be so designed that material moving at different levels could be caught in separate compartments. The one that had the best performance had a $\frac{3}{8}$-in. opening for the wind and sand and a considerable depth parallel to the wind to allow the sand to settle in the trap, while

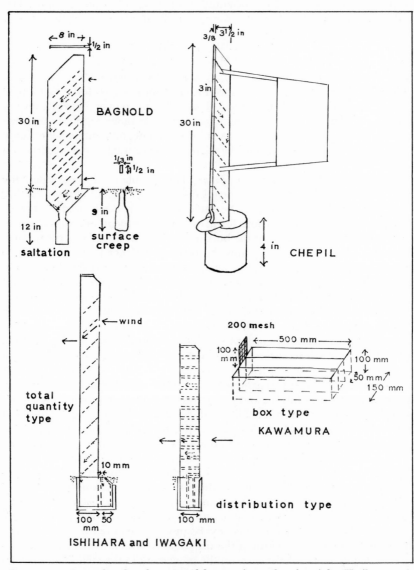

FIGURE 3.10. Examples of sand traps used for experimental testing. (after Horikawa and Shen B.E.B.)

it was designed to let the wind pass out through the trap, behind a curved flange.

ii *Sand movement.* Observations using sand traps in the field are not very numerous but a lot of fundamental work has been done by Bagnold. Many of the basic observations have been made in wind tunnels, and therefore methods and results of these experiments will be considered in the following chapter, but Bagnold has also made many useful observations on actual desert dunes. The observations, which were carried out in the Libyan desert in 1938, were concerned with measuring the wind at several heights with a series of pitot tubes fixed to a vertical mast at different levels above the ground. These wind observations enabled the vertical wind profile to be obtained, and they were combined with observations with sand traps. The pressure wind measurements were made at 1, 4, 16, and 64 inches above the ground, the readings being recorded on a manometer. The sand movement was measured in two traps, one small horizontal trap to collect the sand moving by creep, and a narrow vertical trap to catch the sand moving by saltation, The vertical collector was $\frac{1}{2}$ in. wide and 30 in. high, while the creep trap was buried to leave only a small opening for the creeping grains to pass into (see figure 3.10). It was placed at some distance from the other trap, which disturbed the movement of the sand so that a hollow formed round its base.

One of the difficulties was the fact that observations to be of any value had to be taken during a storm and, as the direction and timing of strong winds could not be forecast, the apparatus had to be set up during the sand storm. A set of observations took about one hour to make.

The wind velocity was found to increase logarithmically with height above the surface, when sand was moving on the dune. One problem of field observations was the fact that the dune surface was always curved and the sand was unsorted; however, the curvature of the dune did not seem to affect the change of wind velocity with height. The volume of sand moved correlated with the cube of the wind speed, in the field, thus checking the laboratory results.

The size of the grains must also be considered, as this affects their mobility. Bagnold has shown that in air the most easily moved grains are of about 0·1 mm diameter; these will start to move when the velocity is about 15 cm/sec. For smaller grains of silt and clay the velocity must be much greater; thus once the grains have settled to form a smooth surface, they are not readily picked up again until they are disturbed. It is interesting to note that the mean diameter of the thick loess deposits of areas such as China is about 0·05 mm, this is just below the critical size, so that once the deposit has settled it will not be so likely to be blown away again, unless it is disturbed. Hence the roads in such an area become deeply sunk. Another factor that tends towards the immobility of fine material is its capacity to collect moisture. In natural sand the sizes are mixed and as the wind increases in strength the smaller particles that are exposed move first, and the ultimate threshold velocity is that moving the largest grains, but in dune sand the sorting is usually such that the wind fairly rapidly reaches the velocity at which all the grains can be moved.

c) *Desert dunes.* In considering the formation of dunes in the desert the nature of the desert floor must be observed, as the supply of sand may depend upon its characteristics. The only area of a desert where sand forms a complete surface covering is on the actual dunes; the floor of the intervening area may contain sand, but it is usually hidden beneath pebbles. A pebbly desert floor is a sort of reservoir for sand as the sand grains move across the floor and lodge in the cracks between the pebbles. A floor with pebbles can hold sand during periods of gentle wind and this material is available during periods of strong winds, when it is removed downwind. Sand will tend to accumulate on any sand patch that alreadyexists,causing it to extend upwind during the action of strong winds. The direction of the wind and its strength in relation to the sand supply is very important in considering the characteristic form of desert dunes and the processes by which they are built. Thus it is essential that observations concerning the wind regime and local sand sources be obtained. It is also important to differentiate between the effects of strong and gentle winds. Bagnold defines a strong wind as one whose velocity gradient increases upwards above a certain critical value, where the velocity is just over $2 \cdot 5$ cm/sec at a height of $0 \cdot 3$ cm. The figure depends partly on the roughness of the surface, given by the spacing of pebbles, rocks or vegetation. As the roughness increases so must the wind gradient before dune-building can take place; thus dunes will be less likely to form in a rough area than one which is rather smoother. The strong wind will tend to increase the bulk of the dune, and such winds will be called the dune-building winds, while the gentler winds will tend to increase the length of the dune at the expense of its bulk.

In studying the types of sand accumulation it is necessary to have details of the proportion of gentle and strong winds and their directions relative to each other. The major types of sand accumulation probably depend on the character of the wind regime. One type of dune, the crescentic barchan dune, is probably formed by undirectional wind systems. This is one of the smallest types of independent dune; the other smaller features are dependent on some obstacle in whose shadow they form, their size being related to the dimensions of the obstacle. The barchan on the other hand can form and move independently as a unit. One of the critical steps in the formation of a dune of this type is the initial formation of a slip face. This can be explained by the nature of sand movement over the dune; Bagnold has shown that the rate of deposition or removal depends on the tangent of the angle of slope of the surface. Thus there is no change at the crest of a smooth heap of sand, but deposition on the lee side must reach a maximum where the slope is steepest, and if this is not at the base of the dune, the lee side will steepen, Once the steepening has gone beyond a certain critical point the flow of air over the dune is modified and eddies form, while the increased steepness will lead to instability and the slope will shear. The maximum angle of repose of dry sand has been measured to be 34 degrees, As the wind can no longer follow the shape of the dune surface, all sand that is driven up the windward side becomes trapped as it moves over the slip face, building up the angle until shearing takes place.

Observations in the field have shown that the rate of advance of a dune depends on the height of the slip face. This is a minimum of 30 cm, owing to the average jump of a sand grain. If the height of the slip face is less than 30 cm the sand grain can reach the foot of the dune and so will not necessarily lead to over-steepening. Bagnold has shown that the forward movement of the dune varied directly with the rate of sand movement over the brink of the slip face, but inversely with the height of the slip face. The slip face will move most slowly where it is highest in the centre of the dune and lowest near the edges, and this accounts for the characteristic crescentic form of a barchan dune. Sand can only leave the dune at the trailing wings, which are too low to develop a slip face. It is clear that a slip face can only be maintained if the wind is always blowing sand over the brink; if the direction changes the form of the slip face must be modified. This type of barchan dune, therefore, can only form effectively where the wind is unidirectional.

An interesting relationship has been observed in the Kharga oasis area between the distribution of barchans and their size. Beadnell has observed the rate of movement of five barchans over the period of one year in this area. His results show a close correlation with the size of the dunes, the largest, 20 m high, travelled 10·9 m in one year, the smallest, 4 m high, travelled 18·4 m during the year. By extrapolating from these observations of movement, it can be shown that the barchan belts originating from the oasis depression of south Egypt and north Sudan have advanced 120 km and this should have taken about 7000 years. It was at about 5000 B.C. that there is evidence of migration of the pre-Dynastic folk to the Nile valley, presumably as a result of desiccation in their previous home; the same desiccation is presumed to have caused the erosion which initiated the barchan belt. Thus observations of dunes and their movement can yield useful corroboration of historical data, while the historical information, in turn, supports the geomorphological results.

The other main type of dune is the seif dune, which depends for its characteristics on the wind regime having two dominant elements. The internal structure of such dunes is not so orderly as that of barchans, but field observations of the internal structure can yield valuable data concerning the building of the dune and the wind regime that is responsible for its formation. Sand deposits are of two types: the accretion deposits are built up of sand driven up the windward side of a dune, while the avalanche layers are those which have been pushed over the slip face and have fallen loosely at their angle of rest and are not well-packed and, therefore, have a loose texture. It is normally difficult to appreciate the bedding of a dune, each layer is very thin and the difference in particle size is often not sufficient to reveal the layers clearly. However, a method by which the structure can be revealed has already been mentioned on p. 73. By this method the internal structure of the dune can be studied, and such studies are of value in comparison with older deposits of sandstones. A barchan dune that is not growing in height will consist of avalanche deposits throughout, except for a thin layer on the windward side, up which sand is being moved, and the crest of the dune above the level of the slip face brink. If the dune was growing in height the junction between the avalanche or encroachment deposits and the overlying accretion deposit will slope up in the direction of dune advance. This direction is readily apparent from the angle of the encroachment bedding planes.

d) *Coastal dunes*. Although coastal dunes have some features in common with desert dunes, in other respects they are more complex, as their character depends to a considerable extent on the vegetation that grows on them. In many areas, where the supply of sand is not great, the coastal dunes are limited to fairly simple foredunes. These normally form low ridges parallel to the shore, indicating that their source of sand is from the beach, and that their stabilisation by vegetation is so rapid that the sand cannot travel far inland. Information concerning the growth and establishment of vegetation on new dunes has been gained by repeated surveys across a line at right angles to the shore. These revealed the way in which beach ridges were

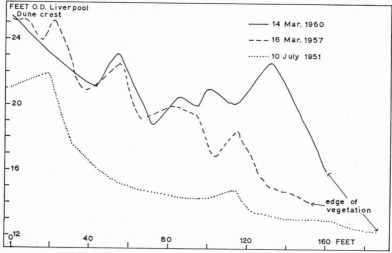

FIGURE 3.11. Dune growth in south Lincolnshire at Gibraltar Point, illustrated by repeated surveys.

built up by the waves, and stabilised and protected by growth of further ridges to seaward, which allowed the ridge to gain height by addition of blown sand, on which dune plants soon became established, thus allowing the accretion to continue. In this area of south Lincolnshire of fairly restricted wave action, the first dune plants, *Cakile maritima* and *Salsola kali*, come in when the sand has built up to a height of only $1\frac{1}{2}$ feet above the mean high spring tide level; the figure for more exposed areas, such as western Ireland, was about 3 feet. The growth of marram grass at rather higher levels greatly speeds up the process of sand accumulation, and repeated surveys along the

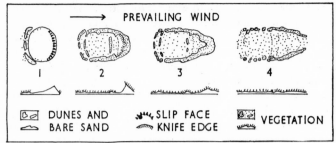

FIGURE 3.12. (*a*) Diagram to show U-dune formation.

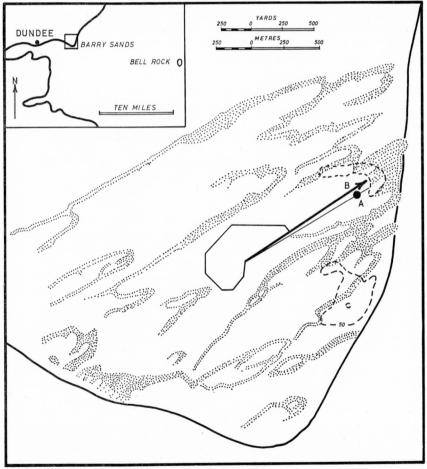

FIGURE 3.12. (*b*) The relationship between dune orientation and the wind vector on the Sands of Barry. (after Landsberg)

same line can readily demonstrate that up to 5 feet of sand can accumulate in this way over a period of six years (figure 3.11). The value of this grass is such that it is frequently planted to help stabilise dune areas. Where sand is more plentiful and winds blow predominantly onshore the area of the dune-covered ground may increase considerably so that the dune pattern is no longer one of simple foredunes.

Observation of these larger dune areas shows that they no longer lie parallel to the coast, but that their orientation depends more on the wind regime. In form the individual dunes characteristically assume a parabolic or U-shape. Unlike barchans in the desert, however, the dunes are aligned so that the open arms of the U face upwind. At first the dune appears to be a more or less symmetrical mound of sand, with only a limited cover of marram or no vegetation; the lee face may be a slip face at this stage, as in the desert. The sand tends to be diverted round the dune, and vegetation becomes more firmly established as the water supply is better at the lower levels, and this and the dampness traps sand on the flanks. The centre on the other hand can continue to move forward. At this stage the dune can move relatively fast, often covering several miles, leaving trailing flanks behind to mark its passage. The central part may eventually be removed altogether to form a blow-out (see figure 3.12). The orientation of the long flanks shows a clear relationship to the wind regime; this can be established by plotting the vector diagrams for the wind as already described (Landsberg, 1956).

Thus observation of dune form and internal structure in relation to the wind regime can lead to a better understanding of the larger scale effects of the processes involved in dune-building both in the desert and on the coast.

6. MARINE PROCESSES

The processes discussed already can all be grouped together as subaerial processes; they may be contrasted with marine processes, operating at the edge of and beneath the sea. In the early days of geomorphology there was considerable argument about the relative efficacy of these two major forms of erosional and depositional process, but now it is realised that each plays its own part by different mechanisms to produce very different landforms; the action of both may be recognised on the present land surface. The method of study of marine processes will be divided into three sections, dealing respectively with wave action, tidal action and the processes operating beneath the sea.

A. *Wave action*

a) *Wave observation.* In order to understand wave action on the shore it is necessary to have reliable observations of wave characteristics as a basis for the analysis. Methods of recording wave dimensions have improved a great deal recently, and there are now instruments available that can measure waves reasonably accurately in the open ocean with a ship-borne wave-recorder (Tucker, 1956). This instrument can record the profile of the waves with an accuracy of about 10%. It has been shown, however, that there is a considerable difference between the wave dimensions in the open ocean and in coastal waters, so that measurements made closer to the shore are perhaps of more value as far as geomorphological analysis is concerned. These observations may be made by ships close to the shore or with shore-based equipment. For example wave records have been taken from a light-ship in Morecambe Bay; from an analysis of these it is possible to obtain a reasonable idea of the dimensions of waves generated in an enclosed sea, such as the Irish Sea. These records indicate that the most common significant period was 5 seconds, only exceeded in January and December by periods averaging 7 seconds. The heights only exceeded 10 feet for 2% of the time while waves occurring 20% of the time or more were only 1 foot high or less. It is significant to compare these values with recordings made with a pressure wave gauge off the coast of Cornwall, where long Atlantic swells can reach the shore. On such an open coast wave periods can exceed 15 seconds for 45% of the time in some months, while heights at the coast in February averaged about 11 feet, compared with over 23 feet at a weather-ship in the mid-Atlantic, where periods, on the other hand, were shorter.

This type of observation is of considerable importance for an understanding of coastal processes, and, when long enough records are available, it is possible to evaluate the 'wave climate' of the area concerned. For example the coasts of south Australia are dominated by long swells of 14 seconds, generated by the strong westerly winds of the Southern Ocean (Davies, 1959). On the other hand, the coasts of the Irish Sea and southern North Sea are dominated by relatively short waves, generated locally. These waves are, therefore, affected by the local winds to a greater extent than coasts exposed to long swells generated by far distant storms. The coastal features will react to the dominant waves reaching the area, so that precise knowledge of the wave pattern is a very valuable preliminary to coastal work.

The problem of the analysis of the wave record must be mentioned (Tucker 1962), because the recorded waves show a great variety of height, on account of the wide spectrum of waves that is usually present at any one time. The value that is often considered the most satisfactory for practical purposes is the height of the average of the highest $\frac{1}{3}$ of the wave heights recorded, although Tucker suggests that, if the records were really reliable, the best values to use would be the two highest waves, measured from the still water-level to the highest crest and trough respectively. The best value to use for the period is T_z, given by the number of times the record crosses the mean water-level in an upward direction divided into the length of the record in time, or its duration. This is probably the most significant period as it is often the period of the largest waves in the record.

Instrumental wave records are not always available for the particular locality that is under consideration, so that it is useful to make approximate measures of wave dimensions at the study site. The period can be relatively easily measured by using a stop-watch to note the time it takes ten wave crests to pass some fixed object. The mean of this value will give a reasonable idea of the period, especially when the wave pattern is fairly simple, such as a long,

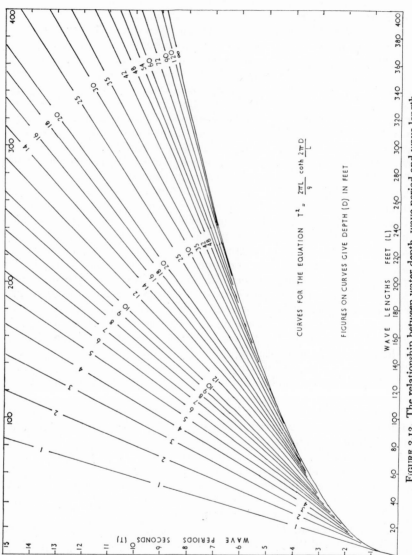

FIGURE 3.13. The relationship between water depth, wave period and wave length.

even swell. The wave period can be converted into wave length by means of the formula

$$L = 5 \cdot 12 \ T^2,$$

where L is the length in feet and T is the period in seconds. This gives the theoretical deep-water wave length, where deep-water is defined as greater than half the wave length. If lengths are required at intermediate and shallow depths, the full formula

$$T^2 = \frac{2\pi L}{g} \coth \frac{2\pi d}{L}$$

must be used, d being the depth and g gravity. The calculation of the wave length is necessary to estimate the wave steepness, as this is an important parameter in assessing the effect of the waves on the shore forms. The relationships are shown on figure 3.13.

The height can be measured against any structure that is available, such as a pier, but it is sometimes possible to measure the wave height by using a theodolite, if this can be set up at some distance above the sea surface. To measure wave height it is necessary to fix a buoy so that it can float in the waves; this can often be done conveniently at low water, the buoy being in fairly deep water at high tide, where the tidal range is great. Vertical angles can then be read on a succession of wave crests and troughs, the difference being converted into a measure of wave height by calibration with a graduated staff set up at the same distance from the theodolite as the buoy. A series of such observations in different depths can give useful information concerning the change of wave height as the waves move into shallower water. However, fairly simple pressure wave gauges are available and these give better results as their record is continuous. In estimating wave steepness it is important that the height and length dimensions should be comparable; both must be adjusted to the deep-water values preferably. The direction of wave approach should also be noted by using a compass.

The dimensions of the waves are vital to an understanding of coastal phenomena, but note should also be taken of the wind direction and force, as a strong onshore wind can noticeably affect the movement of sediment by setting up strong offshore currents along the sea-bed, while offshore winds tend to increase the shoreward movement of sediment. The importance of this factor was demonstrated on the beach at Marsden Bay, Co. Durham (King, 1953).

Not only is it the actual size of the waves that influences the movement of sediment, but the movement of the water within the waves is also important. An instrument used by Inman and Nasu (1956) to measure the orbital velocities of waves in the surf zone proved effective. The measurements were made at La Jolla in California by using a specially designed current measuring device in water depths of 5 to 15 feet. This is the zone where the movement becomes very complex near the breaker line, but in which a large proportion of the movement of sediment takes place; thus any observations

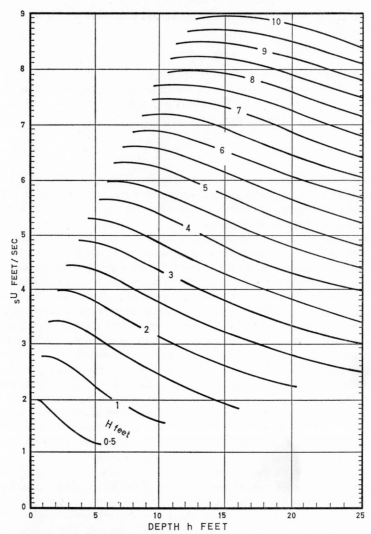

FIGURE 3.14. The relationship between the maximum horizontal orbital velocity at the bottom and water depth for various wave heights. (after Inman and Nasu B.E.B.)

that can be made in this zone are of great value. The observations were obtained with a current meter attached to a tripod, to which a pressure-type wave gauge was also fixed. The current measurements were made 25 cm above the sandy bottom. The instruments recorded both the horizontal and the vertical orbital motion and the profile of the wave form simultaneously. The velocities were measured in the direction of wave propagation. The wave periods were obtained from the wave recorder, and the heights were checked by visual measurements on a graduated staff attached to the Scripps Institution Pier, where the observations were made.

The records show that the orbital velocities follow the pattern of the wave form very closely, and compare favourably with those calculated using the solitary wave theory; these theoretical values may, therefore, be used as a first approximation for the actual values of orbital velocities near the break-point; they are shown on figure 3.14. The velocity increases with decreasing depth for any one wave height, and increases very rapidly at any one depth with increasing wave height, thus in 15 feet of water a $1\frac{1}{2}$ feet high wave will have an orbital velocity of 2 ft/sec but if the wave were $8\frac{1}{2}$ feet high its orbital velocity would have a maximum value of about 8 ft/sec. The orbital velocity is such that there is a mass transport velocity towards the shore, which Longuet-Higgins (1953) has analysed theoretically, showing that it takes place largely in a landward direction near the bed with long, low waves in shallow water. This landward movement of water must be compensated by a seaward return flow; this at times becomes concentrated into strong currents, localised in position, that are known as rip currents.

Useful observations have been made on the nature and distribution of rip currents by Shepard and Inman (1950) and McKenzie (1958). Their presence can often be seen from the shore, because where they are flowing strongly seaward through the surf, the line of breakers no longer turns over and the water often appears to carry more sediment that is dispersed beyond the breaker zone. They can also be identified in the water by strong and localised seaward flowing currents. The position of rip currents was found by Shepard and Inman to depend on the nature of the waves and the general pattern of inshore circulation. Their observations were made in California near La Jolla, where the bottom relief is complicated by submarine canyons; these cause much refraction of the long swells, and this results in the development of longshore wave induced currents and rip currents.

The methods used to study this circulation were not elaborate, but they yielded very useful data. Measurement outside the breakers was made with triplanes or current crosses, which were attached by lines to small surface floats, but moved with the current near the bed. These floats were released outside the breaker zone and the positions of recovery on the shore were noted. Surface currents were measured by drift bottles. The position of the markers was recorded at intervals by taking horizontal sextant angles to fixed marks on shore. Where the water became so shallow that the triplanes grounded, observations were made by using dye on the surface and weighted balls on the bottom. Care was taken to observe wave currents on days when there was little wind, so that the observed currents were the result of wave action only. Longshore currents can be generated either by the oblique approach of short waves, or by the uneven distribution of energy, and with it wave height along the coast; this sets up currents flowing from zones of high waves to zones of low waves. Thus the pattern was found to be more complex when long swells reached the coast, than with shorter, more oblique waves. The strongest rip currents were associated with the longest waves and the greatest

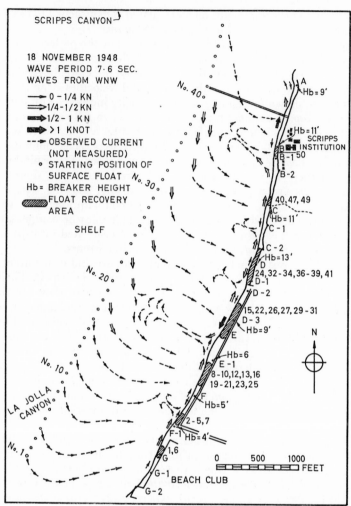

SCRIPPS CANYON

18 NOVEMBER 1948
WAVE PERIOD 7·6 SEC.
WAVES FROM WNW

→ 0 – 1/4 KN
⇒ 1/4 – 1/2 KN
⇒ 1/2 – 1 KN
⇒ > 1 KNOT
--→ OBSERVED CURRENT
      (NOT MEASURED)
○ STARTING POSITION OF
   SURFACE FLOAT
Hb = BREAKER HEIGHT
▨ FLOAT RECOVERY
   AREA

SHELF

No. 40

No. 30

No. 20

No. 10

LA JOLLA CANYON

No. 1

A
Hb = 9′

Hb = 11′
SCRIPPS
INSTITUTION
B-1 50
B-2

40, 47, 49
C
Hb = 11′
C-1

C-2
Hb = 13′
D
24, 32 – 34, 36 – 39, 41
D-1
D-2

15, 22, 26, 27, 29 – 31
D-3
Hb = 9′
E

Hb = 6
E-1
8 – 10, 12, 13, 16
19 – 21, 23, 25
F
Hb = 5′

2 – 5, 7
F-1 Hb = 4′

1, 6
G

G-1   BEACH CLUB
G-2

N

0   500   1000
▭▭▭▭▭▭ FEET

FIGURE 3.15. (*a*) Typical nearshore circulation pattern resulting from waves of less than 10 seconds period approaching normal to the Scripps beach in California with a southerly flowing coastal current.

amount of refraction. Thus observations of wave characteristics, both in the short term to interpret day-to-day changes, and in the long term to establish the wave climate of the area, are essential to any complete understanding of marine processes (see figure 3.15).

The study of wave attack on solid rock is difficult to carry out quantitatively, but some attempts have been made to measure the pressures set up by breaking of waves against structures, whether they be natural cliffs or man-made sea defences. For example, de Rouville (1938) used pressure gauges to

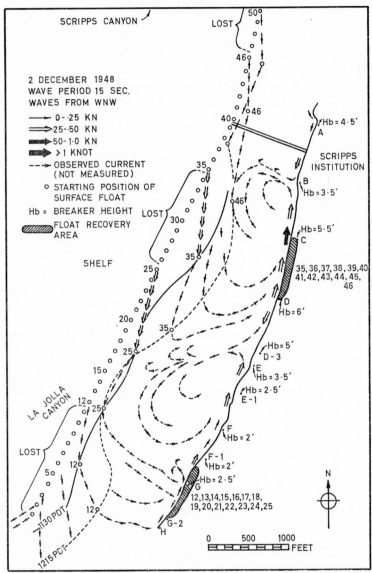

SCRIPPS CANYON

LOST

50°

2 DECEMBER 1948
WAVE PERIOD 15 SEC.
WAVES FROM WNW

— 0 - ·25 KN
⇒ ·25-·50 KN
50-1·0 KN
> 1 KNOT
--→ OBSERVED CURRENT
   (NOT MEASURED)
o STARTING POSITION OF
   SURFACE FLOAT
Hb = BREAKER HEIGHT
FLOAT RECOVERY
AREA

SHELF

LOST

46°

40°

/Hb = 4·5′
A

SCRIPPS
INSTITUTION

B
Hb = 3·5′

Hb = 5·5′
C

35, 36, 37, 38, 39, 40
41, 42, 43, 44, 45,
46

D
Hb = 6′

Hb = 5′
D - 3

E
Hb = 3·5′

Hb = 2·5′
E - 1

F
Hb = 2′

F - 1
Hb = 2′

Hb = 2·5′
G

12, 13, 14, 15, 16, 17, 18,
19, 20, 21, 22, 23, 24, 25

G - 2
H

LA JOLLA CANYON

LOST

1130 PDT

1215 PDT

N

0   500   1000
          FEET

FIGURE 3.15. (*b*) Typical nearshore circulation pattern resulting from long
waves of 15 second period coming from the west-north-west.
(after Shepard and Inman)

measure the force exerted by waves against sea-walls at Dieppe. The results
he obtained showed that the high pressures were very short lived, but very
high; with a wave about 6 feet high and 132 feet long, a maximum pressure
of 12,700 lb/sq. ft was recorded, but the pressure only exceeded 6000 lb/sq. ft

for $\frac{1}{100}$ second. Such very high pressures depend on very critical conditions that only occur rarely, but they can be very damaging in well-jointed rocks.

The very high pressures are set up when a wave encloses a pocket of air as it breaks against the cliff, so that the depth of water in front of the structure, which determines the position of the break-point, is an important factor. Where there is deep water offshore most of the wave energy will be reflected and shock pressures will not be set up; on the other hand, where the water is very shallow the wave will break before it reaches the structure and again shock pressures will not be set up. However, both the depth and character of the breaker are critical to the setting up of damaging pressures.

b) *Movement of sediment by waves.* Waves are in many areas the most effective agent that moves loose material on the beach, and several methods have been developed to measure and record their effect in the foreshore and nearshore zones. There are various methods of approach to the problem of movement of sediment by waves: the amount of sediment in the water should be assessed, the nature of the bottom and the changes in beach level can be recorded, the depth to which sediment is moved and the disturbance depth provide useful data, and the profiles that result from these movements can then be studied and their seasonal and periodic changes recorded and analysed. Another very important aspect of sediment movement by waves is the longshore transport of sediment, because on this factor the incidence of coast erosion and accretion largely depends.

i *Sediment in suspension.* Observations were made by the Beach Erosion Board (1943) at Long Branch, New Jersey, to measure the amount of sediment in the water under different parts of the wave. The results were obtained by taking samples of water of known volume at different depths above the bottom and at varying distances from the break-point of the waves. The sand was filtered out and the amount was expressed as parts per million by weight. The results showed that there was only a large amount of sand in suspension near the break-point, and here it amounted to 5% of the total moved, being about 17,000 parts/million. Only 25 feet seaward the amount fell to 4000 parts/million and was less than 1000 a further 275 feet seaward. For all the waves measured, sand in excess of 200 parts/million was confined to within 2 feet of the bottom.

Watts (1953) developed a pump type of instrument to measure the amount of suspended sediment, and although his results show considerable scatter some useful data were obtained. However, the equipment was bulky and had to be based on a pier. He found the greatest volume in suspension in depths of 4 to 8 feet, just inside the break-point.

ii *Sediment movement in the nearshore zone.* Some valuable observations have been made by Trask (1955) and Inman (1957) on the processes operating on the sea-bed. The method used by Trask was to collect samples from the offshore zone; their analysis gave an indication of the character of sediment movement by the waves. Trask noted that the sea-bed beyond a depth of 60 feet was rarely disturbed and he called this the passive zone, the zone between 30 and 60 feet depth was an intermediate zone, with occasional sand

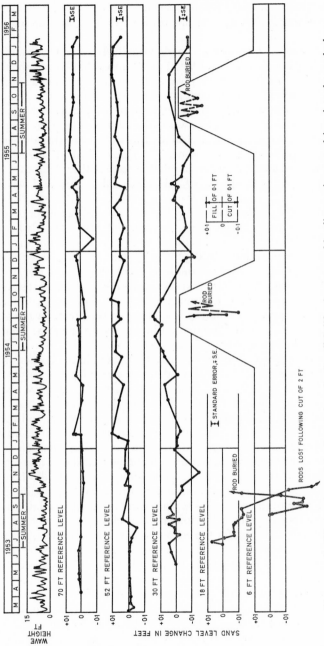

FIGURE 3.16. Changes in sand level at various depths off California measured by divers using pegs driven into the sea-bed. (after Inman and Rusnak, B.E.B.)

disturbance, while the zone shallower than 30 feet was the surf zone and was frequently disturbed. In the passive zone it was observed that the bottom was frequently covered by a layer of fine brown sediment, and the material did not move.

Inman described observations made visually by direct measurement by divers in depths up to 170 feet. One of the features studied was the character of the bottom in relation to the wave size. He showed that the brown sediment, described by Trask, was not a permanent feature and with some high waves could be disturbed and a ripple pattern develop. However, when the waves decreased in size the ripples were soon destroyed by burrowing animals and the brown sediment was deposited; this state was estimated to last for 39% of the time in the passive zone. The ripples formed when the orbital velocity exceeded a critical value in relation to the other significant controls. At a depth of 52 feet the period of quiescence fell to 12% and was nil at 30 feet.

To obtain more precise evidence of the amount and character of the movement of bed material, experiments were carried out with rods fixed in the sand at different depths, the length of rod projecting being measured by divers. The rods were fixed in depths of 30 feet, 52 feet, and 70 feet. The deepest rods showed changes of sand level of less than ± 0·1 feet (range 0·15 feet) over the three years of observations, while the one at 52 feet showed only slightly greater movement, the range being 0·16 feet; at 30 feet the total change over the period amounted to a range of 0·29 feet. In the shallower depths there was a seasonal fluctuation in level, with the sand being higher in summer and lower in winter (see figure 3.16).

The precise measurements made on the rods fixed in the bottom were used to check the accuracy of acoustic methods of surveying the bottom profile, and the results showed that the echo-sounders tested could give results that were accurate to within ± 0·5 feet. Echo-sounding has one advantage over the rod method of measuring the change in beach elevation, and this is that a complete profile is obtained. On the other hand the direct method of measurement is considerably more accurate for noting small changes that occur in the deeper water and has the advantage that the bottom conditions can be examined at the same time. Some information can also be obtained about the actual movement of sand under different wave conditions, as the depth in which movement first takes place can be seen. The relative accuracy of the two methods of measuring under water change of level is ± 0·05 feet for the rods and ± 0·5 feet for the echo-sounder. Direct underwater methods of observation of sand movement under wave action can only be carried out in clear seas, such as those off California, where the observations described were made. In more sediment-laden waters the visibility would render such methods very difficult to operate, as has already been mentioned.

Another method that has been used to study the changes in level of the sea-bed offshore is to measure the movement of artificially dumped material. An example of this occurred at Long Branch, New Jersey: 601,991 cu. yd of sand were dumped in the sea about half a mile offshore, with the intention of nourishing the beach, which was suffering from a loss of sand. The depth of the dumping area was 38 feet at mean low water. The offshore area was surveyed before, during and at various times after the dumping. By correlating the movement of sand from the stock-pile offshore with the waves that were affecting the area Manohar showed that only 3·4% of the waves acting in the area were able to move the sand from the stock-pile. The minimum waves that could affect the sand in this depth were 4 feet high and had a period of 6 seconds; these dimensions were only exceeded by 3·4% of all the waves measured. As a result, after four years the stock-pile was still substantially intact; it had originally been a ridge 7 feet high, 750 feet wide and 3700 feet long; it only became slightly flattened out in the interval. There was also a slight decrease in the median diameter of the sand.

From the evidence already given and the methods used to arrive at the results, it should be evident that the depth to which waves can effectively change the bottom relief is relatively small. On sand beaches the methods used have shown that there is little change in level of sand in depths greater than 30 to 40 feet. Other experiments have been carried out to test the depth at which material offshore can be moved by waves. The experiments made with radio-active tracers at Tomakomai in Japan have shown that sand, with a median diameter of 0·13 mm, started to move in a depth of 6 m (19·7 feet) when the wave height exceeded 5·8 feet. Shingle appeared to move in even smaller depths than sand, although experiments made with radio-active pebbles off Scolt Head Island (Steers and Smith, 1956) did indicate that pebbles could move in depths of 16 to 20 feet. Over a period of about 6 weeks the pebbles had moved up to 450 feet from the point of injection.

Another line of evidence that can be used to assess the depth of wave action is that used by Bradley. He based his views on observations of the rounding of pyroxene grains; he found that the grains of pyroxene were much more rounded in the surf zone than they were in water deeper than 30 feet. The grains were derived in an angular state from the land, but became rounded unless they moved quickly through the surf zone and came to rest in the deeper, quieter water beyond. Thus all methods of analysis point to the same conclusion, that waves cannot disturb bottom sediment, whether it be sand or shingle, in depths greater than about 20 to 30 feet for shingle and 30 to 40 feet for sand. This depth is very much less than that suggested by D. W. Johnson.

iii *Sand disturbance depth on foreshore.* It is also of interest to measure the depth to which waves can disturb the sand as they pass over it, and a convenient method can be used to measure this (King, 1951). The experiments can be carried out on any tidal beach. At low water two thin pegs were fixed in the sand as reference points and at a known distance between them a vertical face was cut in the sand, a vertical strip of dyed sand, contrasting with the natural sand, was placed along the face. The hole was then filled in and smoothed over. After the tide had risen and fallen again the change in level of the sand was measured on the pegs. Observations of disturbance depth were made whenever possible when the change in level had been very small. The position of the dyed sand was noted with reference to the pegs, and the site was carefully undermined from below until the base of the dyed column was located; this was followed up until the dyed sand ended abruptly at the level to which the disturbance had reached. This value could then be correlated with the observations made of the wave dimensions at high tide. It is clear that if the maximum disturbance takes place in the swash zone or the breaker zone, it will not be possible to measure exactly the disturbance in the deeper water outside the break-point. As the results of all the observations made on any one day, regardless of the depth of water over the site at high water, were similar, it may be assumed that the maximum amount of disturbance occurs in the shallow water at and inside the break-point. This is what would be expected and agrees with the findings of measurement of the amount of sand in suspension, which was also at a maximum at and inside the break-point.

In order to find out what variables affect the depth of disturbance, this value was plotted against the wave height and other wave dimensions. The results showed that there was a linear relationship between the depth of disturbance and the wave height for observations made on the beaches at Rhossili, South Wales, Blackpool and Whitbeck, Cumberland. These beaches all had sands of nearly the same size, but the sand at a fourth beach, in Druridge Bay, Northumberland, was coarser, and the disturbance depth was greater than in the finer sands. Thus both wave and sand size affect the disturbance depth and both should be observed.

iv *Beach profiles.* Much useful information can be obtained by studying the change in beach profiles under different conditions of wave attack. It was early observed that beaches tended to be combed down after attack by storm waves and built up by the more gentle waves of the fair-weather interludes. Thus by surveying the changes in the beach profile and correlating these with accurately determined wave observations it has been possible to show that it is probably the wave steepness that is the critical factor in determining the nature of wave attack. Waves can be divided into constructive waves and storm waves, the destructive effect of the latter increasing if there is a strong onshore wind. However, note must be made of the beach material concerned; in shingle it has long been recognised that the major ridges, extending highest above the mean sea-level, are the work of the largest storm waves, as only these can throw shingle to such heights. Steep waves acting on sand, on the other hand, tend to be entirely destructive, unless the coastal protections are breached and sand is washed inland, as occurred on the east coast of England during the 1953 storm-surge. Surveys of the beach before and after the action of steep storm waves can readily show this effect. In some areas it is possible to show that there is a seasonal effect of constructive and destructive waves. A very good example of this has been studied by Shepard (1950) in California; he superimposed pairs of surveys, one of each pair being taken in the autumn and the other in the spring, along the Scripps Institution pier. They showed very clearly that during the summer the beach gained sand at the top. This belt of accretion extended to about 10 feet below

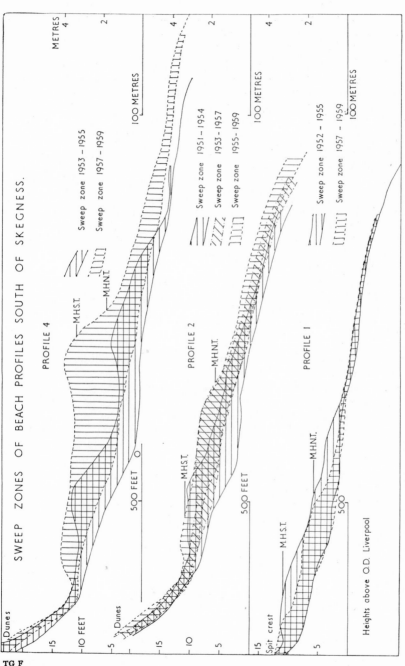

SWEEP ZONES OF BEACH PROFILES SOUTH OF SKEGNESS.

FIGURE 3.17. Sweep zones of the Lincolnshire coast beaches south of Skegness, showing coastal accretion on profiles 2 and 4, but slight loss of sand on profile 1.

TG F

mean low water. During the winter, however, when destructive waves reach the coast more frequently, the sand was cut away and carried out to deeper water offshore, where it accumulated in depths up to about 20 feet below low water. The changes in beach level involved amounted at times to about 7 feet of sand vertically. It is interesting to note that the winter profile nearly always had a submarine bar, marking the deposition of sand combed down from the foreshore, while this feature was eliminated in the summer as the sand was moved up the shore, and the beach gradient often became steeper.

Similar but smaller changes can be recorded over much shorter time intervals, and these changes have allowed the correlation of beach gradient with relevant parameters of the waves. Thus it has been shown that long waves are associated with a flatter swash slope gradient (King, 1953). There was also a tendency for the steeper waves to be associated with a flatter beach. More noticeable is the relationship between the gradient of the beach and the size of the material. The gradients of different beaches are closely related to the size of the beach material; this is due to the variation of permeability with grain size. In fact the Beach Erosion Board, Washington, found a straight line relationship between the tangent of the slope angle and the median diameter of the material.

In order to study the change in a beach profile over a number of years using a large number of observations, these must be arranged in a way that enables the changes that are taking place to be appreciated. This can be done conveniently if a considerable number of profiles are superimposed; then the upper and lower envelope curves provide a limit within which the profile lay at any one time, depending on the weather conditions and wave type. If the area between the curves, called the sweep zone, is narrow, then the beach is in a stable state of equilibrium (see figure 1.3). This method provides more useful results if the sweep zones are constructed for different periods of years. Then the temporary changes, due to changing wave conditions, can be discounted and the longer term changes become apparent. If the coast is accreting the whole sweep zone will be raised, although any one individual profile of the later period may lie near or below one of the high ones of the former period. The reverse will apply to a beach undergoing erosion. Examples of these changes have been demonstrated on the Lincolnshire coast (King and Barnes, 1964), where in the south accretion is proceeding rapidly. The whole sweep zone is considerably higher for the period 1957-1959 than it was in the earlier period from 1952-1955 as shown on figure 3.17. The sweep zone in the south is also wider because the accretion has been accompanied by the growth of large beach ridges on the foreshore. In the zone of erosion to the north, however, the sweep zone has become narrower as the beach has come into equilibrium with new coastal defences, established since the 1953 storm-surge that did so much damage along this coast.

v *Longshore drift*. It has been shown that observations in the field indicate that movement of the beach material normal to the shore can only take place in relatively shallow water, and that material eroded at one season or during one storm, is returned to the beach during the other season, or when constructive waves begin to counteract the effect of the destructive ones. It is, therefore, of great importance to study the movement of material alongshore, because only when more material is taken away from one area by longshore movement than is brought into it will serious erosion result, because of the inability of a low, thin beach to protect the coast. A wide, high beach is the most effective protection for any coast, as it absorbs all the wave energy.

Longshore drift is difficult to measure accurately in the field, but fairly new methods have been devised that are providing more quantitative data on this subject. Some of the earlier estimates of longshore movement of material were based on the change of beach configuration as the result of upsetting the natural movement of sand along the shore by building breakwaters or other structures. A good example of this type of study is that carried out in California at Santa Barbara. A break-water was built here in 1929 resulting in the disturbance of the natural longshore movement; erosion took place downwave of the breakwater, extending 10 miles in a few years, while accretion took place in the harbour and on the upwave beaches. Between 1932 and 1951 the estimated amount of accretion in the harbour averaged 279,650 cu. yd/year. In order to study this longshore movement of sand more fully, wave recorders were set up and frequent surveys of the harbour were undertaken. In analysing the data, the wind direction and speed, the wave height and period, and associated steepness and the wave power were used, and these variables were plotted against the rate of movement of sand alongshore between the periods of observation, which extended altogether from April 1950 to February 1951. No record of wave approach was available, but very rarely did the waves approach from a point that caused a westerly drift. On nearly all occasions when the longshore transport was greater than average, it was found that the wave power was also great; the only exceptions appeared to be due to smaller waves approaching from a direction which induced rapid drift. During the period of survey the waves were on the whole of very low steepness, so that sand was moving onshore, and much of the transport was taking place in the swash and backwash zone.

Other experiments of this type have been carried out in Anaheim Bay, California, where Caldwell, as a result of careful surveys during 1948 and 1949, was able to relate the amount of longshore transport with the wave energy, taking into account the direction of wave approach. The wave data were obtained from two gauges, and synoptic charts were used to estimate the direction of wave approach. On the whole there was a close linear corrrelation between the volume of sand moving alongshore and the longshore energy. Both variables were plotted on a logarithmic scale, so that there was a rapid increase of transport as the longshore energy increased. Various other estimates of longshore transport have been made on the basis of beach changes resulting from the interference of the natural state of movement. All the studies revealed very considerable rates of movement, but nearly all of them were undertaken where the coast was open and movement alongshore was unimpeded by headlands.

Field studies along indented coasts have tended to show that each small bay has its own characteristic type of sand, as revealed by a study of the heavy mineral assemblage. This applies to the work of Baak (1936) in the small bays of the west coast of Brittany and Normandy, where the complex geology facilitated the study.

The other main method of assessing the amount and direction of longshore drift is to follow the movement of marked material. Many of the recent studies of this type have used markers of radio-active or fluorescent material. Such methods require very elaborate preparation and equipment, so that before describing them a simpler method of marking pebbles, and the results that can be obtained, will be mentioned. The measurements made by Kidson and Carr (1961) in Bridgwater Bay illustrate the method. The markers consisted of fireclay bricks pierced with holes, which had the advantage of being easily distinguishable from the Lias Limestone and purple sandstone pebbles already on the beach. They were angular to start as were the limestone pebbles amongst which they were sited, and they were of the correct density to travel in the same way as the local pebbles. Each pebble was marked with a label attached through the hole, so that its final position and state could be compared with the initial state. Three sizes were used, whole, half and quarter bricks, each being placed with similar-sized pebbles on the beach. The tracing of the movement of the markers was carried out at first after every tide, but subsequent searches were made less frequently. The pebbles that were located during the experiment were fixed in position by pacing or taping from the original line and the beach crest. The rate of recovery was very high near the bottom of the lines normal to the beach as little movement took place, and elsewhere 50% of the markers were recovered during the first six months. Thereafter a large proportion became buried owing to disturbance of the beach crest. The movement on the whole was very slow in this sheltered area and only very few of the markers moved from the lower beach to the crest. The greatest movement recorded was only 7500 feet and the area was unusual in that the movement only took place over a very narrow height range near the top of the beach, and no shingle occurred below low water, so that there was no possibility of movement proceeding undetected in this zone. Another interesting point that emerged from the study was that the shingles of different dimension moved at different rates and sometimes in different directions. This area was particularly suited to this type of experiment on account of the slow movement. Elsewhere short-term tracing of pebble movement can be carried out by using the local pebbles painted to contrast with the normal ones.

Jolliffe (1964) has reported experiments with painted shingle and artificial fluorescent pebbles at Deal and Winchelsea in south-east England. The aims of the experiments were to test the relative rate of travel of abraded and non-abraded artificial tracer pebbles, to determine differences in rate of travel of natural shingle and artificial tracer pebbles, and finally to examine the relative rate of travel of different sized shingle. Pebbles were collected from the beaches and covered in marine paint and then baked at 160 to 170 degrees

C for 2 to 3 hours. 'Araldite' can also be used successfully for coating pebbles. A range of pebble sizes were coloured and fluorescent tracer pebbles were also used. At Deal the experiment only lasted one week and after six days the lateral spread of the pebbles was only 150 feet to the north. At Winchelsea the marked material was placed between high water and the lower limit of the shingle, and two lines of ranging rods were fixed along the beach crest at 50-feet intervals to facilitate location of marked pebbles. The beach between the crest and the lower shingle boundary was divided into ten stretches and observations were made every 10 feet along the beach. Counts were made by using a sampling grid frame in each section. The general conclusions reached concerning the movement of the natural pebbles are interesting; the larger pebbles, 2 to 3 inches in size, travelled considerably further than the smaller ones, about $\frac{1}{2}$ inch in diameter, while the largest, 3-4 inches in diameter, travelled a little less far than the 2 to 3 inch ones. These relative rates appeared to increase as waves became higher. The artificial stones moved at a different rate from the natural pebbles.

In attempting longshore movement studies it is very important that the material used for tracing experiments should have the same properties as the normal beach material; thus it is best to mark the actual beach material. This is easier to accomplish with shingle than sand. Other problems must be considered, such as safety precautions with radio-active materials, and tracing problems with fluorescent material. If the latter is used samples have to be collected for laboratory analysis or the sampling must be carried out at night under ultra-violet light, with the attendant surveying problems. The difficulty of marking finer grade materials, such as silt and sand, has been partly solved by using soda-glass instead of natural material. However to provide useful results the material must behave like the natural material, and resemble it in density and size and other essential characteristics.

There are some advantages in the use of radio-active tracers, for example, no laboratory work is required in assessing the movement, especially of shingle. It also has the advantage that material can be located even if it is buried under the surface layer of shingle or sand. However, it must be borne in mind that all the tracing experiments carried out suffer from the same drawback to a greater or lesser degree: they can only record the movement that is going on during the time of the experiment. With radio-active tracers, that have a relatively short half-life, this may only be a period of a few weeks, and fluorescent sand may also be dispersed after only a short period of time. This means that, unless the wave and weather conditions are similar to those of the long-term average during the progress of the experiment, the results will not be typical, and can even be misleading if the conditions are abnormal.

This effect was seen in the experiments carried out on Orford Ness from January to March 1957 (Kidson, Carr and Smith, 1958). The shingle in this experiment was marked with the isotope barium-140—lanthanum-140, which has a half-life of 12 days, and allows tracing to continue for seven weeks. The 2600 marked flint pebbles were traced with a set of geiger-counters for underwater detection and a scintillation counter for detecting pebbles above the low water mark; both instruments were mounted on sledges. Pebbles could be located at a distance of 10 inches under water, but 15 feet away above water, while buried pebbles above water could be located at a depth of 6 to 9 inches. The pebbles were injected at two points along a fixed line of transit. The underwater pebbles were located by towing the geiger-counters behind a boat and, when a pebble was contacted, the boat was positioned above the pebble and its position fixed by horizontal sextant angles to fixed points on the shore. One set of pebbles was deposited in water varying from 19 to 28 feet in depth according to the tide and about 700 yards offshore. These pebbles did not move at all during the time of the experiment. Other pebbles deposited just seaward of low water level recorded considerable longshore movements.

Orford Ness has clearly grown southwards by movement of shingle from the north, so that it was interesting to note that, under the conditions of the experiment, the pebbles moved northwards by a mean distance of 600 yards in 4 weeks. During this time winds blew from a south-west, south or south-easterly quarter. Had the experiment only lasted these four weeks, an entirely misleading impression of the normal movement would have resulted; however, before the end of the experiment winds from the north and north-east blew, and under their influence the direction of movement was rapidly reversed and the pebbles moved very fast to the south. This indicates the danger of placing too much reliance on short-term experiments that may not operate under typical conditions. It also shows that on any coast drift can occur in more than one direction, and that although the dominant direction of drift may be quite clear, longshore movement may well occur in the opposite direction under suitable wave conditions.

Sand on the whole is less easy to mark than shingle, in which each individual pebble can be separately marked and traced again. However, Inman and Chamberlain (1959) record a method whereby sand may be marked and traced. One of the difficulties with sand is that large quantities must be marked, if it is to be traced for any length of time, and the sand used must behave like the natural sand. As most natural sand is formed of quartz, this material was used and it was marked by phosphorus-32; this does not lead to any health hazard. It has a half-life of 14·6 days and can be traced for several months. Sand was taken from the experimental area and treated by irradiation, it was then reintroduced into the test area by divers, and was traced at intervals to determine the rate of dispersion. Samples for analysis were obtained in two ways: firstly, from the upper layer of the bottom by pressing a grease-coated card 3 by 5 inches on to the sea bed, or, secondly, by pressing a plastic tube into the bottom. The amount of treated sand in the first sample could be found by exposing the card on a photosensitive film, which after exposure and development showed the treated grains as spots. The cores were solidified with resin and then sectioned for examination. The sand was released at a depth of 10 feet, where the wave height was $1\frac{1}{4}$ feet and the period about 14 seconds. The sand was dyed an intense blue to allow visual tracing in the first stages of the experiment, which lasted for 24 hours, although tests showed that the irradiated particles could be detected for four months. The treated particles were released on the bottom in an area of about 3 sq. ft. Samples were taken at positions fixed by a grid of reference stakes fixed in the bottom at 10-feet intervals; the samples were taken at intervals of $\frac{1}{4}$, 1, $3\frac{1}{2}$, $7\frac{1}{2}$ and 24 hours after the time of placing the sand.

The experiment showed very rapid dispersion of the grains, especially in view of the low waves acting at the time. Particles moved at 1·5 ft/min. during the first $\frac{1}{4}$ hour. The bulk of the movement took place in an onshore-offshore direction, and after the 24-hour period the main movement had been towards the shore. The presence of ripples on the bottom may account for the rapid dispersion as the grains were lifted into suspension. Measurement of the reference rods showed that slight erosion of 0·1 feet took place at the site of injection, but accretion took place on the foreshore. The depth of mixing was found to be a maximum of 0·06 feet at 10 feet from the release point after 7 hours. The treated sand dispersed over an area of 0·75 sq. miles after only 24 hours. The results of this experiment clearly produced very different information from that made with marked shingle. It is a useful means of assessing the effect of different waves over a limited period in a small area.

A problem remains in all these methods of measuring longshore movement with tracers; the marked material forms only a very small fraction of the total material in movement, and there is the difficulty of relating the movement of the tracers to the total movement of material along the shore. A method of overcoming this problem has been suggested by R. C. H. Russell (1961) of the Hydraulics Research Station in connection with work on sea-defence schemes, including the effect of groynes. The work included a study of the character of the beach in question at Deal. The movement of material alongshore was traced by using marked pebbles on the half-tide line. It was argued that if the movement were in one direction only at a rate of M tons/year, and tracer pebbles were put on the beach at m tons/year, after mixing the concentration of tracer to beach pebbles would be m/M downwave. Littoral drift could then be found by multiplying the number of beach pebbles moved with each tracer pebble by the rate at which tracer pebbles were being placed on the beach. The problem is more complex if the drift occurs in two directions; in this case, with regular placing of pebbles at the initial point, the maximum number occurs here, and there are more on the downwave than the upwave beach. In order to calculate the drift mathematically under these conditions it is necessary to assume that the drift is evenly distributed throughout the period of observation. Reasonably accurate results by this method can only be achieved if there is no loss of shingle offshore.

The pebbles in this experiment were traced by making them fluorescent, and they were located by ultra-violet lamps at night. The concentration could be found by counting the marked pebbles in a given area. Tracer pebbles were placed on the beach at the rate of 1 cwt/day for 21 days. The net drift was calculated as being at the rate of 720 tons to the north. However, in a later experiment lasting 83 days the net drift was shown to be 1310 tons to the south (both figures during the time of the respective experiments).

On beaches where the drift is variable and small, the errors in the method of calculating net drift are as great as the estimated movement.

An interesting example of the use of naturally radio-active sand as a tracer is described by Kamel (1962). The material traced was radio-active thorium, and samples were collected at mid-tide level both from the surface and from a depth of one foot along the 90-mile stretch of coast near San Francisco, from Russian River to Point Pedro in California. The heavy minerals in a small specific size-range were separated out and the radio-activity was measured with a two-channel gamma-ray spectrometer. The reduction in concentration of thorium and other heavy minerals from their source area in the Russian River basin gave an indication of the longshore drift direction. The results were checked by correlation with calculated wave-induced currents derived from wave refraction diagrams. The general direction of drift was from north to south, but a few localities showed a reversal of the general direction owing to local configuration of the coast.

B. *Tidal action*

In the past the effect of tidal action on coastal phenomena was over-emphasised, but then it became virtually ignored and all features were explained in terms of wave action. Now its importance is being appreciated again, especially in some areas, where it clearly plays an important part in shaping the coast and offshore zone. In considering tidal action, and its effect on the shore, two aspects have to be taken into account, firstly, the actual movement of the water under the influence of the tidal streams, and, secondly, the effect of the variation of water height on coastal processes during the tidal cycle.

a) *Tidal streams*. The measurement of tidal streams is an essential part of the study of their effect on the nearshore zone. This is not a very straightforward operation, as the tidal streams are combined with other types of currents and long continued records are required to obtain an accurate estimate of the tidal part of the total current. Another difficulty is that the observations must be made from a floating station which may itself move. Surface movement can be measured fairly reliably from the deck of an anchored ship by log line, by noting the time the log takes to cover the length of the line and its direction. The ship must face into the current so that it does not move during the observations. To obtain the current speed below the surface a large submerged kite can be used, attached to a light spar 30 to 35 feet long that just emerges above the water surface so that it can be followed from the ship. To overcome the difficulty of wind drift the result may be more accurate if a small floating object, not so subject to influence by the wind, is followed by the boat, whose positions can then be fixed at intervals by horizontal sextant angles to fixed positions on shore, if these are available. If not, a buoy can be used as a reference point, but in any case observations must be continued throughout the tidal cycle of about 12 hours and at different states of the tide from spring to neap tide.

The other method by which currents can be observed is to use current meters. There are many types of current meters; some record continuously, others can be lowered to different depths for short-term readings. The direction is less easy to measure than the velocity, but it is very necessary, and is usually obtained by fitting a magnetic compass in the instrument; this leads to errors unless the meter is some distance from the ship.

Because of these difficulties the recorded tidal streams that are published on Admiralty charts and given in Admiralty publications may not always be absolutely accurate. Nevertheless they do provide very useful data concerning the variations of tidal streams from hour to hour in relation to the time of high and low water, and also the difference between the streams at spring and neap tide. Tidal streams in some narrow straits can reach velocities of up to 7 or 8 knots at spring tide, and such fast-moving water must clearly exert a strong influence on the bottom. Unlike wind waves, tidal waves are long compared to the depth of water and they do not show much reduction of velocity with depth; from this point of view also they exert a considerable influence on the bottom.

A useful and relatively simple method of measuring bottom currents has been devised by J. N. Carruthers (1962). It can be used in depths up to 60 fathoms. Experiments were made with it off Great Yarmouth at two points, at depths of 43 feet and 23 feet on the chart. These measurements were made at the same site as radio-active markers were put down to trace the movement of material by tidal streams. The radio-active tracer experiment indicated a mean southward movement of 2000 feet in three months, with some of the sand covering one mile. The movement of sand on this offshore shoal showed no indication of the effect of wave action, the sand moving south only under current action due to tides. On the other hand, evidence of sand waves suggested northward movement of sand in this vicinity, so that current measurements were required to check the other types of evidence. The current measuring device of Carruthers has the advantage that it measures the current very close to the bottom, where the sediment is moving.

The instrument consists of a bottle containing 4 fluid ounces of a hot gelatine solution, which was lowered to the sea-bed. A compass card was allowed to float in the hot jelly and the top of the bottle was fixed by a short length of twine to a sinker. The whole apparatus was allowed to sink to the bottom at the end of a line, and the bottle then floated upside down, as it was $\frac{3}{5}$ full of air. The jelly solidified as the water cooled it, setting the compass card pointing to north, while the angle of the bottle depended on the strength of the current; it would stand vertically in still water, and increase its angle of inclination as the current increased. The surface of the jelly set horizontally, so that the angle of the bottle could be measured to give the speed of the current; for example a slope of 80 degrees corresponded with a speed of $\frac{1}{4}$ knot, while a slope of 39 degrees corresponded with 1 knot, $14\frac{1}{2}$ degrees with 2 knots, and 2 degrees with 3 knots. Speeds up to 6 knots can be measured with suitable adjustments. Measurements made with jelly-bottles were compared with current meter results; the latter gave a maximum speed of 1·8 knots flowing south at high water and 0·9 knots flowing north 3 hours before local low water; at spring tides the south and north flowing peak currents were 2·1 knots and o·8 knots respectively. The jelly-bottle, with an intermediate tidal range, gave a maximum flow to the north of 2·35 knots, as against o·9 knots by current meter, while the southerly flow was o·65 knots faster than that recorded by the current meter, giving a bottom speed of 2·75 knots. Both observations agree that the southerly flow is greater than the northerly, which is the essential point concerning the residual movement.

When considering the effect of bottom currents on the movement of sediment it is important to bear in mind both the strength and duration of the flow in different directions, because there is a certain threshold velocity below which flow will not cause movement of bed material; a long period of gentle flow may move less material than a shorter period of greater flow, as the amount of material moved increases with a certain power of the velocity of flow of the water. The velocities that were observed on the bottom with the jelly-bottles were such that sediment must have been moving for most of the tidal cycle, going north at one stage of the tide and returning south as the tide reversed, but in each instance going a little further south than north, to produce the pattern revealed by the experiments with the radio-active material.

These experiments show clearly that in the offshore zone the tide plays the most important part in the movement of bed material, and that this is essentially alongshore. The jelly-bottle method of measuring bottom currents gives very useful information of the tidal stream at the time of observation, but in considering the long-term development of coastal forms and the long-distance movement of bed material, methods that can measure movement over longer periods are required.

A method of this type has been developed by the Fishery Research Establishment at Lowestoft, primarily to trace the movement of bottom water in connection with fishery research, but this method has also been used with success in estuaries and inshore. The Woodhead Seabed Drifter (see figure 3.18a) consist of a plastic cup to which is attached a brass weight to cause it to sink to the seabed; this must be adjusted in estuaries to the prevailing salinity, as it must reach the bottom, but not be too heavy to move. Attached to the pastic cup is an addressed post-card, which entitles the person who finds and returns it to a small reward. The recovery rate of the cards is remarkably high. They have a map on the back and a space for filling in details and plotting the exact site and date of location, so that it is possible to plot the travel of the plastic markers from their original position to their stranding point. It is not possible to obtain any precise information concerning the rate of travel or the route, but some indication of travel time is obtained and the dispersion of the markers from their origin throws much light on the movement of sediment by tidal streams.

Robinson (1964) has described the recovery of markers released off Spurn Head in Yorkshire. Most of the markers were recovered on the Lincolnshire coast to the south, but their distribution along this coast is of interest (see figure 3.18); many of them were found in the area to the north of Mablethorpe, particularly around Saltfleet, while another area where a number

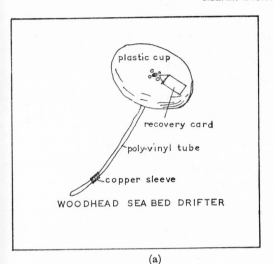

(a)

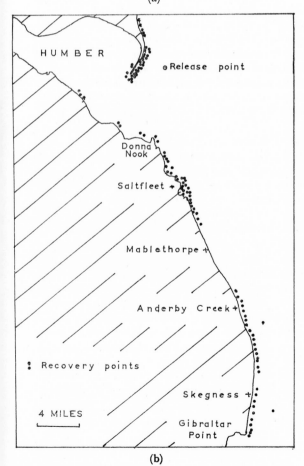

(b)

FIGURE 3.18. Sketch of Woodhead sea-bed drifter and an example of distribution of recovery points from a set of drifters released in the Humber estuary off Grimsby. (after Robinson)

came ashore was in the southern part of the coast near Gibraltar Point. Between Mablethorpe and Anderby none was recovered. It is significant that this last area is the stretch along which erosion has been taking place slowly for several centuries, while the areas where most were recovered are the parts of the coast that are building out by accretion of beach material. The suggestion that the tidal streams play an important part in providing sediment for accretion on the shore is, therefore, given greater weight as a result of these observations. The method also has useful applications to the problem of sediment movement in a tidal estuary, and studies in the west coast estuaries show that the direction of movement depends to a considerable extent on the tidal cycle, being different during spring and neap tides, the former being associated as a rule with stronger currents.

When the tidal streams are reversing at high and low water it is relatively easy to see which is the dominant direction of movement of water and sediment. However, the tidal streams are often rotatory in character. To establish the direction of net transport of sediment it is useful to work out the resultant direction of flow. This can be done by constructing a vector diagram. Each observation of the tidal stream covering one hour is plotted as a line in the correct direction and proportional to the strength of the current, the second hour being drawn from the point reached in the first hour, and so on through the complete cycle. The distance between the initial point and the final point indicates the movement of a particle of water during the cycle and the direction and distance of the resultant of its movement can be measured. Such a diagram depends on the accuracy of the observations, but it can give a useful indication of the probable direction of transport of material under the influence of tidal streams.

b) *Tidal banks and channels.* Features that are well developed in some coastal areas depend entirely on the tidal streams for their characteristics; These are the offshore tidal banks and channels that are common, for example, in the southern North Sea and in many tidal estuaries. Study of these features and their movement depends on the knowledge of the tidal streams in the vicinity. The banks only form where there is a large supply of loose sand on the sea-bed and where the tidal streams are rectilinear. They form between interdigitating channels, which are kept clear by the concentration of the tidal streams within them, while the sediment is deposited in the relatively quiet water on either side. The tidal stream through one channel tends to continue flowing for rather longer as the tide changes, and the stream in the adjacent channel may do the same in the opposite direction; thus most channels are used more by streams flowing in one direction than the other, and become shallower in the direction of the dominant tidal stream. Each element of the system may move independently of its neighbour, while the whole system moves bodily in response to larger-scale changes in the whole vicinity.

A good example of a study of these features is the hydrographic analysis of the banks at the approaches to Lowestoft Harbour (Cloet, 1963). The information available for the analysis consisted of 44 surveys made by the Hydrographic Department of the Admiralty on a scale of 1:20,000 or larger, extending from 1835 to 1962; 40 of the surveys were made between 1923 and 1962. When the latest survey was made, a line of special echo-sounding was run, with the intention of identifying any sand waves that might be present, and bottom samples were also collected.

An analysis was carried out to establish the amount of movement of the different elements in the offshore zone. A chart of stability was prepared, which attempted to delimit the extent of the stationary substratum of the banks. An envelope of movement was formed by taking each fathom line in turn on the superimposed charts; the minimum extent of the envelope indicated the furthest incursion of that fathom line. The minimum extent of all the fathom lines could then be assembled on a chart, which showed the minimum extent of all the banks during the period of survey. Similarly a chart showing the maximum extent of each contour was prepared. By superimposing the two charts, a chart showing the thickness of the zone of movement was produced. The movement was also assessed by plotting the movement of conspicuous features, such as the head of a deep or shoal as it was traced from map to map (see figure 3.19). The chart of minimum extent suggests that there is a solid spur off Lowestoft Ness, and that this area shows very little change in level; in fact over the period the level has changed only through 1 fathom. The movement of the banks showed that different features moved in a variety of directions, each under the predominant influence of the ebb or flood tidal streams. This very detailed study shows clearly that, where the pattern of banks and channels is intricate, the complexity of movement in such areas is very great.

The area off south Lincolnshire also exhibits well-developed offshore banks. Surveys of this area, together with analysis of sediment samples, revealed that their movement was complex. The coarser material was found in the channels, indicating that in these the currents were stronger, the intervening banks were formed of fine, well-sorted sand. This also suggests that movement directly across the channels is limited, and that most of the movement takes place in the direction of the tidal streams, sediment moving up one channel and down the next, until it may reach the shore eventually by a rather circuitous route. Movement under the influence of tidal currents is probably the major form of offshore movement of sediment in this type of area with strong coastal tidal currents and limited wave attack by waves of generally small length.

Considerable attention has been paid lately to the micro-relief forms of the submarine features formed by tidal streams; these features can now be detected fairly easily on records made with precise echo-sounders. Stride (1959, 1963) in particular has studied and interpreted observations of these minor relief features. The sand waves are the most conspicuous; they often have asymmetrical cross profiles, and Stride argues that the movement of sand is towards the steeper side of the wave, and that they can, therefore, be used to establish the general direction of movement of sediment. Carruthers has, however, pointed out that, where the tidal streams flow fast, it is likely that the

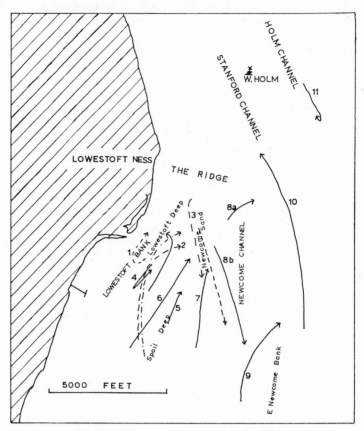

FIGURE 3.19. Tracks of the movement of specific features off Lowestoft
Harbour traced by analysis of repeated surveys.

1. Lowestoft Bank 1947-62	7. Spoil Deep 1923-38
2. Lowestoft Bank 1923-45	8a, *b*. Newcome Channel 1947-62
3. Newcome Sand 1947-62	9. East Newcome Bank 1948-62
4. Lowestoft Deep 1951-62	10. Stanford Channel 1923-62
5. Lowestoft Deep 1923-38	11. Holm Channel 1945-62
6. Spoil Deep 1947-62	

(after Cloet)

Based on extracts from Admiralty Marine Science Publications No. 6, 1963, with the sanction
of the Hydrographer of the Navy.

asymmetry of the waves changes with the direction of the tidal streams.
Surveys should, therefore, be made both at ebb and flood tide to enable this
effect to be allowed for. Where the streams are not so strong it seems likely
that the asymmetry of the wave gives a reliable indication of the net direction
of transport.

Particularly interesting are the sand waves that have been recorded near
the edge of the continental shelf off south-west England. These waves were
recorded at a depth of 90 fathoms, and were aligned normal to the direction

of the tidal currents, thus suggesting a connection between the two factors. The waves had an average height of 25 to 40 feet, and a crest separation of about 2800 feet; they ended abruptly at the edge of the continental shelf. Samples taken from the vicinity showed that the waves were mainly of sand, with some shell gravel, the median diameter being 0·5 mm. The waves were larger than those found in shallow water, indicating that tidal streams were strong. The form of the waves suggested that sand was carried westward towards the edge of the shelf.

More recent observations have been carried out in this area by Carruthers (1963), who has measured the bottom currents in the area of the sand waves on La Chapelle Bank, 100 miles off Ushant. The observations were made with a lightly modified version of the jelly-bottle at hourly intervals throughout a complete tidal cycle. The results showed rotatory tidal streams, the maximum velocity being 0·55 knots in a direction of 190 degrees, and a velocity of 0·42 knots in the reciprocal direction. The observed currents were normal to the wave crest direction. The current was never weaker than 0·25 knots and the overall average speed was 0·40 knots. These observations were made very close to the bottom and reveal that present tidal currents can move material in these depths. An alternative suggestion is that these large waves are the result of the generation of internal waves by the tidal streams. Internal waves should be best developed in September, when the thermocline, on which they partly depend, will be most marked. Temperature observations have supported the view that internal waves may be well developed in this region.

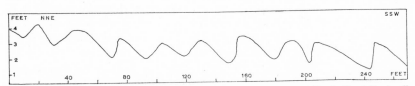

FIGURE 3.20. Sand waves formed by the ebbing tide on the Inner Dog's Head Bank off south Lincolnshire, surveyed by levelling at low water. For position of survey see figure 2.8.

In the shallower water, where most of the observations of sand waves have been carried out, they are probably formed directly by tidal streams, and on the whole their dimensions are smaller (see figure 3.20). The sand waves of the southern North Sea average 15 feet in height and about 450 feet from crest to crest and they are orientated normal to the tidal streams. Repeated surveys with an accurate echo-sounder showed that the waves maintained the direction of asymmetry; this supports the view that they can be used to assess the net direction of movement of sediment. It is possible to calculate the net transport of sand from the estimated rate of advance of the sand waves. This was done for the 40-mile wide stretch of sand waves that appear to be moving north off the coast of Holland. The result suggested a tentative estimate of 4 million cu.m/year passing across a plane 40 miles wide. This illustrates some of the types of information that can be gained by studying the nature of the sand waves.

c) *Effect of tidal range on beach processes.* A study of any beach problem should take into account the tidal range, as this plays an important part in explaining the nature of the beach profile. When the tidal range is great, the waves cannot break at the same position for very long at a time, so that beach features that depend on the constancy of the break-point are affected by a large tidal range. A good example of such features is the submarine bars that are characteristic of many tideless seas and those where the tidal range is small. Surveys carried out on the south coast of France revealed the character of these submarine bars; their movement could be related to the changing position of the break-point of the waves, when these were steep enough to cause a seaward movement of the sand inside the break-point and large enough to break on or near the bar. There were often three submarine bars present, the outermost at the break-point of the highest storm waves, the middle at the break-point of the smaller storm waves, while the inner bar, often in only a few feet of water, was much more mobile than the others as it was influenced by the waves most often. Its movement could be correlated with the size of the waves; when these got slowly larger they would break in slightly deeper water, as waves break when the water depth is about $\frac{4}{3}$ of the breaker height, and hence the bar moved offshore. When the waves decreased slowly in height the bar crest moved slowly inland. Such features cannot form so readily on tidal beaches, as the waves do not break for long enough at any one position even if their height does not change.

The other type of beach feature which probably owes its character to the tidal range is the ridge and runnel beach. Where the ridges lie parallel to the beach it can be shown from field observations, for example at Blackpool, that the ridges form most permanently at the mean tide levels, because it is at these positions that the waves can act for longest in each tidal cycle. It is at these positions, therefore, that the constructive wave action can build up the ridge to fit the equilibrium slope under the conditions prevailing, when the natural slope is too flat.

The range of the tide also plays an important part in the development of salt marshes, as these depend for their sediment on the tide flooding over the marsh at each high water, bringing silt with it to deposit around the growing vegetation. Observations of the accretion in a tidal salt marsh can be carried out by spreading a layer of distinctive material, such as coloured sand, on the surface at fixed positions. The silt and other deposited material will cover the coloured material, then after a period of time the coloured material can be re-exposed by cutting a vertical section, and the depth of accretion can be measured accurately.

Interesting observations have also been made concerning cyclic changes on a beach caused by the tidal cycle. Sometimes these changes are sufficiently regular for fish to adapt their breeding habits to them; this applies to the grunion, *Leuresthes tenuis*, which spawns on some Californian beaches. At neap tide sand deposition occurs just above mid-tide level, and this buries the fish eggs that were laid two days after spring tide at high water level. Then as the next spring tide approaches, erosion takes place just above the mid-tide level, releasing the eggs as they are due to hatch. This spawning takes place from March to August, during the period when the beach changes are most regular in respect of the tide and waves; because wave action is not variable at this time of the year, the tidal beach cycle is well developed.

C. *Submarine processes*

It is much less easy to obtain detailed observations of the processes operating in the deeper parts of the ocean, but they are of interest because they differ so greatly from subaerial processes. Erosion over a long period of time is dominant on land, but in the sea the material worn from the land finds a resting place, so that the dominant processes in the sea are depositional. However, just as deposition occurs on land, so erosion can take place deep beneath the sea, and the operation of these erosional processes may be mentioned first.

A method of measuring currents at great depth in the ocean has been developed by J. C. Swallow at the National Institute of Oceanography. This technique allows the current speed to be measured at any depth over a considerable period of time. Floats, the density of which is adjusted so that they remain at a predetermined depth, send out acoustic signals that can be picked up by the ship above; these signals allow the position of the float relative to the ship to be fixed, then if the position of the ship is known accurately the absolute movement of the float can be determined. In the open ocean it is difficult to fix the positions with great accuracy, so that a method has been developed whereby the position of the ship is determined relative to some conspicuous bottom feature, such as a guyot or sea-mount, by echo-sounding. This feature is then used as the datum point for observing the movement of the float. In the western Atlantic floats have been followed at depths of 2500 m and 2800 m, where current velocities were recorded between 2·6 and 9·5 cm/sec and 9·7 and 17·4 cm/sec respectively. In the eastern Atlantic velocities up to 5 cm/sec have been recorded, but directions in this area appear to fluctuate widely and rapidly (Swallow and Worthington, 1957, 1961 and Swallow and Hamon, 1960).

Laughton has used another method to record water movement on the bottom in great depths; this is done by photographing a ball fixed to the bottom. The ball is deflected in the direction of the current as it floats on a short line. Results with this instrument showed bottom velocities of up to 5 cm/sec at a depth of 3200 m, only 50 cm above the bottom in the western North Atlantic. Velocities such as these show that the bottom of the ocean is by no means as still as was thought at one time. In fact observations with under-water photography have shown that currents are sufficient to cause rippling of the bottom, and the scouring of rocks or the winnowing away of finer sediments to a depth of 4000 fathoms. In the latter depth rock bottom, scoured by ocean currents, was revealed in the Romanche Deep in the equatorial Atlantic (Heezen, 1963). Ripple marks have been observed in the

Atlantic down to depths of 2000 fathoms. It has been suggested that the Blake Plateau, which is a flat shelf at 300 to 400 fathoms on the continental slope off eastern U.S.A., owes its flat character and bare surface to erosion by the Gulf Stream which flows rapidly north-east across this part of the slope. On the other hand the view has been expressed that the Blake Plateau consists of several basins filled to overflowing with sediment. This opinion is based on the results of seismic-refraction work in the area, which has revealed many deep basins beneath the recent sediment. The more upstanding parts of the area, however, have probably been smoothed off by the fast flowing currents. Thus the conclusion is reached that nearly all the upstanding parts of the ocean floor are liable to some slight erosion, or at least the movement of water in these areas is sufficient to prevent deposition.

The large areas of accumulation must be sought in the basins and deep abyssal plains of the ocean floor. However, not all the areas of erosion are upstanding. Perhaps the most spectacular features of the ocean floor, and certainly those that have caused most speculation concerning their origin, are the submarine canyons, forming deep gashes down the continental shelf and slope and reaching at times right to the floors of the deep basins. Clearly both erosion and deposition are associated with these features, and work done on them may be taken as an example of the type of observations and measurements that will in time reveal the processes at work in the sea. After the discussion of many possible methods of formation, most authorities now believe that turbidity currents play a considerable part in the formation of many of the submarine canyons. One of the strongest supporters of the turbidity current theory of submarine canyon formation has been P. H. Kuenen (1952, 1956).

An opportunity to study turbidity currents in action was provided by the effects of the Grand Banks earthquake in 1929. The earthquake, centred just south of Newfoundland, broke a considerable number of submarine cables, and by plotting the time and place of the cable breaks some direct information on the speed and effect of the turbidity currents could be obtained. The submarine cables were broken in succession from north to south down the continental slope. Heezen and Ewing consider that the breaks were caused by the slumps initiated by the earthquake. Turbidity currents appear to have been generated by the movement and travelled down the slope and continued far out on to the abyssal plain, extending for a total distance of over 450 miles from their source. It is estimated that the current velocity exceeded 50 knots on the slope, where gradients of 1 in 10 to 1 in 30 occur. Even on the abyssal plain the velocity appears to have been as much as 12 knots, on a slope of only 1 in 1500. The original movement that set up the turbidity current must have been a disturbance of the deposits. An examination of the characteristics of fine grain sediments shows that, once the sediment is disturbed, its thixotropic character is such that the mass is rendered into the state of a turbulent liquid, which can flow rapidly downslope. This is partly the result of the large amount of water included in newly deposited fine sediment, which may amount to 60-80% by volume (Kuenen, 1952).

The high velocities suggested by the timing of the cable breaks could be reached under these conditions; the frictionless nature of the movement would allow a velocity of 30 m/sec. to be attained in $\frac{1}{2}$ minute on a slope of 1 in 10. Thus addition of material is not necessary to induce sliding, and once the liquefaction has taken place as a result of the disturbance the material will flow downslope. The slowing down of the turbidity current is mainly due to the decrease in thickness of the layer of turbid water. The breadth of the current caused by the 1929 earthquake reached 350 km at one point. Kuenen has calculated that the total amount of material moved by this current was between 100 and 250 cu.km.

The velocities reached in this type of turbidity current appear to be very high, and such rapidly moving material gathers more as it moves, causing erosion, at least in the softer sediments. Whether it can also erode in solid rock is still a debated question. A turbidity current requires sediment and a trigger action in order to operate; the former is normally available on the sea floor, and the latter may be provided by earthquakes, as in the example discussed, or hurricanes impinging on the shore, or possibly extra large volumes of sediment brought down by flooded rivers. The common association of deep sea canyons with large river mouths points to the importance of sediment supplied from the land in providing the trigger, if only because the same mechanism can operate in the same position many times and thus be more likely to erode a definite channel.

In considering the movement of sediment through a canyon as a result of a turbidity current, it is natural to look for the evidence of its flow in deposition of material at the mouth of the canyon, where the slope diminishes and the current comes to rest. Such evidence has been found in abundance, by taking cores at the bottom of submarine canyons and on the flatter parts of basins. Ericson *et al.* (1961) have shown clearly that there are two distinct types of sediment deposits in the ocean; the first type consists of sand and silt, sometimes even gravel, each bed with a well defined base and often graded bedding. The second type consists of slowly deposited grain-by-grain sedimentation of pelagic oozes. The first type is clearly the result of the action of turbidity currents. The graded bedding is a particularly diagnostic factor, the beds become finer upwards as the coarser particles settle out first when the current comes to rest, and the finer are deposited last. The sharp base results from the initial erosion by the current before sedimentation starts, while the inclusion of coarse sediments, often with shallow water fauna or sediment, clearly denotes the transport of the sediment from shallow depths over long distances. The natural levees alongside the channels, and the deep sea fans, also give evidence of turbidity current activity. This method of spreading out sediment over the basins and deep abyssal plains is the major factor in accounting for their flatness.

The study of cores from deep water and the examination of the more accessible upper part of the canyons by diving and underwater photography have solved many of the major problems concerning these intriguing features,

7. EARTH MOVEMENTS—ENDOGENETIC PROCESSES

The external or exogenetic processes are those which mainly concern the geomorphologist, but some attention should at times be paid to the internal forces, especially where these directly affect the landscape, and observations in the field can provide data concerning their character. Four types of internal movement will be mentioned very briefly to indicate the type of problem that may require solution and the sort of evidence available; firstly, earthquake activity and faulting; secondly, warping; thirdly, isostatic adjustment; and fourthly, volcanic activity.

While the exogenetic processes can be studied instrumentally and in detail, the interpretation of the endogenetic processes and their effects on the external form of the earth depends on geomorphological observation and mapping of the landscape by the methods discussed in chapter 2.

a) *Earthquake activity and faulting.* The relief effects of recent earthquakes are seen only in some particularly unstable parts of the earth, such as New Zealand, where fault traces can be seen in the landscape and some small scarps are the direct and little-modified result of faulting. It is valuable in a larger area to be able to recognise the landscapes that still bear the imprint of tectonic activity in the form of faulting, giving rise to tectonic relief. Even in more stable landscapes it is often possible to recognise the influence of faults, although subsequent erosion has often modified their form. The Pennine Faults, bounding the Eden valley on the east, are a good example of a fault system that has moved at different periods in the past, with the last major movement probably having taken place in the early Pleistocene. The abrupt truncation of erosion surfaces at the fault and their continuation at different elevations on the other side indicate that faulting has occurred since the formation of the surface (Trotter, 1929).

On a larger scale, and more clearly displayed, is the blockfaulted landscape of Central Otago in New Zealand; this good example of tectonic relief has been called a 'concourse of earth blocks' by C. A. Cotton (1917). This area, shown on figure 3.21, consists of a hard rock undermass, which was covered by a thick layer of sediments mainly during the Tertiary period. The area then suffered upheaval during the Kaikoura orogeny in the late Tertiary and Pleistocene periods. These earth movements produced the pattern of earth blocks that are still clearly visible in the landscape, despite the removal of nearly all the covering strata. Thus geomorphological evidence is available in the nature of the landforms, and this can be used to elucidate the nature of the earth movements. The evidence is found in the nature of the mountains, which consist of tilted blocks, producing parallel ranges with asymmetrical valleys between them. The ranges include the Dunstan Range, the Raggedy Range, Rough Ridge and Rock and Pillar Range, with the intervening valleys, the Manuherikia Valley, the Ida Valley and the Upper Taieri Plain. These features are all aligned north-west southeast, in the general direction of the faulting responsible for them.

The other major source of evidence for the tectonic nature of this and similar landscapes is the drainage pattern. Not all the faulting occurred at one time; this complicates the drainage evolution, and Cotton has introduced the term 'anteconsequent' to describe one type of river associated with this relief. He suggests that the main drainage lines were consequent upon the initial faulting and uplift, but that subsequent faulting may not be sufficient or act fast enough to change the course of an established river, which is therefore antecedent to the later movements. This often has the effect that the rivers flow in alternate gorge and basin sections; the gorges occur where they

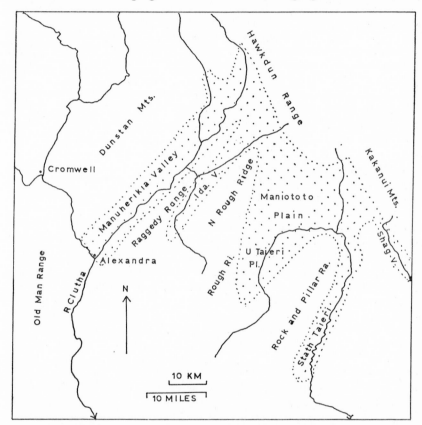

FIGURE 3.21. Map to show ridges and fault-angle valleys and depression in the block-faulted landscape of Central Otago, New Zealand, showing tectonic relief.

cross the rising fault blocks and the down-faulted troughs fill with recent sediment to form the basins. The rivers do not necessarily use the lowest sag along the mountain range as they flow out of a basin, if erosion is ignored. This occurs if the outlet to the basin set up at an early stage continues to be cut down by the river as deformation continues causing greater uplift across the course of the river. The Waiau gorge as it leaves the Hanmer basin in Canterbury is probably anteconsequent; observations of the river in the gorge reveal clear signs of recent uplift of the mountains relative to the river, in the formation of terraces and a high stack in the river. Not all the gorges are anteconsequent, however, and the River Clutha is classed as consequent by Cotton.

Many of the faults in New Zealand, and particularly the great Alpine Fault, have large transcurrent movements, and evidence for this type of movement can also be seen in the landscape. The off-setting of spurs is a very conspicuous feature, and the movement of terraces can give information of both vertical and lateral movement. The need to shorten the telegraph wires as they cross the north-south fault from north-east to south-west, gives good measurable evidence of the movement of the land on the western side of the Alpine fault to the north relative to the eastern side. This movement is still actively progressing and appears in the past to have moved altogether about 300 miles, according to the pattern of outcrops on either side of the fault.

b) *Folding and warping.* Not all recent uplift and subsidence is the result of faulting, some earth movements have been caused by folding; often in fact the two types of movement are closely associated and blend into one another. The effects of upwarping and upfaulting are, therefore, closely comparable, but in the former there are no sharply defined fault blocks and fault scarps.

An area showing clearly the effects of recent local uplift is the Rhenish Uplands. This district, discussed recently by Yates (1963), has risen up across the course of the Rhine, producing features characteristic of antecedence. In the Rhine gorge, cut across this rising area, the terraces give evidence of the differential Pleistocene uplift; their gradients become greater as they increase in age and height. On either side of this localised area of uplift, the Rhine Rift valley and the lower Rhinelands have undergone subsidence. Yates comes to the conclusion that tectonic forces have been of major importance in the formation of the Rhine terraces.

Other areas where warping has produced a visible effect on the drainage and landforms is in association with some of the rift valleys of Africa. Part of this area has been studied in detail by J. C. Doornkamp using field morphological mapping methods to establish former stages of landscape development. In East Africa, for example, the rivers Kafu, Katonga and Kagera once flowed westwards into the Congo drainage basin. The dismemberment and reversal of this drainage took place as a consequence of the formation of the Western Rift valley across their paths. Along a zone on the eastern side of the Rift valley there was a general uparching of the relief, while further to the east, in the areas now occupied by Lakes Kioga and Victoria, there was a corresponding tectonic depression of the surface. These warps, in their final stages, were sufficient to decrease the gradient of the westward flowing streams, until they could no longer keep pace with the rising land and their flow was reversed, resulting in a ponding back of these rivers against their watershed to form Lake Kioga at the head of the Kioga valley, and Lake Victoria across the heads of the Katonga and Kagera valleys. The former westward flow is still reflected in the pattern of the drainage network (see figure 3.22).

The tectonic deformation associated with rift valleys may not only affect the drainage, it may also lead to the warping of erosion surfaces. The continuity of such surfaces cannot, therefore, be mapped on a basis of absolute heights. In any area marked rises can occur, for example, because of changes in lithology or through faulting; such causes have to be eliminated before warping can be established as the factor responsible for creating height differences in any one landscape, and even here the known geological history of the area must be taken into account. In the area between Lake Victoria

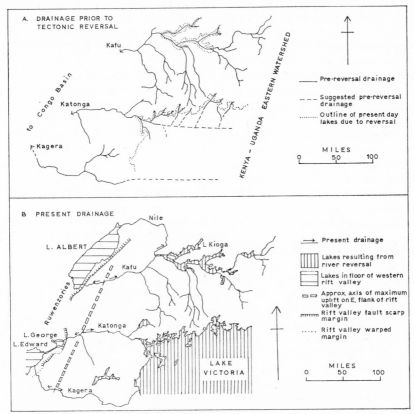

FIGURE 3.22. Map to illustrate the effects of warping on the drainage pattern of part of Uganda, East Africa. (after Doornkamp)

and the Western Rift valley, as in other warped areas, surface continuity can readily be traced in the field when only a small amount of dissection has taken place; greater difficulty arises when the former continuity of isolated erosion remnants has to be considered. Near the western shores of Lake Victoria isolated remnants of an erosion surface occur on the hill tops, and further to the west more continuous remnants occur, but at a somewhat higher level. This difference in height is partly brought about because the boundary between the two areas coincides with the geological junction between more resistant beds forming the higher ground to the west and less resistant beds to the east. However, the Rift valley upwarp will also have caused a rise in absolute height to the west; but the problem of showing that the two sets of remnants formerly belonged to one continuous surface remains. In this instance field mapping of landscape stages, by the techniques of morphological mapping described in chapter 2, showed that the rise from any-one valley floor to either group of remnant summits involved the same number of landscape stages, and the summits are themselves, therefore, at the same stage. Pallister's (1956) analysis of hill form and the amounts of hill-crest reduction within this area led him to the same conclusion as that reached by Doornkamp. Further west, towards the area of maximum uplift, surface continuity and evidence of former continuity are again the only criteria by which one erosion surface or landscape stage may be distinguished. Because of the warping, only field mapping, and the careful recognition of each significant slope boundary, can lead to valid conclusions; cartographic analysis of contour maps is not sufficient.

The direct effects of warping in Britain are not so great, but nevertheless there are interesting examples of the effect of warping that can be seen in the present landscape. A good example of this is seen in the Alston Block, discussed by Trotter in 1929. A study of the outcrop of the Main Limestone in relation to the ground slope reveals the recent warping, which has left its mark also on the relief and drainage of the area. Faulting and folding have dislocated and warped an earlier erosion surface. The discontinuous surfaces on either side of the most recently moved Pennine Fault lines have already been mentioned. The drainage on the Alston Block can be seen to follow the direction of the greatest slope on the warped surface of the older peneplain, which was uplifted along the fault lines to west and north. The recent date of these movements can be inferred from the relatively small amount of subsequent erosion in the river valleys; these are still deep and narrow, such as the West and East Allendales. The pattern of the drainage, flowing away on both sides from the crest of the Teesdale anticline, indicates the nature of the warping. Trotter believes that this movement took place in the earliest part of the Pleistocene.

Evidence of warping has also been brought forward by Straw (1961) from work done in Lincolnshire. He has shown that the land surface of east Lincolnshire has been affected by the Audleby monocline, the land to the south being noticeably higher than that to the north, and the drainage pattern and scarp alignment have also been affected. A similar feature is found in the north of the area along the Humber gap, suggesting that the Northern Wolds have been let down and moved west along these two dislocations. Straw has shown, by a careful study of the distribution and height of erosion surfaces in the field, that all those younger than the summit surfaces must have been formed after the movement along the structural features. The summit surface, probably of early Pleistocene age, seems to predate the structures. These must, therefore, have moved during the Pleistocene.

There is very clear evidence for downwarping in the eastern part of England since the early Pleistocene. Deposits of this age are found at a height of about 600 feet above sea-level in the North Downs and Chilterns; however, the evidence of other deposits shows clearly that east of a north-south line, which Wooldridge and Henderson (1955) consider runs through Braintree in Essex, the land has been downwarped. Deposits of the same age are at about sea-level in East Anglia and in Holland they are found at a depth of 1200 feet below sea-level. This downwarping is associated with long continued subsidence in the southern North Sea basin, which is an area with geosynclinal tendencies.

Warping may also play a considerable part in accounting for the abrupt change of relief at the coast around Britain; the steep, dissected country inland contrasts strongly with the flat nature of much of the sea-bed. This type of warping has been called continental flexure by Bourcart, and appears to have been taking place around the shores of Britain for a long time.

c) *Isostatic adjustment.* The crust of the earth responds to the addition and removal of weight, and as a result isostatic adjustments occur wherever conditions are such that weight is added to or removed from the crust. The best documented and most closely studied example of isostatic adjustment has been caused by the recent removal of load by the melting of the great ice-sheets that until about 10,000 years ago mantled large areas in high latitudes in the Northern Hemisphere. This reduction of the load of the crust has allowed it to rise up towards the pre-glacial state of isostatic equilibrium.

The rate and type of isostatic recovery has been established as a result of a large amount of field work carried out in the areas where this process has been most active, such as Scandinavia, Scotland, and northern Canada. The study has been based on the measurement and dating of raised coastal features, much of the classic work having been done in Finland and Sweden. Details of the methods of study of raised shorelines have already been considered in chapter 2. In Finland Sauramo has shown that the uplift has not been uniform, but has taken place along hinge lines, sometimes forming actual faults. This can be established by the accurate dating of raised shorelines, many of which are associated with glacial limits and morainic features formed near the ice limit.

Evidence of the contemporary isostatic recovery can be obtained by a study of modern tide gauge data; the results of such a study show that the head of the Gulf of Bothnia is rising at about 9 mm/year, while in southern Finland the rate is about 3 to 4 mm/year rise. The line of zero uplift runs through northern Denmark, extreme southern Sweden and southern Latvia. The uplift is greatest in the zone where ice thickness was at a maximum. Here the previous uplift has also been greatest, amounting to an uplift of 120 m since the time of the Littorina Sea, by which time the rate of uplift was beginning to slow down. Thus the shorelines of earlier stages become increasingly warped up towards the centre of glaciation as they become older.

The rate of uplift at any one stage can be conveniently shown by constructing the isobases of that particular stage on a map, which will indicate the pattern of isostatic recovery since that time. By this method the centre of uplift of a glaciated area can be located, if this cannot be done by other means. For example, the work of Donner on the raised beaches of Scotland has suggested that the centre of isostatic uplift, and hence probably of the thickest ice, is in the neighbourhood of Callander on the Highland margin. The work of Ives and Andrews in north-west Baffin Island has shown that the marine limit slopes down inland, thus suggesting that ice thickness was greatest in Foxe Basin, a long way west of the present remnant of the ice-sheet, the Barnes Ice cap. Evidence of erratics supports the conclusion that Foxe Basin was a centre from which ice dispersed in all directions at one stage of the glaciation.

Crustal downwarping can be studied by examining the deposits of the shore zone. Submerged forests supply useful data, as these can often be accurately dated by carbon-14. An example of the use of this method is the work of Harrison and Lyon (1963) on the coast of New England. They have established the date of three drowned forests whose level relative to modern sea-level can be established. Then, by allowing for the eustatic rise of sea-level that was taking place during the period under consideration, 4500 to 3000 B.P., the crustal warping of this stretch of coast could be evaluated. The results showed that part of the coast has been stable for most of the period, but Nova Scotia showed first downwarping at 2·6 ft/century, then upwarping at 4 ft/century, and finally renewed downwarping. Thus detailed work has shown that crustal warping can be of very local occurrence in the recent past, with two areas quite close to one another moving at different rates or in different directions. Areas of deltaic sedimentation, such as the Mississippi, have shown marked downwarping, in contrast to the uplift of the previously glaciated areas.

d) *Volcanic processes.* Volcanic activity is one of the most violent mani-festations of endogenetic forces to affect the surface of the earth directly, and the study of the actual processes of volcanic eruption is the work of the volcanologist and not of the geomorphologist. However, the geomorphologist is interested in the volcanic features as landscape forms, and from this point of view must know something of the nature of the eruption and the products that build up the volcano. These features may vary from the very nearly perfect concave cones, such as Mount Egmont and Fujiyama, although both have their symmetry spoilt by parasitic cones, to the great spreads of plateau basalt or acid ignimbrite, and the steep cones of acid lava.

Volcanoes provide a useful means of assessing the rate of geomorphological erosion, in that the volcano is often formed very quickly from the geological point of view and its subsequent dissection can be studied closely. Where a volcano has grown up very recently, for example Paricutin in Mexico, it provides a well defined starting point from which the action of processes of erosion may be dated and their rate studied. Paricutin was born in February 1943 and reached a height of 410 m in 1952 when eruptions suddenly ceased. This provides a known datum from which to follow its dissection. However, other volcanoes in the district, which must be post-glacial, show little effect of erosion yet.

The work done in analysing the landscape of the Banks Peninsula in the South Island of New Zealand is a good example of the study of volcanic scenery. These hills still show clear evidence of their volcanic origin. Although they are now only about 3000 feet high, their original height has been assessed at about 10,000 feet. The hill group consists of two large interlocking volcanic piles; there are two centres, from which lava flows emanated to give the elliptical form to the hill group as shown on figure 3.23. The centres of the volcanoes have been eroded out to form two large erosion calderas, from the

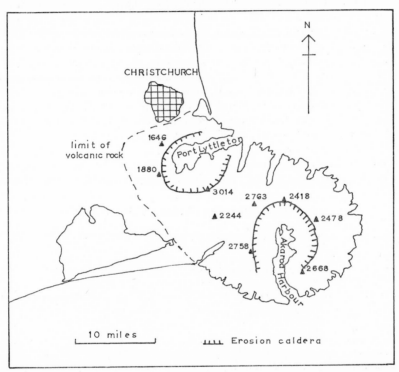

FIGURE 3.23. Map of Banks Peninsula, New Zealand, to show the position of the two erosion calderas and the effect of subsidence in drowning the coastline to form Port Lyttleton and Akaroa Harbour.

crest of which the original lava slope still forms part of the landscape; these remnants have the shape of a flat-iron, and have been called 'planezes'. They form as a result of the radial drainage; the interfluves between the streams get wider away from the caldera, leaving the triangular remnant of the original surface pointing up the slope. Probably because of the large amount of material erupted through the central vents, the area has since subsided, and the sea has flooded into the erosion calderas. Not all the height reduction has been caused by erosion, therefore, but some is accounted for by the subsidence of the foundations of the volcanoes.

The lahars that occur on the flanks of Mount Egmont in the North Island are interesting minor volcanic forms. This volcano has only very recently become inactive, and during one of the latest eruptions material was thrown out of the volcano and its deposition was accompanied either by very heavy rain, or more likely, the melting of the snow cover, or draining of a crater lake. The resulting deposit looks superficially very like a coarse, blocky moraine landscape, as it is formed of uneven hillocks in which are incorporated large blocks of rock. The deposits, on close inspection, can be differentiated by the lack of foreign material in the lahar and the non-striated nature of the boulders, while its position in relation to the volcano is another factor, which may not be diagnostic as many volcanoes carry small ice-caps.

Volcanicity may provide a useful means of dating some landscape features; for example, when the volcanic material rests on an erosion surface. The Napak volcanic rocks in Karamoja, north-east Uganda, are associated with a site of fossil mammalian fauna. The fossils rest on an erosion surface and are covered by volcanic material and incorporated within it. The fossils have strong affinities with the Miocene period and could be older; thus the volcanic material is dated and the erosion surface on which it rests must clearly be older (Bishop, 1962).

Volcanic landforms add interest to many geomorphological problems and their volcanic character must be considered when these regions are studied.

REFERENCES

PART I

BLENCH, T. 1957. *Regime behaviour of canals and rivers.* 138 pp. London.

COLBY, B. R. 1961. Effect of depth of flow on discharge of bed material. *U.S. Geol. Surv. Water-supply paper* 1498 D, 1-10.

DANIELS, R. B. 1960. Entrenchment of the Willow drainage dirch, Harrison County, Iowa. *Amer. Journ, Sci.* 258, 161-176.

DURY, G. H. 1958. Tests of a general theory of misfit streams. *Inst. Brit. Geog.* 25, 105-118.

DURY, G. H. 1961. Bankfull discharge: an example of its statistical relationships. *Int. Assoc. Sci. Hydrol.,* 6th Year. *U.S. Geol. Surv.* 3, 48-55.

EINSTEIN, H. A. 1944. Bed-load transportation in Mountain Creek. *U.S. Soil. Conserv. Paper* SC S—TP 55. 47 pp.

HUBBELL, D. W. 1963. Apparatus and techniques for measuring bed load. *U.S. Geol. Surv. Water-supply paper* 1748.

HJULSTRØM, F. 1935. Studies in the morphological activity of Rivers. *Bull. Geol. Inst. Upsala.* 25, 297.

INGLIS, C. C. 1949. The behaviour and control of Rivers and Canals. *Res. Publ. Central Board Irrig. India,* no. 13, 2 vols.

LACEY, G. 1946. A general theory of flow in alluvium. *Journ. Inst. Civ. Eng.* Paper 5518, 27, 16-47.

LEOPOLD, L. B., WOLMAN, M. G. and MILLER, J. P. 1964. *Fluvial processes in Geomorphology.*

NELSON, M. E. and BENEDICT, P. C. 1951. Measurement and analysis of suspended loads in streams. *Trans. Amer. Soc. Civ. Eng.* pap. 2450, 116, 891-918.

NIXON, M. 1959. A study of the bankfull discharge of rivers in England and Wales. *Proc. Inst. Civ. Eng.* 12, 157-174.

ØSTREM, G. 1964. A method of measuring water discharge in turbulent streams. *Geog. Bull.* 21, 21-43.

SCHUMM, S. A. 1963. Sinuosity of alluvial rivers on the Great Plains. *Bull. Geol. Soc. Amer.* 74, 1089-1100.

WOLMAN, M. G. 1959. Factors influencing erosion of a cohesive river bank. *Amer. Journ. Sci.* 257, 204-216.

WOLMAN. M. G. and MILLER, J. P. 1960. Magnitude and frequency of forces in geomorphic processes. *Journ. Geol.* 68, 54-74.

WOLMAN, M. G. 1954. A method of sampling coarse river-bed materials. *Trans. Amer. Geoph. Un.* 35, 951-956.

WOLMAN, M. G. and LEOPOLD, L. B. 1957. River flood plains. *U.S. Geol. Surv. Prof. Paper 282 C.*

PART 2

AHLMANN, H. W. 1948. Glaciological research on the north Atlantic coasts. *Roy. Geog. Soc. Research Series* 1. 83 pp.

ANDREWS, J. T. 1963. Cross-valley moraines of North Central Baffin Island: a quantitative analysis. *Geog. Bull.* 20, 82-129.

BATTLE, W. R. B. 1960. *Norwegian cirque glaciers.* Ed. W. V. Lewis. Chap. 8, Temperature observations in Bergschrunds and their relationship to frost shattering, 83-95.

Glaciological Society Glacial research sub-committee. *Tech. Note* no. 1.

GLEN, J. W. 1956. Measurement of the deformation of ice in a tunnel at the foot of an icefall. *Journ. Glaciol.* 2, 735-745.

GLEN, J. W. and LEWIS, W. V. 1959. Measurements of side-slip at Austerdalsbreen. *Journ. Glaciol.* 3, 1109-1122.

GROVE, J. M. 1960. *Norwegian cirque glaciers.* Ed. W. V. Lewis. Chap. 3, The bands and layers of Vesl-skautbreen, 11-23.

HARRISON. P. W. 1957. A clay-till fabric: its character and origin. *Journ. Geol.* 65, 275-308.

HARRISON, P. W. 1957. New technique for three-dimensional fabric analysis of till and englacial debris containing particles from 3 to 40 mm. in size. *Journ. Geol.* 65, 98-105.

KAMB, B. and LA CHAPELLE, E. 1964. Direct observation of the mechanism of glacier sliding over bedrock. *Journ. Glaciol.* 5, 159-172.

LEWIS, W. V. 1949. An esker in process of formation, Boverbreen, Jotunheim, 1947. *Journ. Glaciol.* 1, 314-319.

LEWIS, W. V. (Editor) 1960. Norwegian cirque glaciers. *Roy. Geog. Soc. Res. Series.* 4, 104 pp.

McCALL, J. G. 1960. *Norwegian cirque glaciers.* Ed. W. V. Lewis. Chap. 5, The flow characteristics of cirque glaciers and their effect on glacial structure and cirque formation, 39-62.

MEIER, M. 1962. Proposed definitions for glacier mass budget terms. *Journ. Glaciol.* 4, 252-261.

MELLOR, M. 1958. Photogrammetric flow measurements on Antarctic Glaciers. *Trans. Amer. Geoph. Un.* 39, 1158.

MILLER, M. M. 1958. Phenomena associated with the deformation of a glacier borehole. I.G.G.U. *Ass. d'Hydrog. Sci. Toronto* 4, 437-452.

NYE, J. F. 1957. The distribution of stress and velocity in glaciers and ice-sheets. *Proc. Roy. Soc.* A 239, 113-133.

NYE, J. F. 1958. A theory of wave formation in glaciers. U.G.G.I. *Ass. Int. d'Hydrol. Sci. Chamonix* 139-154.

NYE, J. F. 1959a. A method of determining the strain-rate tensor at the surface of a glacier. *Journ. Glaciol.* 3, 409-419.

NYE, J. F. 1959b. The deformation of a glacier below an ice-fall. *Journ. Glaciol.* 3, 386-408.

NYE, J. F. 1960. The response of glaciers and ice-sheets to seasonal and climatic changes. *Proc. Roy. Soc.* A 256, 559-584.

NYE, J. F. 1963. The response of a glacier to changes in the rate of nourishment and wastage. *Proc. Roy. Soc.* A 275, 87-112.

ØSTREM, G. 1961. A new approach to end moraine chronology. *Geogr. Ann.* 43, 422-423.

ØSTREM, G. 1963. Nigardsbreen Hydrologi, 1962. *Norsk. Geog. Tidskr.* 18, 156-202.

SHREVE, R. L. 1962. Theory of performance of isothermal solid nose hot-points boring in temperate ice. *Journ. Glaciol.* 4, 151-160.

SHREVE, R. L. and KAMB, W. B. 1964. Instruments and methods, portable thermal core drill for temperate glaciers. *Journ. Glaciol.* 5, 113-117.

WARD, W. H. 1958. Surface markers for ice movement studies. *U.G.G.I. Ass. Int. d'Hydrol. Sci. Chamonix* 105-110.

WEERTMAN, J. 1964. The theory of glacier sliding. *Journ. Glaciol.* 5, 287-304.

PART 3

ANDREWS, J. T. 1961. 'Vallons de gelivation' in Central Labrador-Ungava; a reappraisal. *Canadian Geog.* 5, 1-9.

ANDREWS, J. T. 1963. The analysis of frost-heave data collected by R. H. J. Haywood from Schefferville, Labrador-Ungava. *Canad. Geog.* 7, 163-174.

BLACK, R. F. 1964. Periglacial studies in the United States, 1959-1963. *Biul. Periglac.* 14, 5-30.

CORTE, A. E. 1962. Vertical migration of particles in front of a moving freezing plane. *Journ. Geoph. Res.* 67, 1085-1090.

CORTE, A. E. 1963. Particle sorting by repeated freezing and thawing. *Science* 142, 499-501.

COSTIN, A. B., JENNINGS, J. N., BLACK, H. P. and THOM, B. G. 1964. Snow action on Mount Twynam, Snowy Mountains, Australia. *Journ. Glaciol.* 5, 219-228.

DIMBLEBY, G. W. 1952. Pleistocene ice wedges in north-east Yorkshire. *Journ. Soil Sci.* 3, 1-19.

FITZPATRICK, E. A. 1958. An introduction to the periglacial geomorphology of Scotland. *Scot. Geog. Mag.* 74, 28-36.

FITZPATRICK, E. A. 1960. Geomorphic notes from West Spitzbergen. *Biul. Periglac.* 7, 159-164.

IVES, J. D. 1962. Iron mining in permafrost, Central Labrador-Ungava: A geographical review. *Geog. Bull.* 17, 66-77.

KELLAWAY, G. A. and TAYLOR, J. H. 1953. Early stages in the physiographic evolution of a portion of the East Midlands. *Quart. Journ. Geol. Soc.* 108, 343-376.

LACHENBRUCH, A. H. 1961. Thermal contraction cracks and ice wedges in permafrost. *U.S. Geol. Surv. Prof. Paper* 400 B, 404-406.

LEWIS, W. V. 1939. Snow patch erosion in Iceland. *Geog. Journ.* 94, 153-161.

MILLER, R., COMMON, R. and GALLOWAY, R. W. 1954. Stone stripes and other surface features of the Tinto Hills. *Geog. Journ.* 120, 216-219.

PATTERSON, T. T. 1940. The effects of frost action and solifluction around Baffin Bay and the Cambridge district. *Quart. Journ. Geol. Soc.* 96, 99-130.

PÉWÉ, T. L. 1962. Age of moraines in Victoria Land, Antarctica. *Journ. Glaciol.* 4, 93-100.

PÉWÉ, T. L. 1963. Ice wedges in Alaska,—classification, distribution and climatic significance. *Abst. Geol. Soc. Amer. Sp. Pap.*

PISSART, A. 1964a. Vitesses des mouvements du sol au Chambeyron, Basses Alpes. *Biul. Perigl.* 14, 303-310.

PISSART, A. 1964b. Advancement des recherches periglaciaires en Belgique de 1956 à 1963. *Biul. Perigl.* 14, 67-74.

POULIN, A. O. 1962. Measurement of frost formed soil patterns using airphoto techniques. *Photogram. Eng.* 28, 141-147.

RAPP, A. 1959. Avalanches boulder tongues in Lappland, description of little-known forms of periglacial debris accumulation. *Geogr. Ann.* 41, 34-48.

RAPP, A. 1960. Recent development of mountain slopes in Karkevagge and surroundings, North Scandinavia. *Geogr. Ann.* 42, 65-200.

SHOTTON, F. W. 1960. Large scale patterned ground in the valley of the Worcestershire Avon. *Geol. Mag.* 97, 404-408.

SMITH, J. 1960. Cryoturbation data from South Georgia. *Biul. Perigl.* 8, 73-79.

TABER, A. 1943. Perennially frozen ground in Alaska: its origin and history. *Bull. Geol. Soc. Amer.* 54, 1433-1548.

WASHBURN, A. L. 1956. Classification of patterned ground and review of suggested origins. *Bull. Geol. Soc. Amer.* 67, 823-866.

WILLIAMS, R. B. G. 1964. Fossil patterned ground in eastern England. *Biul. Perigl.* 14, 337-349.

PART 4

ANDREWS, J. T. 1961. The development of scree slopes in the English Lake District and central Quebec-Labrador. *Cahiers de Geog. de Quebec* 5, 219-230.

BLACKWELDER, E. 1928. Mudflow as a geological agent in semiarid mountains. *Bull. Geol. Soc. Amer.* 39, 465-484.

COTTON, C. A. and TE PUNGA, M. T. 1955. Solifluxion and periglacially modified landforms at Wellington, New Zealand. *Trans. Roy. Soc. N.Z.* 82, 1001-1031.

JOYCE, J. R. F. 1950. Stone runs of the Falkland Islands. *Geol. Mag.* 87, 105-115.

KING, C. A. M. and HIRST, R. A. 1964. The Boulder-Fields of the Åland Islands. *Fennia* 89, 5-41.

PARIZEK, E. J. and WOODRUFF, J. F. 1957. Mass wasting and the deformation of trees. *Amer. Journ. Sci.* 255, 63-70.

RAPP, A. 1960a. Talus slopes and mountain walls at Templefjorden, Spitzbergen. *Norsk. Polar. Skrift.* 119. 96 pp.

RAPP, A. 1960b. Recent development of mountain slopes in Karkevagge and surroundings in North Scandinavia. *Geogr. Ann.* 42, 65-200.

SMITH, H. T. U. 1953. The Hickory Run boulder field. *Amer. Journ. Sci.* 251, 625-642.

STEVENS, G. R. 1957. Solifluxion in the Lower Hutt area. *N.Z. Journ. Sci. Tech.* B 38, 279-296.

WARD, W. H. 1945. The stability of natural slopes. *Geog. Journ.* 105, 170-197.

WILLIAMS, P. J. 1957. The direct recording of solifluction movements. *Amer. Journ. Sci.* 255, 705-715.

WILLIAMS, P. J. 1957. Some investigations into solifluction features in Norway. *Geog. Journ.* 123, 42-58.

YOUNG, A. 1960. Soil movement by denudational processes on slopes. *Nature* 188 (4745), 120-122.

PART 5

BAGNOLD, R. A. 1954. *The physics of blown sand and desert dunes.* London.

HORIKAWA, K. and SHEN, H. W. 1960. Sand movement by wind action—on the characteristics of sand. *B.E.B. Tech. Memo.* 119. 51 pp. Washington.

JENNINGS, J. N. 1957. On the orientation of parabolic or U-dunes *Geog. Journ.* 123, 474-480.

LANDSBERG, S. Y. 1956. The orientation of dunes in Britain and Denmark in relation to the wind. *Geog. Journ.* 122, 176-189.

PART 6

BAAK, J. A. 1936. *Regional petrology of the southern North Sea.*

Beach Erosion Board, Washington 1933. *Interim Report.*

BRADLEY, W. C. 1958. Submarine abrasion and wave-cut platforms. *Bull. Geol. Soc. Amer.* 69, 967-974.

CARRUTHERS, J. N. 1961. A simple current measuring bottle for fishermen. *Fishing News* 1961, 2-4.

CARRUTHERS, J. N. 1962. The easy measurement of the bottom currents at modest depths. *Civil. Eng.* 57, 484.

CARRUTHERS, J. N. 1963. History, sand waves and near-bed currents of La Chapelle Bank. *Nature* 197, 942-946.

CLOET, R. L. 1963. Hydrographic analysis of the sandbanks in the approaches to Lowestoft harbour. *Ad. Marine Sci. Pub.* 6.

DARBYSHIRE, M. 1958. Waves in the Irish Sea. *Dock and Harbour Auth.* 39, 245-248.

DARBYSHIRE, J. 1961. Prediction of wave characteristics over the North Atlantic. *Journ. Inst. Navig.* 14, 339-347.

DAVIES, J. L. 1959. Wave refraction and the evolution of shoreline curves. *Geog. Studies* 5, 1-14.

DOODSON, A. T. and WARBURG, H. D. 1941. *Admiralty Manual of Tides.* H.M.S.O.

ERICSON, D. E., EWING, M., WOLLIN, G. and HEEZEN, B. C. 1961. Atlantic deep sea sediment cores. *Bull. Geol. Soc. Amer.* 72, 193-286.

HEEZEN, B. C. 1963. Chap. 27, Turbidity currents, in vol. III *The Sea.* ed. M. N. Hill, 742-775. New York.

HEEZEN, B. C. and MENARD, H. W. 1963. Chap. 12, Topography of the Deep Sea floor, in vol. III *The Sea.* ed M. N. Hill, 233-280.

INMAN, D. L. 1957. Wave generated ripples in nearshore sand. B.E.B. *Tech. Memo.* 100. Washington.

INMAN, D. L. and NASU, N. 1956. Orbital velocity associated with wave action near the breaker zone. B.E.B. *Tech. Memo.* 79. 41 pp. Washington.

INMAN, D. L. and Rusnak, G. A. 1956. Changes in level on the beach and shelf at La Jolla, California. B.E.B. *Tech. Memo.* 82. Washington.

INMAN, D. L. and CHAMBERLAIN, T. K. 1959. Tracing beach sand movement with irradiated quartz. *Journ. Geophys. Res.* 64, 41-47.

JOHNSON. J. W. 1953. Sand transport by littoral currents. *Proc. 5th Hydraul. Conf.* 89-109.

JOLLIFFE, I. P. 1964. An experiment designed to compare the relative rates of movement of different sizes of beach pebble. *Proc. Geol. Assoc.* 75, 67-86

KAMEL, A. M. 1962. Littoral studies near San Fransisco using tracer techniques. B.E.B. *Tech. Memo.* 131. Washington.

KIDSON, C., CARR, A. P. and SMITH, D. E. 1958. Further experiments using radioactive methods to detect the movement of shingle over the sea bed and alongshore. *Geog. Journ.* 124, 210-218.

KIDSON, C. and CARR, A. P. 1961. Beach drift experiments at Bridgwater Bay, Somerset. *Proc. Bristol Nat. Soc.* 30, 163-180.

KIDSON, C. and CARR, A. P. 1962. Marking beach materials for tracing experiments. *Journ. Hydraul. Div. Proc. Amer. Soc. Civ. Eng.* 4, 43-60.

KING, C. A. M. 1951. The depth of disturbance of sand on sea beaches by waves. *Journ. Sed. Petrol.* 21, 131-140.

KING, C. A. M. 1953. The relationship between wave incidence, wind direction and beach changes at Marsden Bay, Co. Durham. *Inst. Brit. Geog.* 19, 13-23.

KING, C. A. M. and BARNES, F. A. 1964. Changes in the configuration of the intertidal beach zone of part of the Lincolnshire coast since 1951. *Zeit. für Geomorph.* N.F. 8, 105*-126*, Sonderheft.

KUENEN, P. H. 1952. Estimated size of the Grand Banks turbidity current. *Amer. Journ. Sci.* 250, 874-884.

KUENEN, P. H. 1956. The difference between sliding and turbidity flow. *Deep Sea Res.* 3, 134-139.

LONGUET-HIGGINS, M. S. 1953. Mass transport in water waves. *Phil. Trans. Roy. Soc.* A 245, 535-581.

McKENZIE, P. 1958. Rip current systems. *Journ. Geol.* 66, 103-113.

REID, W. J. and JOLLIFFE, I. P. 1961. Coastal experiments with fluorescent tracers. *Dock and Harbour Auth.* 41, 341-345.

ROBINSON, A. H. W. 1961. The hydrography of Start Bay and its relationship to beach changes. *Geog. Journ.* 127, 63-77.

ROBINSON, A. H. W. 1964. The inshore waters, sediment supply and coastal change of part of Lincolnshire. *East Midland Geog.* 3, 307-321.

ROUVILLE, de A. 1938. Annales des Pont et Chaussées.

RUSSELL, R. C. H. 1961. The use of fluorescent tracers for the measurement of littoral drift. *Proc. 7th Conf. on Coastal Eng.* 418-444.

SHEPARD, F. P. and INMAN. D. L. 1950. Nearshore circulation related to bottom topography and wave refraction. *Trans. Amer. Geoph. Un.* 31, 196-212.

SHEPARD, F. P. 1950. Beach cycles in southern California. B.E.B. *Tech. Memo.* 20, Washington.

STEERS, J. A. and SMITH, D. B. 1956. Detection of movement of pebbles on the sea floor by radioactive methods. *Geog. Journ.* 122, 343-345.

STRIDE, A. H. 1958. Sand transport at the southern end of the North Sea. *Dock and Harbour Auth.* 38, 323-324.

STRIDE, A. H. 1959. A pattern or sediment transport for sea floors around southern Britain. *Dock and Harbour Auth.* 40, 145-147.

STRIDE, A. H. 1963. Current-swept sea floors near the southern half of Great Britain. *Quart. Journ. Geol. Soc.* 119, 175-199.

SWALLOW, J. C. and WORTHINGTON, L. V. 1957. Observations of deep currents in the western North Atlantic. *Nature* 179, 1183-1184.

SWALLOW, J. C. and HAMON, B. V. 1960. Some measurements of deep currents in the eastern North Atlantic. *Deep Sea Res.* 6, 155-168.

SWALLOW, J. C. and WORTHINGTON, L. V. 1961. An observation of a deep counter current in the western North Atlantic. *Deep Sea Res.* 8, 1-19.

TRASK, P. D. 1955. Movement of sand around southern Californian promontories. B.E.B. *Tech. Memo.* 76, Washington.

TUCKER, M. J. 1956. A shipborne wave recorder. *Trans. Inst. Nav. Arch.* 98, 236-250.

TUCKER, M. J. 1962. Analysis of records of sea waves. *Journ. Inst. Civ. Eng.* 26, 305-316.

WATTS, G. M. 1953. Development and tests of a sampler for suspended sediments in wave action. B.E.B. *Tech. Memo.* 34.

PART 7

BISHOP, W. W. 1962. The mammalian fauna and geomorphological relations of the Napak volcanics. *Records of Geol. Surv. Uganda* 1953-58, 1-18.

BLOOM, A. L. 1963. Late-Pleistocene fluctuations of sea level and post-glacial crustal rebound in coastal Maine. *Amer. Journ. Sci.* 261, 862-879.

BOURCART, J. 1950. La théorie de la flexure continentale. *Compte Rendu Inter. Geog. Un.* Lisbon, 16, 167-190.

COTTON, C. A. 1917. Block Mountains in New Zealand. *Amer. Journ. Sci.* 44, 249-293.

DONNER, J. J. 1963. The late and post-glacial raised beaches in Scotland. II. *Ann. Acad. Sci. Fennica A III Geol. Geog.* 68, 5-13.

DOORNKAMP, J. C. and TEMPLE, P. H. 1966. Surface, drainage, and tectonic instability in parts of Southern Uganda. *Geogr. Journal* (in press).

HARRISON, W. and C. J. LYON. 1963. Sea-level and crustal movements along the New England-Acadian shore. *Journ. Geol.* 71, 96-108.

IVES, J. D. and ANDREWS, J. T. 1963. Studies in the physical geography of north-central Baffin Island, N.W.T. *Geog. Bull.* 19, 5-48.

PALLISTER, J. W. 1956. Slope form and erosion surfaces in Uganda. *Geol. Mag.* 93, 465-472.

SAURAMO, M. 1955. Land uplift with hinge lines in Fennoscandia. *Suom. Tied. Toim. Ann. Acad. Sci. Fennica A* 44, 5-25.

STRAW, A. 1961. The erosion surfaces of east Lincolnshire. *Proc. York. Geol. Soc.* 33, 149-172.
TROTTER, F. M. 1929. The Tertiary uplift and resultant drainage of the Alston Block. *Proc. Yorks. Geol. Soc.* 21, 161-180.
WOOLDRIDGE, S. W. and HENDERSON, H. C. K. 1955. Some aspects of the physiography of the eastern part of the London Basin. *Inst. Brit. Geog.* 21, 19-31.
YATES, E. M. 1963. The development of the Rhine. *Inst. Brit. Geog.* 32, 65-81.

4   EXPERIMENT AND THEORY-MODELS

TYPES OF MODELS

The part played by analogy in the formulation of theories to explain geo-morphological phenomena has already been mentioned. In this connection it is useful to consider the application of the methods of study which use models. The term 'model' can imply two very different ways of approaching a problem; this may be attacked by using a conceptual model, relying to a certain extent on the method of analogy, and the theoretical model, using deductive reasoning, or on the other hand the approach may be made by using a scale model. Most of this chapter will be devoted to the geomorpho-logical work that can be done in scale models, but it is worthwhile to con-sider briefly some aspects of the conceptual and theoretical models.

The setting up of a conceptual model is often basic to the development of a theory. The behaviour of the model must correspond in a certain degree with the object of study, but it cannot, of course, be completely similar. The properties of the model that are known to behave in a similar way to those of the prototype may be called the positive analogy, while those that are known to differ may be termed the negative analogy; there remain the un-known properties, that may be called the neutral analogy. It is possible by analogy with the model to predict the behaviour of the prototype, which is one of the main points to be satisfied in testing theories.

A good example of this type of model, and its use in developing and testing theories, is Nye's (1960) work on the effect of climatic change on glacier length and behaviour. His analysis was based on the theory of kinematic waves, developed by Lighthill and Whitman to study the movement of flood waves in rivers, the flow of traffic on roads, and similar problems re-lated to group velocity phenomena. Thus the kinematic wave theory has certain properties that allow valid analogies to be made with greatly varying factors, such as those listed; it provides a theory, based on a model, that can then be tested. This can be done in the case of glaciers by studying the glacier budget and measuring the variations in the length and volume of the glacier.

In testing the theory certain simplifying assumptions must be made be-cause of the complexity of most natural phenomena, but the theory deter-mines which are the most important variables affecting the issue. If the correspondence between the observed results and the predicted changes is not close, then it may be assumed that some important variable has been omitted from the model. Its inclusion in the model will modify the theory and the next testing may provide a more reliable result, as far as correspondence with prediction is concerned. Hence the second modified theory, using the modified model, will be better than the first.

Krumbein (1961) has discussed the setting up of a conceptual physical or mathematical model for the study of beach phenomena in nature. The model specifies the physical processes occurring along the beach and, using these processes, attempts to deduce the resultant features. The main problem is that there are so many physical processes operating on a large number of variables. However, the advantage of setting up this type of theoretical model is that it enables a reasonable choice of variables to be made for observation. Such a choice can conveniently be based on a division of the variables into two groups. These groups consist, firstly, of the process model, which should include features that can be differentiated from the second, the response model. The two groups can be considered in the formula

$$F\left(p,\ G,\ P,\ S,\ T\right)\ =\ \mathrm{o},$$

where p represents the physical, chemical and mineralogical properties of the beach sediment, p_1, p_2, etc., G represents the geometrical properties of the beach as a three-dimensional body, such as width, slope and such factors. P represents individual shore processes, such as waves, tides etc., S represents geographical co-ordinates along the beach S_1, and S_2, and elevation S_3, while T is the time factor. The process model includes the factors P, S and T, which are the factors that produce the change in the other group, called the response model. Thus the equation can be expressed as

$$\left(p,\ G\right)\ =f\left(P,\ S,\ T\right).$$

The response elements are on the left and the process elements on the right. This connection is not such that the two sides cannot, to a certain extent, influence each other. However, on the whole the process elements are the independent variables and the response elements are the dependent variables.

It is clear that this same principle can also be applied to other phenomena, such as rivers and slopes, all of which depend on a large number of variables in each group; both response and process factors are numerous and involved. This complexity causes the major problem in analysing geomorphological features on the basis of field work, even if a good conceptual model is used as a basis for the observations and their analysis. Because of the large number of variables involved it is difficult to assess the true effect of any one variable. In fact there may be a connection between two apparently unrelated variables as a result of the particular situation of the area. For example, wave height and wave length may not be unrelated on any one beach, on account of the characteristics of the exposure of the area to wave attack; thus on this particular beach it would not be easy to study the effect of different wave steepnesses on the nature of the beach profile, for example, because certain critical steepness values may never occur under natural conditions.

Another type of model is the theoretical model of slope development, which can be deduced on the basis of specific assumptions; such models have been developed by W. Penck, by Bakker and Le Heux, and more recently by A. Young (1963). The latter may be taken as an example of this type of model, in which the theoretical development of slopes is worked out step by step assuming different sets of controls in the various models considered. Young's slope models have been constructed on the basis of the operation of different processes on the slope. The first model assumes that transportation of material down the slope is proportional to the slope angle; movement of this type probably takes place in soil creep. The second model assumes downslope transportation varying with the slope angle and with the distance from the crest of the slope, such as the process of slope wash in nature. The third process considered is the direct removal of weathered material without transportation to the base of the slope; this is achieved mainly by solution. The slope models show how slopes will develop under the operation of these different processes on the assumption, firstly, that the material is removed from the foot of the slope, and secondly, that river incision is taking place at the base of the slope. The method of calculation is by successive approximation, giving a series of stages of development on the slope.

The results of this deductive model analysis suggested that processes involving downslope soil transportation will tend to cause slope decline, while processes of direct removal will tend to cause parallel slope retreat; the processes of direct removal will tend to operate more rapidly than those of transportation, if the rates observed in the field, for example those discussed in chapter 3, are substituted in the equations. This method of slope analysis forms a useful link between field studies of processes operating on slopes, discussed in chapter 3, and the field studies of slope form by profile surveying and regolith analysis, described in chapter 2. Theory can both use field observations and direct them; field observations can be used to substitute values in the theoretical equations to arrive at the deduced rates of development and these in turn can be checked in the field.

In one model for a rate of transport of 0·5 cm³/cm/year for a slope 10 m high, assuming that the slope is rectilinear at an angle of 35 degrees, with level ground above and below, and no erosion at the foot of the slope but unimpeded removal from the base, and that the rate of removal varies with the sine of the slope angle, the time taken to reach the final profile calculated would be 1½ million years; for a slope 100 m high the time would be 150 million years. In a second model with direct removal, however, assuming a rate of 0·02 cm/year, the time would be 25,000 years for a 10-m slope and 100,000 years for a 100-m slope. Other assumptions made are similar to those for the first model slope, except that the direct removal acts uniformly on all slopes greater than zero degrees and that no transportation takes place on the slope. The change in the second model would take place by parallel retreat and in the first by slope flattening. In this way theoretical concepts can be used to direct the measurement of actual slopes and the study of processes acting on them in the field. This type of model is clearly very different from the scale models discussed in the rest of the chapter, but it is a useful approach to a problem.

SCALE MODELS

To overcome the problem of the large number of uncontrollable variables that are involved in any process and its effect on the natural landforms, scale models may be used. They have the advantage that the variables may be controlled and the initial conditions may be set up as required, but they have the serious disadvantage of the scale problem. The results of model experiments will be of relatively little value unless they can be related to the effect of similar conditions in the prototype. The scale factors, therefore, are very important, and before discussing the types of problems that can be investigated by the use of models it is necessary to consider briefly some of the scale relationships that must be fulfilled in the model experiments.

In order to relate the model to the prototype, the model must be undistorted and the similarity must be maintained as far as possible between the geometrical, kinematic and dynamic dimensions of the model and prototype. If the model is undistorted geometrically, it can readily be shown that the co-ordinates of a point in the model and the prototype will bear a direct linear relationship to each other; X/X' will equal $\Upsilon/\Upsilon' = A$, where A is the length ratio and is a constant. The time scale is important in establishing the kinematic similarity of model and prototype; in the model a point takes time t to travel from X to Υ, and in the prototype the time taken to travel from X' to Υ' is t'. The ratio t/t' may be called B and is the time ratio. The velocity ratio can be called C and will equal V/V'; this is equal to

$$\frac{X\Upsilon}{t} \bigg/ \frac{X'\Upsilon'}{t'} = A\, t' \,/\, t;$$

now V/V' is equal to A/B. The acceleration ratio is equal to $A\,/\,B^2$. In considering the dynamic similarity the ratio of forces must be considered. Taking, for example, inertia and gravity, the inertia in nature on a particle of volume Q' is $Q'\,r'\,a'$, where A' is the acceleration and r' is the density. The inertia in the model is $Q\,r\,a$. The ratio of forces, Fi is $Q\,r\,a\ /\ Q'\,r'\,a'$, $Q/Q' = A^3$, and $a\,/\,a' = A\,/B^2$. Taking the density ratio as R, then

$$Fi = \frac{R\,A^3 \times A}{B^2};$$

this equals $\dfrac{R\,A^4}{B^2}$. R is 1 if the fluids are the same in the model and the prototype. Considering gravity, which is the same in the model and prototype the same formula applies, $Q\,r\,a\ /\ Q'\,r'\,a'$ equalling Fg, and $Fg = R\,A^3 \times 1$, owing to gravity having the same value in both model and nature. The same ratio of forces must hold for gravity and inertia, therefore $Fi = Fg$, and if $R = 1$, $A^4/B^2 = A^3$ and $A/B^2 = 1$, so $A = B^2$. The ratio of velocities C is equal to $A\,/\,B$, therefore C equals B. From this Froude's law is derived; this states that

$A = B^2 = C^2$, showing that the time and velocity scale are equal to the square root of the linear scale.

Allen (1947) has shown that because of the square factor in the velocity scale it is often not possible to use the correct corresponding speed, this term implying the actual speeds at which similarity exists between model and prototype. He shows that it is impracticable to ensure that the forces caused by a number of different effects should all be in the correct ratio to each other at the same time. In considering the problem of corresponding speeds it is useful to take into account the principle of dimensional homogeneity. This means that all the terms of a true physical equation should possess the same units of mass, length and time, denoted by M, L, and T. Taking, for example, the factors on which the beach slope, i, depends, they can be given as h, l, p, v, d, u, s, E, g; their dimensions are as follows:

i beach slope, dimensionless
h wave height, L feet
l wave length, L feet
p wave period, T seconds
v settling velocity LT^{-1} feet/second
d density, ML^{-3} lb/cubic foot
u viscosity, $ML^{-1} T^{-1}$ lb/feet/second
s median diameter of sand, L feet
E wave energy, $M L^2 T^{-2}$ foot-lb
g acceleration of gravity, $L T^{-2}$ feet/second/second

Taking E, l and v, as they include all three units of mass, length and time, dimensionless equations can be solved for the other variables in turn, giving six dimensionless ratios:

$$i = f\left(\frac{h}{l}, \frac{vp}{l}, \frac{v^2 l^3 d}{E}, \frac{l^2 v u}{E}, \frac{s}{l}, \frac{l g}{v^2}\right).$$

These ratios then give the factors on which the beach slope should depend, and if these variables are used in the model tank, the fact that they consist of dimensionless ratios will help to reduce the scale problems and allow closer correspondence. Thus the beach slope may be related to the wave steepness h/l, and this can be varied by changing either h or l in the experimental wave tank.

The range of problems that can be studied in model conditions is large, including the investigation of wind action in a wind tunnel, fluvial flow in a stream trough, wave action, in two or three dimensions; tidal action can be studied in estuaries, including both wave and tide variations as well as river flow. Other more specialised models include those of glaciers and turbidity currents. The models can be used to test fundamental physical relationships that have been established by theoretical and mathematical reasoning. For example it is possible to calculate theoretically the movement of grains of sediment under different conditions by using the fundamental physical relationships between the particles and the forces acting upon them. These theoretical values can then be tested in the controlled conditions of the model tank, and, using the model laws for relating these values to natural conditions, estimates can be made of the probable values of the same factors in nature. These can then be checked by field work. Alternatively, empirical relationships may be set up as the result of field work, but there may be some doubt as to the part played by the different variables in the field in producing the relationships; this doubt may be resolved by use of controlled experiments in the model.

SCALE MODELS OF DIFFERENT PROCESSES

a) *Wind action.* In considering the movement of sediment by wind, it is necessary to consider first the character of the wind, from the point of view of model similarity. Osborne Reynolds has developed the fundamental connection between the wind in the model and the prototype in terms of the Reynolds' number, *Re*. If the size of the model is *l*, and the velocity of flow is *V* and the state of the fluid can be determined by the kinematic viscosity, *v*, then the movement of the fluids will be comparable and pressures will remain unchanged if *l V* / *v* remains equal to a constant number, called the Reynolds' number, *Re*. The value of *v* in air is 0·14 in C.G.S. units, but varies somewhat with temperature and pressure. It is important to know for model conditions when the air becomes turbulent in its flow characteristics; this occurs when *Re* exceeds about 1400. In a model tank, where *l* = 30 cm, the wind is turbulent at speeds over 7 cm/sec, or when *l* × *V* exceeds 1400 × 0·14. For the atmosphere Brunt gives the value for turbulent flow as 1 m/sec. In calculating the movement of sand by wind in the model tank and in nature, the drag velocity V^* is an important value. The drag velocity is equal to the velocity gradient perpendicular to the surface; this is the change of wind speed with height. The drag velocity V^* is equal to $\dfrac{\sqrt{\tau}}{\rho}$, where τ is the drag per sq.cm and ρ is the density of the fluid; under normal conditions this is $1·22 \times 10^{-3}$ grams/cm³. The value of V^* is directly proportional to the rate of increase of the wind velocity with the logarithm of the height (Bagnold, 1941). The value of the velocity gradient changes as soon as sand is picked up by the wind and V^* must become V'^*, which is the drag velocity when sand is being moved by the wind. Bagnold, as a result of his wind tunnel experiments, was able to show that the wind velocity at a height of 3 mm above the surface always remained the same, regardless of the wind speed and vertical gradient. In fact with a higher wind speed the velocity close to the surface actually decreased. Bagnold has established experimentally the basic relationships between the wind and the movement of sand caused by it. One of the important relationships that he set up was the amount of sand moved, *q*, in relations to the strength of the wind and the character of the sand; he gives

$$q = C\sqrt{\frac{d}{D}\frac{\rho}{g}}\ V'^{*3},$$

where q is the total sand flow, C is an empirical co-efficient, d is the grain diameter of the sand under consideration and D is the grain diameter of the standard 0·25 mm sand, and g is gravity. C is equal to 1·5 for nearly uniform sand, 1·8 for naturally sorted sand and 2·8 for poorly sorted sand, $\frac{\rho}{g}$ is 1·25 × 10^{-6} in C.G.S. units. The sand flow varies also as the cube of the excess wind velocity above the threshold velocity Vt, the wind velocity being measured at 1 m above the ground surface.

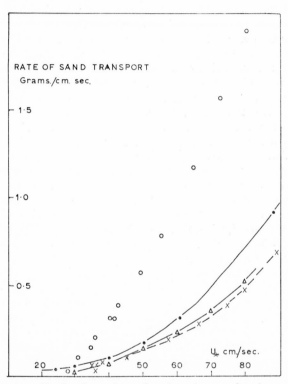

FIGURE 4.1. Results of experimental work on the rate of sand transport for different workers, using sand of grain diameter 0·25 mm. U_* is the shear velocity of the wind. Circles refer to the results of Kawamura, dots to those of Bagnold, triangles to those of Zingg and crosses to those of Harikawa. (after Belly C.E.R.C.)

More recent work on sand movement by wind has been reported by Belly (1964), in which some of the theoretical relationships have been tested experimentally. The difficulty of establishing formulae for sand movement is shown by the different experimental results obtained by various workers. It can be seen from figure 4.1 that Bagnold's results are fairly close to those of Zingg and Horikawa, but that Kawamura's are considerably different. The formula derived by Kawamura for the rate of sand transport can be compared with the one already given. Kawamura gives

$$q = k \frac{f}{g} (U^* - U^*t) (U^* + U^*t)^2,$$

where k is a constant, found experimentally to be 2·78, U^* is the shear velocity and U^*t is the threshold shear velocity. Experiments were carried out to test these different formulae and to obtain other basic information concerning sand transport by wind. These studies provide examples of the type of work that can be done under experimental conditions, the equipment that can be used, and the results that are obtained.

The experimental equipment consisted of a wind tunnel 100 feet long, 4 feet wide and 2½ feet high. Wind velocities of 24 to 40 ft/sec could be achieved by the operation of a fan at the exit end. Wind velocities were measured with a pitot tube and sand movement was measured by using the vertical trap, suitable for both field and laboratory work that has been described on p. 131. A horizontal trap was also used; this was 8 feet long, divided into 18 compartments, and was emptied by using a vacuum cleaner. Each run lasted from 5 to 30 minutes. Experiments were made to test the variation of wind velocity due to the side walls, and vertical wind profiles were also investigated. The vertical velocity profiles formed straight lines when plotted on semi-log paper. The focal point was found to be 0·0144 ft, which agrees with Zingg's estimate, but is rather greater than Bagnold's 3 mm being 4·4 mm. The threshold velocity was also established and was found to be lowered with a sand feed-in, falling from 40 cm/sec without sand feed-in to 30 cm/sec with sand feed-in. The lower value agrees well with Bagnold's formula, which gives 34 cm/sec.

The rate of sand transport was also measured experimentally, and again differences were noted between results with and without sand feeding. This changes the amount of sand moved at the lower velocities, but at wind velocities in excess of about 30 ft/sec there was no difference. The results agreed more closely with those of Kawamura than those of Bagnold and Horikawa, possibly because of differences in the sand sizes used, and the fact that Belly's sand was not nearly so well sorted as the other experimental sands. If Bagnold's formula is modified for poorly sorted grain size, the experimental results fit the curve plotted from the formula fairly closely for the maximum rate of sand transport. Kawamura's formula can also be made to fit the experimental result if his constant k is made equal to 3·1. The latter formula fits better than Bagnold's for the lower velocities.

Other experimental results included a study of ripples; these appeared on the sand surface as soon as there was any movement, but disappeared with velocities in excess of about 36 ft/sec. There was no observable correlation between the ripple wave length and the strength of the wind, the length of the ripples varying little from about 3 inches. Another point measured was the average flying distance of the grains. A slow increase of flying distance with increasing wind velocity was noted, the values ranging from about 1·3 ft to about 1·6 ft, with wind velocities increasing from 28 to 35 ft/sec. No correlation could be found between flying distance and ripple wave length, as recorded by Bagnold, on account of the very small variation in ripple wave length. The grain size, however, was found to have a marked effect on the flying distance, there being a particularly rapid increase of flying distance as the grain size was reduced from 0·5 mm, when the wind velocity was 31 ft/sec.

Experiments were also carried out to measure the length of time it took for the sand transport to become adjusted to a new wind speed; two wind speeds of 31½ and 35 ft/sec were used and observations recorded the amount of sand caught after every two minutes. The results of this test showed that the sand bed adjusts itself immediately to the wind velocity, probably within 4 minutes.

The efficiency of the vertical trap was tested by comparison with the horizontal one, which was assumed to have trapped all the sand in transit. The results showed that with wind speeds above 31·5 ft/sec the vertical trap had an efficiency of more than 100%, but that at lower speeds its efficiency was considerably less than 100% and rather variable. Scour round the base of the vertical trap caused loss of sand moving by creep in long experiments. All the experiments were then repeated with a smaller sand size of 0·30 mm, which was much better sorted. The threshold shear velocity was 16 cm/sec, agreeing well with Bagnold's figure, and the rate of transport values no longer showed the change of values at lower velocities, moreover the results agreed well with both Bagnold, using $C = 2·8$ and Kawamura, with $k = 3·1$.

A further set of experiments was then made with very fine sand, having a diameter of 0·145 mm. To enable measurement to be made with lower wind velocities the trap was used partially uncovered. In testing the results of the experiments with Bagnold's and Kawamura's formulae the constants $C = 1·5$ and $k = 1·0$ were used. The results agreed rather more closely with Bagnold's, although many were very slightly smaller.

Other interesting results were obtained by testing the influence of moisture on the threshold of sand movement. In order to measure the effect of moisture the wind had to be saturated so that it did not dry out the moistened sand. The moisture in the sand was measured by weighing it wet and then after it had been dried. A heated pan supplied moisture to the air in the tunnel. Sand with a mean diameter of 0·44 mm was used. The experiments showed that the moisture increased the threshold shear velocity of sand movement. When the moisture was in the atmosphere the variation was only small for the normal range of humidities. On the other hand, the dampness of the sand had a very considerable effect on the sand movement when the water content reached values of 2 or 3%; the wind strength needed to initiate movement was greatly increased. The threshold shear velocity for a water content of 0·1% was about 34½ cm/sec, but when the moisture increased to 3% the corresponding velocity was 58 cm/sec. This is clearly of importance in natural conditions, especially in coastal dunes, where the moisture factor is more likely to be important.

Thus experimental work has enabled the theoretical equations of sand motion to be checked under controlled conditions, and the value of the constants to be established for different conditions. These results can then be used for field observations and provide a basic understanding of the physics involved in the movement of sand by wind.

b) *Fluvial action.* Studies of flowing water under model conditions can be approached in a variety of ways; the basic physical relationships that have been considered concerning movement of sand in air can be applied to the movement of cohesionless grains in water; alternatively, the flow of rivers may be studied in stream troughs to establish relationships between different variables, such as load and discharge; finally, models may be made of specific rivers to study special engineering problems.

Bagnold (1956) has done much basic work on the physical controls of sediment movement by flowing water. Few experiments had been made previously on the problems of the basic physical movement of grains in flowing water, although it had been shown that the fluid threshold for grains in water differs from that in air. The velocity of flow required to initiate grain movement in water is lower than that for air, owing to the difference in density between the water and the sand being very much smaller than that between the air and the sand. The critical diameter at which sand grains in air move most readily is 0·08 mm, but in water it is 0·2 mm; these values of sand size require the lowest velocity, about 15 to 18 cm/sec. As the material becomes coarser or finer higher velocities are required to initiate movement.

Work in experimental flumes and natural rivers (Leopold, Wolman and Miller, 1964) has shown that there is an almost straight line relationship on log-log paper between τ_c, the critical shear stress required to initiate movement, and the grain size, the two factors increasing together. There is a considerable scatter for fine sediment between 0·1 and 1·0 mm size. A plot of the data from the U.S. Waterways experimental station for transport rate against shear stress shows that the transport starts at about 0·003 g/cm², which gives a reasonable critical shear stress for this size of sand.

Some early experiments on the basic relationships of river channels, for example between the character of the channel and the load-discharge ratio, have been made by W. V. Lewis (1944, 1945) in a small stream trough. The apparatus consisted of a tilted wooden trough 4 m long and 50 cm wide. The tilt of the trough was adjustable and sand could be fed into the apparatus at a known rate, and the rate and volume of water being fed into the stream could also be adjusted. The first experiment was designed to illustrate the change of channel gradients resulting from changes in the proportion of sand and water entering the trough. The gradient of the stream was measured by noting the elevation every 10 cm. The water supply was 118 cm³/sec. The first runs showed that a slope of 1 in 37 was set up and that this value could be repeated in successive runs. The water supply was then halved and the tilt of the trough increased to hasten the attainment of a constant profile. After equilibrium had been attained the gradient was 1 in 27. The sand supply was then doubled and the equilibrium slope became about 1 in 19 to 20. However, when the sand supply was reduced to its former value the profile did not return to the initial gradient, but remained at 1 in 21. This was probably because a higher velocity is required to erode a bed than to transport the material. Other experiments tested the effect of tributaries and the changing of base level in producing knick-points. The profile of the stream with constant load and discharge appeared to be a straight line and no concavity was formed. However with the presence of tributaries a rather uneven concave curve was produced, due to erosion below the junction of the tributaries. The experiment concerned with the behaviour of knick-points was carried out with a mixture of sand and mud, which was more resistant to erosion than pure sand. The experiment made to investigate the development of tributaries showed that knick-points developed which had no connection with changes of base-level; this provides a warning that natural breaks of slope need not necessarily be caused by changes of base-level.

Rather more elaborate experiments have been carried out to establish the regime character of self-formed river channels in alluvial areas. The experiments (Stebbings, 1963) were carried out in a tilting flume 27 ft long, 3 ft wide and 10 inches deep. Water circulated in a closed circuit and sand was caught by filtering at the outlet of the flume. The sand used for the experiments was mostly between 0·6 and 1·2 mm in size. In most of the experiments the stream bed was given a cross-slope of $\frac{1}{2}$ inch from the edge to the centre, and a small initial channel was formed to guide the water, in order to concentrate all the discharge into one channel at first. The sand moving downstream increased the slope in that direction, causing a gradual increase in the bed-load down the channel, and the depth decreased as the surface width of the channel increased. At the upper end of the channel the bed-load decreased to zero with time as the slope decreased, while the bed-load downstream increased to the critical point where braiding took place. The slope of the channel was adjusted so that the start of braiding took place near the bottom end of the channel and the transport was zero near the top of the trough. A steep slope caused braiding to start too far up the channel. Where the bed-load was zero the cross section of the channel was a continuous curve, with the deepest water in the centre, but just before braiding started it was wider and shallower, and bed-load transport was at a maximum.

The section between the two extremes demonstrates all conditions of regime for a given bed material and discharge as far as shape and slope are concerned. The regime charge was given by the volume of bed-load at the point in question. Sand-feed was required to maintain this state of equilibrium. When the bed-load in the lower section was reduced by cutting off the sand supply beyond a certain value the channel became narrower and deeper again. This process continued to extend upstream until a channel of uniform character was set up along the whole length of the flume with a form similar to that of the upper section. The braided length also reverted to a single channel.

Experiments were then carried out with a gentler bed slope and these again showed that a uniform channel with zero bed-load transport was established throughout the flume, the final slopes being less steep in the second experiment. None of the runs showed the formation of ripples, possibly because the sand was too coarse. When the channel was eroding, the particles moved in straight lines parallel to the banks, although at times the flow became sinusoidal and shoals and deeps developed.

The braiding pattern started as the result of the formation of an overtaking-shoal, which caused erosion on two banks opposite each other. Although the cross sections changed in character from the point of zero bed-load to the start of braiding, the cross-sectional area was the same for any one discharge. The analysis of the experimental results was based on a theoretical approach, in which the forces acting on the bed were calculated from physical principles. The correctness of the theoretical curve could then be related to the experimental results. An alternative method of analysis is the empirical one. By this means it can be shown that there is a close correspondence between the breadth of the channel and the discharge, which agrees with Lacey's formula,

$$P = 2 \cdot 67 \ Q^{0 \cdot 5}$$

where P is the wetted perimeter; or this can be given in terms of the breadth. Two lines must now be considered, one for B_2, the breadth at which braiding starts, where $B_2 = 1 \cdot 6 \ Q^{0 \cdot 5}$, and one for B_1, the breadth at which bed transport begins, where formula is $B_1 = Q^{0 \cdot 5}$. The two lines are parallel and the value

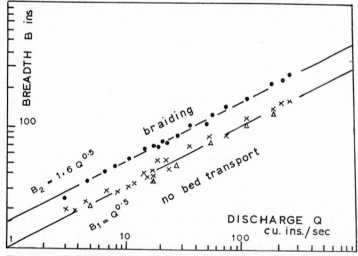

FIGURE 4.2. Relationship between river breadth and discharge in model studies, dots refer to series 1 with maximum bed-load, crosses to series 1 with zero bed-load and triangles to series 2 with zero bed-load. (after Stebbing)

for the regime channels lies between the two as shown on figure 4.2. The same sort of variation can be shown for the changes of cross-sectional area with discharge, where $A = 0 \cdot 14 \ Q^{0 \cdot 9}$, with A in sq.in. and Q in cu.in./sec. The points on the graph have little spread because the slope factor was omitted. The equations are useful in providing a correlation between breadth and depth limits for a given discharge.

Flow resistance is influenced both by the bed configuration and by the damping effect of turbulence. Both effects can be studied experimentally in a flume. The bed configuration can be shown to vary with velocity of flow and in turn to affect flow resistance; with low flow, less than 1·5 ft/sec, the bed was flat and the resistance small, then as flow increased to 1·5 to 2·5 ft/sec dunes formed, moving downstream, and flow resistance greatly increased. As the velocity increased further up to 4 ft/sec the bed again became smooth and the flow resistance decreased again, but as the velocity increased beyond 4·5 ft/sec antidunes formed, moving upstream, and the flow resistance again increased; there was a steady and rapid increase of transport as the velocity increased. The damping effect of turbulence was studied in experiments by Vanoni and Nomicos (1960). Dunes formed by moving sediment were stabilised, and sediment-free water was allowed to flow over the fixed bed. The resistance co-efficient was found to be 5 to 28% smaller when sediment was present, due to the dampening effect of sediment on turbulence. Thus by eliminating one variable in a controlled experiment, the effect of another can be studied and a theory could be confirmed.

Some of the problems of river models have been mentioned by Blench (1957). He shows that in practice it is very difficult to fulfil the model laws for dynamic similarity and to obtain comparable results. These problems can be seen by considering a hypothetical example; it is required to make a model with a discharge of 10 cusec to simulate a prototype with a discharge of 10,000 cusec. The discharge scale should be 1/1000. In designing the model it is likely that the bed slope and the cross section would be made geometrically similar. If this were done then the model would be too flat to carry its load, which would not be similar to the prototype, which would have dunes on the bed. Eventually the model channel would develop a slope and depth-to-breadth ratio that would be on a scale of $1000^{1/6}$. It would then run in a comparable way to the prototype and both would be in regime. In order to get the model to form its bed like the prototype geometrical similarity cannot be maintained any longer. Thus dynamic similarity cannot always be maintained at the same time as geometrical similarity; this illustrates the complexity of model working. In dealing with the problem of model scale, the vertical exaggeration must be considered. If a small model is to be made to react like the prototype, there must be some vertical exaggeration, because if the scale is made correct the depth will be so small in the model that other effects, such as surface tension, will make the results unreliable. Characteristics of the bed may also be greatly exaggerated in the model, especially near the sides of the stream. The time scale is also likely to give trouble in models, and results may well be out by ten times because of the difficulty of scaling down the bed-load satisfactorily.

A problem arises when the bed-load in the model is different from that in the prototype, in that its reaction to flow at different velocities may not be comparable. It has already been pointed out that a specific size of material, from about 0·1 to 0·5 mm, will be most readily picked off the bed as flow increases. If the model material is smaller than the critical size then it may well require a greater velocity than the prototype material, if this falls into the range of size mentioned above. Thus the lower velocity of the water in the flume will not cause bed-load movement comparable with that of the prototype. To overcome this difficulty it may be necessary to use the same bed-material in the model as in the prototype, although other factors bear a different scale ratio to one another.

In all model work dealing with river flow it is difficult to achieve an exact scale copy of the prototype in all its characteristics, as each factor may bear a different scale relationship to its prototype counterpart, and thus quantitative predictions may be difficult to make with accuracy. Nevertheless the models can give very valuable data of a more qualitative type, which are of particular value to engineers working on specific problems in natural rivers. The models that have provided the basic data dealing with the reaction of the river bed to the load and discharge are of great interest to both engineers and geomorphologists; they enable the processes operating in the formation of the river channel to be more fully understood.

It is important to realise that the model results should form a continuous sequence with the results of field measurements. The model is at the bottom of the scale, but the small river can be considered as a model for a larger one and so on, until a continuous relationship between any two variables can be set up, with the model at one end and the large river at the other. The table given in chapter 3, p. 86, illustrates this point, as far as the dimensions of regime channels are concerned.

Models of actual rivers may also provide valuable evidence on the operation of particular rivers in special circumstances, and although nearly all these studies have been made for specific engineering problems, the results are of more general interest to geomorphologists. It is, therefore, worthwhile to describe briefly one or two specific river models, as given by Allen (1947). The examples quoted are of non-tidal rivers, as the tidal type will be considered later.

In creating a model of a specific river it is necessary to work to a certain extent by trial and error in establishing the most suitable scale ratios for different factors. Thus it is generally agreed that there must be a vertical exaggeration of scale if the model is to simulate the prototype successfully. The general principle on which the model is designed is to construct it so that it can be made to reproduce known changes in the prototype river; then the effect of specific engineering works, or its future changes, can be assessed by continuing to run the model, taking the present conditions as the starting point. It is generally found that the scale of velocity should be proportional to the square root of the vertical scale of the model and not the horizontal scale. This distortion of the vertical scale is found also in nature as a larger channel runs considerably flatter than a smaller one, and the breadth to depth ratios in large and small rivers also illustrate this point. The larger river is much broader in proportion to its depth than the smaller one, so the model must continue this trend.

One of the models described by Allen (1947) is that constructed of part of

the Mississippi at the U.S. Waterways Experimental Station. The problem
was to consider methods of improving the river at Brooks Point. The crossing
below the Point had given trouble and required a lot of dredging for navigation purposes, and the bank was being attacked below Saladin Towhead (see
figure 4.3), which could have resulted in the river creating a major cut-off
where two bends were less than 1½ miles apart, thus threatening the town of
Cairo, Illinois.

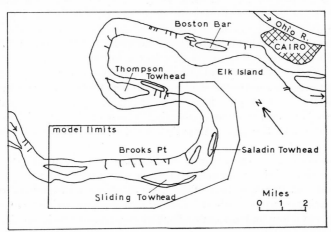

FIGURE 4.3. Map of part of the Mississippi river to illustrate the model
study of the river near Cairo, Illinois.

The horizontal scale of the model was 1 in 1000 and the vertical scale 1 in
125, the prototype length was 10 miles and this was 53 feet in the model. The
stages of the river were known from records for a period of 12 years, and the
operating time to cover the range of stages used in the model was 16 hours;
the level between high and low water varied by 5 feet, and the durations of
the high and low stages were correlated with those recorded on the actual
river. The model was adjusted to conditions of the bed in 1932, and the preliminary operating of the model showed that the bed was correctly designed,
as few changes occurred. The effects of various improvements were then
studied, such as building spur dykes, and these showed a very close similarity
with changes actually taking place in the channel as the result of full-scale
improvements made in the same way.

Another interesting example of improvements to the Mississippi tested by
model construction concerned the erection of pile-dykes in the same reach
of the river. These dykes were built into the river and they produced no
apparent good result for some time, so a model was built to study the problem. The model indicated that the dykes had been correctly placed to
achieve their aim, though this would take some time to happen; the forecast state of the river according to the model results showed that the necessary scouring should have taken place in about a year, and in fact the scour-

ing did take place as forecast by the model. The two models were on the same scale and had the same vertical exaggeration; this gave a model slope of 0·0015 at mean low water, compared with 0·0001 in nature. These two examples illustrate the sort of help a river model can give to engineers studying the effect of different remedial measures, but they also provide valuable data concerning the actual operation of fluvial processes.

c) *Wave action.* Wave action is in some respects more complex than river action, as the flow in waves is oscillatory, and the problems are often complicated by the presence of tidal and other currents as well as a pattern of waves from several directions arriving simultaneously. Thus models can play an important part in establishing the fundamental relationships under the controlled conditions that are possible in the laboratory wave tank. There remains, however, the problem of scale; this is complicated by the fact that wave steepness is an important factor in the operation of waves on the shore, so that there can be no vertical exaggeration where wave action is being simulated. The same problem concerning the use of bed material to scale is also encountered if the same scale ratio is applied to this factor as to the other factors.

As with rivers, the problem of wave action can be approached from different points of view; the nature of water movement under waves will be considered first, then the effect of waves on structures and sand transport by waves, leading on to the study of beach profiles. All these studies can be made most easily in a long narrow tank, which gives a two-dimensional view of the effect of waves. The study of longshore movement by waves is, however, a very important one, and this can only be studied in a three-dimensional model, while models of actual stretches of coast must naturally be of the three-dimensional type.

i *Two-dimensional models—waves.* It is known from theory that the particles in wave motion move in open circular orbits in deep water, and that the particles do not come back precisely to the point they left. This small movement is the velocity of mass-transport, and the changes in its pattern from deep water into shallow water and at various depths within the water form a topic that can be examined theoretically, as Longuet-Higgins (1953) has done, or experimentally in a model tank, as illustrated by the work of Russell and Osorio (1958). Their work has supported the theoretical conclusions of Longuet-Higgins. The nature of mass-transport in waves was established in a two-dimensional tank with a smooth bottom. The waves were allowed to run for some time until they had reached a steady state, then a piece of dye was dropped through the water; this formed a thread that could be followed as the waves moved past, and its distortion indicated the nature of the mass transport in different depths of water.

The results showed that in deep water the movement was at a maximum in the direction of wave propagation on the surface, falling off rapidly to no movement at a short distance below the surface; but in shallow water, where beach changes take effect, the movement was different. An interesting point, forecast by the theory and confirmed by the experimental results, was that there was a surge of water towards the shore very near to the bed as the waves moved into shallow water. This is accounted for in the theory by taking into account the boundary effects and the viscosity of the water. Above the thin tongue of forward moving water, the central layers tended to move seawards, while the upper water also moved towards the shore. The seaward movement of the central layer is the result of the return drift, which on an open shore or in three-dimensional models may become concentrated to form rip currents. This basic pattern of water flow in a wave is important in understanding the movement of sediment. It is worth considering some of the experimental apparatus developed to study other aspects of waves and their action.

Experiments have been carried out to study the generation of waves in a tank 60 feet long and 1·28 feet deep and 1·0 feet wide. The wind was generated by a blower set up at one end of the tank, the wind velocities varying from zero to 50 ft/sec, gentle slopes of 1 in 10 allowed the wind to reach the water gently, while the downwind beach allowed the waves to break (Sibul, 1955). Wave heights and periods were measured at four points, the records being taken at intervals after the wind had started to modify the calm surface, and the effects of different types of bottom were studied. The results showed the relationship between the wind duration and the wave height, and also the relationship between the wave height and the wind velocity and fetch. The graph of Bretschneider's relationships between these variables fitted the experimental data fairly well, if they were continued to the experimental scale, although there was a considerable scatter of the points. The results only applied satisfactorily to deep water conditions; the wave heights were lower when d/L_0 was less than 0·2 (when d = depth of waves and L_0 is deep water length).

Shock pressures are known to have destructive effects on shore structures, but the measurement and study of these pressures are difficult in nature. Laboratory work on this problem has been done by Ross (1955), using a 96 feet long tank, which was 2 feet deep and $1\frac{1}{2}$ feet wide. Waves were generated by a moving bulkhead type of equipment, with periods varying from 1 to 5 seconds and a good range of heights. The waves broke against a bulkhead, whose slope could be varied and in which piezometric gauges were fixed. The angle of the bulkhead and the concrete slope in front of it could be adjusted to cause the waves to break. Recording wave gauges were also installed. The pressure gauges had to be calibrated to give results in lb/sq.in. The first few waves to arrive were the most reliable because when the reflected waves were set up they affected the size of the oncoming waves. In applying the results to full-scale conditions the scale ratio must be known, but the results covered too small a range to allow this to be done accurately; larger-scale experiments would enable a scale to be worked out. The maximum observed shock pressures were 21 lb/sq.ft, and these sometimes occurred over a considerable area at any one time, but the shock pressure only accounted for about 10% of the total wave momentum.

Other problems that can be studied in wave tanks include the wave runup on different types of slope and overtopping of shore structures. These types of experiments provide useful data on the effectiveness of different types of sea-wall for example. One set of experiments (Savage, 1959) showed that the run-up is greater for waves of low steepness when the slope is about 1 in 4; for steeper waves the run-up is greatest on a steeper slope of 1 in 2. The work was done in a tank of the same dimensions as that used for the previous experiment described. The effect of the roughness increased as this factor increased and this applied also to the permeability. These factors have more effect with waves of lower steepness and as the slope flattens. According to tests in two models of different size the scale effect caused the run-up in the smaller model to increase by about 10 and 20%, for smooth slopes at a gradient of 1 in 6 and 1 in 3 respectively.

Sediment transport. Basic experiments on the transport of sediment by wave action have been carried out by a number of workers. The same problem of the reaction of the sediment to the forces is encountered, and one method that has been adopted to overcome this difficulty is to use sand of a lower density than normal quartz sand. Bagnold (1947) used Perspex sand ground to the same dimensions as quartz sand. This material is so mobile, as shown by other experiments with it, that it cannot be used for all types of observation; it was found useful, however, in studying the effect of an onshore wind in creating a seaward under-current, when it was not strong enough to generate measurable waves.

For certain purposes the use of lighter than normal sand may be justified, and the results of Ippen and Eagleson's (1955) work illustrate this point. Spheres of plastic material and glass were used to investigate the nature of sediment movement. The plastic spheres had a specific gravity of 1·29, and they were set in motion before the heavier glass particles. The movement of the light particles revealed a null point, where movement was nil; to seaward of it they moved seawards, while landwards of it they moved towards the shore. The heavier glass particles moved only within the shoreward range of movement for the experimental conditions, which allowed a range of wave steepness between 0·02 and 0·06. The particles were considerably larger than normal sand. This type of experiment is useful in indicating the movement that is going on close to the shore, and the results support the theoretical and experimental work on mass-transport velocities. As a result of these experiments the offshore zone was divided into three parts, firstly a zone of equilibrium, in which movement was neither onshore nor offshore, secondly a zone of onshore movement lying landward of the first zone, and thirdly, a zone of offshore movement, lying seaward of the first zone and null point. As a corollary to the results the sorting of sediment in the offshore zone seaward of the break-point can be worked out. If the finest particles are set in motion near the null point, some will move onshore and some offshore, and closer to the break-point larger and larger particles will be set in motion, while all grades will move to the break-point; thus the smaller grains will be leaving the offshore zone in increasing proportion towards the shore, and so the median diameter will increase towards the shore. This can be tested and has been found correct on many natural shores. The experiments just described were carried out with artificial particles, lighter and larger than normal sand, but interesting results can be obtained by using normal sand.

For most experiments it seems best to use the same type of material as that found in the prototype; this is because shingle on a natural beach behaves in a different way from sand, and by scaling down the material to fit other scale factors its behaviour is completely altered, as already mentioned in connection with river work. On the other hand, if the same size sand is used in the laboratory wave tank as that found on natural beaches, a continuous relationship between some parameters is found. For example, when wave length is plotted against beach slope in the swash zone there is a linear relationship as shown on figure 4.4.

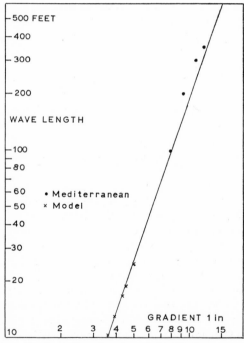

FIGURE 4.4. Graph to show that the relationship between wave length and gradient holds continuously from model to prototype conditions, as a straight line relationship.

In order to measure the amount of sand moving in a two-dimensional tank, normal to the shore, traps were used. They were arranged in such a way that the sand moving seaward fell into one partition and that moving landward fell into the other. The traps extended across the full width of the tank, which was 1 foot wide and 30 feet long. The size of the openings was such that sand fell into the part nearest to the direction from which it was moving.

The difference in the amounts caught in each side of the trap then gave the net amount of sand moved and the direction of movement. By varying the wave height and length systematically and by placing the traps in different depths of water it was possible to measure the volume of sand moving under different conditions, and the results showed that the amount of sand transported increased with the wave height, the wave length, and hence with the wave energy, in any one depth of water. The amount also increased as the depth decreased or the break-point was approached, and as the slope flattened (see figure 4.5).

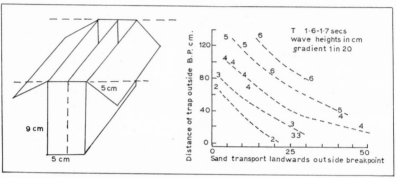

FIGURE 4.5. Sketch of trap used to measure net sand transport in the model wave tank, and some of the results of observations with the trap outside the break-point. The figures give the wave height in cm.

Experiments were also made with the bottom of the tank both rippled and smooth, and the results showed that the movement increased when the bottom was rippled, as more sand was thrown into suspension. Throughout the zone seaward of the break-point, whatever the wave dimensions, the sand was found to move inland, which can be explained by the theoretical and experimental results already mentioned.

Inside the break-point, however, the movement was more complex. Bagnold (1940) has shown, as a result of experiments made with dye, that there were usually two separate circulations, one inside and one outside the break-point, and that material did not readily move from one zone to the other. Experiments made with the sand trap set up inside the break-point showed that the direction of movement appeared to depend on the wave steepness, although more recent work, to be mentioned later, suggests that perhaps the steepness is not the true controlling factor. However, with shorter, higher waves sand was found to move seaward inside the break-point, while with waves less than a critical height-to-length ratio the movement was landwards in all depths.

The only conditions that reversed this pattern of flow were found in experiments that were carried out with an onshore wind accompanying the waves. The wind by itself was not strong enough to move the sand, although it did move the light Perspex sand, as already mentioned. It did, however, set up a seaward current on the bottom, which was strongest in the shallowest water, but which was still noticeable beyond the break-point. This had the effect of reversing the constructive action of the waves inside the break-point, even for the lower steepness values, and also produced the only conditions in which offshore movement was recorded outside the break-point. The destructive effect of onshore wind action was particularly noticeable inside the break-point when the waves were steep.

Before considering the different profiles that can be studied in the laboratory tank, the measurement of sand in suspension will be considered. Experimental work on this topic has been done by Fairchild (1959). The sand moved in suspension is liable to movement by slight currents and it may therefore move in a different direction from the sand on the bed, so that an accurate means of measuring this is of value, especially if it can be adapted for full-scale observations in the field. The experiments are also of interest as they were carried out at different scales, using waves of 2 to 6 inches in height and waves 2 to 6 feet in height. The most common method of collecting the samples has been by pumping, a method that works best in unidirectional flow, although the nozzle does cause some disturbance to the flow. The tests to be described were carried out by using a vacuum pump with a $\frac{1}{4}$-in. nozzle in the two smaller tanks that were used, while a submersible pump with a $\frac{1}{2}$-in. nozzle was used in the large wave tank, in which 6-foot waves could be generated.

The smallest tank was 42 feet long, $1\frac{1}{2}$ feet wide and 2 feet deep and the sand used had a median diameter of 0·22 mm. The effect of an important variable that is sometimes neglected was studied; this was the effect of temperature. It has been shown that a lower temperature is associated with a higher load of sediment in suspension in a river; the Colorado for example has $2\frac{1}{2}$ times as much sediment in suspension in winter as in summer; even a ratio of 5 to 1 has been recorded with temperature variations from 40°F in winter to 80°F in summer. The temperatures used for the present experiments were 53°F for the colder conditions and 80°F for the warmer ones. This is about the recorded difference between winter and summer water temperatures off eastern U.S.A. Although there was a considerable scatter of points, the results showed that there was appreciably more sediment in suspension under the colder conditions—about 50 to 75% more—the higher percentage values occurring at greater relative elevations above the bottom. Near the bottom the difference was not so great, and it is in this zone that most sediment is in suspension. In fact under some conditions a higher temperature may lead to greater suspension very near the bottom.

The second tank in which experiments were carried out was 300 feet long, 150 feet wide and 3 feet deep, but the waves were small, 3 to 5 inches in height, and the sand in suspension was found to be between 0·1 and 10 parts/ 1000. The shorter waves on the whole threw more sand into suspension. The largest tank was 635 feet long, 15 feet wide and 20 feet deep so that ocean-sized waves could be generated, having heights up to 6 feet and periods of

2 to 16 seconds. The sampler has already been described and the results showed that the amount of sand in suspension was greater for the shorter waves of 11·3 seconds than for the longer ones of 16 seconds period (see figure 4.6).

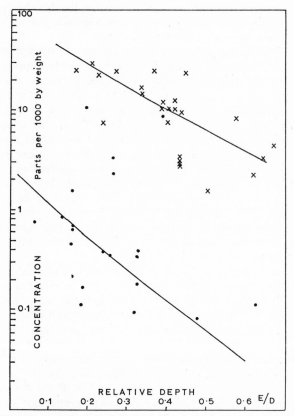

FIGURE 4.6. Experiments to measure the sand in suspension in a large wave tank. The crosses refer to observation with a wave of period 11·33 seconds and breaker height of 3·5 to 6 feet, and the dots to a wave of 16 seconds period and breaker height of 3 to 4 feet. (after Fairchild B.E.B.)

The amount of sediment in suspension is affected by the development of ripples, and a very detailed theoretical and experimental study of ripples has been carried out by Manohar (1955). His experimental work on ripples was done by oscillating a section of the bed harmonically in still water of relatively great depth, a method used earlier by Bagnold. Manohar showed that the stable profile of a ripple depends on the velocity at the interface, and each velocity has its own appropriate profile, the wave length and height of the ripple increasing up to a certain point beyond which the ripple length goes on increasing but the height diminishes until the ripple disappears. These results only apply to water deeper than 25 feet.

Beach profiles. As a result of the movement of sediment under the action of the waves a variety of beach profiles builds up; the character of these and their changing form can be readily examined through the glass sides of the wave tank, and the variables on which they depend can be assessed by changing these one by one. Experiments on the building up of beach profiles have shown that the wave character is the fundamental factor on which they depend. This can be appreciated when the results of the experiments already described are taken into account. The flat waves tend to build up a profile by constructive action, creating a berm at the limit of the swash, while the steep, destructive waves tend to comb down the foreshore sand and move it seaward to the break-point, where it accumulates as a break-point bar. This feature is probably the model counterpart of the submarine bars found in such seas as the Mediterranean and Baltic, which are tideless. The break-point bar can be shown to build up to a height where its crest above the original profile in the model tank is twice the depth of water over the crest and this same relationship seems to hold under natural conditions also. The effect of a changing tide level can also be studied in the model tank; the experiments showed that a falling water-level, simulating an ebbing tide, destroyed the break-point bar.

Similarly the berm built up by the model constructive waves seems to react to the waves in a similar way to the ridges and runnels found on some tidal beaches; both seem to be the result of the constructive activity of flat waves. Their swash slope gradients in each instance can be shown to be related to the length of the waves for any one sand size, showing that there is a continuous gradation from model to full-scale conditions, as already mentioned (see figure 4.7a-d).

Other more elaborate experiments on the equilibrium character of beaches deal with the development of a stable beach profile under different conditions (Eagleson *et al*, 1961). Associated with the development of the equilibrium beach profile the sorting of sediment in the offshore zone was also studied. The equipment used was a wave tank 100 feet long, 2½ feet wide and 3 feet deep, and for the equilibrium beach experiments the sand used was a well-rounded silica sand with a mean diameter of 0·37 mm, while the sorting experiment made use of three different types of sand. Different initial slopes were used: 1 in 20, 1 in 30 and 1 in 45. The waves affecting the beach ranged in steepness from 0·025 to 0·048 and they were allowed to act on the beach until equilibrium was reached. The results showed that previous theories could correctly account for the beach changes in a qualitative sense, but that quantitatively values were only reasonably accurate when the depth at which movement first started lay within the tank. The experiments were continued with each wave type until the beach showed no change; this time varied from 121 to 222 hours. The wave dimensions were designed as far as possible to ensure that the depth at which sediment first started to move lay on the beach. Four tests were made using different gradients and two wave steep-

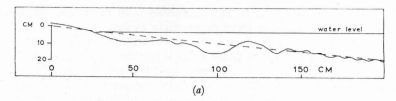

(a)

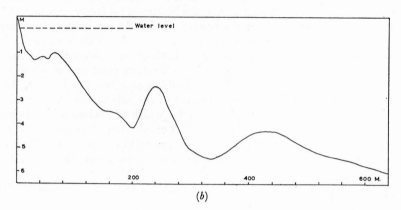

(b)

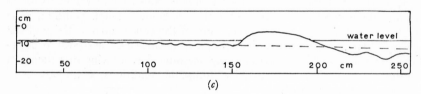

(c)

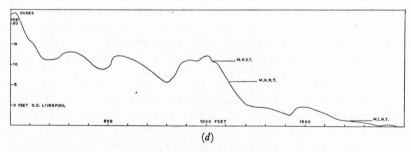

(d)

FIGURE 4.7

(a) Profile of a break-point bar formed by a steep wave in a model wave tank. Wave height 9·0 cm, wave length 240 cm, time of run 10 min.

(b) Profile of a beach with submarine bars at Les Karentes in the south of France on the Mediterranean coast.

(c) Profile of model beach to show a swash bar, built up by flat waves, 5 cm high and 624 cm long, steepness 0·008, from an original gradient of 1 :50, time of run 40 mins.

(d) Profile of ridge and runnel beach south Skegness, Lincolnshire. Mean tide heights are shown.

nesses, 0·0297 and 0·0464; the 1 in 30 gradient was tested with both wave steepnesses, the 1 in 20 with the steeper wave and the 1 in 45 with the flatter wave.

The conclusions from the experimental results suggest that the breaker is one of the essential features governing the nature of the profile in the inshore zone in particular. The available sediment is another important factor, and this depends partly on the initial slope and the depth at which sand movement begins. The offshore equilibrium is only established very slowly, as the material from the breaker zone does not influence the offshore zone once the profile has reached an equilibrium value in the breaker zone.

The sorting experiments were made in 8 runs with the three different sands, and the results showed that the sediment changed progressively in size towards the break-point, the diameter increasing slowly shoreward of the point at which movement first started until the influence of the breaker was felt, after which the diameter tended to decrease as the coarse fraction was removed. The sorting improves in an onshore direction. Both these findings agree with the theoretical results, if the size increase is limited to the deeper water.

The experiments of Fairchild (1959) with different water temperatures showed that this factor also affected the beach profiles; slightly more material appeared to move seaward under the colder conditions, and the beach berm maintained a higher level under warm than under cold conditions; the bars and troughs were sharper in the warm water. The most important difference, however, appeared to be the more rapid rate of movement under the cold conditions, which seems to be independent of the type of load, so that a beach may be expected to react to waves more rapidly under cold conditions.

ii *Three-dimensional models.* The main factor that can be studied in a three-dimensional model but not in a two-dimensional one is the longshore transport of sediment under wave action. This is very important because most problems of serious coastal erosion are caused by longshore movement of sediment, whereby more material is carried out of the area than is carried into it from alongshore. The experiments discussed in the previous section showed that sand can be moved onshore only from a certain depth and that there is a limit to the material available from offshore because of this factor. Any long continued loss of material must be due to longshore transport and the same is true of an accreting shore, where the extra material must come into the area from alongshore or inland. The difficulties of measuring the movement of material alongshore on natural beaches has already been discussed, so that any information that can be gained on this important topic from the study of models is of considerable interest and value, not only for specific engineering problems, but also in accounting for the development of many coastal landforms.

An important factor relevant to the longshore movement of material is the refraction of the waves, so a model experiment to test the reliability of Snell's law is of interest (Wiegel and Arnold, 1957). Snell's law can be stated in terms of the relationship $\sin a_2 / \sin a_1 = C_2 / C_1$, where a_2 and a_1 are angles between adjacent wave fronts and the respective bottom contours, and C_2 and C_1 refer to the wave velocity at the two positions, and can be obtained from tables relating wave velocity to water depth and wave period. The experiments were carried out in a model wave basin 150 feet long and 64 feet wide and $2\frac{1}{2}$ feet deep. Waves were generated to approach the shore at different angles up to 60 degrees, the wave heights used were 0·05 and 0·25 feet, and the wave periods ranged from $\frac{1}{2}$ second to $7\frac{1}{4}$ seconds. Some difficulty was experienced in measuring the orientation of the wave crests correctly, but the results confirmed that Snell's law predicts the refraction of waves correctly for the shorter period waves. The longer waves sometimes caused peculiar results, but on the whole the law was still found to be correct. The effect of wave height on the angle of refraction was found to be negligible.

The study of longshore transport of material depends on the generation of longshore currents. An example of model work designed to investigate this point may be described (Saville, 1950). This work was carried out in a tank 66 feet by 122 feet and the model beach was set up at a gradient of 1 in 10, the waves approaching the shore at an angle of 10 degrees. The speed of the longshore current was obtained by timing the movement of dye across a 10-ft length parallel to the beach. The velocity of the current was found to range between 0·066 and 0·4 ft/sec. The current increased with increasing wave steepness partly because the flatter waves were longer and these were more refracted; an increase of wave height was also found to cause a more rapid current. The fastest current was found to occur at the break-point, where a break-point bar had formed; it is in this area that most sand is in suspension and liable to be moved by the longshore currents, when the waves are steep. There was a critical steepness between 0·02 and 0·03 at which the transport was most rapid. The wave-induced currents naturally affect the sediment transport, and this was also measured by using traps at various positions down the beach, so that not only could the optimum wave steepness and direction for longshore transport be ascertained, but the position of this movement on the profile was also indicated. Saville showed that with a relatively flat wave the bulk of the transport took place in the swash zone, just above the still water level; about 80% of the transport was retained in the uppermost trap, while with steep waves about 70% of the sand was caught in the trap at which the waves broke. The percentage of sand carried in suspension was far greater with the steep waves and the value was as great as 60%, while with flat waves, when the bulk of the transport was by beach drifting, only about 20% of the sand was carried in suspension. Saville's work was extended by Shay and Johnson (1953) to establish the optimum direction of wave approach. The results of the tests with waves approaching from greater angles than the 10 degrees adopted by Saville revealed that the optimum direction of wave approach was an angle of 30 degrees to the shore.

A larger tank was available for a more recent set of experiments carried out by Savage (1959), who also studied the effect of groynes on the movement of material alongshore. The tank was 300 feet long, 150 feet wide and 3 feet deep, thus scale effects would not be so serious in attempting to relate the results to prototype beaches as for the previous experimental results. Extrapolating the data measured in natural environments, it was found that the results of the smaller-scale experiments fell considerably below the curve, indicating much smaller transports, and the scatter was considerable, owing to the variety of wave conditions tested.

The experiments carried out by Savage were done with a beach slope of 1 in 20 and the sand transport was measured in traps arranged at right angles to the shore at the end of the straight beach. In all 15 traps were used, each covering 3 feet of beach normal to the shore, but varying in width. The wider traps were fitted with a series of narrow rotatable covers, so that the sand settled on the top of the covers, and these were then rotated to allow the sand to sink into the metal cone below and be washed along by pumped water into the weighing machine. The results of five tests, the first without groynes, the second with low short groynes, the third and fourth with high short groynes and the last with high long groynes showed that most sand was moved alongshore with no groynes and that the high long groynes were much the most effective in slowing down sand movement; after 50 hours of test time the amount of sand moved in the first test was 18,600 lb, or 374 lb/hour; for the second test the result was 329 lb/hour, the third 302 lb/hour and the fourth 271 lb/hour, whereas in the fifth it was reduced to 154 lb/hour. The drift rate tended to be greater in the second period of 25 hours than the first, so there is some doubt whether a stable state had been set up. The greatest bulk of the movement took place in the zone between the break-point and the swash limit. Current measurements showed that the long, high groynes almost stopped the littoral current (see figure 4.8).

The Hydraulic Research Station (1956) have also carried out experiments on the effectiveness of groynes and the transport of sand alongshore, basing their model on a particular stretch of coast at Dunwich in Suffolk. The model was constructed with a horizontal scale of 1 in 30 and a vertical scale of 1 in 20, the beach being moulded to represent the actual beach at Dunwich, and the waves and tides were also adjusted to give comparable values by trial and error, until the profile remained in adjustment. The direction of wave approach was set at 30 degrees north of normal to the shore and the wave height would be the equivalent of 2 feet in deep water, increasing to 3 feet at the break-point in the prototype. The longshore movement of sand was measured by trapping the sand in trays that were 2 feet in the model, representing a zone 60 feet wide on the prototype. The transport scaled up to prototype dimensions was equivalent to 455,000 cu.yd/year when no groynes were present on the beach; the transport took place in the zone occupied by the three upper trays, or 180 feet of the prototype beach, the greatest movement taking place in the high tide area and about half as much just above low tide, where the prototype tidal range was 6 feet. Only a very small amount moved below low water. Groyne spacing used in the experiment was the equivalent of 180 feet and 360 feet in the prototype; the groynes, which were 3 feet high to scale and normal to the beach, greatly reduced the volume of longshore transport, and with the wider spacing this was reduced to only

120,000 cu.yd/year. These values must clearly exceed the actual values as they are based only on the optimum angle of wave approach, and do not allow for any counter-drift, which has been shown to occur in nature; they do, nevertheless, at least give some indication of the probable effect of groynes on a specific beach.

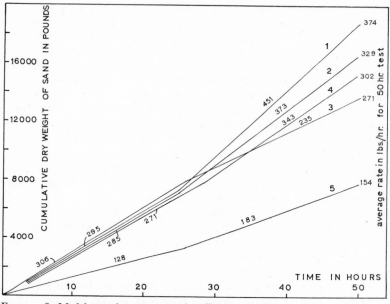

FIGURE 4.8. Model experiments to test the effectiveness of groynes. The numbers on the curves indicate the transport rate in pounds/hour for the straight portion of the curve. No. 1, no groyne; No. 2, low short groynes at station 30; No. 3, high short groynes at station 30; No. 4, high short groynes at station 45; and No. 5, high long groynes at station 45. (after Savage, B.E.B.)

Another recent experiment carried out on the subject of longshore drift and the behaviour of the beach in relation to groynes is that made by Kemp (1962). The tank used for the experiment was small and this renders the results rather more difficult to scale up to natural dimensions; it was 15 feet by 9 feet and only small waves could be used. The work included some preliminary studies without groynes, before testing the effect of impermeable groynes. Tidal variations could also be included in the model. The littoral drift material was fed into the model by a conveyor belt which fed in a known amount of damp sand, while material at the down-drift end was caught in a trap and measured by volume. The changes in the beach profile during the tests were recorded by laying a fine brass chain along each contour, delineated by allowing the water to drop by successive amounts, and then photographing the beach area from vertically above. Waves were recorded and the longshore currents were measured by using liquid dye and solid particles. Unlike most of the experiments described so far the material was chosen to simulate a shingle beach in nature. It was, therefore, adjusted so that the bulk of the transport took place as bed-load, as it does on a shingle beach. The material also had to fulfil the requirements listed: firstly, it must move under the action of waves no higher than 1 cm, secondly, it must produce consistent results, thirdly, it must show a high rate of littoral transport, fourthly, it must be such that the profile rapidly reached adjustment with the waves acting. The material chosen after some tests was pumice, with a specific gravity of 2·0, a median diameter of 0·9 mm and a fall velocity of 4·1 cm/sec. This material moved 14 times as fast alongshore as quartz sand and the beach adjusted itself 20 times as quickly as with quartz sand.

The results of the experiments on the changing beach profiles suggested that it was not the wave steepness that determined whether the beach formed a storm profile or summer profile, the former associated with the break-point bar and the latter with the berm, but that the ratio t/T was the critical factor, t being the time of the uprush or swash and T the wave period. These factors do depend on the height and length of the waves, and the bar became most fully developed when one wave reached the limit of the swash just as the next was breaking. The time of the swash was also affected by the character of the beach material. The effect of groynes was tested under both destructive and constructive conditions, the waves producing those conditions had periods of 0·554 seconds and 0·422 seconds, and heights of 1·2 cm and 3 cm, respectively. The tidal range was 3 cm and the beach slope was 9 degrees. Before the groynes were added the waves were allowed to act on the beach for 30 minutes; only two groynes were used owing to the size of the tank, but three types were tested: low groynes, high long groynes, and high short groynes. Each was tested in three alignments, normal to the shore and trending 30 degrees in an up-drift or 20 degrees in a down-drift direction, while the shoreline was at an angle of 15 degrees to the wave crests.

The results can be expressed in a table, the figures representing percentage of the drift measured without groynes.

	Wave A: T—0·544 sec, H—1·2 cm		
Groyne type	*Alignment*		
	30° Up-drift	0°	20° Down-drift
Low	48	61	95
High long	35	42	48
High short	58	63	56
	Wave S: T—0·422 sec, H—3·0 cm		
Low	57	57	70
High long	59	65	68
High short	86	86	88

The up-drift alignment clearly trapped more material, except in the high short groynes. The least effective are the low groynes, facing down-drift. It is interesting to note that the high short groynes are least effective with the storm waves, which agrees with the findings of other workers that under these conditions movement would be at the break-point and not in shallow water. Scour round the end of the groynes can be reduced by the adjustment of the beach orientation, which lowers the rate of littoral flow.

As a result of the types of model tests that have been described a much better idea of the fundamental processes operating on the beach has been achieved. Although there is still some doubt as to the applicability of the results of small model tests to full-scale prototypes, with the increasing use of larger models that provide an intermediate step in the scale ratios this difficulty should be overcome.

d) *Tidal action.* One of the first attempts to construct a tidal model was that of Osborne Reynolds, who built a model of the Mersey estuary; his model was on the horizontal scale of 1 in 31,800 and the vertical scale was 1 in 960, giving a vertical exaggeration of 33 to 1. He was the first person to realise that the time scale of a model must be equal to the square root of the linear scale. In dealing with tidal phenomena it is necessary to reproduce the tidal cycle correctly, and the speed of propagation depends on the depth of the water. Reynolds found that only one tidal period would give the correct tidal pattern in his model estuary, this was about 40 seconds. That this is about the correct length in view of the size of his model can be shown by considering the propagation of a tidal wave. If d is the depth of water in the model and D is the prototype depth, and v and V represent the model and prototype velocities respectively, then $v \mid V = d \mid D$. The time that the wave takes in travelling a distance l or L is given by $l \mid v$ or $L \mid V$; therefore, the time t and T must be connected by

$$t \mid T = \frac{l \mid v}{L \mid V} = \frac{l \times V}{L \times v} = \frac{l}{L}\sqrt{\frac{H}{h}}$$

where h and H are the range. This can be written

$$t \mid T = 1 \mid x.\sqrt{y}$$

where x is the horizontal scale and y is the vertical scale. If the tidal periods are t_0 and T_0 respectively in model and prototype, then

$$t_0 \mid T_0 = \sqrt{y} \mid x .$$

Given the figures for the example cited, then T_0 will be 12·4 hours or 44,600 seconds and x is 31,800 and y is 960. Then

$$t_0 = \frac{44,600 \times \sqrt{960}}{31,800} = 43\cdot5 \text{ seconds,}$$

which agrees closely with the period Reynolds used of 42 seconds. This example illustrates the use of vertical exaggeration in a tidal model, which is necessary to produce results comparable with the prototype, and the way in which the time scale must be adjusted to the linear scales (Allen, 1947).

Before considering in more detail the functioning of models of specific areas in which tides play an important part, it is useful to consider one of the relatively few experiments that have been made to study tidal phenomena in general. Bruun and Gerritsen (1960) state that there is relatively little accurate knowledge of the relationship between tidal flow and sand transport in an inlet channel, so that a laboratory experiment to study this connection is worth mentioning. Saville *et al.* (1957) have described a series of experiments to test the effect of an uncontrolled tidal inlet on the adjacent beaches. The work was done in a large semicircular wave basin of about 50 feet radius and 1½ feet depth. The mechanism included tide producing machinery and a movable wave generator that could be used to make waves approach the inlet from various directions. The sand used for the experiment was well sorted and had a median diameter of 0·23 mm. The tests were run first without a tidal inlet into the lagoon behind the barrier beach; then an artificial straight inlet was cut through the barrier beach and the experiment was repeated with the same wave sequence until stability was reached. The width of the inlet was cut so that it was ¼ of its length, and its size was limited by the fact that sufficient length of beach had to remain on either side to include the whole area affected by the inlet. The dimensions chosen for the inlet were 2 feet wide and 8 feet long, leaving 60 feet of beach on the up-drift side and 70 feet on the down-drift side of the inlet. Sand was fed on to the beach on the up-drift side and traps caught what moved out on the down-drift side. The wave steepness chosen for the experiment was 0·025; these waves were of intermediate steepness as far as beach reaction was concerned, but they produced maximum longshore drift of sand. The initial beach gradient was 1 in 20 and the crest elevation 0·35 feet, while the water depth in the deeper part of the tank was 1·15 feet and the initial depth in the tidal inlet was 0·2 feet at mean tide level; the inlet side slopes were 1 in 5. The lagoon area was 2800 square feet and in the first 5 tests its depth was − 1·15 feet, but in the sixth it was decreased to − 0·20 feet. The tidal range was 0·1 feet and the tidal cycle lasted 20 minutes, while the wave height was 0·1 feet and the period 0·884 seconds. Each test was run with a variety of wave types and directions, but the drift was always predominantly in one direction.

The first four tests showed the rapid closure of the inlet, after it had become curved as a result of the littoral drift. The closure was effected by the development of a curved bar at both the lagoon and the open sea end of the channel, while a deeper channel was maintained in the centre (see figure 4.9). At first the channel was more open to the sea, but as longshore drift continued the channel became more oblique to the coast and the tips of the opposing channel banks became interlocking spits, the up-drift one curving into the hollow of the down-drift spur, until they finally linked at the lagoon end of the inlet. In the first test the closure was effected after 42 tidal cycles, and in the second the closure took place after 30 tidal cycles. The same waves were used for the first two tests, but in the second sand was not pumped alongshore artificially, as it was in the first, and this increased the rate of longshore transport by reducing eddies present in the first set-up. In the third test the waves came from the same direction and closure took place during the 31st tidal cycle. In test 4 the inlet only closed after 60 tidal cycles and it did not migrate so far. The closure in these first tests seemed to be due more to weak currents flowing through the inlet than to the longshore movement of sand; the smaller distance the inlet migrated in the fourth test was probably due to the lesser angle of wave approach causing less drifting.

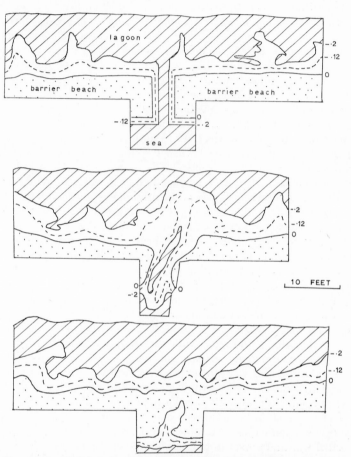

FIGURE 4.9. Model study of the effect of tidal inlets on adjacent beaches. The upper diagram shows the inlet in test 5 as it was when first cut. The middle diagram shows the inlet in test 5 after 90 tidal cycles, the lower diagram shows the closure of the inlet in test 1 after 42 cycles. Contours are shown in feet. (after Saville, Caldwell and Simmons, B.E.B.)

Owing to the rapid closure in the first four tests the effective area of the lagoon was increased during the last two tests; this had the effect of increasing the velocities of the tidal currents to 1·5 ft/sec instead of 1·0 ft/sec in the earlier series. The wave sequence in test 5 was the same as for test 2. Again a large bar formed on the inside of the inlet, but the channel through it deepened at first. Between 80 and 90 tidal cycles the bar was broken through by a channel, which was maintained for 300 cycles, while the depth of the channel in the main inlet was maintained at a greater value than the initial figure. The channel through the bar was again broken through before the 420th cycle, and by the 450th cycle a complex series of channels existed on both sides of the deep trough in the centre. In test 6 the deep lagoon was exchanged for a more natural shallow one, as it was felt that the deep lagoon trapped too much sediment carried into it on the flood tide. The channel in test 6 did not maintain its depth as well as in test 5 and the inlet became much longer and more oblique, with a long spit forming on the up-drift side of the lagoon. A channel through the bar was not maintained at so great a depth as formerly; it was no deeper than it had been originally, but much wider. It was, in fact, necessary to simulate a storm tide between cycles 301 and 310 to keep the channel open, because the outer bar had grown to such a height that high-tide waves could not wash over it. The results showed that with a shallow lagoon a large tidal flow is required to keep the channel open owing to the formation of bars both at the entrance and the lagoon end of the inlet. These features are very often a menace to navigation in natural tidal inlets so that the study relating to their maintenance has a practical value as well as illustrating the interaction of wave and tidal action in an interesting way.

An example of a recent study of tidal siltation in a real estuary may now be considered. The Mersey was the area first used for tidal model work, and a more recent model has given valuable information concerning the movement of sediment in the estuary; field work has also been carried out to support the model work and to help in its interpretation (Price and Kendrick, 1963). The model was built at the Hydraulics Research Station and was used with a second model, designed to test the effect of training walls. These models showed the importance of taking the salinity of the water into account when both river flow and tidal flow are involved in the transport of sediment in an estuary.

The Mersey estuary consists of an outer portion in which large sand banks are exposed at low water, and across which the navigational channel has been trained between stone walls for nine miles (see fig. 4.10). This channel leads to the Narrows, a single deep channel six miles long, 3000 feet wide and 60 feet deep at low spring tide, when the tidal range is about 27 feet. The upper estuary then opens out into a large tidal basin of maximum width of 18,000 feet and 26 miles in length, extending to Warrington; this area largely dries out at low water, there being three tidal channels in the lower part, but only discontinuous and changing channels in the upper part. This part is by-passed by the Manchester Ship Canal.

The field work that was carried out in the estuary was designed to give data necessary for the construction of the model; tidal and river currents, salinity and amount of material being moved in suspension were all measured in many places. The field experiments also included the use of radio-active tracer in Liverpool Bay. Admiralty charts of the area were also analysed to

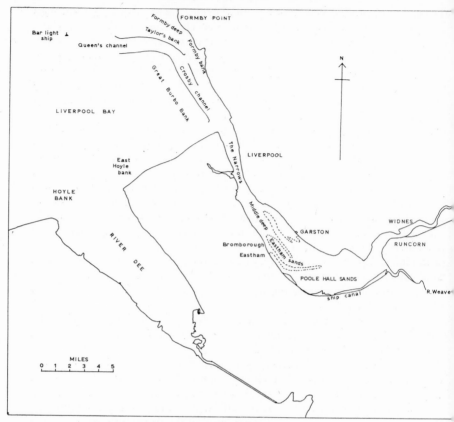

FIGURE 4.10. Map of the Mersey area to illustrate the model studies of the Mersey estuary and Liverpool Bay.

provide a historical view of the development of the estuary. This was again necessary for the setting up of the model; known changes could then be simulated and future ones extrapolated with more confidence.

Of the two models that were constructed one had scales of 1 in 3200 horizontally and 1 in 120 vertically, and the other 1 in 550 and 1 in 60. The larger area covered by the first model included Liverpool Bay, and the upper Mersey estuary, as well as the Dee estuary and the north coast of Wales as far as Rhyl. Its main object was to study the effect of the training works on the circulation in the estuary. The second model was the larger of the two and had a movable bed, unlike the first model, which had a fixed bed. The second model covered the Mersey estuary upstream from the Narrows; its purpose was to study the circulation pattern in the upper estuary, particularly the shoaling of the two channels that are closest to the shores near the downstream end of the upper estuary. These are called the Garston Channel on the north and the Eastham Channel on the south. The amount of sediment in the upper estuary has increased by siltation, and this material comes mainly from the sea, although there must clearly be a net flow of water out of the estuary. However, saline water coming in from the sea is denser than the fresh water and flows in along the bottom, bringing the sediment with it, while the fresh water flows out along the top; salinity differences of between 1 and 2% have been recorded in the Narrows channel. In the Mersey much of the material being deposited is sand, and this is more influenced by the bottom currents.

Field observations were made with current meters near the bed, at mid-depth and near the surface, and water samples for sediment and salinity analysis were taken with a pump sampler. A net drift landward was found on the bed for a variety of tidal ranges varying from 9000 to 15,000 feet per tide; near the surface there was a seaward drift. The transport of sediment also showed a landward drift on most occasions, although at times a seaward drift was indicated. The volume increased rapidly with the tidal range, although the results cannot be considered entirely accurate, owing to rapid variation in values; nearly all the material was silt. At another position, however, sand was recorded in the transported load. The salinity difference increased the effectiveness of the flood tide at the expense of the ebb.

The model was fitted with a tide-generating machine which could produce either a sequence of tides from spring to neap, or a continuous series of tides of the same range. The natural pattern of tides in the estuary could be reproduced satisfactorily, a miniature current meter being used to measure the model tides. The effect of salinity was tested by first running the model without any saline water; the results of this test showed a poor correspondence with the prototype. With no saline water the net drift was divided across the estuary, a landward drift taking place on the northern side and a seaward one on the southern side. When correct salinity relationships were included drift on the bed was all inland, with seaward flow taking place in the upper water. The salinity that was used in the model was the same as that found in the prototype, and the results then agreed closely with the net flows recorded in the real estuary. In testing the movement of sediment, the addition of saline water reversed the direction of movement in part, so that the importance of correct salinity relationships was clearly shown.

In considering the causes of siltation in the upper estuary, it was argued that at the beginning of the century the system had reached equilibrium, with the material coming up the Narrows into the upper estuary from the sea but not in such quantity as to cause serious loss of capacity in the upper estuary. The training works in Liverpool Bay were thought to have been responsible for changes in circulation in the outer estuary and to have allowed an increased amount of silt to travel into the upper estuary. Hence the smaller model of the larger area was constructed to assess the effect of the training works on the circulation in the estuary. The bed of the estuary in the model was first moulded to that of the 1911 survey and measurements of the currents were made to establish the circulation, after having shown that the prototype conditions could be reliably reproduced in the model. The net drift conditions in the 1911 state could be assessed. The results showed a fairly large rate of seaward drift at the mouth of the Narrows channel. The bed was then moulded to the 1957 survey, by which time the training works had been constructed. The observations of the model currents were again made to establish the net drift direction. The tidal correspondence between the model and the prototype were very close and the model and true current observations agreed well; the prototype showed a net drift of 7900 feet, while the model value scaled up was 7500 feet. The pattern of circulation revealed for the two dates showed very great changes. The flow had become concentrated in the trained channel, but out in the centre of the bay the drift, that had formerly been seawards, was reversed to flow inland, a result confirmed by the radio-active tracer experiments. Thus material that would formerly have moved into deeper water could now find its way up to the upper estuary, and as this area was used for dumping material the situation in the upper estuary was aggravated. The sand banks on the south side of the training wall were shown to provide the material filling in the upper estuary. Between 1906 and 1960 the loss of capacity of the upper estuary was 103 million cu.yd which would cause a reduction of depth of 2·8 feet throughout. Part of the material was derived from the deepening of the trained channel but this cannot account for all the material deposited upstream. Before training, the model net drift pattern suggested that material was moving fairly freely in the bay, ebb channels interdigitating with flood channels, causing a state of dynamic equilibrium of the sediments in the area as the material moved up one channel and down the next. When the training walls were in place the material could only move down the channel with the ebb, and if overflowing of the walls occurred only the upper water flowed over and little sediment was carried as a result.

Although the training works achieved their main aim of keeping a deep channel available to Liverpool, the use of modern methods of investigation, with the aid of models, has shown that these works are the main cause of the deterioration in the upper estuary. But it is not the only one; one of the effects of building training walls is that they prevent the natural tendency of the channel to meander, and meandering leads to erosion as well as deposition, whereas when the channel is forced to flow straight the adjacent area can silt up much more readily. Surveys of the Eastham Channel show that this has meandered very considerably in the past; the main low water channel in the upper estuary moved between 1867 and 1891 to cover at one time or another nearly all positions in the estuary that were possible, but in 1891-1893 the channel became stabilised owing to some artificial check on its movement. Experiments carried out in the upper estuary model to establish the net drift showed that the central of the three channels, already mentioned, is a flood channel and the other two are ebb channels. In order to establish the effects of training works on these channels, the model was used for tests of various types of works, and the results showed that the depths in the Eastham Channel could probably be increased by suitable training works. The possibility of reclaiming an island in the estuary was also considered but model results suggested that such a scheme would cause more problems than it would solve. The more the channels are free to move the less likely they are to lose depth, and silting over a wide area would be prevented, since in the estuary meandering is an erosional process under these conditions.

The model equipment and the experiments that have been carried out with it show that models can provide much material of value in increasing the understanding of the action of processes associated with river flow, waves and tides. The models are, however, elaborate and expensive pieces of equipment, beyond the scope of most individual workers. Nevertheless the results obtained by these means should not be lost sight of in analysing the operation of these processes. Much of the work that has been described has been carried out by engineers, with particular practical problems in mind, but some of the work is pure research, aimed at understanding the basic processes, which in turn can be used for practical problems and for obtaining a better knowledge of the geomorphological processes and the resultant landforms.

e) *Submarine processes—Experiments on turbidity currents.* The investigation of turbidity currents is not of such immediate practical application as the studies already described, but, as was shown by the account of the cable breaks resulting from the Grand Banks earthquake, discussed in the last chapter, sometimes the effect of turbidity currents can have results of direct human significance. Turbidity currents, however, are difficult to investigate actually in progress, so that a model study of the phenomenon can give very interesting and useful results, which help to explain the full-scale processes.

The model investigations can also be of assistance in testing theoretical ideas on the subject of auto-suspension of sediment, which is thought to be an important element in the operation of turbidity currents in the ocean. The most extensive experimental work on turbidity currents of high density has been carried out by Kuenen (1951). The main essential of a turbidity current is that it should be denser than the still water surrounding it. The experiments conducted to establish the factors determining the action of turbidity currents, and the relation between model and prototype dimensions, were carried out in a tank 2 m long, and 50 cm wide and deep, which could be tilted lengthwise. A bucket-full of the sediment, consisting of water, clay, sand and gravel, was stirred up and emptied into the tank near the bed at the upper end, and the progress of the water and sediment was measured with a stop-watch as it travelled down the tank. The effect of different variables could be ascertained by varying the density, volume, slope and the viscosity and noting changes in the velocity under the different conditions.

A second set of experiments was carried out in a longer trough, 30 m in length, with the purpose of studying the nature of the sediments resulting from turbidity current activity, and the nature of flow could also be studied. More sediment was used for these experiments, 100 to 150 litres, as opposed to a maximum of 18 litres in the smaller tank. In the longer trough the sediment was allowed to flow down a slope 20 cm high and 2 m long and then continued by its own momentum along a horizontal part of the floor. A final series of experiments was carried out to simulate a gorge opening out on to a flatter area of a deep sea basin.

The results of the experiments revealed three types of flow depending on the dilution of the sediment with water. When the sediment consists of a pasty mass of clay, with or without sand, it only flows a short distance down the slope before coming to rest. When the mass is slightly more diluted with water and when much sand is present in it, the flow is intermediate in character, a thin wedge of more viscous material moves forward at the base, which is overtaken by a highly turbulent turbidity current above. The upper part of the material in the turbulent flow settles with graded bedding, but the lower wedge does not; it breaks up into slabs and does not spread so far. With still further dilution the whole mass flows as a turbulent current, without the bottom wedge, the deposit settles over a wider area and is graded throughout. As the dilution is still further increased the movement remains similar, but less sand can be carried. In order to measure the density of the current, samples were taken at intervals with a series of siphons arranged along the axis of the trough at different levels above the floor. The glass siphons had a capacity of 80 cu.cm and they were filled by piercing a piece of rubber covering the top of the siphon, while the lower end was open at the required distance above the bottom; by this means the siphon filled in $\frac{3}{4}$ second and although the measured densities were probably too low the results give a correct idea of the variation of density along the trough.

They showed that the densest part was always at the head of the flow and near the base. The velocity of flow was also greatest at the base on account of the retarding effect of the static water and the greater momentum of the densest water on the bottom; it is bottom flow that keeps the head of the current supplied with the sediment that maintains its density. Velocities were measured over each stretch of 3 m from the bottom of the slope along the floor of the long trough, and the results showed a rate of flow of 75 cm/sec at the top of the slope, decreasing to about 50 cm/sec, 10 m from the top; and about 24 m from the top of the slope the speed was still 15 to 20 cm/sec. The rate of release of sediment was then slowed down and the velocities, although following the same shaped curve, were 10 to 20 cm/sec slower. Attempts to measure the effect of variations in viscosity on the velocity led to the conclusion that this factor was probably not of great importance, although the results were not entirely consistent (see figure 4.11).

An analysis of the results from the point of view of comparison with full-scale phenomena was complicated by the processes involved and the variables which included the mechanical properties of the sediment, its thixotropic character, its strength and viscosity, and the fact that the current is flowing through still water, a factor that does not occur in normal rivers. In calculating the velocity of the current the formula

$$V = C\,(m\,.\,s\,.\,d)^{\frac{1}{2}}$$

can be used, which applies strictly to rivers, where V is the velocity, m is the hydraulic mean depth, s is the slope and d the density. C must be given an appropriate value and the sine of the slope was used for *s*, while *d* must be the difference between the density of the current and that of the water above. The results showed that there is a straight line relationship between the velocity and the square root of the effective density, running through the origin, and indicating a velocity of 80 cm/sec with an effective density square root of 1. The value of *C* was found to agree reasonably well between the two

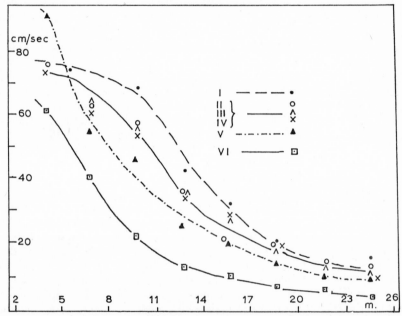

FIGURE 4.11. Results of experiments on model turbidity currents, measuring the velocity along the horizontal floor of the ditch. The distance from the top of the initial slope is shown. Roman numerals refer to the composition of the suspension as follows:

	Water %	Clay kg	Fine sand kg	Coarse sand kg	Density
I	70	30	60	20	1·58
II	70	25	60	20	1·57
III	70	25	60	20	1·57
IV	65	30	60	20	1·58
V	70	40	60	20	1·59
VI	70	40	60	20	1·59

(after Kuenen)

troughs, and a value of 125 gives a good mean; this is about $\frac{1}{6}$ of the value for rivers, probably owing to the effect of turbulence in the flow. In estimating the relationship between model and prototype velocity, it is necessary to make assumptions concerning the dimensions of the prototype; this can be done by considering the area of any one graded bed and its thickness. A volume of $\frac{1}{10}$ cu.km would seem reasonable, if a density of 1·6 is assumed; the full-scale volume of flow would be about 2×10^9 times that in the larger

TG H 2

model trough. It may be estimated by comparison with the model that the depth of the current might have been 100 times that of the model or about 20 m and the velocity 10 times or 7 m/sec.

In the third model a short steep canyon debouched into a basin 3 by 5 m in area and 40 to 50 cm deep, about 40 litres of suspension material was used. The flow spread out to form an almost perfect semicircle at the foot of the canyon. With coarse sand a subaqueous delta was formed. The finer material formed a more horizontal deposit further away, there was a deep hollow at the mouth of the canyon, slightly elongated in its direction of flow, which was oblique to the basin below it. This hollow must have been eroded by the turbidity current, before it deposited the surrounding ring of sediment. The size of the area covered by sediment depended on the density of the current, its velocity and the size of the sediment. These results provide valuable information on a process that cannot be seen actually in operation and demonstrates some of the factors involved and how they operate.

It is worth noting that the theoretical work of Bagnold (1963) on auto-suspension of sediment suggests that the sediment should be uniformly distributed throughout the moving mass. The sediment should move under its own momentum if the internal friction gradient, tan ϕ, is exceeded by the gravity gradient, tan β, so a turbidity current should be able to move by auto-suspension if tan β exceeds the gradient $w / \bar{U}$, where $\bar{U}$ is the mean transport velocity of the suspended load, w is the fall velocity of the sediment grains and β is the angle of inclination of the bed. These conditions are confined to turbulent flow. From these relationships it follows that if the rate of fall of sediment particles is less than the transport velocity of the suspended load multiplied by the tangent of the angle of slope, the transport rate of the grains will be unlimited, except when the concentration of sediment is so great that turbulent flow no longer takes place. Bagnold has applied these views to the development of a formula which might be used to determine the size and character of a turbidity current that would enable it to be self-generating. This formula could usefully be checked by model observations, as it would not be easy to check in the field. These two approaches provide a good example of the experimental and theoretical approach to a problem that is difficult to study under natural conditions, and if the two methods of approach can be linked by the testing of the theoretical results the value of the study is greatly enhanced.

f) *Glacial processes.* Much theoretical work has been done on the problems associated with glacier flow, some of which has already been mentioned in connection with full-scale experiments on the flow of actual glaciers. However, some of the essential properties of ice that occur as constants in many of the formulae can best be measured in the controlled conditions of a laboratory. The work of J. W. Glen, in measuring the strain rate of polycrystalline ice, is a good example of this approach and of the value of laboratory experiment in glaciology. Attempts have also been made to study the whole glacier and its flow characteristics in a model; but before considering these some other aspects of ice study and models will be mentioned.

One interesting possibility has been suggested by Robin (1962) in considering the work done by Weertman (1961); Robin points out that the large ice-sheets, such as that of the Antarctic, deform at a speed intermediate between that of the earth as a whole and the laboratory models that can be devised to study earth movement. Weertman has studied in detail the forces at work in an ice-sheet governing its thickness and the extent and thickness of floating ice-shelves. In these shelves deformation takes place at measurable speeds and the forces that it depends on can be measured, but this is not possible with earth movements, which take place too slowly for noticeable change to be recorded in one life-time. Thus the deformation of the great ice-sheets, that probably resemble the earth's crust in many essential factors, could be used as a model of the earth's crust, enabling the nature of earth movements and the forces that cause them to be studied. As with all models the scale factors and negative analogies would have to be given due weight, but at least some useful indications might well be forthcoming from such a study. Weertman has shown that if a mean temperature difference of no more than 30 degrees existed under the different oceans, the force that causes ice-shelves to spread could produce similar effects in the earth's crust; this would result in continental drift. The movement depends on the deformation of the ice or rock under stress, and this is the aspect of experimental work that can be carried out in the laboratory.

Experiments on the plastic deformation of polycrystalline ice were carried out by Glen (1958a and b). He has shown that polycrystalline ice behaves in a different way from a single ice crystal and, as glaciers are polycrystalline, his results are of value in determining the character of ice movement in glaciers. A single ice crystal deforms along one well established slip plane; but in polycrystalline ice the orientation of the different grains plays an important part. Some interesting work was done on the deformation of ice as the result of a proposal to form an iceberg aircraft carrier in the Second World War. The material tested was a frozen mixture of water and wood pulp. The plastic properties of this material showed considerable similarity to the behaviour of metals at high temperature, and suggested that the analogy of the deformation of ice and metals could provide useful information concerning the plastic deformation of polycrystalline ice. Glen found that in a number of his experiments with ice there was a close similarity with some metals. This illustrates the value of analogy in scientific investigation.

The results of Glen's experiments showed that the flow law of ice, as it has been termed, could be stated as the relationship $\dot\epsilon = k\,\sigma^n$, where $\dot\epsilon$ is the strain rate, and σ the stress; k and n are constants. The values of these constants varied with conditions, but the relationship plotted produced a straight line on log paper. The value of n was found to be $3 \cdot 17 \pm 0 \cdot 2$ for tests with a temperature of $-0 \cdot 02°C$ and $-1 \cdot 5°C$. This value held reasonably well over the stress range of 1 to 10 kg/sq.cm. Similar experiments by Steinemann suggested that n should be $1 \cdot 85$ for low stresses of 1 kg/sq.cm but be increased to $4 \cdot 16$ for stresses of 15 kg/sq.cm. This result may be due to the long time that is needed to reach stability at low stresses. When correlated with observations on an actual glacier the higher value of n seems to be justified. The strain rate was much reduced, by a factor of about 6, when the temperature was lowered to $-6\cdot7$ and $-12\cdot8°C$. Most of the tests were made with the ice in compression or tension, but some shear experiments have also been carried out. The flow law of ice can be used to predict the rate of closure of glacier tunnels under hydrostatic pressure, but if the glacier is also undergoing strong compression, as on the ice-fall in Austerdalsbreen, the rate of closure will be greater than that indicated by the flow law, as other factors are influencing it. The laboratory results provide a very useful relationship that can then be tested in the field and used to calculate further effects resulting from the deformation of the ice under stresses of different types.

The analogy between the behaviour of ice and metals has already been mentioned, and there is another fruitful analogy worth consideration; this is the similarity between rotational shear slips discussed in chapter 3, and the rotational movement of a small corrie glacier, that has also been described (p. 102). This similarity first led W. V. Lewis to suggest that corrie glaciers might erode their beds by rotational slipping. The work described in chapter 3 has shown that this movement does not take place along discrete slip planes as Lewis (1949) at first suggested, but that the glacier rotates as a whole with some deformation as well. There is thus a fairly close analogy between the movement of a small cirque glacier and that of a rotational shear slip in cohesive strata, as described by W. H. Ward.

This led Lewis to search for some material that might simulate the movement of a glacier under model conditions. The material had to be such that its strength corresponded to the glacier ice in the correct scale ratio, the linear scale being between 1 in 1000 and 1 in 10,000. The material would have to be rigid enough to crack to form crevasses and yet able to yield to stresses by plastic deformation, and it would have to be able to slip on a rigid bed. An organosilicon product, or bouncing putty, was selected for experiments carried out in the Physiographical Laboratory at Cambridge University; this material has several interesting properties, it deforms plastically under small stresses and imitates the viscous flow of a glacier very well, but it does not often produce crevasses, although it will break abruptly if a sharp, sudden force is exerted. The bouncing-putty glacier showed the normal curvature of a line of stakes across a glacier, and the match sticks, used to simulate the stakes, leant forward, indicating a more rapid flow on the surface. The material also slipped on a greased bed.

The bouncing putty, apart from being very expensive, also had qualities that did not conform to those of ice, so a new material was tested and found to be suitable. This was kaolin, mixed in a proportion of two parts of kaolin to one of water; this mixture showed many features simulating similar ones on real glaciers. The strength of the mixture could be determined by the amount of water used with it, although there were some problems of drying out, so that experiments could not be too lengthy; alternatively the atmosphere had to be kept damp. One way of overcoming the drying out was to use light engine oil instead of water. The drying out had one advantage that the small cracks, simulating crevasses, tended to widen and become more conspicuous as the surface dried. One of the problems of simulating glacier flow is the difficulty of allowing for the accumulation and ablation that play an important part in the glacier behaviour.

The model glacier was 150 cm long and 30 cm wide. Its bed was modelled in plaster of Paris and included a cirque basin at the head, reversals of slope on the floor and a plain for the tongue to extend on to below. At one point the glacier was made to flow along the glass wall of the trough, to enable the internal movement to be observed; the kaolin slipped past with little drag if the glass was well greased. The kaolin mixture at first filled the corrie and overflowed slightly down the valley. Movement was initiated by tilting the trough. Step faults formed at the brink of the sill out of the corrie and lower down the valley, resembling the tensional crevasses at the lip of ice-falls. A bergschrund formed at the head wall of the corrie and bed slip was observed. An increase of the tilt caused more rapid movement, but a reduction stopped it. The crevasses that formed on the steeper parts of the bed tended to close as the bed flattened and the flow became compressive. Some attempt was made to simulate the annual accumulation of the glacier by adding a wedge-shaped volume of new kaolin to the upper part of the glacier; a layer of dust was spread on the surface, to indicate the summer surface, before putting on the new material. This method showed that the annual layers were tilted, very much as in a real glacier where the upturned annual outcrops may be conspicuous. Thus the model galcier reproduced many of the features of a real glacier.

A second experiment was carried out in which the glacier model was used to reproduce the characteristics of the small corrie glacier Vesl-Skautbreen, already described in chapter 3. A model of the glacier floor was made and cut in half so that a cross section of the flow could be studied along the glass side of the trough, the model being on a linear scale of 1 in 1000. It was difficult to induce movement at a reasonable angle of slope with the glacier thickness to scale, so a thicker glacier was used, representing the glacier at the time of maximum post-glacial advance. This glacier moved mainly by slipping over its bed, but there was some differential movement through the ice, with the most rapid flow within the ice. Wedge-shaped additions of kaolin caused the glacier snout to advance with a very steep front slope, simulating the character of an advancing glacier in nature (see figure 4.12).

Some preliminary experiments with bouncing-putty model glaciers by Lewis have been mentioned, but more recently this material has been used for a different type of study; its movement was speeded up by whirling the model glacier in a centrifuge (Ramberg 1964). The model consisted of a source basin connected to a piedmont flat by a narrow valley. The bouncing putty was placed in the upper basin and was induced to flow to the piedmont flat by the whirling action, which caused a great increase of pressure proportional to the acceleration. In this way the glacier was made to flow in a short time, but it remained static when the rotation was stopped; this facilitated study of the deformation produced. Stroboscopic light allowed the evolution of the structures to be watched as they formed. Powdered wax was used to imitate moraines on the glacier. The whole model was small, fitting into a cup 10·5 cm in diameter. Before centrifuging the model strips of 'moraine' were placed in varying positions on the 'glacier', which was placed in the upper basin. After an initial period, during which the bouncing putty moved into the lower basin, a steady state was set up, when the centrifuge

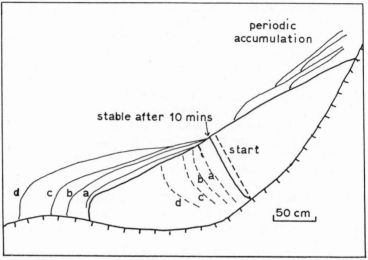

FIGURE 4.12. Scale model of Vesl-Skautbreen at 1:1000. The effect of four additional wedges of accumulation is shown in the flow pattern and snout advance. (after Lewis and Miller)

was run at 1000 *g*. The moraines remained parallel to the direction of flow in the valley, but folding started at the mouth of the valley and became intensified outwards, as in similar natural glaciers, such as the Malaspina. This was due to compression acting in a direction parallel to the moraine elongation, and extension occurring normal to the moraine. The greater viscosity of the moraine material caused the buckling to start at the valley outlet. When the 'moraines' were made of material similar in viscosity to the rest of the 'glacier' its deformation provided a useful means of assessing the geometrical character of the folding and related it to the strain rates of longitudinal compression and lateral extension in the piedmont lobe. There was no indication of shearing even in very sharp chevron-type folds.

The examples of different types of models that have been described should help to give some idea of the great variety of problems that are amenable to model study. The models can be simple or elaborate, the results can be qualitative or quantitative, applicable to general problems concerning the features simulated or to a specific local example to solve a specific problem. The versatility of models must, however, be balanced by the formidable problems of relating all the different aspects of scale ratios correctly between the model and the prototype. Nevertheless the controlled conditions that can be produced in models have enabled a great deal of valuable work to be achieved, many theoretical results have been checked, and many full-scale problems have become better understood, if not fully solved, as a result of model studies.

REFERENCES

ALLEN, J. 1947. *Scale models in hydraulic engineering*. London.

BAGNOLD, R. A. 1940. Beach formation by waves: some model experiments in a wave tank. *Journ. Inst. Civ. Eng.* 15, 27-52.

BAGNOLD, R. A. 1941. *The physics of blown sand and desert dunes*. London.

BAGNOLD, R. A. 1947. Sand movement by waves: some small scale experiments with sand of very low density. *Journ. Inst. Civ. Eng.* 27, 447-469.

BAGNOLD, R. A. 1956. The flow of cohesionless grains in fluids. *Phil. Trans. Roy. Soc.* A 249, 234-297.

BAGNOLD, R. A. 1963. Chap. 21, Beach and nearshore processes, in *The Sea*, vol. III, ed. M. N. Hill, New York, 518-522.

BELLY, P. Y. 1964. Sand movement by wind. C.E.R.C. *Tech. Memo.* 1. 27 pp.

BLENCH, T. 1957. *Regime behaviour of canals and rivers*. London.

BRUUN, P. and GERRITSEN, F. 1960. *Stability of coastal inlets*. Amsterdam.

EAGLESON, P. S., GLENNE, B. and DRACUP, J. A. 1961. Equilibrium characteristics of sand beaches in the offshore zone. B.E.B. *Tech. Memo.* 126, 64 pp. Washington.

FAIRCHILD, J. C. 1959. Suspended sediment sampling in laboratory wave action. B.E.B. *Tech. Memo.* 115. 25 pp. Washington.

GIBSON, A. H. 1934. The use of models in hydraulic engineering. *Trans. Inst. Water Eng.* 39, 172.

GLEN, J. W. 1958a. Mechanical properties of ice, I The plastic properties of ice. *Phil. Mag. Supp.* 7, 254-265.

GLEN, J. W. 1958b. The flow law of ice. U.G.G.I. *Ass. Int. Hydrol. Sci. Chamonix* 171-183.

HARWOOD, F. L. and WILSON, K. C. 1957. An investigation into a proposal to dispose of power-station ash by discharging it into the sea at low water. *Proc. Inst. Civ. Eng.* 8, 53-70.

HESSE, M. B. 1963. *Models and analogies in Science*. London.

Hydraulics Research Board Report 1956. D.S.I.R. 1957 Publ. 33-36.

IPPEN, A. T. and EAGLESON, P. S. 1955. A Study of sediment sorting by waves shoaling on a plane beach. B.E.B. *Tech. Memo.* 63. Washington.

JOHNSON, J. W. 1953. Sand transport by littoral currents. *Proc. 5th Hydraul. Conf. Bull.* 34 89-109.

KEMP, P. H. 1962. A model study of the behaviour of beaches and groynes. *Proc. Inst. Civ. Eng.* 22, 191-210.

KING, C. A. M. and WILLIAMS, W. W. 1949. The formation and movement of sand bars by wave action. *Geog. Journ.* 113, 70-85.

KING, C. A. M. 1951. The depth of disturbance of sand on sea beaches. *Journ. Sed. Petrol.* 21, 131-140.

KRUMBEIN, W. C. 1961. The analysis of observational data from natural beaches. B.E.B. *Tech. Memo.* 130. 58 pp. Washington.

KUENEN, P. H. 1951. Properties of turbidity currents of high density. *Soc. Econ. Paleo. Min. Sp. Publ.* 2, 14-33.

LEOPOLD, L. B., WOLMAN, M. G. and MILLER, J. P. 1964. *Fluvial processes in Geomorphology*. New York.

LEWIS, W. V. 1944. Stream trough experiments and terrace formation. *Geol. Mag.* 81, 241-253.

LEWIS, W. V. 1945. Nick points and the curve of water erosion. *Geol. Mag.* 82, 256-266.

LEWIS, W. V. 1949. Glacial movement by rotational slipping. *Geogr. Ann.* 1, 146-158.

LEWIS, W. V. and MILLER, M. M. 1955. Kaolin model glaciers. *Journ. Glaciol.* 2, 533-538.

LONGUET-HIGGINS, M. S. 1953. Mass transport in water waves. *Phil. Trans. Roy. Soc.* A 245, 535-581.

MANOHAR, M. 1955. Mechanics of bottom sediment movement due to wave action. B.E.B. *Tech. Memo.* 75. 101 pp. Washington.

NYE, J. F. 1960. The response of glaciers and ice sheets to seasonal and climatic changes. *Proc. Roy. Soc.* A 256, 559-584.

PRICE, W. A. and KENDRICK, M. P. 1963. Field and model investigations into the reasons for siltation in the Mersey Estuary. *Proc. Inst. Civ. Eng.* 24, 473-517.

RAMBERG, H. 1964. Note on model studies of folding of moraines in piedmont glaciers. *Journ. Glaciol.* 5, 207-218.

ROBIN, G. de Q. 1962. The ice of the Antarctic. *Sci. Amer.* 861, 14 pp.

ROSS, C. W. 1955. Laboratory study of shock pressures of breaking waves. B.E.B. *Tech. Memo.* 59. 22 pp. Washington.

RUSSELL, R. C. H. and OSORIO, J. D. C. 1958. An experimental investigation of drift profiles in a closed channel. *Proc. 6th Conf. Coastal Eng.* 171-183.

SAVAGE, R. P. 1959. Laboratory data on wave run-up on roughened and permeable slopes. B.E.B. *Tech. Memo.* 109. 10 pp. Washington.

SAVAGE, R. P. 1959. Laboratory study of the effect of groins on the rate of littoral transport: equipment development and initial tests. B.E.B. *Tech. Memo.* 114, 55 pp. Washington.

SAVILLE, T., CALDWELL, J. M. and SIMMONS, H. B. 1957. Preliminary Report: Laboratory study of the effect of an uncontrolled inlet on the adjacent beaches. B.E.B. *Tech. Memo.* 94. 19 pp.

SAVILLE, T. 1950. Model study of sand transport along an infinitely long straight beach *Trans. Amer. Geoph. Un.* 31, 555-565.

SCHEIDEGGER, A. E. 1961. *Theoretical geomorphology.* Berlin.

SHAY, E. A. and JOHNSON, J. W. 1953. Model studies on the movement of sand transported along a straight beach. *Inst. Eng. Res. Univ. California.* Issue 7, series 14 (unpublished).

SIBUL, O. 1955. Laboratory study of the generation of wind waves in shallow water. B.E.B. *Tech. Memo.* 72, Washington.

STEBBINGS, J. 1963. The shapes of self-formed model alluvial channels. *Proc. Inst. Civ. Eng.* 25, 485-510.

VANONI, V. A. and NOMICOS, G. N. 1960. Resistant properties of sediment-laden streams. *Amer. Soc. Civ. Eng. Trans.* 125, 1140-1175.

WEERTMAN, J. 1961. The stability of ice-age ice sheets. *Journ. Geoph. Res.* 66, 3783-3792.

WIEGEL, R. L. and ARNOLD, A. L. 1957. Model study of wave refraction. B.E.B. *Tech. Memo.* 103. 14 pp. Washington.

YOUNG, A. 1963. Deductive models of slope evolution. *Nach. Akad. Wissen. Gottingen* II Maths.-Phys. 5, 45-66.

ZINGG, A. W. 1952. Wind tunnel studies of the movement of sedimentary material. *Proc. 5th Hydraul. Conf.*

5 CARTOGRAPHIC AND MORPHO-METRIC ANALYSIS

Maps on which the surface relief is portrayed by the use of contours provide a valuable tool for the geomorphologist, and many methods of geomorphological map analysis have been developed. The value of the results of cartographic analysis depends on several factors; the quality of the map used is, of course, one of the most important and if contours are not correctly placed the results will be inaccurate, quite apart from any errors in plotting that may arise during the course of the analysis. There are, however, rather more subtle dangers in some cartographic methods of analysing relief forms; these will be considered in relation to the methods concerned. Maps are the basis of many types of work that will be considered in this chapter; the accuracy of the maps being used for any purpose of cartographic analysis must, therefore, be considered before the work is undertaken.

I. ACCURACY OF CONTOURS

The publication by the Ordnance Survey in Great Britain of the 1 in 25,000 maps has provided a very convenient scale for much geomorphological analysis, although the 6 inches to 1 mile map (1 in 10,560) may still be required for some of the more detailed work. One of the great merits of the 1 in 25,000 map, which may be taken as an example of surveys suitable for morphological analysis, is its 25-ft contour interval. This gives a very good indication of the shape of the ground and is very suitable for most techniques.

It is worth considering the accuracy of these contours before the methods of using them and similar maps are mentioned. K. M. Clayton (1953) has gone into this point and has produced some interesting evidence. It must, however, be remembered that his remarks refer to some of the earlier versions of this map, and more recent publications will have a greater number of surveyed contours, much of the more recent work being done by means of stereoscopic aerial photographs, which can be used to delimit the contours with good accuracy. It is intended to survey all the 25-ft contours in this way eventually. In 1953, however, the number of surveyed contours depended partly on the locality; only in the south of England and Wales were the 100-ft contours all surveyed instrumentally up to 1000 feet; above this height the contours were only surveyed every 250 feet. On some of the earlier 6 in. to 1 mile maps only the instrumentally surveyed contours were shown, hence the 100-ft interval on this scale on many of the older maps.

Clayton has found from using the 1 in 25,000 maps for detailed field work that, although there are occasional really serious errors, in many instances the contours portray the landforms very well, as they are often placed at the break of slope between facets; these breaks of slope must have been emphasised on the original hill-sketches used to interpolate the intermediate contours. Until all the contours have been surveyed the results obtained by analysis of maps will have an element of uncertainty.

Nevertheless the 1 in 25,000 maps of the Ordnance Survey do provide useful material for many methods of morphological analysis, and their value will be greatly enhanced when more accurate contours are available. They can be used quite safely to establish a series of surfaces whose separation is greater than that of the surveyed contours; but where the separation of a series of surfaces is less than the surveyed contours then the results may not be justified. In all geomorphological analysis using maps it is necessary to ascertain the accuracy of the contours before work is started. In some countries the contours do not claim to be more than form lines and have no high accuracy. These maps are useful for plotting field surveys, but cannot be used for cartographic analysis.

In any case these cartographic methods should be used with great care, because quite apart from any inherent deficiency in the map itself, the results may be misleading unless they are related to findings in the field. There is a danger that if the cartographic analysis precedes the field work, then the field evidence may be seen in the light of the results already obtained by morphometric methods. It is, therefore, probably better to do the bulk of the field work first, and then use the cartographic techniques to confirm and illustrate the findings of the field survey. It may well happen that the map data reveal points that were not appreciated in the initial field work and these can then be further studied in the field. The danger is particularly great in the case of some of the methods designed to demonstrate erosion surfaces from cartographic analysis; the methods themselves only give positive results if the surfaces are horizontal, but even if the results are negative, it does not mean necessarily that there are no erosion surfaces, but only that if they are present they are not horizontal. This is a very common occurrence when the remnants are of subaerial origin and follow the slope of the valleys.

With these warnings in mind, the methods can still often be used to obtain useful results. The methods that depend only on map evidence will be considered first, then a discussion of some of the ways in which field data can be used to prepare diagrams that allow the data to be more readily analysed and appreciated, such as the height-range diagram and the mathematical extension of river profiles will follow. Air photographs, which are being used increasingly for geomorphological interpretation, will also be mentioned. All the methods to be discussed first apply to the whole landscape, but there are special features that can also be demonstrated from map evidence and techniques that depend on theoretical knowledge, such as the construction of wave refraction diagrams, that can best be included in this chapter.

2. PROFILES

Although for detailed work the longitudinal profile of a river valley should be accurately surveyed, yet a profile constructed from a large-scale map will often provide sufficient evidence to demonstrate a point seen in the field or suggest a possible solution to a particular problem, that can then be checked in the field. As an example of the uses of longitudinal profiles the Upper Wensleydale area and Howgill Fells may be cited. In the latter area some river captures have taken place that can be very convincingly demonstrated by drawing longitudinal profiles of the small streams concerned. These profiles (figure 5.1) show that the former courses of Little and Great Ulgill Beck

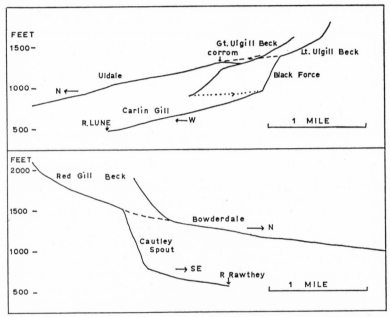

FIGURE 5.1. Longitudinal river profiles drawn from the 1:25,000 O.S. map to illustrate river captures in the Howgill Fells, north-west England.

must clearly have flowed down Uldale prior to their capture by Carlin Gill, which has a double advantage over the north-flowing streams; both these points are clearly demonstrated by the profiles and these therefore confirmed the field analysis. The profiles reveal that the slope of Carlin Gill and its length both act in its favour, and the reason for its greater slope is clearly apparent in the knick-point near Tebay. This shows up very clearly even on a profile drawn from map data alone, and is very easily identified in the field.

The second example from the Howgill Fells also indicates the capture of the head-waters of Bowderdale by the stream flowing over Cautley Spout; this has been hastened by glacial action, forming the corrie of Cautley Crags, which can be identified both on the map and very clearly on the ground.

The longitudinal profiles of the Ure and its tributaries in its upper reaches also reveal points of interest that bear upon its geomorphological development. Again the profiles can be used to support and confirm field observations. By constructing the longitudinal profile of the river from its source to below its confluence with the Cover it can be seen that the main stream hangs to its much shorter tributary, Bishopdale Beck, and, as the amount of hang is of the order of 150 feet, it does not require an accurately surveyed profile to reveal it. By drawing representative cross profiles of the valleys a clue to account for this anomaly is suggested, and this again can be confirmed by field evidence: the cross profile of Bishopdale Beck is deeply U-shaped clearly suggesting glacial scouring, but the profile of the Ure valley shows no similar evidence of excessive glacial erosion (see figure 5.2). An

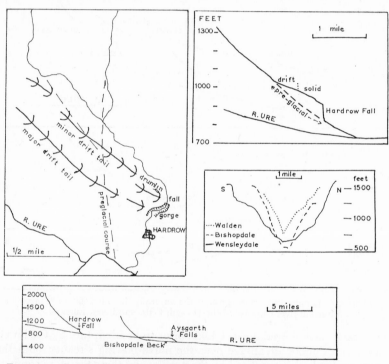

FIGURE 5.2. Longitudinal river profiles and cross profiles drawn to illustrate river development in Upper Wensleydale, Yorkshire. The map shows the diversion of the stream eastwards by drift-tail deposition.

examination of the larger surrounding area on a map provides a possible reason for this difference, which can then provide a basis for further field observations. It is interesting to note that the longitudinal profile of the neighbouring tributary, Walden Beck, shows the same steepening of gradient as the main stream, and its cross profile is steeply V-shaped, showing little glacial modification. The map of the area shows that its head is protected by

high ground from ice, while its neighbour Bishopdale is in a position to receive the surplus ice from Wharfedale. The two very marked breaks of
gradient in the Ure and Walden Beck, revealed by examining their longitudinal profiles, can be shown to have the characteristics of knick-points, and
the Cover shows a similar steepening, although not so marked as in the Ure,
where the knick-point is held up on the hard Great Scar Limestone; in
Bishopdale the knick-point has been removed by glacial erosion.

Further up Wensleydale, Hardrow Beck has a waterfall 100 feet high (see
figure 5.2). By drawing the longitudinal profile of the beck it can be shown
that the fall is not a knick-point due to rejuvenation, but is the result of
glacial drift in drumlinoid drift-tails, which are clearly shown on the map,
diverting the stream into a new course, the upper part of which is gentler in
gradient to compensate for the fall, where the slope is steepened. Above and
below the diversion the profiles clearly belong to one graded pre-glacial
stream. Thus again the profile can confirm a field interpretation and illustrate it.

One use of cross valley profiles was mentioned in connection with the Ure
drainage, where the shape of the profile was diagnostic of the processes
shaping the valley. Cross sections can also usefully be constructed in a polycyclic valley to relate the longitudinal profile to the cross profile. The knick-
points that are revealed in the long profile should be matched by valley
bench remnants on the hill-sides. If the relief of the area is not very great it
may be necessary to supplement the map evidence by additional field surveys, but in areas of relatively high relief at least a first indication or con-
firmation of benches may be sought in the construction of cross profiles.

Where the valley has undergone relatively great incision, as for example
the River Churnet, which has been greatly deepened by fluvio-glacial melt
water, cross profiles may be used to reconstruct the longitudinal profile of the
valley before incision took place (see figure 5.3). In such a situation the cross
profile shows clearly the break of slope at the upper limit of the fluvio-
glacial modification of the valley. The pre-glacial valley can be reconstructed
by joining the two breaks of slope on either side of the valley. Then the base
of the reconstructed cross profile can be used to reconstruct the longitudinal
profile before modification. In this instance the result is fairly clear-cut, as
subsequent erosion has been limited because the fluvio-glacial down-cutting
took place in the Newer Drift period. The reconstructed longitudinal profile
shows clearly the position of the col where the melt-water first overflowed to
cut the spillway gorge, which is 300 feet deep on the col, where its depth is at
a maximum. It must clearly decrease upstream from this point as the drainage of this section has been reversed.

In drawing cross profiles there may be evidence of benches, but these
should be checked in the field to ensure that they are genuine erosional
features. The profiles that have been mentioned to show characteristics of
river development can be extended to illustrate processes operating over the
whole landscape. For example a common and useful way of demonstrating
the relief of an area pictorially is to draw a series of profiles across it at uni-

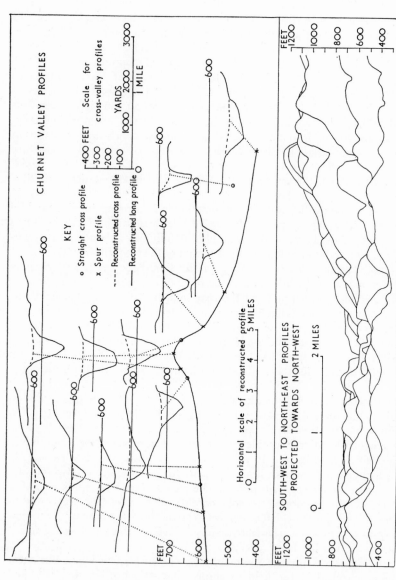

FIGURE 5.3. Cross profiles of the Churnet valley, Staffordshire, to illustrate the method of reconstructing former longitudinal profiles. The projected profiles are drawn looking towards the north-west across the Churnet valley.

form intervals. The kilometer grid lines on the Ordnance Survey maps often make a useful foundation for the drawing of a series of profiles. The most suitable direction in which to draw the profiles will clearly depend on the nature of the country, and it is usually best to draw them at right angles to the grain of the country. There is always the danger that the line may in some parts of the map run along the contour, giving the false impression of a flat area, when in fact the ground may slope steeply at right angles to the profile line. Nevertheless a series of such profiles gives a very good visual impression of the landscape.

The profiles may be arranged in a number of ways; superimposed profiles include the most complete evidence, in that the whole of the series of profiles is plotted on the same graph. If more than five or six are included, however, the result becomes very confused, so the profiles are often drawn as projected profiles. In this type it must be decided from which direction the landscape is to be viewed, and if, for example, this is from the west, then the most westerly profile in a north-south series is plotted, the next one to the east is drawn where it projects above the first and so on to the most easterly profile, as shown on the figure 5.4. The result gives almost a panoramic view of the landscape and provides a very good pictorial impression of the landforms, on which any consistent flatter areas can be readily picked out.

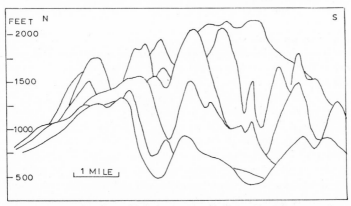

FIGURE 5.4. Projected profiles of the Howgill Gells. North-south profiles projected from the west.

It is often helpful to indicate the geology along the profile, in order to demonstrate that any surfaces that may be apparent are found on a variety of outcrops. The term projected profile is sometimes used to describe a profile constructed along a crest line by dropping perpendiculars from each contour on the crest to a straight line drawn as nearly parallel to the crest as possible. A series of such projected crest profiles can be combined into one diagram as already indicated for the more usual type of projected profile (Miller, 1953). This method has one distinct advantage over the method of using equally spaced straight lines for the profiles; it avoids the difficulty of the contour running along and not across the profile. However multiple projected crest profiles can only be drawn in suitable areas, such as those with a series of nearly parallel ridges or spurs.

A more widely applicable method of delimiting possible erosion surfaces by drawing profiles is to construct a series of spur profiles. The line of profile must follow the highest land along each spur and the resulting profile will show clearly any spur flats suggested by the contours, as shown on figure 5.5;

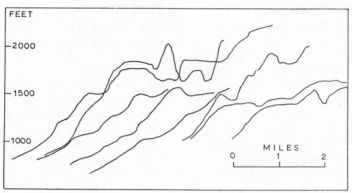

FIGURE 5.5. Spur profiles drawn along the northern spurs of the Howgill Fells.

these are often the most conspicuous remnants of former erosion surfaces in regions of fairly high relief and deep dissection. The Howgill Fells provide an area where spur flats are very conspicuous in the field and on the map. Where the spurs form minor divides in a major river valley or along the coast, the spur profiles can be arranged *en échelon* or staggered so that the flats on one profile can be linked by dotted lines to the adjacent profile, thus revealing the form of the valley side benches clearly; the steeper part of the spur slopes can be shaded in to make the flats show up better. This method can give a very good visual impression of the landscape and the erosion surfaces. In drawing the profiles it is important that the vertical exaggeration be carefully considered; the longitudinal profile will need considerably more vertical exaggeration than the cross profiles and the other types.

3. GENERALISED CONTOURS

Methods using profiles take into account the whole landscape along selected lines. Generalised contours attempt to reconstruct the whole landscape before dissection took place. The method is based on the fact that the erosion surface that may be revealed has been considerably dissected, since its initial formation, by minor valleys of small streams. The aim of generalised contours is to eliminate all the minor dissection of the landscape, thus revealing any large surface, if this is present. The contours can reveal both horizontal and sloping surfaces. In order to draw generalised contours the spur end contours are joined up across the intervening valley. The actual drawing of the contours is not entirely objective, however, as some geomorphologists tend to be more ruthless than others in their elimination of minor valleys. The method works best on a fairly simple slope, such as the dip slope of the Chilterns, where the dissection has not gone so far as to eliminate all evidence of the former landscape, and the significant spurs can fairly readily be recognised.

This method can reveal significant stages in the development of the landscape. For example in the Howgill Fells the generalised contours can be drawn to produce a much more reasonable landscape if they do not pass through the Lune Gorge below 1500 feet. In fact, as shown in figure 5.6, in drawing the contours a col at the present site of the deepest part of the gorge is suggested at a height of about 1500 feet. Other methods of cartographical analysis in this area also point to the importance of erosion when the baselevel was at about this height (see figures 5.5 & 9 and 2.3). Although this

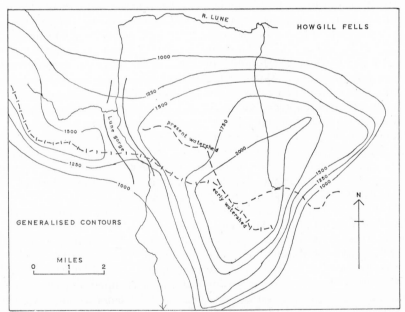

FIGURE 5.6. Generalised contours in feet of the Howgill Fells showing the former and present water sheds and the position of the Lune gorge.

method does not give any definite evidence in support of a former col across the site of the present gorge, it does provide a hypothesis which is worthy of further investigation in the field, and whose implications should be borne in mind when other hypotheses are being tested. It can be associated with the capture of Uldale by Carlin Gill, which has already been commented upon, providing a ready explanation for the pattern of Uldale and the upper Lune, which first flow north, then west before turning south.

4. ALTIMETRIC ANALYSIS

The highest parts of the landscape will be the last to lose remnants of former erosion surfaces as later dissection spreads up from the valleys, so that it is reasonable to look here for remnants of erosion surfaces, particularly when these are part of an original summit surface. The landscape may be investigated by means of altimetric analysis; one method is to count the numbers of spot heights and closed contours within each height range. On the 1 in 25,000 map, for example, the numbers of spot heights or closed contours can be counted for each 25-ft group, but, owing to the problems of contour inaccuracy already mentioned, there are some advantages in grouping the results into 100-ft groups, although by doing so closely spaced surfaces cannot be identified. The graph can be drawn by plotting the number of occurrences of each height range against that height, as shown in figure 5.7. Where there are peaks on the curve there are larger numbers of remnants at that height, and it may be inferred that this represents an erosion level.

It will be obvious that this method can be misleading; for example, one large flat plateau, which is very significant morphologically, will only count one point, while a very dissected upland may produce many points near the same height. Also in some terrains the results will be meaningless; if the area covered includes a field of drumlins, the top of each may well be recorded and suggest an important erosion surface.

The first problem may be overcome by using a different method; this is to sample the area evenly, and although not all the points selected will be on a hill top, if the spread of points is even there will be a greater number where the area at any height is greatest. This method is preferable to the former, and the results may be compared in figure 5.7. The map grid again provides a convenient method of obtaining a uniform spacing of points. The method consists of recording the highest point in each square and plotting the number of points against the height (see chapter 7, p. 308).

O. T. Jones (1951) has carried this method one stage further; he has noted the highest points in each kilometre grid square and for each 10-km square he has worked out the mean height and the standard deviation of the highest points. As a result of using this method, which he applied over the whole of Wales, he was able to demonstrate that the mean height of adjacent squares varied in a systematic way, suggesting warping of the upland surface, which was the most important surface revealed by this method of analysis. The calculation of the standard deviation of the heights for each square and within each set of levels, gives some indication of the subsequent dissection; the value increased upwards, as the dissection became more marked.

H. Baulig has used this method extensively in his work in France, but it should be noted that unless the area is subdivided only horizontal surfaces will be apparent; this may give a misleading impression of the landscape. If the method is too rigidly adhered to, without critical appraisal in the field, it may give apparent support to the eustatic theory that is not justified. That the method need not only reveal horizontal surfaces is shown clearly in the example of the Yorkshire Wolds. Three east-west squares of 10 km side were

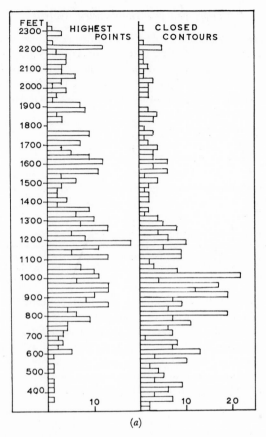

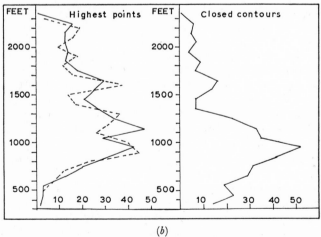

FIGURE 5.7. Altimetric analysis of the Howgill Fells, showing two methods of obtaining and plotting the data. The lower figure shows the same data plotted in 100 feet groups, the full line shows the data centred on every 50 feet and the dashed line shows the data centred on every 100 feet.

used and the highest points in each 1-km grid square were noted. The mean elevation and standard deviation of the three squares were calculated and they showed very clearly that the summit surface, which was clearly revealed on the three graphs, declined gently and regularly eastwards, as shown on figure 5.8. This suggests that one erosion surface has been warped; this could

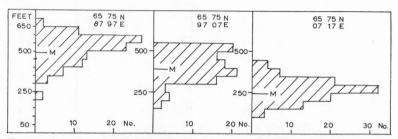

FIGURE 5.8. Altimetric analysis of the northern part of the Yorkshire Wolds; each graph covers 10 by 10 km. The mean elevation is indicated by the M. The gentle easterly decline in elevations is shown.

not have been shown if the three squares had been combined into one graph, as the maxima would have been blurred and no single level would have stood out. One of the obvious drawbacks of the altimetric method of analysis is that it takes into account only a very small portion of the total landscape, and the fact that a dissected surface may be given much more prominence than an undissected one leads to the conclusion that it is much more satisfactory to take the areas between given heights into account in analysing the landscape.

5. AREAL ANALYSIS

This method has many advantages over the former one, but its main drawback is the difficulty of measuring accurately the areas between closely spaced contours on a map. This problem may be overcome by several methods; the simplest is to outline on tracing paper the area to be measured and to lay this over graph paper and count the number of squares on the graph paper. Another relatively rapid method of measuring the area of a fairly small figure is to draw a series of parallel lines on a piece of tracing paper at a unit distance apart on the scale of the map; this is then laid over the area to be measured and small vertical lines are made where the boundary of the figure comes, so that an equal area is left on either side of the vertical line. The length of the lines between the verticals is then measured and the area is given directly. Another rather similar method is the sampling technique, where again a series of vertical lines is drawn over the contoured area. Along each line the length between each successive contour is noted and entered opposite the appropriate contour on a table, the values for each strip are then summed for each height and a cumulative list can be made, giving the area above each contour in turn. This method has the advantage that all the areas can be found at the same time, and is therefore quicker than the previous two methods, which apply to only one height at a time.

Another method which can be employed, but which again takes considerable time, is to use a polar planimeter. This instrument is designed so that as the pointer is moved in a clockwise direction round the area to be measured so the area is recorded on a wheel. The result can be read with a vernier scale to a high degree of accuracy, but it is best to check each reading by going round the area twice, as the result depends on the smooth running of the recording wheel; this records when the instrument moves in one direction, but slips sideways when it moves at right angles, and unless the wheel can move freely over the paper the result will not be reliable. The instrument is the best means of measuring area accurately, but it is very laborious in complex country, where each contour may be split up into several smaller units. Clayton (1953b) has devised another method, but again it is laborious. He used the 1 in 25,000 maps and cut them up along the contours, keeping the area between two adjacent contours separately. He then weighed the areas between contours separately on a very delicate torsion balance, having taken the precaution of testing the maps for uniformity of paper and thereby providing a conversion factor to turn weight into area. As the area above each contour can be used in a considerable variety of different techniques it is worth determining the values accurately before any further analysis is attempted. Any errors in the measurement of the areas will clearly lead to misleading results.

The results of the measurement of area between contours can be plotted in a number of ways, the simplest of which is to plot the area between two successive contours against the elevation; this is called the frequency curve and it shows clearly by maxima of the graph if there is more ground at one height than at another. The example of the Howgill Fells, shown in figure 5.9, clearly demonstrates the importance of the surface between 1500 and 1600 feet, which has already been revealed by other methods, as illustrated in figures 5.5, 5.7, 2.3, but which shows more distinctly in the frequency curve than in the altimetric curve. The other main method of showing the area height data is to construct a hypsographic curve, in which the area above any one contour is plotted against the height.

The hypsographic curve for the earth as a whole is well known and illustrates the principles of the method; it shows that there is far more land at 600 to 3000 feet above sea-level than at any other height, and that the area of ground at greater elevations is severely reduced. It also reveals the importance of the areal extent of the deep sea plains, which form the other major step on the graph, and the greatest deeps again occupy only a very small area. The slope of the curve is steep between the main land level and the deep ocean level, indicating the significance of the continental slope as a major feature of the relief of the earth as a whole. However, for geomorphological analysis the areas chosen for study are much smaller and more compact, and more subtle differences are significant in the areal distribution.

The development of the techniques of morphometric analysis in America in particular is based on the drainage basin as a unit of study. The work of Horton (1945) on various relationships within a drainage basin has stimu-

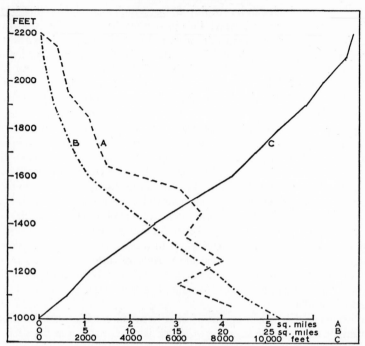

FIGURE 5.9. Aerial analysis of the Howgill Fells. A, Frequency curve. B, Hypsographic curve. C, Clinographic curve shown with a 10 times vertical exaggeration of the slope.

lated a study of the height-area analysis of particular drainage basins, to provide criteria against which each individual basin may be judged. The contribution of Strahler (1952) is valuable in this respect. He has rationalised the study of the many complex aspects that determine the geometry of a drainage basin. A morphological analysis of the type he suggests forms a useful preliminary step in the study of the dynamic quantitative development of the landscape by river action and mass-movement. The features that must be considered include the characteristics of the drainage network, the channel gradients, the form of the slopes, the density of drainage and the hypsometric properties of the basin. The type of hypsometric analysis of the basin advocated by Strahler is not primarily designed to show erosion levels, but is more for comparative purposes between one basin and another, to establish stages of denudation that can be applied to any basin. Thus it is necessary that one basin should be directly comparable with another and therefore the units used to plot the data should be dimensionless and not absolute; they should be reduced to proportions of the total basin, so that the values range between 0 and 1 on both axes of the graph (see figure 5.10a). The values that form the basis of the graph are the area above a certain contour as a ratio of the total area of the drainage basin, as measured on the map, and the height of the particular contour as a ratio of the total height range between the lowest and highest point in the basin. The y axis of the graph may be the height ratio h/H, and the x axis the area ratio, a/A. The curve so formed is called the hypsometric curve and must always run from the top left-hand corner of the graph to the bottom right-hand corner, but the variations between these points give useful information concerning the state of denudation of the basin.

The first step in the analysis is to outline the drainage basin under con-

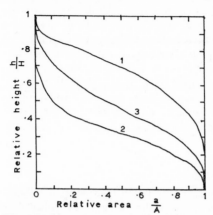

FIGURE 5.10. (*a*) Hypsographic curves plotted on a dimensionless basis. Curve 1 is for a plateau region with deep canyons, r is 0·05, z is 0·125, and the integral 0·676. Curve 2 is for a butte rising above a shale lowland, r is 0·01, z is 0·27 and the integral 0·329. Curve 3 is for a shale lowland, r is 0·05, z is 0·275 and the integral is 0·478. (after Strahler)

sideration, then the areas above each contour in the basin must be measured, preferably with the polar planimeter, and the ratios calculated. It is useful to be able to calculate the volume of ground involved in the basin and this will indicate the amount of erosion that has already been accomplished and what still remains to be achieved. This can be done by assuming that the area is divided up into a number of thin slabs; each slab has a volume equal to $a \Delta h$, where a is the area of the slab and Δh is its thickness; the volume of the whole area can be found by integration so that V, the volume equals

$$\int_{\text{base elevation}}^{\text{summit elevation}} a\ dh.$$

If both sides of the equation are divided by H and A the formula can be written

$$V/HA = \int_{\text{base elevation}}^{\text{summit elevation}} a/A\ d\ (h/H);$$

this is the volume beneath the level of the contour concerned as a ratio of the total volume. The formula can now be written as

$$V / HA = \int_0^{1 \cdot 0} x \, dy;$$

thus the hypsometric function, $x = f(y)$, can be integrated between the limits 0 and $1 \cdot 0$, and this will give a measure of the landmass volume remaining of the whole basin projected on to a horizontal plane multiplied by the height from the highest point to the lowest point; thus it indicates the volume before any erosion at all has taken place. The integral found in this way is called the hypsometric integral and defines the ratio of the area under the hypsometric curve to the area of the whole square forming the graph, which must be unity as both axes are one unit. It can be obtained by measuring the area under the hypsometric curve with a planimeter. The hypsometric curve normally has an S-shaped form, being concave upwards in the upper part and convex upwards in the lower part; but the degree of sinuosity is very variable, and the slope of the curve at the point of inflexion is very variable. These points can be further examined by use of a function in the form

$$y = \left[\frac{d - x}{x} \cdot \frac{a}{d - a} \right]^z;$$

a and d are constants, with d being greater than a, and z, the exponent, is positive or zero. The slope of the curve at the point of inflexion depends on the ratio a / d and is called r. The location of the curve on the graph depends upon the exponent z. The scale on the abscissa is required to run from 0 to 1; therefore the formula is modified so that the abscissa is R, which equals $\frac{x - a}{d - a}$. When R equals 0 then x equals a, and when R is 1 then x equals d. Using these variables it is possible to plot a family of curves for a selected value of r, the family of curves being derived by varying the exponent z (see figure 5.10b). Strahler includes in his paper a series of the families of curves, which provide a basis against which a particular drainage basin may be assessed. As the value of r is decreased so the sinuosity of the curve is increased, and the slope of the curve in the area of the point of inflexion is reduced. A graph from which the value of z may be obtained from the measured integral for any curve is given by Strahler; this also requires the value of r, which may be obtained by inspection from the curve families. The inflexion point can also be found from the graphs, and this has some morphological significance; the inflexion point marks 'the level at which the rate of decrease of mass upwards changes from an increasingly rapid rate of decrease to a diminishing rate of decrease'. It may also have further dynamic significance, which may be revealed by further work on the processes acting; it may differentiate the area where creep is dominant above from the area where channel erosion is more important below. In order to match the actual curve to the correct curve in the family of curves r can be estimated by measuring the slope of the integral at the point of inflexion. The hypsometric integral can be used to assess the geomorphological stage of development of the drainage basin, because in the stage of youth the hypsometric integral is large, but it decreases as the landscape is denuded towards a stage of maturity and old age. A youthful basin will have an integral of about 0·8, the broad convexity in the lower part of the curve showing the initiation of steep-sided valleys; in maturity the hypsometric integral falls to about 0·5 and in old age is reduced to about 0·125, but this low value is only maintained as long as a few monadnocks give a relatively great difference in height between the highest and lowest points; when the monadnocks are consumed the integral returns to about 0·4 to 0·6. Strahler considers that the early stage of landscape development is one of inequilibrium, in which the hypsometric integral exceeds 0·6; when this value is reached the equilibrium stage of maturity has been established and lasts until the integral falls below 0·35, at which stage monadnocks are conspicuous.

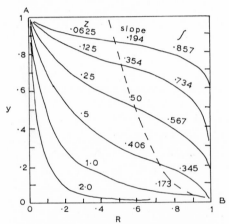

FIGURE 5.10. (*b*) An example of a set of curves for selected values of z with r equal to 0·1. The dashed line joins the points of inflexion on the curves and the slope at this point is given. (after Strahler)

This method of map analysis provides a means whereby the qualitative ideas of W. M. Davis may be expressed quantitatively. The suggestion that the state of maturity, as indicated by the value of the hypsometric integral, is a state of equilibrium, when each basin is in contact with its neighbours and the channels and slopes are in harmony with each other, is supported by the great similarity of hypsometric curves for areas in which the controls are very different. These controls include the relief, size, drainage density, climate, vegetation and rock type.

The use to which hypsometric curves can be put in analysing the processes that produce the representative curves has also been considered by Strahler. He chose five areas of different relief and other conditions, in a mature state of fluvial erosion, and in each area six small drainage basins were outlined and measured to find the hypsometric curve. The mean value for the six basins was found and the one nearest to this value was used for comparison, giving one curve for each area. The analysis was done on good 1 in 24,000 maps and the values of r and z were obtained by comparison with the theoretical curves. The hypsometric integrals ranged from 40·8 to 59·7%, and r was 0·1 for three areas and 0·25 for the other two; z varied between 0·25 and 0·5. The hypsometric results were compared with other variables, such as slopes and drainage pattern, in an attempt to find correlations that might point to important formative processes.

The results showed that on the whole the basins with a high integral had the lower relief and gentler slopes, while the steeper slopes and high drainage density tended to have a lower integral. Two of the basins that showed dissimilar integrals were of the same rock type, so that it could be shown that it was some other factor that caused the difference. Similar rocks, therefore, do not necessarily produce similar landforms; differences of geomorphological development are more likely to cause the variations. There are interesting variations in the curves when structural control is a significant factor in the drainage basin, and the actual curve may depart from the theoretical and develop more than one point of inflexion. The dissected plateau of the basin of the Aisne near Soissons in France illustrates this point; this is an area where Tertiary chalk forms a resistant cap to the plateau, while the river is cutting into weaker sands and clays below the chalk. The streams have steep inner slopes, but there is an undulating broad interfluve with only gentle slopes.

Chorley and Morgan (1962) have suggested another method of recording data concerning drainage basin characteristics, using a technique that allows dimensionless comparison between two basins in different areas and of different dimensions. The type of data that they used for this work is based on a comparison of different variables with the stream order. The factors included the drainage area, the stream lengths, number of stream segments, stream slopes, drainage density, mean relief and basin shapes. It was found that parallel lines define the relationships for different basins, plotting the stream order on the x-axis and the logarithmic value of the other variable on the y-axis. The lines were found by regression analysis to obtain the best fit relationships. Thus a correlation was found between stream order and the other variables in the areas chosen, which were Dartmoor in England and the Unaka Mountains in America. From the results obtained an idealised basin was reconstructed for each area, in which the relationships could be shown visually by contours and stream outlines for an ideal fourth order basin in each area. These were then converted into block diagrams, giving a very useful impression of the character of the basins in an idealised form. Although the areas show great contrasts, they have both been developed on hard rocks by fluvial erosion. The drainage density showed the greatest difference and this could explain many of the other differences. The two factors that probably determined this difference were the relief and run-off intensity, which were very different in the two regions. The higher run-off was due to greater rainfall intensity and more rapid run-off was due to the steeper slopes, and it was the maximum and not the mean run-off that was significant.

The clinographic curve is another method of presenting area-height data. This method, first suggested by Hanson-Lowe (1935), is concerned with the average slope of the land between contours. He pointed out that the hypsographic curve can give a misleading impression as the slope of the curve becomes very steep near the top in some circumstances. This can be seen by considering a hypsographic curve that defines the area-height relationships for a straight-sided cone, which bears some resemblance to a normal type of mountain. The hypsographic curve for the cone will be strongly concave, showing a great change of gradient along its length, although the ground slope of the cone is constant. The only figure that will give a straight hypsographic curve is the paraboloid. In particular the hypsographic curve does not bring out small flat surfaces near the hill tops, that may be important geomorphologically. Especially is this true if the aim of the analysis is to identify erosion surfaces, rather than to consider the relief of the area as a whole as was Strahler's aim. The clinographic curve shows the average slope between two contours.

When the areas have been measured it is a relatively easy operation to plot them in the form of a clinographic curve. The area enclosing the lowest elevation may be called A and the area of the next lowest contour may be termed a, while h is the contour interval. The radii of the circles of area A and of area a are calculated; calling them R and r respectively, then $A = \pi R^2$ and $a = \pi r^2$. R and r will now be in the units of measurement on the map, and can be converted into feet. The value of $R - r$ in feet may be called L, then the average gradient will be tan $\alpha = h \,/\, L$, where h and L must both be in the same units. The curve can be drawn either by obtaining the correct angle from tangent tables and drawing this on the graph with a protractor, or better, the length L can be used, and can be worked out cumulatively to avoid a cumulative error in plotting. When the graph is completed the breaks of slope are easy to identify; the zones of relatively less slope can easily be picked out, and indicate heights at which erosion surfaces may exist. It is often useful to plot the hypsographic curve and the clinographic curve on the same graph, so that the area and slope relationships may be readily compared. The frequency curve can also be added; the three may be compared on figure 5.9.

In a region with only moderate relief it may be necessary to exaggerate the vertical scale on the clinographic curve, this can be done very easily if the method of plotting L is adopted. It can be shown that in some instances, particularly near the upper part of the curves, the hypsographic curve shows an increase of slope upwards, while the clinographic curve shows that in fact the slope is less steep on the average; thus the clinographic curve can correct certain misleading features of the hypsographic curve.

Chorley (1958) has shown that in some circumstances the hypsographic curve will not reveal the character of an obviously polycyclic drainage basin. He takes as an example the Heddon River basin in north Devon. This small basin has a steeply incised lower stream course, with very much gentler slopes above the incised section of the stream. The marked break of slope occurs about 520 feet in the river profile. The areas above the different contours of the basin were measured by polar planimeter, and the resulting hypsographic curve is a very symmetrical one with a fairly deep concavity in the upper part and an equal convexity below, the point of inflection being nearly in the centre of the graph. Strahler has shown that the drainage basins in an equilibrium stage of development with a single cycle of relief have a statistically normal distribution for their hypsographic curve; the curve for the Heddon basin can be shown by statistical analysis to be normally distributed. This normality can be readily appreciated by plotting the area axis of the graph on arithmetical probability paper, which has the property of showing a normal curve as a straight line. Thus on this type of paper the Heddon hypsographic curve shows an almost straight line relationship of area against height. This result would not be expected with a drainage basin that shows such obvious signs of its polycyclic character, but it is due to the fact that the basin is divided into approximately two equal halves, each representing the steeper and the less steep portions of the landscape, also the division between the two lies at about 720 feet, which is almost half way between the lowest and highest points. Had the erosion been considerably less far or further advanced the curve would have been skewed to a considerable degree and would no longer show normality. The hypsographic curve, however, clearly indicates that there is a considerably greater area around 700 to 900 feet than would be expected if the region showed no polycyclic characteristics, owing to the marked degree of convexity and concavity at the upper and lower parts of the graph, but this cannot be defined precisely.

The clinographic curve can be used to give greater precision to the height of the break of slope. The mean slope in feet/mile can be plotted against the elevation to give a clinographic curve; on this graph it is immediately apparent that the slope falls into two distinct parts, which can be expressed by regression line equations, in the form

$$S = 3779 \cdot 75 - 4 \cdot 191 \, H, \text{ and } S = 825 \cdot 55 - 0 \cdot 88 \, H,$$

where S is the slope in feet/mile and H is the elevation in feet. In the last formula the regression co-efficient is almost zero, which indicates that there is no appreciable change in slope in the upper part of the basin for which this second formula is designed. Thus a uniform slope of 729 feet/mile is indicated in the upper part of the basin. Below the break of slope, however, the clinographic curve shows that the slope becomes steeper as the elevation diminishes. By joining the two straight regression lines it is found that they meet at 720 feet, indicating the elevation of the major break of slope.

It is interesting to note that in this instance the break of slope in the stream occurred at 520 feet, whereas that in the landscape as a whole was at 720 feet; this difference can probably be accounted for by the fact that the newer steeper surface is advancing upslope at the expense of the lower gradient upper surface and that where the break of slope occurs it will be modified by creep and slumping of the upper surface downwards, creating a convexity at the expense of the upper surface, which is losing area, and this results in the higher break of slope in the landscape as a whole. This example shows that care must be used in the interpretation of hypsographic relationships and that it is useful to compare them with clinographic curves.

Another method of using the area-height data is to calculate the available relief. Dury (1951) has indicated a method by which this can be done. The available relief is that part of the land that is available for erosion in any particular area. The base plane of the area must first be defined, and this is called the streamline surface. This passes through the bases of the major valleys and can be drawn by joining the contours that cross each major valley together across the interfluves in smooth curves. The area of the surface of each contour can be measured and the volume of material between sea level and the height concerned can be calculated. It is also possible to measure the areas of the streamline surface, and from this, the volume of material between the streamline surface and sea-level can be determined. The difference between these two values will give the total volume of the interfluve areas above the assumed base surface. If this value is divided by the total area it will give the mean available relief. The volume calculations are done fairly simply by using the formula

$$V \text{ (the volume)} = \text{V.I.} \left(\frac{l^0 + l_n}{2} + l_1 + l_2 + \ldots l_{n-1} \right),$$

where V.I. is the vertical contour internal and l^0 l_1 $l_2 \ldots l_n$ are the areas enclosed by the respective contours. This summation need not be done if the mean height only is required; this is given by the formula

$$h = \text{V.I.} \left(\Sigma l - \frac{l^0 + l_n}{2} \right)$$

where l_n is the mean height. Then the mean height of the streamline surface has to be determined in a similar way and the difference between the two gives the mean available relief.

The map of the streamline surface can be used to give an estimate of the depth of dissection of a landscape in which there is clear evidence of an erosion surface. This estimate of dissection can be obtained by first drawing in the streamlines on the map and superimposing on this the contours of the reconstructed surface, drawn on tracing paper, then the two maps can be used to plot differences of height between the two surfaces, this is done at the points where the two sets of contours cross. Then using the plotted points as a guide, isopleths showing line of equal depth of dissection can be drawn on the map. This method can only be used where the original surface can be reconstructed with a fairly high degree of certainty. The volume of material involved can then be calculated, if the areas are measured by planimeter.

6. SLOPE MAPS

There are a number of methods by which slope maps may be constructed and these will be described briefly, but it should be pointed out that such maps are of no value for detailed work of slope form and analysis; for such a purpose field surveys are essential. The slope maps, however, provide a useful visual impression that can then be used to relate to some other geographical variable, or they can be used merely for illustrative purposes to draw attention to particular ranges of slope angle.

It is sometimes useful to obtain a value for the average slope of a specified area, and this can be done easily by a method proposed by Wentworth (1930). The map is first covered by a grid of straight lines at right angles. The total length of the grid lines is measured over the area being studied, and the number of contour crossings per mile length of grid is counted. This number is then multiplied by the contour interval in feet and the result divided by 3361. The resulting figure is the tangent of the angle of slope, and represents the mean slope of the whole area. The figure 3361 is derived from the value of 0·6366, which is the mean of all possible values of sin ϕ (where ϕ is the horizontal angle between the contour and the grid line), multiplied by 5280, the number of feet in a mile. A different constant must, therefore, be used if the metric scale is adopted.

A contour map gives a good indication of slope on an areal basis suitable for most purposes, but there may be some occasions when it is necessary to draw attention to particular grades of slope and there are various methods by which this can be achieved. One method of producing a slope map is to divide the area concerned, which may be quite extensive, into a number of squares by using a grid; the difference in height between the highest and lowest points in each square is noted in the centre of the square, and isopleths, joining points of equal relative relief, are then drawn. The divisions can then be shaded appropriately.

Another method, based on slope, has been devised by Raisz and Henry (1937), which is more useful geomorphologically. The method is to outline those areas in which the contour spacing remains more or less uniform, then these are differentiated by shading according to a graduated scale of gradients. This method can be usefully applied to fairly large-scale maps. A graphical scale of gradients for the map used must first be constructed. This consists of sample distances apart of contours for different gradients, and these can conveniently be marked on the edge of a piece of tracing paper. This can then be moved over the map and separate regions of approximately constant slope can be delimited, and numbered according to the scale selected. When the whole map has been covered the areas can be shaded. Areas of any significant slope can be made to stand out, but the map shows no indication of altitude, so there is no means of differentiating a summit surface from a valley flat.

Another rather laborious method of slope plotting on an areal basis is that of Robinson. The map is covered by a small grid, and the average slope of each square is estimated, a dot is put in the square for each degree of average slope, the dots being placed with regard to the contours and dots in neighbouring squares. The measurement of the average slope is the main problem in this method, and this can be done with a scale of gradients. The map gives a visual impression of slope, but it is doubtful if all the work involved is worthwhile.

7. BLOCK DIAGRAMS

A good block diagram can be a very effective method of illustrating some geomorphological work, and it is more suited to this purpose than to any other. Block diagrams can be drawn to illustrate general principles or to show specific features in a special area on the map. The area to be drawn must first be selected and the view-point considered. It is desirable that the angle of tilt of the block be about 35 to 40 degrees. Block diagrams can be drawn either with a one-point or two-point perspective. The one-point perspective block will be described first; a vertical line BA (see figure 5.11) is drawn on the edge of the paper and a line AV, at right angles to it is drawn at the top of the paper. A point X on AB is selected so that the ratio AX / BX is equal to t the tangent of the angle of tilt, a convenient value is to draw AX to BX in the ratio 7 to 10. A line XY is drawn perpendicular to AB, and on it the rectangle of the block diagram CDEF is drawn, so that the angle VAC is not less than 30 degrees, or the block becomes very oblique. C is then joined to A and D to A, and F is joined to B. The lines BF and DA cut at T. A line parallel to CD is drawn from T to cut CA, then the figure CSTD forms the top of the block and this represents the area CDEF. Perpendiculars are dropped from C, D and T and the front of the block GH is joined, H is continued to A and a perpendicular from T is dropped to meet it, forming the side of the block. The parent area is then divided up into squares with a grid and this is transferred on to the top of the block.

Before continuing it is as well to mention the method of drawing the two-point perspective block. Draw a line at the top of the paper horizontally GH, to show the horizon (see figure 5.11). Draw EF at right angles to it so that EA / AF is the tangent of the angle of tilt. Draw the parent rectangle at A, this is ABCD. Draw FG parallel to AB and FH parallel to AD. Join AG and AH. Join BF and DF, then AJ and AK are the front of the block. Join KG and JH to meet at L, then AJLK is the top of the block. Draw AM along EF, join MG and MH and complete the block by dropping perpendiculars from J and K to cut MH and MG respectively. The grid on the parent rectangle can then be transferred to the top of the block.

The same stage is then reached in both blocks and there are several methods of proceeding, but the raised contour method is probably the most satisfactory. The contours must first be transferred from the parent rectangle to the top of the block, and the rivers should also be added, to act as a guide. It is very important that the contours should be clearly labelled. When the contours have been transferred to the block top, CSTD or AJLK, a vertical line is drawn up from C in the first block or J in the second. This line is marked off according to the range of contours and the required vertical scale, which for an area of high relief on the 1 in 25,000 scale can conveniently be $\frac{1}{10}$ inch to 200 feet. The scale is numbered with the greatest elevation at

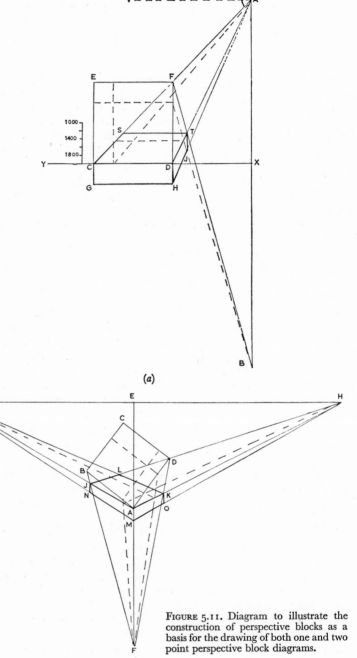

(a)

FIGURE 5.11. Diagram to illustrate the construction of perspective blocks as a basis for the drawing of both one and two point perspective block diagrams.

(b)

the bottom and so on upwards to cover the full range of heights on the area. A vertical line is then drawn on a piece of tracing paper and an index mark made. The vertical line is then fitted over the vertical line from C or J, with the index mark on the highest contour. This is then traced from the top of the block. The tracing paper is then raised until the index mark reaches the next contour, which is traced off, except where it disappears behind the higher one, and this is repeated until all the contours have been traced. The ends of the contours are joined to form the edge of the block. The corners can be fixed by marking a point in the correct line according to their height. The raised contours themselves give a good idea of the relief and can be used as a guide to shade this in. The front and side of the block can be used to indicate the geology, if this is relevant, the geological section can easily be drawn in perspective by joining significant points to the vanishing point A in the first block and G and H in the second. An alternative method of guide line drawing is to construct sections along the grid lines, which must be adjusted to the perspective scale, and these can be used as a basis for shading the relief.

Another much more rapid method of illustrating a special area in relief is the terrain representation method of Robinson and Thrower (1957). This method is based on the inclined contour; this is the projection on a datum plane of the outline of the intersection of the ground surface with an inclined plane. The diagram gives an oblique view of the landscape. The spacing of the horizontal lines used to draw the diagram controls the apparent vertical exaggeration. The closer the lines are the flatter the landscape appears. This spacing can be calculated by using $D = (12\ h \cot \theta)\ /\ S$, where h is the contour interval, θ is the viewing angle and S the scale denominator of the map and D is the distance in inches between the parallel lines on the map. For example, with a scale of 1 in 25,000 and a contour interval of 100 feet and θ equal to 45 degrees, then $D = (12 \times 100 \times 1)/\ 25,000 = 0.05$ inches, and 45 degrees is a useful angle. If the traces drawn from the lines do not coalesce a back-slope can be drawn. The view shows no foreshortening because the ground traces and the inclined planes are planimetrically in their proper positions, although there is an illusion of foreshortening. The procedure is as follows: firstly, the contour map is prepared, with the required contours marked, then secondly the drainage should be added, thirdly the horizontal lines in another colour, fourthly the inclined contours in a third colour by joining points where the contours cut the horizontal lines, and finally the landscape is shaded in, using these lines as a basis as shown in figure 5.12. The shading can be heavier on the right and front slopes to give an impression of north-west lighting. The front facing slopes are the most difficult to shade as they have fewer inclined contours.

8. METHODS OF ANALYSIS—RIVER PROFILES AND PATTERNS, HEIGHT-RANGE DIAGRAMS

Much use has been made of the logarithmic curve for the extension of river profiles, with the aim of establishing the former base-level to which the rivers

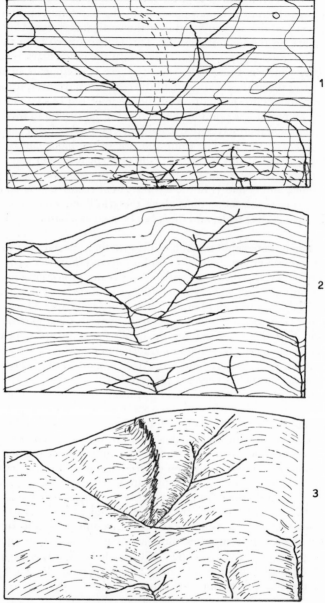

FIGURE 5.12. Example to illustrate the method of drawing terrain diagrams, based on a map of part of the Howgill Fells.

were graded, if they have knick-points. Green first developed the method for use on the River Mole and it has since been used in many analyses of river long profiles. It has already been shown that the profile should not be drawn from the map, but should be surveyed, or at least important points should be checked in the field. But when the surveyed profile has been plotted it can then be analysed. R. F. Peel's (1941) work on the profile of the North Tyne is a good example of the application of this mathematical technique to use the graded upper portion of the profile to determine the base-level at the time of rejuvenation. The knick-point that is revealed on the North Tyne is very clearly marked, occurring at a height of 350 feet. The basis of the method of mathematical extension is to fit a curve to the supposedly graded upper part of the river above the knick-point and then to extrapolate this down to the end of the river. The method is clearly based on the assumption that the river was graded throughout its course before rejuvenation took place. This in itself is a dangerous assumption, as it can be shown that the graded profile of a river is not necessarily an even logarithmic curve, especially if it receives large tributaries at intervals. The fundamental premise on which the method is based is therefore open to doubt. The other problem is that the unrejuvenated part of the river is usually only a small proportion of the whole length, and there is no guarantee that this part has not been upset in its profile by factors depending on change of climate, which can influence the load-discharge ratio and hence the gradient. Considering these factors it is surprising that the method can give such reasonable results as it often does. However, Miller (1939) has shown that the curves themselves can be based on a wide variety of formulae, all of which give reasonable results.

The usual formula adopted for the purpose of mathematical extension of longitudinal profiles is in the form

$$y = a - k \log (p - x)$$

where y is the height of any point on the profile, p is the total length of the stream in miles, x is the distance from the mouth of the stream; thus $p - x$ is the distance from the source; a and k are constants. The major problem is to find values for a and k that fit the upper graded part of the curve. A preliminary value for testing the formula can be found by taking two points on the graded profile and substituting the known values of y and $p - x$ in the formula, the two formulae can then be solved as simultaneous equations to give the value of a and k for those two points, then these values of the constants can be tested at other points on the unrejuvenated curve, and if the fit is good these values can be adopted for the extrapolation; but normally they will require some adjustment to make them fit well throughout the upper reaches. It is possible to get two different values of a and k both of which give fairly reasonable values for the upper curve, but yet yield very different results when extrapolated down to the mouth of the stream. The constant a is based on the height of the source of the stream, while k is connected with the radius of curvature of the concavity of the stream profile.

Peel found that the value that fitted best for the North Tyne was

$$y = 870 - 380 \log (p - x),$$

a being 870 and *k*, 380. These values for the constants gave differences between the actual profile and the curve given by the formula that were as follows every mile down the profile from 9 to 26: -3, -3, 0, 0, $+3$, $+1$, -1, $+3$, -2, -1, -1, 0, -3, -4, -3, -1, -4, -5 feet. Below the knick-point the differences rapidly increased to -16, -32, -45, -53, -58 feet and so on in increasing values, until at the confluence with the South Tyne the value was -143 feet. The final amount of rejuvenation suggested by this method was 150 feet. A similar value has been found for the River Lune, which also has a very well developed knick-point.

Kidson has also used this method to reconstruct a number of levels of rejuvenation in the Rivers Exe and Barle, but instead of only extrapolating one curve he extrapolated a large number of curves from only short lengths of graded river above each knick-point. This method, relying on only short lengths of river, is liable to lead to uncertain results, as he fully realised, and in order to overcome this difficulty he adopted the same method for the two tributaries above their confluence, extrapolating the curves to this point. The close fit of the extrapolated curve at this point gave confidence in the results of this method.

However, it is not a method that should be given too much weight in the analysis of the landscape development, unless it is supported by other evidence. It is in this situation that a study of the cross profiles of the river valley can give very valuable support to the mathematical extrapolation, and diagrammatic methods of presenting the data from longitudinal profile extensions and cross profiles will be considered later. Mention should first be made of another method of plotting the extrapolated curve that may facilitate its analysis. Chorley (1958) has shown how a river profile can usefully be plotted on logarithmic normal probability paper. This type of paper is so designed that it has a probability scale on the *y*-axis and a logarithmic scale on the *x*-axis. Thus if the river profile is a logarithmic curve it will appear as a straight line on this paper if the distribution is logarithmically normal. The Heddon basin stream profile was plotted in this way, and the result showed two straight line reaches joining at the knick-point at 520 feet; this stream has already been mentioned in dealing with areal analysis. This method of plotting an accurately surveyed river profile with many breaks of slope might help to indicate which of the breaks of slope are genuine knick-points.

It is valuable to be able to plot river terraces, normally located and mapped in the field, in association with its longitudinal profile. The problem is that these valley flats are three-dimensional features, with a slope both down the valley and towards the stream, and they are variable in width. One method of representing the terrace remnants, suggested by A. Coleman (1954), is to plot a rectangle whose length is proportional to the length of the flat, and whose height is proportional to the vertical distance between the front an back of the remnant, while the whole rectangle is placed at the correct alt tude according to the height scale on the ordinate of the graph. The abscissa is a length scale on which the valley is straightened out. One of the disadvantages of the method is that steeply sloping remnants come out as high rectangles, whereas the more significant flat terraces only appear as very thin rectangles. In some instances it is not obvious which is the best direction for the vertical plane of the diagram; the direction should be such that the flats show the minimum fall. This would be parallel to an old cliff or along a valley. This method should reveal a marine surface clearly, as it will appear horizontal in the absence of warping. The weakness of the method is that the rectangle shows the same vertical height range at both ends. To overcome this problem the height range diagram was modified into the form of quadrilaterals or triangles. The height ranges at both ends of the feature as well as its state of preservation are indicated. When the diagram reveals a series of former levels, these may usefully be differentiated by shading each series by a different symbol.

This method of plotting data may reveal problems for further investigation, or it may be used to illustrate a complex system of erosional remnants diagrammatically so that they can be more easily appreciated. The method itself, however, is not enough to provide any definite conclusions concerning the landforms, though it can be useful supporting evidence. Miller has indicated that this means of showing erosional remnants is open to misinterpretation, and that, becuse it is based on information gleaned in the field, it is to a certain extent subjective, depending on the methods adopted in the field mapping. Another difficulty is that if the number of remnants is great the difficulty of interpretation is much increased as a result. However, used with care in suitable areas with well defined valley flats, it can be useful.

The drainage pattern is one of the most obvious features of many maps, and the orderly relationship between various parameters associated with the drainage pattern is of considerable interest and can be studied from map data. Horton's classic work in this field has revealed many interesting relationships. Stream order has been found to be a significant variable. First order streams on any map are those with no tributaries, second order streams only have first order tributaries, a third order stream only receives first and second order tributaries and so on. Horton extends the highest order stream of each drainage basin up to the end of the longest tributary, but Strahler restricts the higher orders to the segments between the start of one order and the next higher downstream. The relationships to be mentioned are based on Horton's method. He has shown that the stream order correlates directly with stream length and drainage area and inversely with number of streams; similarly channel length correlates closely with drainage area, the correlations being linear when the variables are both plotted on the logarithmic scale. Drainage density is calculated by dividing the total stream length by the drainage area. The size of the first order streams will depend on the scale of the map; the 1 in 25,000 map is usually as large as necessary, and on this scale a river such as the Mississippi would be designated as a twelfth order stream, neglecting the rills (Leopold, Wolman and Miller, 1964). The drainage density can be used to assess the texture of the landscape from map data. This does not necessarily depend directly on the drainage density; K. G. Smith (1950) has defined 'texture' or dissection as the ratio of the contour with the most crenulations divided by the perimeter of the drainage basin. The number of stream crossings of the mid-elevation contour can also be used to assess this factor. On the former system values between 1 and 1000 were found in nature.

Another method of considering the longitudinal profile of a stream, discussed by Leopold, Wolman and Miller (1964), is to work out the most probable profile by the random walk model. In this model the probability of a decrease in unit elevation in a horizontal unit distance decreases as the elevation approaches zero of base level. Taking as an example a profile with 5 vertical steps and 10 horizontal ones, the average elevation values derived from 100 random walk trials give the following elevations for each horizontal step:

Horizontal distance	0	1	2	3	4	5	6	7	8	9	10
Vertical height	5	4·17	3·48	2·90	2·42	2·02	1·68	1·40	1·17	0·98	0·81

Such a curve has the form of many river profiles, being concave up. The concavity of the profile can be related to the river length, as suggested by the random walk trials. This relationship can be confirmed by plotting the profile concavity for streams of constant discharge against the specific length, $L/\sqrt{Q}$, where L is the length and Q, the discharge, is a function of the width; this allows different rivers to be compared. The stream concavity is defined as the ratio between a and b, a being the vertical distance from the plotted profile to the mid-point of a straight line joining the top and bottom of the profile, and b being the elevation of this mid-point above the river mouth or base-level. The relationship between stream concavity and specific length is a straight line for rivers of constant discharge, that is those flowing through deserts and receiving no tributaries. The concavity increases with increase of specific length. The random walk method also suggests a relationship between concavity and relative river length L_0 and relief H_0, where L_0 is the ratio of distance from the headwaters to total length of river and H_0 is the ratio of height to total height. By plotting H / H_0 and L / L_0 against each other in dimensionless units it can be shown that the greater the relief relative to the length, the less is the concavity of the profile; so far this suggested relationship has not been tested against field data.

9. GLACIAL FEATURES

Various glacial features such as hanging valleys, valley steps and diffluent channels can be recognised on good contoured maps. The distribution of drumlins, which often show up conspicuously on topographical maps, can also be mapped. These features need not be described, but two methods of illustrating and analysing the characteristics of certain glacial forms may be mentioned, one dealing with features formed by glacial erosion, the other with depositional forms.

The study of late-glacial corries in the mountains of Snowdonia by Seddon (1957) is concerned with their distribution and height in relation to the factors determining their formation. In order to illustrate the significance of the orientation and height of the corries in the three separate mountain groups, Snowdon, Glyders and Carnedd, a system of polar diagrams was devised. The circles were arranged so that each corrie could be plotted to show its orientation to the nearest 10 degrees, and its elevation was shown by the use of concentric circles, the highest elevation being nearest the centre of the circle. This enabled an immediate visual impression of the relationship between height of corrie and orientation to be obtained; the dominant importance of the north-easterly quadrant was very marked in all the groups, while in general the lowest corries were those facing most nearly due north-east. This could be demonstrated by linking the lowest corries for each direction with a dotted line.

When all the corries from the three groups were shown on one diagram and the lowest of each group were indicated, as shown on figure 5.13, then a significant difference between the three groups became apparent. The Snowdon corries clearly were the lowest for any particular orientation, then came the Glyders, and the Carnedd were the highest. This could clearly be related to the position of the three groups; the most westerly have the highest precipitation now, and this falls off eastwards, in the same way as the snow-fall presumably did in the past, when the corries were being formed. Hence the highest corries lie to the east. This point was brought out clearly by drawing a diagram indicating the three-dimensional pattern of the lowest corries in the three groups in relation to their spatial relationship to each other. Elliptical lines were drawn to include all the corries in each group on the basis of their altitude, the altitude scale being shown on the ordinate of the graph, and the distance along a north-east to south-west line of section being indicated on the abscissa. The aspect was shown as the third dimension in the lower shaded part of the diagram, in which all the corries occur, as this was the semicircle from south-east to north-west via north-east. South-east and north-west were drawn isodiametrically, as though on a plane at right angles to the paper. The lowest moraine to the north-east determined the lower end of the long axis of the ellipse. The centre of the ellipse was fixed by noting the average altitude of the moraines in the south-easterly and north-westerly aspects; this was 1700 feet for Snowden, 2000 feet for the Glyders and 2200 feet for the Carnedd group, while the lowest moraines were at 900 feet in Snowden, 1300 feet in the Glyders and 1600 feet in the Carnedd group. These methods of plotting the data in diagrammatic form provide useful evidence pointing to the factors that were of significance in accounting for the formation of the corrie groups.

Drumlins are often conspicuous features of a topographic map but there is still considerable doubt as to their method of formation. A study of the form of drumlins, which can be obtained from map data if the scale and contour interval are suitable, has been given by Chorley (1959). A drumlin field is often called 'basket of eggs' relief, and Chorley has compared the shape of drumlins with eggs: both show streamlined characteristics. The drumlins have a steeper side against which the ice flowed; this steepness reduced the formation of vortices. A method of describing their shape might well throw

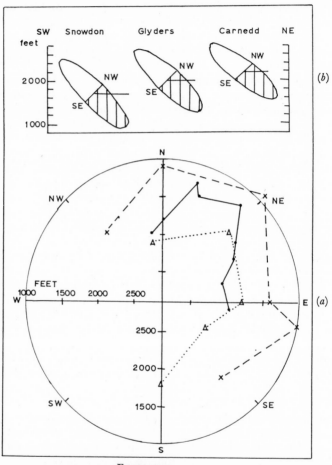

FIGURE 5.13

(a) Rose diagram to show the relation of corrie height with aspect in the corries of the Snowdonian mountains. The dots refer to the Glyders, the triangles to the Carnedd group and the crosses to Snowdon.

(b) Diagram to illustrate the respective elevations of the lowest mean elevation of the three groups. The lowest moraines of each corrie group are shown at the lowest part of the shaded area, and the centre of the ellipse is given by the average of the altitudes of the cirque moraines of the south-easterly and north-westerly aspects in each group. (after Seddon)

light on their origin. In a streamlined form there must be no region of dead flow between the object and the moving medium, whether it be air, water or ice. This is illustrated by the shape of aircraft wings, snow and sand and other forms moulded by the wind. A type of geometrical form which has the necessary characteristics to form streamlined shapes is the lemniscate loop. The equation for this figure in its simple polar co-ordinate form is

$$\rho = l \cos k\,\theta,$$

l is the length of the long axis, and is the value of ρ when $\theta = 0$; *k* is a dimensionless number expressing the elongation of the lemniscate loop. *k* is 1 when the form is circular and increases with the elongation of the loop. *k* is given by

$$k = \frac{l^2\pi}{4A},$$

where A is the area of the loop. Lemniscate loops can be fitted to an actual drumlin by measuring the values of l and A; from these k can be found, and then l and k can be substituted in the first equation. It can be shown that this type of curve fits many drumlins fairly closely.

There is the difficulty, however, that for reasons of surveying the outline of the drumlin on the map sometimes does not show the complete tapering of the drumlin in a down-ice direction. However, if drumlins are specially surveyed this characteristic of their shape is often clearly revealed; but at times this extreme tapering is missing in the actual drumlins, because if the streamlining medium is only moving slowly, as in the instance of ice compared with other media, the tapering form does not develop so fully. Some drumlins, particularly the smaller ones, seem to show a more symmetrical form that approaches an ellipse, which is symmetrical about two axes, instead of only one. The reason for the greater symmetry of the smaller drumlins may possibly be illustrated by reference to bird's eggs. An egg is always laid with the blunt end foremost, where the pressure is greatest, as with the stoss end of a drumlin. Nonturbulence is also characteristic of the formation of both features, and there is another similarity, which helps to explain the observation that smaller drumlins are more symmetrical than large ones; it can be shown that the most asymmetrical eggs are those that are largest in relation to the bird laying them. The more symmetrical drumlins may, therefore, be due to the limiting amount of till available, which would account for their small size. The value of k increases as the asymmetry of the egg increases, and this value, measured from the outline of the drumlin, may be inversely proportional to the relative resistance presented by the equilibrium form of the drumlin. This resistance may be due to the strength of the till or the low velocity of flow of the ice. Thus the calculation of the appropriate lemniscate loop provides a useful quantitative method of describing the shape of drumlins and may also suggest some of the factors that are important in their genesis.

10. WAVE REFRACTION DIAGRAMS

The construction of wave refraction diagrams can give valuable evidence concerning the distribution of wave attack on the shore. They are drawn on the basis of submarine contours obtained from marine charts, and this demonstrates the importance of the offshore zone in determining the character of the foreshore, especially in areas where the coastline is formed by berms built up by the long, constructive ocean swells. These swells are greatly influenced by refraction, and the coastal outline is built up to lie parallel to the crests of the refracted waves, as shown by Davies (1959). Thus in these areas the drawing of wave refraction diagrams can provide the explanation for the orientation of the coast. In other areas a wave refraction diagram may help to explain the incidence of coastal erosion and deposition, and give some indication of the direction of longshore transport of material.

The depth contours should be drawn out to a depth equal to half the deep-water length of the wave for which the refraction diagram is to be drawn. The wave length can be simply found from the period by using $L = 5 \cdot 12\ T^2$ where L is the deep-water length in feet and T is the period in seconds. If wave records are available, these will give useful indication of the most common periods of waves in the particular locality concerned, and the direction of approach can be obtained partly from fetch and partly from wind data. It is often necessary to draw diagrams for a variety of directions and periods, each diagram being drawn for a different wave.

The simplest form of wave refraction diagram shows the wave crests and the orthogonals; the former are drawn at convenient intervals according to the scale of the chart and the length of the waves; the latter are drawn everywhere at right angles to the wave crests. The orthogonals are important as they indicate the distribution of wave energy along the wave crest and the shore. It is assumed that in deep water the wave energy is evenly distributed along the wave crest and there the orthogonals are, therefore, equally spaced along the wave crest. However, as the waves enter shallow water the crests usually bend and the orthogonals no longer remain equally spaced. The wave energy distribution along the wave crest is thus no longer uniform, and this is reflected in changes of wave height. Where the orthogonals converge the wave energy is concentrated and the waves are high, and vice versa.

The principle on which the diagrams are drawn is based on the fact that the wave velocity and length decrease in a known way as the waves enter shallow water. This principle is used to construct a scale on tracing paper on which the actual length of the wave or set of waves for the selected period is drawn to scale for a series of depths, the figures for depth on the scale must be the same as the depth contours on the chart. A central line must be included on the scale. The scale must then be cut out. A line is drawn on the chart to represent a wave crest approaching from deep water in the required direction. Lines can then be drawn to scale parallel to this at a distance equal to the chosen number of wave crests until the depth is such that it is less than half the deep-water wave length. Where the depth becomes less than half the wave length the wave crest bends and each must be followed individually into shallow water. This is done by placing the wave scale on the chart so that its centre line cuts the required depth contour at the same contour on the scale, while the straight edge of the scale is made tangent to the preceding wave crest. The point where the depth line cuts the curved edge of the scale then marks the point to which the wave crest will have advanced, and this is marked on the chart. The process is repeated for the other depth contours, and the points so fixed are joined to form the next wave crest, and this is used to plot the subsequent one and so on until the wave is traced into very shallow water, where the spacing is much reduced. Where the bottom contours are not too complex this process is fairly simple. The orthogonals are then drawn by spacing them equally in deep water and then tracing them shorewards by keeping them everywhere at right angles to the wave crests, this can be done with a protractor.

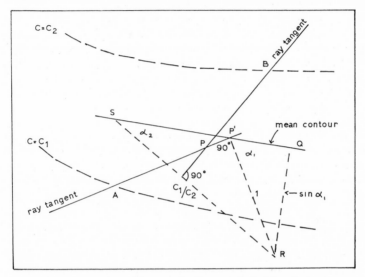

FIGURE 5.14. Diagram to illustrate the direct method of drawing wave rays in refraction diagrams. (after Arthur, Munk and Isaacs)

The orthogonals are the most important part of the diagram and a method has been devised by Arthur, Munk and Isaacs (1952) to draw these directly, without the first stage of constructing wave crests; this has the advantage of eliminating one step and hence increasing the accuracy of the result. The orthogonals can be traced either from deep water towards the shore or from shallow water offshore. The method depends on the ratio of the wave velocity at two successive contours on the chart, relative to the deep-water velocity. Taking two contours, as shown in figure 5.14, on the chart a mean contour between them is sketched in by eye. The orthogonal cutting the first contour, which will be the deepest if the wave is being traced towards shallow water, is prolonged to cut the mean contour at P'. A line is then drawn perpendicular to the prolonged orthogonal AP' from P' to R; this is a length equal to unity on any convenient scale. Then C_1/C_2 is drawn on the same scale from R to S, where it cuts QP' produced. The new direction of the orthogonal is given by PB, which is drawn so that it is perpendicular to RS, and so that PB = AP'. For reasonable accuracy the angle between the two tangents should not exceed 15 degrees. The calculation of the ratio C_1/C_2 can be facilitated by the use of a table, relating the depth on one scale to the wave length and period on another scale with the ratio C/C_d on a central scale. The value of the velocity ratio can be very easily found by laying a straight line between the deep water period or length and the required depth, then the value can be read off directly on the central scale in terms of C/C_d. This latter method is thought to be the best one for drawing wave refraction diagrams, and is considerably more accurate for detailed work although the first method may give a useful visual impression.

Where the underwater relief is complex it is frequently found that the orthogonals will cross; this will occur particularly where the waves are refracted round an island and meet on the far side, they may also cross where a submarine valley, running in close to the shore bends the waves to such an extent that the orthogonals cross. That this can happen can be verified on aerial photographs. Thus it is possible for the waves to move through each other in different directions without losing their identity. The interpretation of crossed orthogonals complicates the analysis of data from wave refraction diagrams, and where the pattern becomes very complex, as when waves move in across a series of submerged offshore banks, the wave refraction diagram loses much of its value, as the orthogonals cross and recross so often as to result in an extremely complex diagram that is very difficult to interpret.

The methods that have been described so far produce a diagram that indicates the extent of refraction for one special set of conditions, determined by the directions of approach of the waves in deep water and by their period or length. The diagram can, however, illustrate the effect of refraction over a considerable length of coastline for those particular conditions. An alternative method of presenting wave refraction data is to show the effect of a variety of different lengths of waves, coming from different directions, at one particular point on the coast. The diagram prepared by Munk and Traylor (1947) for the area near the Scripps Institute of Oceanography indicates the type of information that can be obtained by this method. The refraction factors for waves of 6 to 16 seconds and coming from directions between south-south-west and north-north-west at $22\frac{1}{2}$ degree intervals can be read off the diagram. The factors are shown on concentric circles, each representing one period, with the longer periods having the longer radii; isopleths joining points of equal refraction according to the two factors are then drawn and these can be used to obtain results for intermediate periods and directions of approach. One of the two factors is the angle of approach of the wave crest, and this gives the angle between the approaching wave crest and the shoreline; the initial L indicates that the wave is closer to the shore to the observer's left when looking out to sea, and R indicates the opposite orientation. These values are clearly greater for the shorter waves, approaching from an oblique angle, when they may reach 20 degrees. The other factor,

K_b, is the refraction factor, which is a measure of the wave energy approaching the coast under the conditions specified. It can be given as

$$K_b = \sqrt[3]{S_0 / S_b},$$

where S_0 is the distance apart of the orthogonals in deep water and S_b is the spacing in shallow water at the break-point. The value of K_b approaches unity as the waves become shorter and their angle of approach becomes more normal to the shore. This method of plotting the data makes it possible to obtain all the necessary information concerning refraction of waves on one diagram for the place concerned.

11. AERIAL PHOTOGRAPHS

Aerial photographs provide information of great value to many geomorphological studies. The detail shown on the photographs will depend on the scale of the photograph, which is determined by the flying height of the aircraft (H) and the focal length of the camera (f). Thus the scale of the negative and direct contact print will be equal to f / H. A photograph taken from 30,000 feet with a camera with a 36 in. focal length would have a scale of 1 in 10,000, for example. Air photographs are commonly taken on a scale of about 6 inches to 1 mile. If stereoscopic pairs are available, height determinations can be made from the photographs with suitable instruments to measure the parallax. The amount of parallax depends on the distance apart of the points from which the two photographs of the stereoscopic pair were taken; this is called the air base. The human eye can appreciate angular differences of 30 seconds of arc, so that with an eye-base of about 60 mm, 30 seconds is subtended at an object 440 m away; beyond this distance binocular vision is no longer effective. If, however, two photographs are taken 1000 feet apart at a height of 5000 feet, a mountain 1000 feet high will subtend an angle of 14 degrees 15 minutes, while the ground at its foot will subtend an angle of 11 degrees 26 minutes, and this difference can be readily appreciated with the aid of a stereoscope. This enables the two photographs to be fused into one image, and allows the third dimension or height to be readily appreciated.

The parallax of any object viewed on two photographs in a stereoscope may be computed from the formula

$$p = \frac{f B}{(H - h)},$$

where f is the focal length of the camera, B is the air base, H is the height above sea-level of the aircraft, and h is the height of the ground point. If the height of one point is known, its parallax can be calculated absolutely, but if there is no known height, relative heights can be assessed by measuring the parallax of different points by means of a floating mark, which is adjusted to rest on the ground. If a suitable instrument is available, such as a Barr and Stroud Z.D. 15 Stereoscope, the parallax can be measured by micrometer to 0·01 mm. A more rapid method is to plot p against h on a graph, which should be applicable to a strip of photographs if the air base is of constant length; then the heights can be read off directly. Slopes can be measured by noting the distance between two points at the top and base of the slope, and then measuring their difference of parallax; from this the height difference can be obtained. If tilt can be eliminated from the photographs very accurate results can be obtained, the accuracy increasing with the scale, so that the maximum error should not exceed 1 foot for a scale of 1 in 5000.

Photographs are particularly valuable in regions where base maps are not available, as they can give a good idea of the general characteristics of the country and can be used to plan more detailed field work. Sometimes features show up clearly on the photograph which are difficult to appreciate on the ground, especially when the relief changes are small and the differentiating factor, such as vegetation, is not obvious at ground level. This is particularly true of features such as polygonal patterns that are only identifiable by very slight changes of crop density, invisible on the ground, but shown up very clearly on aerial photographs under some conditons. The aerial photograph in this instance, by showing a much larger area than can be appreciated from a ground view-point, where perspective can be misleading, can reveal the whole pattern of the polygonal features much more clearly than any other method could. Other patterns revealed much more clearly on aerial photographs than by other means include features such as drumlins, and many other characteristics of glaciation, such as eskers and moraines, and structural lineations brought out by glacial scouring. If stereoscopic pairs of photographs and instruments suitable for measuring parallax values are available, then the photographs can be used to obtain the heights of the features as well as their shapes and distribution.

In glaciology also aerial photographs are of great value; they show the pattern of crevasses very clearly, and this evidence can then be used to test the theories of crevasse formation and their patterns that have been put forward. In many instances a photograph of a glacier can give much more information than a good map, and a good series of aerial photographs will produce a map that is not much less accurate than one surveyed by normal ground methods. The extent of height errors found in glacier mapping in Alaska (Case, 1958) showed that with two different plotting instruments errors of ± 0.5 and ± 0.9 m were obtained. Case considers that aerial photographs provide better results than terrestrial photographs taken with a phototheodolite for mapping glaciers. Aerial photographs of glaciers are also particularly useful if they can be repeated at intervals, because then they can be used to give an accurate measure of the glacier fluctuations; this can be done much more easily than by periodic field mapping, although it may be considerably more expensive.

The main value of aerial photographs for geomorphological interpretation is that they enable many features to be recognised that are not shown on topographical maps, even if these are available on a large scale. Structural features such as the lines of faults, and minor intrusions, often show up very clearly on aerial photographs. They may be used to reveal the joint pattern, particularly in areas where the vegetation cover is not complete. A very good example is the pattern of joints on limestone pavements, which is very clearly revealed on aerial photographs, but would require a great deal of detailed ground survey to reveal it so clearly. Rock dips and strike lines are also shown clearly, again if the vegetation cover is not too thick. On other occasions the change in vegetation itself may reveal the pattern, if its distribution depends on the character of the rock. Details of drainage patterns on pediment slopes and seepage lines on areas of low relative relief, boulder distributions and similar features can often be studied usefully on aerial photographs. Photographs are particularly useful when the area to be covered is large and where the surface expression of the features of interest is relatively small but the features produce a colour or texture change that is revealed on the photograph and thus shows up clearly.

Aerial photographs are also very valuable for coastal studies. The vegetation pattern of a salt marsh, in which only two or three plant species occur, is often very clearly revealed on a photograph. Creek banks are frequently higher than the interfluves in a salt marsh, and this small difference in height allows another plant species to become dominant; these belts can be very clearly differentiated and thus the creek pattern is clearly revealed, even when the marsh is fully vegetated in the salting stage. Photographs also reveal very well the pattern of coastal dunes and can be used to differentiate and map different coastal environments, although this use of aerial photographs can only be used in conjunction with field work, and this is true of most geomorphological work with aerial photographs. It is, however, a rapid and reasonably accurate method of mapping zones that have been identified in the field. Aerial photographs taken at low water reveal many features of interest on the foreshore that cannot be shown on published maps owing to their frequent movement. Ridges and runnels are a good example of this type of feature; they can be readily identified and their orientation with respect to the coastline can readily be determined. This is an important property as it influences their movement.

It was not until aerial photographs were available that the widespread distribution and patterns of submarine bars were appreciated. These features, characteristic mainly of tideless seas, show up very clearly on aerial photographs in some conditions. When the sea is calm the bars can be seen because the shallower water over their crests allows the sand beneath to reflect more light than is reflected from the deeper troughs. When the sea is rough enough to break on the bar crests, these can be identified by the lines of breakers, the waves reforming after breaking on the bar before breaking again on an inner bar or at the water line. The aerial photographs can be used to measure the distance from the shore of the bar crests and troughs, and if the general slope of the beach is known an estimate of the water depth over the bar crest can be made. Most of the submarine bars revealed on aerial photographs are straight and parallel to the coast, but in some rather more sheltered areas with access of waves restricted, such as bays, the pattern shown is sometimes of crescentic bars, with the points of the crescents facing inland. The origin of this pattern is still not fully understood.

Aerial photographs have also been used to determine the gradient of beaches. This can be done when long swell waves are shown on the photograph that are fairly even in crest separation in deep water. A photograph of such a swell will show that the waves gradually get closer together as the shore is approached, and if the photograph includes the waves before they have begun to be influenced by the bottom, the depth being more than half the wave length, it can be used to measure depths offshore. The gradual reduction of the wave length can be converted into diminution of depth on a table correlating wave length, wave period and water depth (see figure 3.3, p. 140). Thus the distance is measured from a fixed point on the shore horizontally, and at this point the wave length on the photograph is measured; it is converted according to the scale of the photograph into feet, and the corresponding depth for that particular deep water wave length can be read off the table and the profile plotted. The result can give reasonably accurate figures of the underwater profile. It is not a method that would normally be used and was developed during the Second World War to obtain an estimate of the profiles of enemy-held beaches (Williams, 1947). Aerial photographs can, however, be used to indicate the nature of wave refraction and to provide a check on wave refraction diagrams, as was noted in the previous section.

A useful collection of aerial photographs with notes on their interpretation is given by Walker (1953), which gives some indication of the wide range of geomorphological features that can be identified and studied on aerial photographs. He shows that in measuring height differences with stereoscopic pairs, heights ranging from 1 in 500 to 1 in 1000 of the flying altitude can readily be measured with modern equipment; this gives a fair degree of accuracy, as the planes taking photographs normally fly at between 10,000 and 30,000 feet. However, not all geomorphological problems can be solved by aerial photographs; the poor results obtained in attempting morphological mapping with aerial photographs in some areas of gentle and subtle relief, discussed in chapter 2, illustrate this point; however in many areas of bolder relief and with field checks they can be used successfully for mapping geomorphological features.

The interpretation of aerial photographs depends on an understanding of the various textures of grey colouring on the photographs; this again depends on the reflecting quality of the surface. Some surfaces are smooth and reflect either maximum or minimum light, while the more irregular surfaces reflect an intermediate amount of light. In interpreting aerial photographs it is necessary to make field checks, and then features can be recognised with confidence in areas not visited in the field. Air photographs do not provide an alternative to field work, but they help to direct it into profitable channels and extend its coverage in suitable country.

REFERENCES

ARTHUR, R. S., MUNK, W. H. and ISAACS, J. D. 1952. The direct construction of wave rays. *Trans. Amer. Geoph. Un.* 33, 855-865.

CASE, J. B. 1958. Mapping of glaciers in Alaska. *Photogram. Eng.* 24, 815-821.

CHAPMAN, C. A. 1952. A new method of topographical analysis. *Amer. Journ. Sci.* 250, 428-452.

CHORLEY, R. J. 1957. Illustrating the laws of morphometry. *Geol. Mag.* 94, 140-150.

CHORLEY, R. J. 1958. Aspects of the morphometry of a polycyclic drainage basin. *Geog. Journ.* 124, 370-374.

CHORLEY, R. J. 1959. The shape of drumlins. *Journ. Glaciol.* 3, 339-344.

CHORLEY, R. J. and MORGAN, M. A. 1962. Comparison of morphometric features Unaka Mountains, Tennessee, and North Carolina and Dartmoor, England. *Bull. Geol. Soc. Amer.* 73, 17-34.

CLAYTON, K. M. 1953a. A note on 25-ft contours on O.S. 1 : 25,000 maps. *Geog.* 38, 77-83.

CLAYTON, K. M. 1953b. The denudation chronology of part of the middle Trent Basin. *Inst. Brit. Geog.* 19, 26-36.

COLEMAN, A. 1954. The use of height range diagram in morphological analysis. *Geog. Studies.* 1, 19-26.

CULLING, W. E. H. 1960. Analytical theory of erosion. *Journ. Geol.* 68, 336-344.

DAVIES, J. L. 1959. Wave refraction and evolution of shoreline curves. *Geog. Studies,* 5, 1-14.

DERBYSHIRE, E. 1958. The identification and classification of glacial drainage channels from aerial photographs. *Geogr. Ann.* 40, 188-195.

DURY, G. H. 1951. Quantitative measurement of available relief. *Geol. Mag.* 88, 339-343.

HANSON-LOWE, J. 1935. The clinographic curve. *Geol. Mag.* 72, 180-184.

HOLLINGWORTH, S. E. 1938. The recognition and correlation of high-level erosion surfaces in Britain: A statistical study. *Quart. Journ. Geol. Soc.* 94, 55-84.

HORTON, R. E. 1945. Erosional development of streams and their drainage basins; hydrophysical approach to quantitative morphology. *Bull. Geol. Soc. Amer.* 56, 275-370.

JONES, O. T. 1924. The Upper Towy drainage system. *Quart. Journ. Geol. Soc.* 80, 568-609.

JONES, O. T. 1951. The drainage systems of Wales and the adjacent regions. *Quart. Journ. Geol. Soc.* 107, 201-225.

KING, W. B. R. 1935. The Upper Wensleydale river system. *Proc. Yorks. Geol. Soc.* 23, 10-24.

KING, C. A. M. 1960. The Churnet Valley. *East Midland Geog.* 1, 33-40.

LEOPOLD, L. B., WOLMAN, M. G. and MILLER, J. P. 1964. *Fluvial Processes in Geomorphology,* New York.

MILLER, A. A. 1939. Attainable standards of accuracy in the determination of preglacial sea levels by physiographic methods. *Journ. Geomorph.* 2, 95-115.

MILLER, A. A. 1953. *The skin of the Earth.* London.

MILLER, A. A. 1955. Notes on the use of the height range diagram. *Geog. Studies* 2, 111-115.

MORISAWA, M. E. 1962. Quantitative geomorphology of some watersheds in the Appalachian Plateau. *Bull. Geol. Soc. Amer.* 73, 1025-1046.

MUNK, W. H. and TRAYLOR, M. A. 1947. Refraction of ocean waves; a process linking underwater topography to beach erosion. *Journ. Geol.* 55, 1-26.

PEEL, R. F. 1941. The River North Tyne. *Geog. Journ.* 98, 5-19.

RAISZ, E. and HENRY, J. 1937. An average slope map of Southern New England. *Geog. Rev.* 27, 467-472.

ROBINSON, A. H. 1948. A method of producing shaded relief from areal slope data. *Survey and Mapping* 8.

ROBINSON, A. H. and THROWER, W. 1957. A new method of terrain representation. *Geog. Rev.* 47, 507-520.

SEDDON, B. 1957. Late-glacial cwm glaciers in Wales. *Journ. Glaciol.* 3, 94-98.

SHEWELL, H. A. L. 1951. The accuracy of contours. *Journ. Roy. Inst. Chart. Surv.* 31.

SMITH, K. G. 1950. Standard for grading texture of erosional topography. *Amer. Journ. Sci.* 248, 655-668.

STRAHLER, A. N. 1952. Hypsometric (Area—altitude) analysis of erosional topography. *Bull. Geol. Soc. Amer.* 63, 1117-1142.

WALKER, F. 1953. *Geography from the air.* London.

WENTWORTH, C. K. 1930. A simplified method of determining the average slope of land surfaces. *Amer. Journ. Sci.* 20, 184-194.

WILLIAMS, W. W. 1947. The determination of the gradient of enemy-held beaches. *Geog. Journ.* 109, 76-93.

Sediments are laid down in a wide variety of environments by many different depositing agents. They can be broadly divided into subaerial and submarine deposits, but within these two broad classes there are many subdivisions. Subaerial deposits include glacial tills (and some methods of analysing these in the field have already been mentioned), fluvio-glacial deposits, fluvial and aeolian deposits. Subaerial deposits also include the many forms of deposition by mass-movement, such as solifluction and soil creep. In the coastal region both fluvial and marine processes play their part in determining the character of the sediment; this is most noticeable in deltaic, estuarine and lagoonal deposits. In studying these depositional environments it is useful to be able to determine the source of the sediment and the nature of the depositing agent. The truly marine environment includes the nearshore zone just below the lowest low water, because in the foreshore zone, between tidal limits, the wind as well as the sea may play a part in the sedimentary characteristics. In some areas the foreshore zone is an important source of sand for coastal dunes. In the offshore zone, however, all the forces are marine; as on land, however, there are a number of submarine forces that can be differentiated from the point of view of sediment character. The most important of these are the waves and tides in the shallower water, and it is useful to be able to differentiate deposits laid down by these two agents. In the deeper water other processes become significant from the point of view of sedimentation, such as organic activity in the formation of the deep sea oozes and the effect of turbidity currents; these produce many interesting sedimentary features, some of which have already been mentioned.

There are several reasons for studying sediments from the geomorphological point of view; firstly, the analysis of the sediment can provide data concerning the source of the material. This is particularly clearly shown in the study of erratics in glacial till, and sometimes river capture can be demonstrated by the distribution of rock type in the fluvial deposits, but more subtle studies can be made to indicate the source of many types of sediment. This in turn will provide data for the second major purpose of sediment study; this is the elucidation of the processes operating and the climatic conditions prevailing at the time of their deposition, which give the sediments their particular characteristics. This purpose, apart from providing greater knowledge concerning the sediments themselves, may also throw valuable light on other geomorphological problems. For example if, by examining the nature of sediments resting on an erosion surface, it is possible to determine whether they are marine or subaerial in type, this will provide very important evidence on the origin of the surface and the base-level at the time of its formation. Also by a detailed study of the nature of sediments in a series of river terraces, it is sometimes possible to determine which remnants belong to which stage of development, when this is not possible by purely morphological methods. It is also useful at times to be able to distinguish between sands laid down by tides, waves, rivers or the wind; this can be attempted by studying their sedimentary character. The third purpose of sediment analysis is to establish the age of the deposit; this often requires elaborate equipment, but can produce accurate and valuable evidence. Some of the methods by which these aims can be approached will be considered, including studies of size distribution by mechanical analysis and of shape character.

I. SIZE OF SEDIMENT ANALYSIS

The first operation that must be carried out when a sample is to be analysed for size distribution is to sort it into size groups. The method adopted for this purpose depends on the nature of the sample; coarse sediments, sand grade and larger, can best be mechanically analysed by dry sieving, but boulders and the finer particles cannot be so readily treated by this method. The coarser particle methods, applying mainly to sand and gravel, may be described first.

The most common method of analysing sand is to weigh 100 or 200 grams and to place it in the top of a nest of sieves of decreasing size of aperture downwards. An automatic shaking instrument is necessary to obtain similarity of treatment of the samples, and this should be allowed to operate for 15 to 20 minutes with each sample. The proportion of the total sample retained in each sieve, of which up to ten can be used for each sample, can then be weighed, and the closeness to which the results add up to the original weight of sand provides a check on the results. The sizes of aperture of the nest of sieves used can be adjusted according to the character of the sediment, so that the coarsest and finest fractions are if possible not more than 1 or 2% of the total sample. The reason for this is that the tail of the sample is often of considerable diagnostic value, in assessing the process by which the sediment was deposited.

The finer sand-sized particles can be analysed by other methods as described by Poole (1957), some of which are considerably more rapid than dry sieving and of comparable accuracy. One method makes use of an Emery settling tube (Emery, 1938) which is based on the terminal velocity of fall of the sediment grains in water. The advantage of this is that there are no arbitrary limits determined by the sieve size, and that it is more comparable to the processes of natural sedimentation. Poole's experiments were designed to establish the difference between the settling velocity of experimental spherical samples falling singly, and a group of natural grains falling together. He then tested the relative values obtained by using three methods of analysis, settling tube, sieving and microscope measurement, and compared these with a known-sized sample of glass spheres. The glass spheres were carefully checked for density and sphericity before they were used as a basis for comparison with the natural grains. The time of fall of grains was measured in distilled water at a constant known temperature, and compared well with other standard curves giving the velocity of fall of quartz grains, when adjustments for density had been made. The experiments showed that the grains dropped in groups fell at about 10 to 15% greater velocity of fall than single grains. The group of grains weighed 3·5 grams. If no allowance is made for the group velocity the results would give an error of about $\frac{1}{8}$ ϕ units coarser. If a large sample is dropped at one time the velocity is reduced and not increased.

Four samples were analysed, two being well sorted sand of median diameters 0·42 and 0·21 mm; the third contained 40% heavy minerals and the fourth 40% mica by weight. The finest silts were washed away and the rest of the sample dried and split into three parts for analysis by the three methods and a glass particle sediment was similarly divided. The microscope analysis was done by measuring 300 to 400 grains of each sample with a micrometer using the intermediate diameter and converting to weight for comparison. The results showed that the microscope gave consistently coarser values, the settling tube results using single grain velocity conversion were very close, while the sieving results were slightly finer. The sand with the high proportion of heavy minerals produced the greatest range of median diameters, with the mica sand the tails of the distribution differed. The shape of the particles dominated the sieve results, while density, volume and shape all determined the settling tube results. The single grain settling velocity seemed the most satisfactory for the settling tube analysis.

Summarising the advantages and disadvantages of the three methods, Poole comes to the conclusion that the microscope method has the advantages that shape and roundness can be assessed at the same time as size determination, and size data can be expressed as a number frequency. The disadvantages are the tedious and time-consuming nature of the work, and that the size distribution must be converted to weight to make it comparable with other methods. The settling tube method has the advantage that it is rapid and easy, and takes into account shape, volume and density; it also bears a closer relation to natural deposition. Its disadvantages are that the sample tends to fall as a unit which may give rather erroneous settling velocities. The result gives volumes rather than weight. Sieving has the advantage that it is easy to use, and that, as most size analyses have been made by this method, it is more useful for comparison. The disadvantages are that the shape has an adverse effect on the results, density is not taken into account, and the specified sieve openings are smaller than the effective openings and are liable to change with usage.

Methods that are available for assessing the size distribution of finer material include the hydrometer and pipette methods, and their relative merits have been discussed by Sternberg and Craeger (1961). They divided a sample of silt and clay into nine parts with increasing concentrations from

5 grams/litre and subjected these samples to analysis both by hydro- and by the pipette method. The results showed that the two methods produced very different results for the smallest concentrations, particularly for the coarser sizes, around 5 ϕ units. However the mean values for all the concentrations were closer together in the coarser grades, and were statistically similar for grades from 5 to 7 ϕ; they were on the borderline of rejection of the hypothesis that the samples were significantly the same for 8 and 9 ϕ, and were not similar for 10 ϕ. The conclusions of the study suggest that the accuracy of the hydrometer as a method of assessing the size distribution of fine sediment improves with increasing concentration of silt and clay in the sample, and is not practicable with concentrations of less than 6 g/l; on the other hand the pipette method does not give accurate results with concentration over 24 g/l. With ranges of concentration between 6 and 24 g/l the two methods give results that are significantly similar between the size range of 5 and 9 ϕ. The pipette method is on the whole better within the ranges already stated.

Having mentioned methods of obtaining the volume or weight of sediment in different size groups, it is now necessary to consider methods of plotting and analysing the data. There are a number of scales for describing the size of sediment; one that is quoted in the British Standard Code of Practice (1947) gives the following subdivisions:

Type	Predominant particle size in mm	Field identification
Stones, boulders	200	Larger than 8 in. diameter
Cobbles	60	Mainly 3-8 in, diameter
Gravels	60-2	Mostly between 3 in. and no. 7 B.S. sieve
Sand { coarse	2-0·6	Particles visible to the naked eye
Sand { medium	0·6-0·2	No cohesion when dry
Sand { fine	0·2-0·06	
Silt	0·06-0·002	Particles mostly invisible to naked eye. Some plasticity and dilatancy, dry lumps possess cohesion but can be powdered easily in fingers
Clay	more than 30% of particles less than 0·002 mm	Smooth to touch and plastic, no dilatancy, sticks to fingers. Shrinks on drying, dry lumps cannot be powdered but can be broken.

This method of classification is useful for rapid field identification of sediments, but for more detailed laboratory use the more comprehensive system of Wentworth and the use of ϕ units are more suitable. These two systems can be compared in the table:

Type	φ units	mm Wentworth scale
Boulder	more than −8·0	more than 256
Cobble	−8·0 to −6·0	256 to 64
Pebble	−6·0 to −2·0	64 to 4
Granule	−2·0 to −1·0	4 to 2
Very coarse sand	−1·0 to 0	2 to 1
Coarse sand	0 to 1·0	1 to 0·5
Medium sand	1·0 to 2·0	0·5 to 0·25
Fine sand	2·0 to 3·0	0·25 to 0·125
Very fine sand	3·0 to 4·0	0·125 to 0·0625
Coarse silt	4·0 to 5·0	0·0625 to 0·0312
Medium silt	5·0 to 6·0	0·0312 to 0·0156
Fine silt	6·0 to 7·0	0·0156 to 0·0078
Very fine silt	7·0 to 8·0	0·0078 to ·0039
Coarse clay	8·0 to 9·0	0·0039 to 0·00195
Medium clay	9·0 to 10·0	0·00195 to 0·00098

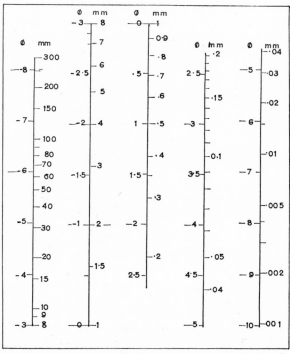

Figure 6.1. Conversion table from mm to φ units. (after Inman)

The ϕ units are found by conversion from the mm scale, where ϕ is $-\log_2$ of the diameter in mm, a conversion table is shown on figure 6·1. This conversion means that one division of the Wentworth scale is the equivalent of one unit on the ϕ scale, as shown on the table. It will be apparent from the table that for every unit on the ϕ scale the value of the Wentworth scale in mm is halved or doubled, that the negative values of ϕ units are the values coarser than 1 mm, and that as the ϕ unit increases the size of the particle decreases.

This method has the advantage that small fractions are not required for the smaller particles and that for many of the common sediment sizes the results in ϕ units are positive. The logarithmic scale also has other advantages from the point of view of statistical description of the sample, as pointed out by Inman (1952). This is because the size-frequency curve of most sediments becomes more symmetrical when the diameter of the grains is plotted as a logarithm of the real value. The symmetry of the curve when plotted frequently approaches the normal distribution. In order to obtain the parameters required for describing the sample most effectively, the results of the size analysis are usually plotted on a curve giving the percentage coarser above each fixed value, if sieves have been used. Thus on the ordinate of the graph ø units increase from left to right, which means that the finer sediments are at the right side of the ordinate. The abscissa is used for the cumulative frequency, showing percentage coarser increasing upwards. This can be plotted on ordinary graph paper, but in this case the curve at the top and bottom becomes very difficult to interpret. A normal sediment on this type of graph will be shown as an S-shaped curve, starting at the bottom left of the graph and trending to the top right. As the tail of the curve is of considerable importance in analysing the characteristics of the sediment, it is important that values of percentage coarser should be accurately read from this part of the curve. This can be done if the figures are plotted on arithmetic probability paper, the probability scale being used on the abscissa for plotting the percentage coarser values. This type of paper has the advantage that the normal distribution curve is a straight line

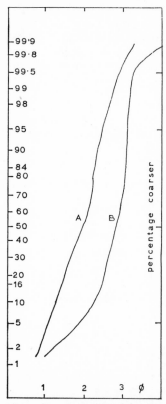

FIGURE 6.2. Examples of size distribution of sand samples analysed by dry sieving and plotted on arithmetic probability paper in ϕ units. Sample A from beach-cusp trough on Trahane beach, Co. Donegal. Sample B from mid-tide level on Dooey beach, Co. Donegal.

on it, so that this provides a useful means of assessing the normality of the distribution at a glance. A sample plot is shown in figure 6.2. The values of significant percentage coarser figures can be read direct from the graph, and the ones that are mainly used are the 5, 16, 25, 50, 75, 84 and 95% coarser figures. Using these values it is possible to describe the sediment in terms of various qualities, including the mean and median, giving a measure of the central tendency; the sorting, skewness and kurtosis can also be considered. These various measures will be described.

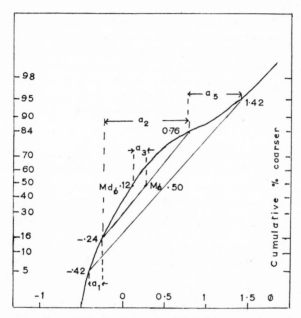

FIGURE 6.3. Graphic illustration of the descriptive measures obtained from a cumulative frequency curve on probability paper. ø mean = $Md\ ø + a_3$, sorting $\sigma\ ø = \frac{1}{2}\ a_2$, Skewness $a\ ø = a_3\ /\ \sigma\ ø$, second skewness $a_2\ ø = a_4\ /\ \sigma\ ø$. Kurtosis $\beta\ ø = \frac{1}{2}\ (a_1 + a_5)\ /\ \sigma\ ø$. (after Inman)

Central tendency. The measure of central tendency most often used for a long time was the median diameter; this is the 50% value on the cumulative frequency graph, and defines the size separating the sample into two equal halves by weight. The median, however, takes no account of the distribution of the grain size on either side of the 50% value. The other method of expressing the central tendency is to use the mean value; if the sample has a symmetrical distribution the mean and the median are the same, but if the sample is asymmetrically distributed the mean will differ from the median. Inman (1952) defines the mean value as

$$M\ \phi = \frac{1}{2}\ (\phi\ 16 + \phi\ 84)$$

TG K

(see figure 6,3). The advantage of the arithmetic mean is that it is more suitable for mathematical analysis; it is the average of a series of samples and can be obtained simply by summing and dividing by the number in the sample. The values chosen by Inman were selected as they give the value nearest to that obtained by other mathematical methods of analysis not using the cumulative frequency graph, but as the use of the graph is so much quicker than other mathematical methods it is preferable, and is nearly as accurate. The median is the value of the ordinate that divides the frequency distribution curve into two equal areas, while the mean value gives the diameter value of the centre of gravity of the frequency distribution curve. If the mm scale is used instead of the ϕ unit scale, the mean, $M \phi$, will give a logarithmic mean of millimetres, but an arithmetic mean in ϕ units; if the ϕ value is converted into millimetres it will give the geometrical mean of the size distribution in millimetres.

Folk and Ward (1957) have shown that Inman's value for the mean provides a good result for fairly normally distributed curves, but if these are very asymmetrical or bimodal in character then the results are not so satisfactory; they suggest a modified value of the mean,

$$Mz = \frac{\phi\ 16 + \phi\ 50 + \phi\ 84}{3}.$$

This value is suggested because ϕ 16 gives a reasonable average for the coarsest third of the sample, and ϕ 84 for the finest third, while ϕ 50, in giving a value for the middle third, provides a more complete view of the distribution. This mean Mz was found to give a more accurate value when compared with the method of calculating the mean of moments. Folk and Ward recommend that the mean value is a better measure of the sediment size than the median, and that this latter value should not be used, as it can be very misleading.

Another measure of central tendency is the mode, but this is difficult to assess accurately. Folk and Ward suggest that it may be found by trial and error, the aim being to locate that $0.5\ \phi$ class in which the weight of sediment is greatest. Thus they assess the percentage between $1.1\ \phi$ and $1.6\ \phi$, and then between $1.2\ \phi$ and $1.7\ \phi$ and so on until the maximum value is found. The use of the result, when it has been established, is that it gives some measure of the degree of sorting in the part of the curve near the mode. It is, however, not often used, the mean and median being more useful.

Sorting. The degree of sorting in the sample is another important aspect of sediment analysis. The standard deviation can be useful as a measure of dispersion. The reason for using the ϕ value for the 16th and 84th percentiles is that these can be used directly to give the standard deviation of the distribution. On a normal curve about $\frac{2}{3}$ of the sample lies within the values given by the standard deviation. Inman suggested a parameter called the ϕ deviation measure, which is given by

$$\sigma\ \phi = \tfrac{1}{2}\ (\phi\ 84 - \phi\ 16).$$

The ϕ deviation measure gives the standard deviation of the curve in terms of Wentworth units, because one ϕ unit is equal to one Wentworth division. In a very skewed distribution the ϕ standard deviation may differ from the moment standard deviation calculated mathematically.

This way of obtaining the measure of sorting may be compared with the older way, which has been used a great deal; this is the Trask sorting co-efficient, given by the formula

$$So = \sqrt{Q_1 / Q_3}.$$

In this Trask uses the upper and lower quartiles on the cumulative frequency graph, that is the 75th and 25th percentile on the mm scale. It is clear that this formula takes less note of the tail of the distribution than Inman's formula and is less soundly based mathematically, as it has no connection with the standard deviation. Again Inman's formula gives good results for a sediment of nearly normal distribution but is not adequate to describe all sediments, as it ignores at least a third of the sample at either end of the range of sizes. It may give misleadingly high sorting values if there is a small amount of coarse or fine material present. To overcome this difficulty, therefore, more of the distribution curve should be included in the sorting measure. However, the analysis is often not reliable for the 99th and 1st percentiles, so a compromise is made and the values of the 95th and 5th percentiles are used for the sorting measure. Folk and Ward suggest a sorting measure that they call the Inclusive Graphic Standard Deviation, and this is given by the formula

$$\sigma_1 = \frac{\phi\,84 - \phi\,16}{4} + \frac{\phi\,95 - \phi\,5}{6 \cdot 6}.$$

This formula was found to provide a value close to the mathematically determined standard deviation. Folk and Ward suggest a verbal scale that can conveniently be used to describe sorting, as follows:

σ_1 under 0·35	very well sorted
0·35 – 0·5	well sorted
0·5 – 1·0	moderately sorted
1·0 – 2·0	poorly sorted
2·0 – 4·0	very poorly sorted
over 4·0	extremely poorly sorted

Values ranging from 0·2 to 8·0 were found in their study of the Brazos River bar. It should be noted that sorting depends to a certain extent on the grain size of the material and is likely to be better in sand than in coarser material but deteriorates again for very fine sediment; thus a statement of the degree of sorting may be misleading, unless two materials of the same general size are compared. This association between sorting and size can be clearly demonstrated by plotting the two variables against one another on a graph, and an example of such a correlation shows that the relationship is very close.

That shown in figure 6.4 has a correlation co-efficient of 0·95 for samples taken offshore in south Lincolnshire, from offshore banks and the channels between them.

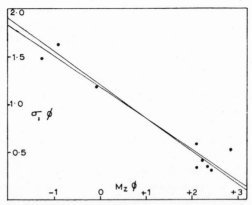

FIGURE 6.4. Correlation of sorting and mean diameter, using Folk and Ward's measures, for samples obtained from offshore in Lincolnshire. The positions from which the samples were obtained are shown in figure 2.8.

Folk and Ward have plotted data showing this relationship over a wider scale of ϕ values ranging from -3 to $+3$ at the coarse and fine ends respectively. Their curve shows an inverted V relationship, with sorting values decreasing in degree of sorting from poor to very poor sorting in the range from -3 to $-0·5$ ϕ; but the sorting improves to well sorted as the size decreases to 2 to 3 ϕ. The part of the curve that shows the latter relationship is covered in the south Lincolnshire data. There is a slight indication that the curve may turn upwards again, indicating that as the mean size decreases below 3 ϕ the sorting may again deteriorate. At one end of the scale are the clean river gravels, which are well sorted; but as the sand content increases the sorting deteriorates, until sand and gravel are about equal in the sample; the pure sands then increase to very good values of sorting, and often these values are less than 0·5 when the mean size is about 2·1 to 2·7 ϕ. Thus pure sand is about twice as well sorted as pure gravel.

Folk and Ward suggest that the true relationship between size and sorting may be a sine curve, whose peaks are dependent upon the modal values of the different types of sediment, gravel sand, silt and clay; thus where the sediment is bimodal the sorting is likely to be rather poorer than when it is unimodal. The degree of sorting will depend to a considerable extent on the method of transport of the sediment. It has been suggested that sorting improves with transport, but this is probably partly due to a decrease in size with transport, if the values fall on that limb of the curve on which sorting is improving with decrease of mean size.

McCammon (1962) has discussed the efficiency of graphic methods of estimating mean size and sorting and has come to the conclusion that of the seven measures used for estimating mean size and sorting some are more valid than others. His valuation of the efficiency of the estimates is based on the minimum possible variance for any unbiased estimate. His results may be expressed in tabular form:

Current measures	Efficiency (percentage)
Mean $(\phi\,16 + \phi\,84)/2$	74
$(\phi\,25 + \phi\,75)/2$	81
$(\phi\,16 + \phi\,50 + \phi\,84)/3$	88
Sorting $(\phi\,75 - \phi\,25)/1\cdot35$	37
$(\phi\,84 - \phi\,16)/2$	54
$(\phi\,95 - \phi\,5)3\cdot3$	64
$(\phi\,84 - \phi\,16)/4 + (\phi\,95 - \phi\,5)/6\cdot6$	79

Proposed measures	Efficiency (percentage)
Mean $(\phi\,20 + \phi\,50 + \phi\,80)/3$	88
$(\phi\,10 + \phi\,30 + \phi\,50 + \phi\,70 + \phi\,90)/5$	93
$(\phi\,5 + \phi\,15 + \phi\,25 + \phi\,35 + \phi\,45 + \phi\,55 +$ $\phi\,65 + \phi\,75 + \phi\,85 + \phi\,95)/10$	97
Sorting $(\phi\,85 + \phi\,95 - \phi\,5 - \phi\,15)/5\cdot4$	79
$(\phi\,70 + \phi\,80 + \phi\,90 + \phi\,97 - \phi\,3 - \phi\,10 -$ $\phi\,20 - \phi\,30)/9\cdot1$	87

These formulae show that the efficiency improves as more of the tail of the sample is taken into account.

Skewness. The skewness of a sediment is indicated by the departure of the mean from the median. In a symmetrical distribution the mean and median coincide and there is no skewness, but the amount and direction of skewness can be obtained, according to Inman's formula, by comparing the mean and median values; thus

$$\alpha\,\phi = \frac{M\,\phi - Md\,\phi}{\sigma\,\phi},$$

that is the median diameter subtracted from the mean and the result divided by the standard deviation. If the skewness is negative the mean is less than the median and the distribution is skewed towards the smaller ϕ values or the coarser particles. On the other hand, if the skewness is positive the distribution is skewed towards the higher ϕ values or the finer particles. This may be compared with Trask's measure of skewness, which is given by

$$Sk. = Q_1 \times Q_3 \,/\, Md^2,$$

where Q_1 and Q_3 are the upper and lower quartiles and Md is the median diameter in mm; this has the same disadvantages as the sorting measure using the quartiles. The sign of Inman's skewness measure can be ascertained visually from the cumulative frequency graph, drawn on probability paper, by joining the 16th and 84th percentile points on the graph by a straight line, representing the normal distribution. If the point where this line cuts the 50th percentile is greater than the median the curve is positively skewed. The ϕ skewness measure gives some indication of the amount by which the curve departs from the normal distribution. It is advisable to take into account the tails of the curve as well, and Inman recommends a second skewness measure to accomplish this, which is given by

$$\alpha_2\ \phi\ =\ \frac{\frac{1}{2}\ (\phi\ 5 + \phi\ 95)\ - Md\ \phi}{\sigma\ \phi}.$$

This value is usually larger than the first skewness measure and indicates the continuity of the skewness; the two values can be combined into a ratio $R\ \phi = \alpha_2\ \phi\ /\ \alpha\ \phi$; this value is often about 2·7 (see figure 6.3).

Folk and Ward suggest a modification to the two skewness formulae of Inman by combining them into one formula, which they call the Inclusive Graphic Skewness and which is given in the formula

$$Sk.\ \mathrm{I}\ =\ \frac{\phi\ 16 + \phi\ 84 - 2\ \phi\ 50}{2\ (\phi\ 84 - \phi\ 16)} + \frac{\phi\ 5 + \phi\ 95 - 2\ \phi\ 50}{2\ (\phi\ 95 - \phi\ 5)}.$$

The mathematical limits of this formula are $+1$ to -1, but few curves have a skewness greater or less than $+0.8$ and -0.8. If the results are positive then the sample has a tail of fine material, if the value is negative there is a tail of coarser grains. Again a relationship has been demonstrated between skewness and size for bimodal sediments, giving a sinusoidal curve; the values were positive for the smaller ϕ sizes or larger grains, falling to negative values for grains between 0 and 1 ϕ, and increasing again to positive values for smaller grains of 2 to 3 ϕ. The skewness is small when the two modes present are nearly equal or if there is only one mode, but as one or other of the modes increases relative to the other so the skewness increases and the relative size will determine the sign.

Kurtosis. One final measure must be mentioned; this is the kurtosis of the sample, which is a measure of peakedness. Inman defines the ϕ kurtosis measure as

$$\beta\ \phi\ =\ \frac{\frac{1}{2}\ (\phi\ 16 - \phi\ 5) + \frac{1}{2}\ (\phi\ 95 - \phi\ 84)}{\sigma\ \phi}.$$

The measure indicates the ratio of the average spread of the tails of the distribution to the standard deviation. The value of $\beta\ \phi$ for a normal distribution is 0·65, but if the curve is more peaked than the normal curve the value will be less than 0·65 and for a less peaked curve the value will be greater than 0·65. Folk and Ward give a rather different method of measuring kurtosis. This is the Graphic Kurtosis and is given by

$$Kg.\ =\ \frac{\phi\ 95 - \phi\ 5}{2.44\ (\phi\ 75 - \phi\ 25)}.$$

Kg. seems to reach a maximum value of about 8·0 under natural conditions, this is for an extremely high and narrow peak; the minimum value mathematically possible is 0·41, but no samples under 0·5 have been found; these are very broadly based and much flatter than a normal curve, which would have a value of 1·0.

The four values described above define the character of a sediment sample, analysed from the point of view of the size distribution of the particles. They may be summarised: the central tendency, best given by the mean: the sorting or standard deviation: the skewness, indicating the relationship between mean and median: and finally the kurtosis, describing the peakedness of the frequency distribution curve. The figures necessary to calculate these values may be read off the cumulative coarser graph.

Use of sediment size parameters. It is useful to consider some of the conclusions that may be drawn from a study of the size distribution characteristics of sediments. Skewness and kurtosis, according to Folk and Ward, provide a valuable means for determining the bimodality of a curve, which on a cumulative frequency graph may only appear as an irregularity or gentle curvature on the probability paper plot, indicating non-normal distribution. Some beach sands exhibit almost straight lines on the probability paper, thus indicating the normality of their particle size distribution, but many sediments from other environments are bimodal and it is important to recognise this. Some dune sands, for example, show a high kurtosis value, and a positive skewness on account of a small volume of fine silt included in the sediment. Very high or low values of kurtosis suggest that one type of material was sorted in a region of high energy, and then transported without change of character to another environment, where it became mixed with another sediment, in equilibrium with different conditions, possibly of low energy. Such a mixed type of sediment will be strongly bimodal. This type of sediment can originate for example where beach sand, sorted in a high energy environment, is washed into a lagoonal area where it may become mixed with sediment of much finer grade, settling under very quiet conditions. If both parts of the sediment had been well sorted before their mixing, then the kurtosis will be very high, and if the sand is in excess the sample will be positively skewed.

Another method of plotting the distribution of sand size of desert sand has been used by Bagnold and Simonett (1950). The log diameter in mm is plotted against the volume of sand by weight in each unit of the log diameter scale, using a log scale for both axes of the graph. In a well sorted desert sand there should be two almost straight lines inclining towards each other. Irregularities in these two lines can give useful evidence of the stage of development of the dunes; this seems to depend on the amount of sand moving.

One of the most useful ways in which size analysis can be used is for determining the type of environment in which a sediment was deposited, and from this basis the processes causing the deposition may be clarified. Some examples of the results of analyses of this sort may be considered; the work of Mason and Folk (1958) on the differentiation of sand in beach, dune and aeolian flat environments on Mustang Island, Texas, indicates some of the ways in which these sedimentary environments may be distingished. They came to the conclusion that skewness and kurtosis were the best parameters for differentiating the environments.

Mustang Island is part of the barrier beach extending along the western coast of the Gulf of Mexico. Winds normally blow onshore, waves are low owing to a gentle offshore gradient, being only 1 to 3 feet high, and the tidal range is only 2 feet. The dunes are stabilised and reach up to 20 to 40 feet, but there are some low foredunes, only sparsely vegetated. The mean values for the four main parameters already discussed were evaluated for each environment. The values for the three environments were then compared and statistical tests applied to establish whether the differences could have been due to chance rather than to inherent differences in the character of the sediments in each environment. The results can best be expressed in tabular form:

Mean size M_z: Beach 2·82 ϕ
 Dunes 2·86 ϕ
 Flats 2·83 ϕ

The statistical tests show that all these sizes are so close that the mean size cannot be used for differentiation of the environment of sedimentation, although the finer character of the dune sand is significant at the 10% level.

Graphic Standard Deviation σ_1 Beach 0·309 ϕ
 Dunes 0·273 ϕ
 Flats 0·286 ϕ

The tests showed that these figures demonstrate a highly significant difference between the beach and dunes, and the beach and flats, but there is only a dubious difference between the dunes and flats.

Skewness values: Beach +0·03
 Dunes +0·14
 Flats +0·17

The difference in these figures is such that the dunes can readily be distinguished from the beach, and the beach from the flats, but there is no significant difference between the dunes and flats.

Kurtosis values: Beach 1·09
 Dunes 1·07
 Flats 1·20

In this factor the differences between the beach and flats and the dunes and flats are very significant, but there is no difference between the beach and dunes. By using all the criteria it is possible to distinguish between the three environments with at least one parameter, and in some instances with three. These differences can be distinguished despite the fact that the material has such a similar mean value. The tails of the distribution are vital to such an analysis. The beach samples on the whole show more normal curves, they are nearly symmetrical and have a medium kurtosis value. The dune samples are also of medium kurtosis, but are skewed to the fine grades, while the flats samples are skewed to the fine particles but have a high kurtosis. Thus the following figures can be used as a basis for differentiating the sources of sediment:

Graphic standard deviation   0·21 to 0·26   probably dune
                                      0·26 to 0·28   dune or aeolian flat
                                      0·28 to 0·30   indeterminate
                                      0·30 to 0·35   probably beach
Skewness   − 0·20 to + 0·02   probably beach
                + 0·02 to + 0·05   beach or dune
                + 0·05 to + 0·13   indeterminate
                + 0·13 to + 0·30   dune or aeolian flat
Kurtosis   0·47 to   0·53   beach or dune
                  0·53 to   0·55   indeterminate
                  0·55 to   0·61   probably aeolian flat

Thus kurtosis is the only way of distinguishing dune and aeolian flat, while beach sands can be identified by their normality and relatively poor sorting.

One method of demonstrating this relationship graphically is to plot the skewness against the kurtosis, and it is found that although there is a zone of overlap between the individual samples from these three zones there are also quite large areas where each environment is represented alone. It is useful to go one stage beyond the specification of values that enable the different environments to be separated on the basis of the mechanical analysis, and this is to explain the processes that lead to the significant differences noted. Then methods of sediment analysis become a tool for research as well as for description and identification.

The fact that the skewness and kurtosis are the most useful factors for differentiating the environments suggests that it is the processes operating to alter the tails of the distribution that must be considered. The bimodal character of the sediment is important in this respect, as it is this factor that upsets the normality of the curve. Methods of modal mixing, particularly in the dune and aeolian flat environment must be sought. Because of the prevailing wind, it may be assumed that the transport is predominantly towards the dunes and flats from the beach. The closeness of the mean values suggests that the beach sand forms a large proportion of the sediment in the other environments, amounting probably to 80 to 95%. There is a small addition to the beach material; at the coarse end of the scale this may amount to only 2 to 5%, but it is nevertheless enough to give the slight negative skewness which is a common characteristic of beach sands and will also account for the rather higher sorting. In this instance the coarser material seems to be a small addition of coarse quartz grains, as it is not shell fragments, although these often add to the coarse fraction in beach samples. As the sand moves to the dunes the sorting is improved and the skewness becomes strongly positive. This could be due either to the addition of fine particles or the absence of the coarse. The second seems the more probable in the area studied, as some of the coarser particles must have been left behind on the beach; this would account for the improved sorting, while also giving a positive skewness to the dune samples. In the aeolian flat the curves become more sharply peaked and the sorting deteriorates. This can best be explained by adding to the fine end of the curve, probably fine wind-borne dust, which is in the silt to very fine sand grade with a ϕ value of 4, and amounts to about 5 to 10% of the whole sample. The fact that the sands are narrowly peaked suggests that they are bimodal, and it seems true that very few natural sands are truly unimodal. Reasons for this depend on the nature of sorting of sand under the influence of waves, wind and currents.

Analyses of sand samples from a variety of environments have been studied by Friedman (1961) and his methods and results exemplify well the value of such work in providing means of identifying the environment of deposition and the processes involved. His 267 samples were derived from dunes, rivers, ocean beaches and lake beaches, and were collected from a very wide distribution, including the United States, Mexico, Canada, the Bahamas, Bermuda, North Africa and Hawaii. 114 of them came from dunes, 80 from ocean beaches, 18 from lake beaches and 55 from rivers. Sands of different mineral content were examined, such as quartz sand, carbonate sands and olivine sands; however 240 of the samples were quartz sand. The samples from the beaches were taken in the swash zone parallel to the bedding. They were all analysed by sieving, using sieves with $\frac{1}{4}$ ϕ interval between two adjacent sieves. In some samples heavy minerals were separated out for separate analysis. The parameters that were used for the analysis were the mean, skewness and kurtosis; these were calculated according to the following formulae: the mean was given by

$$\bar{x} \phi = 1/100 \ \Sigma f m \ \phi,$$

$\bar{x} \phi$ was the mean ϕ grain size, f was the abundance or frequency of the different grain sizes in the sediment, m ϕ was the mid-point of each grain-size grade in ϕ units. The skewness was given by the average of the cubed deviations from the mean divided by the cube root of the standard deviation, σ ϕ; this was given by $\alpha_3 \phi = (1/100) \ \sigma \ \phi^{-3} \ \Sigma f \ (m \ \phi - \bar{x} \ \phi)^3$ and the value of $\sigma \ \phi = (\Sigma f \ (m \ \phi - \bar{x} \ \phi)^2 \ / \ 100)^{1/2}$. The kurtosis was given as $\alpha_4 \ \phi = (1/100)$ $\sigma \ \phi^{-4} \ \Sigma f \ (m \ \phi - \bar{x} \ \phi)^4$. In assessing the results of analyses the various parameters were plotted against each other, and this enabled diagnostic features to be identified. The skewness was plotted against the mean value and the resulting points were widely scattered over the graph, but there was a clear distinction between the beach and the dune sand as shown on figure 6.5. The former showed a very great preponderance of samples with a negative skewness, while nearly all the dune samples were positively skewed. The positive skewness of the dune sands applied to many types of dunes; those formed in the desert, barrier islands, lake and river dunes were all positively skewed. There was one exception to the negative skewness of beach sands, and this applied to sands that probably still had the characteristics of river sands, from which they were derived, and were not yet in equilibrium with their new environment. Some of the coarser beach sands also showed a positive skewness. The mineralogical character of the sand did not appear to influence its characteristic skewness in either environment. Another graph showed the relationship between river and beach sands by plotting the skewness against the kurtosis. The latter factor was not diagnostic of the environment, but again the skewness helped to differentiate the environments, as most of the river sediments were positively skewed, but there were some

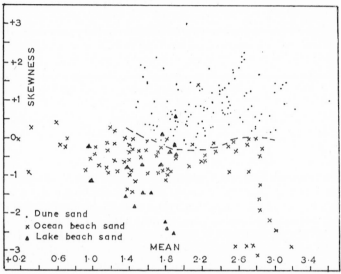

FIGURE 6.5. The relationship between skewness and mean diameter for beach and dune sands illustrates the differentiation of sands from these different environments. The characteristic negative skewness of beach sands is clearly shown. (after Friedman)

exceptions; the coarser river sands did not provide diagnostic results. The sorting and skewness were also plotted against each other, for river and dune sands and the results again helped to differentiate the two types of sediment. Some of the river sands that were negatively skewed could be differentiated from the beach sands by the higher sorting value of the river sands. Only two river sand samples out of 108 lay outside the line separating them from the beach sands. It was found that the ϕ scale showed the separation of sand types much more effectively than the mm scale. Skewness served to differentiate between beach sands on the one hand and dune and river sands on the other, but to differentiate dune and river sands other parameters had to be considered. River sands usually show poorer sorting than dune sands, although there is a large field of overlap when sorting is plotted against mean size for samples from these two environments.

One of the values of a study of this type, which is derived from data from many examples of the various environments studied, is that it can provide evidence of the processes involved in the deposition of the sediment. It reflects the mode of transport and the energy conditions of the transporting and depositing medium. The greater competency of waves on a beach is indicated by the fact that many beach samples have mean ϕ values less than 1·49, but dunes never showed values smaller than this. The positive skewness of the dune and river sands may be due to the unidirectional character of the transporting medium. In a positively skewed curve there is an extra abundance of finer particles, the coarse end of the curve is cut off, showing that these particles cannot be transported in the relatively less effective environment. On the beach, on the other hand, the finer particles are winnowed away by the relatively strong forces that operate in the swash zone where the backwash and swash operate in opposite directions. It is the lack of the tail at the fine end of the curve that gives the distribution its negative skewness. The calculation of the skewness as described by Friedmann, although more accurate than the other methods suggested, is time-consuming.

Fuller (1962) has done work on the way in which the beach sands obtain their characteristic size distribution, by studying sands from shallow water varying from about 6 to 12 feet in depth. The cumulative frequency curves for beach sand sediments from these depths often show two inflection points at 0·8 and 2·0 ϕ. These points may represent grain sizes where processes change, for example, the 0·8 ϕ may separate sand moved by traction from sand moved in suspension. The 2·0 ϕ grade is often lacking in sediments from this environment and this suggests that sand of this size is moved either offshore or onshore from shallow water. The removal of this grade may be due to its relative ease of transport, as it is the size that can be most easily picked up and transported by both wind and water. Thus sand of this size reaching the foreshore may be picked up and carried away by the wind.

It is also worth mentioning some studies that have been made concerning the size distribution of sediments in other environments, such as terraces and alluvial fans. A study of alluvial fan deposits was made with samples collected from fans on the Diablo Mountains on the west side of the San Joaquin valley in California (Bull, 1962). The samples were collected after the rainy season and were analysed mechanically and plotted on logarithmic graphs; the 1% coarser size (C) and the median diameter (M) were used. In the area studied the streams flow in flash floods and vegetation is sparse. By plotting the C and M values for the different samples two different types of sedimentation could be differentiated; these were the traction-current and the mud-flow types. The former had two sedimentary types that could be distinguished: the stream channel sediment and the braided stream sediment. The C, M relationships showed that the mud-flow type of deposit must have a greater density than the traction current type, and the mud-flow deposits showed some similarity with turbidity current deposits. The mud-flow fan deposits showed poorer sorting than the other type in their C, M relationships, and the two types of fan sedimentation could also be differentiated by this method.

Sediment analysis has also been used to differentiate between a series of river terraces, and this method, combined with others can help to confirm evidence of morphology and altitude relationships, and gives more confidence in the correlation of terraces, as well as providing evidence of the character of the river at the time of the terrace formation. The analysis of samples from four terraces in Florida (Lapinsky *et al.*, 1958) illustrates the type of material that can be used and the results obtained. The samples were sieved through ten sieves and the mean size of the samples taken from each of the four terraces showed that the average mean size decreased from the upper terrace of 170-220 feet, where the mean size was 0·357; in the second terrace at 115-150 feet the mean size was 0·298, in the third at 60-150 feet it was 0·286, and in the lowest at 5 to 30 feet it was 0·257 mm. The mean of the curves for the higher terrace, plotted on probability paper in ϕ units, showed a normal distribution, with the exception of a lack of fine particles at one end of the curve. The two intermediate terraces were very similar but finer grained than the upper terrace, while the lowest terrace was finer still and had an excess of the very fine grains. The sands were all well sorted.

In this latter quality they differed from terrace sediments that were analysed by Nossin (1959) in Spain. Here the sediments showed rather poor sorting, which was probably due to variations in flow when the sediments were being deposited, and the addition of fine silt suggests local aeolian action. As this last characteristic was confined to the two lower terraces it provided a criterion by which they could be differentiated from the higher terraces. On the whole these studies were not as helpful in studying these terraces as a study of the shape of the sediment, so that this aspect of sediment analysis should also be considered.

2. SHAPE OF SEDIMENT ANALYSIS

The measurement of the shape of sediment particles can be carried out in a number of ways depending partly on the dimensions of the material. The problem of describing the shape of an irregular pebble accurately is difficult, as there are three dimensions to be considered. Various different methods have been proposed. Consider first a pebble; this has three dimensions, length, breadth and height, and radius of curvature. If l is the length, w the width, t the thickness or height, r the least radius of curvature in the principal plane, and C is the point where w crosses AB or l, the shape of the pebble can be described by three indices (see figure 6.6). Firstly the index of roundness is given by $2r / l \times 1000$, the index of asymmetry is given by $AC / l \times 1000$, and the index of flatness is given by $(w+l)/2t \times 100$. The values, suggested by Cailleux and Tricart, range from a minimum roundness of 0 to a maximum of 1000, the asymmetry ranges from 500 for maximum symmetry to 1000 for maximum asymmetry, and the flatness index ranges from 100 for minimum flatness to infinity, although in fact the value never exceeds 1000. The calculation of these indices can be facilitated by the use of a set of graphs prepared by Berthois (1952). According to Blenk (1960) the roundness index of Cailleux is as good as others that have been proposed subsequently and it has the advantage that many studies have been made by its use, so that the results are comparable, which is an important factor. The measures as suggested by Kuenen, for example, are similar except for a different value of a constant. It seems reasonable, therefore, to use Cailleux's method for determining the shape of pebbles. More recently Tonnard (1963) has tested the various indices proposed to assess the shape of sand grains and comes to the conclusion that Cailleux's index is the most satisfactory.

As pebbles from different rock types tend to have different characteristic

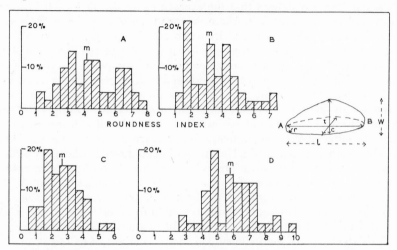

FIGURE 6.6. Measurements required to obtain pebble shape characteristics are shown on the right. The roundness observations on the left illustrate differences between samples measured in Dingle Bay, south-west Ireland. A, south-west corner of Cromane pebble spit. B, north end of Cromane spit. C, central mound of Cromane spit. D, northern end of Rossbehy spit. The mean values are indicated. (after Guilcher and King)

shapes, it is important that, when pebble dimensions are being used to assess method of deposition and for correlation of different sediments, all the pebbles should be of the same rock type. In order to provide valid bases for differentiating various processes or deposits, it is necessary to ascertain that the indices for the different samples differ by an amount greater than a certain value, which can be obtained by statistical analysis of many samples. There is a constant range of standard deviation for each index within which the samples may vary in a random way, so that differences must exceed these values if they are to be significant. The greater the mean value, the greater the standard deviation within which the variations may not be significant. The analysis of pebble shape and character is important in interpreting the origin of a deposit and may also provide evidence concerning the nature of transport, for example the ratio of length to breadth to height can be used to determine whether the pebble has moved by rotation or sliding.

An example of the type of information that can be obtained from a study of pebble dimensions is the work of Nossin (1959), which has already been mentioned. He used Cailleux's method of measurement working in the

Pisuerga drainage of the Calabrian Mountains of Spain. He measured 100 pebbles at each site, using those more than 4 cm in maximum diameter, and confining the measurements where possible to quartzite pebbles. The percentages of pebbles in each group of 100 on the roundness index scale were plotted on a graph; where the pebbles had been shattered after their deposition their roundness was nil and they were not included in the counts, but the number was plotted separately. In some instances the rounding was not the result of fluvial transport to the present position in the terrace deposits, but reflected earlier rounding, the pebbles being derived ready rounded from conglomerate outcrops. Points of this type must be borne in mind when interpreting the results of such a survey. Some pebbles, however, demonstrated clearly the increase of rounding during normal fluvial transport, as the pebbles became measurably rounder at the lower stations. This may be more the result of easier transport of rounded pebbles than of attrition of the pebbles over the relatively short distances involved. Some of the pebbles derived from the conglomerate showed by their roundness index that they had been shattered by frost action and then undergone another phase of rounding; the indices over 400 indicated the original rounding of the conglomerate, while the indices at and below 300 indicated subsequent re-rounding of shattered pebbles. The pebbles of the highest terrace of the Pisuerga were considerably more rounded than those of the lower and middle terrace. The middle terrace samples were all very similar to one another, the pebbles being rather less rounded than those of the lower terrace, although not enough to suggest different methods of deposition under different conditions. The conditions under which the middle terrace gravels were laid down were rather more intense, but of a similar type to those of the lower terrace. The middle terrace deposits showed clearly the resumption of rounding after a period of shattering, as shown by the high peak in the 200 to 300 grade. Such a type of rounding could occur under dry, warm conditions, but if so the pebbles should show a ferruginous coating and the sand fraction should show wind wearing; both these characteristics were missing. Therefore, it was assumed that the sediments showed the effects of periglacial conditions followed by transport. The pebbles of the upper terrace on the other hand, were much more rounded, as already pointed out; this suggested that they must have been laid down under temperate conditions. Weathering must have been active in order to provide the large amount of material in the terraces. Values of over 300 are common for normal fluvial transport over fairly short distances. A high percentage of indices between 0 and 200 suggests deposition under periglacial conditions; this shows a low roundness index. In considering the character of pebble roundness down a river, the material brought into the river from the valley sides must also be considered, and this may account for an uneven change in roundness downstream.

Studies of the roundness of pebbles are also of value in coastal investigations (Guilcher and King, 1961) (see figure 6.6). There are three spits in Dingle Bay in western Ireland, the outer two of which are normal wind- and wave-formed features, largely of sand, with dunes and a wide beach, but also with some shingle. The inner spit, on the other hand, is different; this is clearly indicated by the roundness of the pebbles in comparison with those of one of the outer spits. The distal end of the outer spit has pebbles with the high mean roundness index of 575. These pebbles had clearly travelled for some distance by beach drifting and had been well rounded in the process, pointing to the marine origin of the feature, which must have been built by wave action. The inner spit on the other hand, showed roundness values of 425 on the seaward beach, 325 on the northern, distal tip, but only 275 on the central mound in the spit. Clearly the pebbles at the distal end cannot have come by beach drifting from the inner end of the spit, or they would have been more and not less rounded than those on the seaward beach. Also the pebbles on the crest of the spit were the least rounded and, therefore, must have been least affected by the waves. This shows that the spit is not the work of the waves, which have merely modified its seaward margin and rounded the pebbles here to a certain extent. The inner spit is a deposit of glacial till, shaped by the waves, although they have not affected the spit crest.

The roundness of sand grains can also give useful information concerning the characteristics of the sediment. Finer-grain silt particles can also be analysed from the point of view of their shape by a method suggested by Wright (1957). The method requires a very good electron microscope and is elaborate; it is based on the shadow principle, where the length of the shadow gives a measure of the third dimension of the particle, whose other two dimensions can be seen on the microscope slide; the degree of magnification that is required for silt particles is at least 300 times. The method is slow and difficult, but it is a means whereby fine sediments can be analysed. However, a study of the roundness of sand-sized particles is easier with less elaborate equipment, and can give useful results. It has already been mentioned that Cailleux's indices can also be applied to sand-sized particles. Shepard and Young (1961), however, used a visual system of fitting sand grains, viewed under a microscope, into a predetermined scale of six categories (see figure 6.7). These categories were determined by the pivotability of the grains, as this difference between grains was thought to be significant in determining the variations between grains found on the dunes and on the beach. The highest pivotability was given the highest index and these grains were classed as very angular, while well-rounded grains were the lowest class at the other end of the scale. In each sample 100 grains between 0·062 and 0·125 mm were counted and the roundness value determined for pairs of samples taken from beach and dune in each area. The dune samples showed the greater roundness and this character was much more consistent in areas where the prevailing wind blew onshore. This difference must be due to the capacity of the wind to pick up the rounder grains, whereas the angular ones became more readily trapped amongst their neighbours.

Kuenen (1963) has described an instrument which tests the pivotability of sand grains. It consists of a gently sloping semicircular trough that can be rocked. The sample is placed at the top end of the trough and moves down the gently sloping length of the trough as this is rocked. The samples are separated into twelve categories according to the time the particles take to cover the length of the trough, each size grade being tested separately. The lowest pivotability, number 12, is used to describe the particles left in the trough at the end of the experiment. The results of the tests showed that high pivotability increased the rate of transport by traction, but decreased

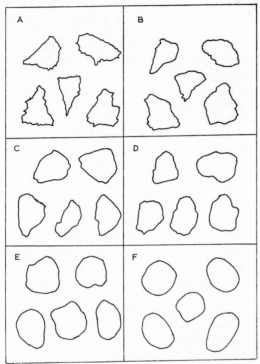

FIGURE 6.7. Scale of roundness and pivotability of sand grains divided into six categories from A-F.
A, Very angular. B, Angular. C, Sub-angular. D, Sub-rounded. E, Rounded
F, Well rounded. (after Shepard and Young, modified)

the movement in suspension. Source materials, such as weathered granite, have low pivotability. It was higher in dune sands than in beach sands supplying the dunes in the fine and coarse grades, but was lower in the medium grades.

Nossin (1959) has used the same measurements for sand grains, viewed under a microscope, as those used for pebble analysis. The sizes of the grains he measured were in the range 0·5 to 1·05 mm and were thus for much coarser sand than the other observations mentioned. In general the sands showed low roundness values, which does not necessarily mean short transport by river action. It is interesting to note, however, that the middle terrace, unlike samples from the other terraces whose maxima fell below 200 and often 100, had indices over 400 and 500 in moderate percentages. The grains also showed a considerable amount of frosting. This points clearly to the importance of wind action in the sediments of the middle terrace and these characteristics occur throughout the sediment and not only at the surface. This could be accounted for by periglacial action for a period before the deposition of the terrace gravel by the river, some of the rounded grains being subsequently reworked into the lower terrace gravel deposits.

The superficial character of the sediment as suggested may give a clue to its origin. The frosting of sand grains is usually associated with wind action, although Kuenen does not consider that wind can frost sand grains. He considered that the frosting of dune sand was a chemical process. The fact that frosting is absent from coastal dunes can be readily explained by the short time that the sand has been under aeolian influence. This supports the view that the roundness of dune sand is the result mainly of selective picking up of the grains by the wind and not of wind modification of the grains. Shepard found that frosting was never diagnostic of coastal sand origin. Biederman (1962) has described detailed studies of individual sand grains viewed under an electron microscope. After careful preparation the water-deposited grains showed regular triangular pits, following the crystal form, which were the result of solution. The wind-deposited grains, on the other hand, showed irregular pitting. Some grains showed evidence of both characteristics and the associated methods of deposition and transport.

The surface markings of larger pebbles may also be helpful for identification at times. Waters (1960) has shown that resistant flint pebbles that were well-rounded, occurring at a height of around 1000 feet in Somerset, showed chatter markings on their surface similar to those of modern beach pebbles, although they probably were last affected by the waves in the early Tertiary period. Thus surface markings give additional valuable evidence of the detailed shaping of pebbles and sand by a special environment, which may have geomorphological significance. The smoothing and striation of pebbles by ice action can also have diagnostic qualities, but is sufficiently well known and easily identifiable to require little further comment; fine-grained hard rocks, such as limestones or fine, hard sandstones, show this characteristic most clearly.

3. CHEMICAL ANALYSIS AND DATING METHODS

It is not possible to do more than mention some of the results that may be obtained from various types of mineral and chemical analyses. These include analysis of heavy minerals and the study of carbonate content of sediments. Heavy mineral analysis was one of the earliest methods of sediment investigation, and it can help with the solution of a number of problems. There are, however, several points that must be borne in mind when heavy mineral analyses are considered; one is the selective wear of heavy minerals under transport. Experiments suggest that different minerals are susceptible to varying extents, but it is not likely that under natural conditions mechanical wear will be sufficiently rapid for a noticeable difference to be found even in long rivers, such as the Mississippi and Rhine, where studies have been conducted. Even on beaches where the wear is more rapid and violent, there is no evidence that heavy minerals are selectively reduced or eliminated.

Another factor that must be taken into account is the selective sorting of heavy minerals in the sediment. The densities of heavy minerals range from 2·89 to 5·0 and their size is also variable, ranging from 0·03 mm to 0·5 mm. It is interesting to note that different heavy minerals tend to be found in different size groups; thus zircons and rutiles are nearly always small. Fine-grained sediments may, therefore, be expected to have higher values of these minerals; this does not necessarily indicate that zircon is especially abundant in the area, but is an effect of sorting. This factor must be taken into account in analyses dealing with fine materials, in the silt and clay grades, which on the whole are less rewarding to study from this point of view. Some minerals such as pyroxene are usually fairly coarse-grained, but may at times be found in the finer sediment. In some instances the effects of sorting are strong, specially when the source provides minerals that cover a wide size range, and where the depositional area also contains a wide variety of environments.

The Rhone delta region provides a good example (van Andel, 1959) for studying the effect of sorting on heavy minerals and their distribution. In the delta and nearshore area there is a heavy mineral assemblage consisting of pyroxene, hornblende and epidote, while in the offshore zone a hornblende, epidote assemblage occurs. The minerals come from several sources, the pyroxene from the volcanic rocks of the Central Massif in France and the hornblende and epidote from the Alps. The assemblage differs on either side of the Rhone delta, which suggests that longshore movement is not taking place. The source of nearshore and delta heavy minerals is clearly from the areas mentioned inland, but the source of the offshore minerals is more obscure. In analysing the samples it was found that the pyroxene grains were always amongst the coarser particles, and the epidote amongst the finest, while the hornblende was intermediate in size. In density the three minerals are fairly closely comparable. In this area the size of the minerals can explain their distribution in the two environments; the finer sediment is deposited in the quieter water offshore, but the coarser particles form a type of lag deposit in the more vigorous environments of the delta, where coarse-grained deposits are found on the beaches and the dunes and in the river sands. Thus the difference of minerals is not due to the difference of source, but to the effects of differential sorting of the originally heterogeneous material, containing all sizes and all materials. It seems, however, that such distinct patterns of sorting are rather rare, and often the heavy minerals are truly diagnostic of material sources. This is true of the whole of the Mississippi delta environment, where the heavy mineral assemblages are very homogeneous, even between sandy and clayey deposits. It is always as well to test for the effects of sand size variations, but it will not often be a vital factor in heavy mineral analyses.

Another factor is the post-depositional alteration of the heavy minerals, but on the whole it seems that this factor is only of significance in special conditions not applicable to recent sediments.

The types of problem that can be helped by a study of heavy mineral analysis include a study of the source of sediment in various environments. For example the different terraces of a river system can at times be differentiated on the basis of heavy minerals, while river capture can also be indicated by this method. Studies, such as that of Baak (1936) in the North Sea are helpful in locating the source of offshore and beach sediment. He has divided the floor of the North Sea into zones based on the heavy mineral assemblages; one group is characteristic of the eastern side and is derived from the Rhine, another group includes glacial and fluvio-glacial material from Scandinavia; there is a mixed group, and another characteristic of the English coast, which is rich in garnet and augite. The sands along the coasts of north France, Holland and Belgium are rather mixed in character, as a result of glacial, fluvio-glacial and marine action at various stages in the deposition and resorting of the sediment.

This state of affairs differs very markedly from that found by Baak further west in the deeply indented coast of western Brittany; here each bay had its own separate heavy mineral assemblage, showing clearly that the sand source was purely local, derived from the complex and variable ancient rocks at the backs of the separate bays. This shows clearly that no longshore transport can take place under these conditions, though, where the shore is open, as in the previous area mentioned, longshore transport can take place readily over considerable distances. Trask has also used heavy mineral assemblages to trace the movement of sand along the coast from river mouths where the sediment has a recognisable heavy mineral content that can be traced alongshore.

Another useful method of chemical analysis is to study the carbonate content of a sediment. This can be done using the Chittick gasometric apparatus described by Dreimanis (1962). The method, which is relatively simple and quick, can usefully be applied to the study of the carbonate content of glacial tills and other deposits. The sample used must weigh 1·7 grams and it must consist of material finer than 0·074 mm. This material is mixed with a 20% solution of hydrochloric acid and the volume of CO_2 driven off is measured. The weight percentage of calcite equals the weight percentage of CO_2 multiplied by 100·09 / 44·01. The calcite dissolves in 5 to 25 seconds, but the dolomite takes a lot longer; thus by taking two readings at different times from the start of the experiment, the amount of calcite and dolomite can be determined separately to an accuracy of ± 0·3. Together they give a good estimate of the total carbonate content as other elements can be ignored. A graph can be used to relate ml CO_2 to percentage calcite and dolomite. Andrews and Sim (1964) have used this method to assess the carbonate content of till in north-west Baffin Island, where localised limestone outcrops occur. By studying the variation of carbonate content in the till samples the source and direction of ice movement could be worked out, and the results suggested a dispersal area over Foxe Basin at one stage of the glaciation.

There are other possible uses for this method of study of glacial tills, such as working out the depth of leaching.

Methods of dating can only be mentioned very briefly; the ones of most interest to geomorphologists are generally those that cover a fairly short period of time with reasonable accuracy. Thus amongst the chemical methods the fluorine and radiocarbon methods are of particular value; they both depend on the preservation of organic material, and can give reasonably accurate results. The fluorine test can be applied to bones and depends upon the fact that fluorine occurs in small quantities in ground water, often about one part in a million. This combines with the calcium phosphate of the bone to form fluorapatite. The content of fluorine increases with the length of time that the bone is influenced by water; thus bones of the lower Pleistocene include about 2% fluorine, the middle Pleistocene about 1% and the upper Pleistocene about $\frac{1}{2}$%.

The carbon-14 method of analysis is more adaptable as it can be applied to any organic matter, but the danger of later contamination by younger organic matter or by other processes is still present. Carbon-14, which is the radio-active isotope of carbon-12, is formed in the atmosphere at high levels from nitrogen under the influence of cosmic rays. The carbon-14 is assimilated by plants and through them by animals, but when the living matter dies the assimilation process ceases and the carbon-14 decays with a half-life of about 5730 years $\pm$ 40 (Godwin, 1962). The range of this method is about 70,000 years (Godwin *et al.*, 1957, 1960) but its great merit is that it is applicable throughout the world, and makes possible comparison of dates on a world-wide basis. Many results are now available by this technique and refinements are making it more reliable. For example, the date of the Alleröd warm period in the late glacial has been accurately fixed in many far separated areas at about 10,800 to 11,044 years ago. Both these methods depend upon the preservation of suitable organic matter, often amongst accumulating deposits.

Another method of dating, dependent on the deposition of sediment itself, consists of counting varves. This method can only be applied in those areas where the annual deposition of varves has taken place in glacial lakes, so that the varve unit, consisting of a coarser summer layer and a finer winter layer, may be counted. De Geer pioneered this method of dating in Sweden and produced an accurate time scale covering about 13,500 years; his results have in part been confirmed subsequently by radio-carbon dating. His zero varve was dated 6850 B.C. and is an extra large varve formed as a result of the bipartition of the Scandinavian ice sheet into two parts. This allowed the sudden drainage of a lake impounded behind the ice, which resulted in the formation of the megavarve. The last varve was formed in A.D. 1710. Varve chronology can only be applied where glacial lakes allowed the accumulation of this particular type of annual deposit, and it has been applied particularly in Scandinavia and the Connecticut valley area of eastern North America, in the latter area by Antevs mainly.

There are several interesting methods of dating by the use of botanical evidence. Dendrochronology, based on the counting of annual tree rings, can carry the record back several thousand years in suitable areas. The giant sequoias live to about 3000 years, and more recently bristle-cone pines growing at 10,000 feet in the White Mountains of California have been found to be more than 4000 years old. These trees are in an area sensitive to climatic change and can therefore record both accurate chronology and evidence of climatic fluctuations. Tree growth is dependent on climate, so it is often possible to correlate the inner rings of one tree with the outer rings of an older one and thus extend the sequence back in time. Tree ring counting can also be helpful in dating glacier retreat by study of trees growing on different terminal moraines.

Tree and other pollen has also been used a great deal for dating and palaeoclimatic studies, where the pollen has been preserved in accumulating sediment, peat being especially important owing to its preservative properties. This method cannot give absolute dates like the others mentioned, but if the pollen can be studied with associated datable archaeological remains, then a relative time scale can be set up. Pollen analysis is particularly valuable in providing a picture of changing climate as it reflects the vegetation from which it was derived. Characteristic pollen diagrams allow correlation between different areas, and it is possible to date deposits to specific interglacial or post-glacial periods by this means.

In arctic areas north of the tree line the problem of determining both a relative and an absolute chronology is exceptionally difficult. In coastal areas marine fossils may be dated by radio-carbon methods, but inland lichenometry, the technique of using the maximum diameter of epipetric lichens as an indicator of the age of the substrate, often provides the only possible solution. Lichens depend for their growth upon the availability of moisture, and Beschel (1961) has summarised the factors affecting and inhibiting growth. The growth curve of a lichen plotted against time is initially sigmoidal, whereas later the curve becomes linear until senescence is reached. However, different environments result in different growth rates so that each area has to be sampled independently. Andrews and Webber (1964) give a table for values of the diameter of *Rhizocarpon geographicum* for different areas. During the linear phase of growth, the length of which varies with the species, the maximum diameter at any site may be considered directly proportional to the age of the site. Growth itself results in no annual structures and the growth rate is the average of the diameter increase of the lichen thallus with time. Sampling involves the recording of the maximum lichen diameters of several different species within an area circumscribed by a circle of 10 m radius. With repeated sampling it was found that the ratio of one species to another was constant and this could be used to extend growth rates from the early lichen colonisers to later and slower growing species. This information provides a relative chronology, but the establishment of an absolute chronology depends on the information available for the construction of a growth curve. In the Alps Beschel was able to use gravestones of different ages to fix the points on the growth rate curves, but in remote arctic areas recourse has to be made to photographic records. Though not as accurate as dendro-chronology, the method of lichenometry does offer considerable possibilities for dating glacial retreat, in particular in areas where it is the only available dating method.

REFERENCES

ANDEL, T. H. van 1959. Reflections on the interpretation of heavy mineral analyses. *Journ. Sed. Petrol.* 29, 153-163.

ANDREWS, J. T. and SIM, V. W. 1964. Examination of the carbonate content of drift in the area of Foxe Basin, N. W. T. *Geog. Bull.* 21, 44-53.

ANDREWS, J. T. and WEBBER, P. J. 1964. A lichenometrical study of the north-western margin of the Barnes Ice Cap: a geomorphological technique. *Geog. Bull.* 22, 80-104.

BAAK, J. A. 1936. *Regional petrology of the southern North Sea.*

BEAL, M. A. and SHEPARD, F. P. 1956. A use of roundness to determine depositional environments. *Journ. Sed. Petrol.* 26, 49-60.

BERTOIS, L. 1952. Abaques pour le calcul des indices des galets. *Rev. Geomorph. Dynam.* 3, 199-205.

BESCHEL, R. E. 1961. Dating rock surfaces by lichen growth and its application to glaciology and physiography (Lichenometry). *Geology of the Arctic* ed. G. O. Rasch, 1044-1062.

BIEDERMAN, E. W. 1962. Distinction of shoreline environments in New Jersey. *Journ. Sed. Petrol.* 32, 181-200.

BLENK, M. 1960. Ein Beitrag zur morphometrischen Schotteranalyse. *Zeit. für Geomorph.* N.F. 4, 202-242.

BRADLEY, J. S. 1957. Differences of marine and subaerial sedimentary environments by volume percentage of heavy minerals, Mustang Island, Texas. *Journ. Sed. Petrol.* 27, 116-125.

BULL, W. B. 1962. Relation of textural (CM) patterns to depositional environment of alluvial fan deposits. *Journ. Sed. Petrol.* 32, 211-216.

CAILLEUX, A. 1945. Distinction des galets marines et fluviatiles. *Bull. Soc. Geol. France* 5 XV, 375-404.

DREIMANIS, A. 1962. Quantitative gasometric determination of calcite and dolomite by using Chittick apparatus. *Journ. Sed. Petrol.* 32, 520-529.

EMERY, K. O. 1938. Rapid method of mechanical analysis of sands. *Journ. Sed. Petrol.* 8, 105-111.

FOLK, R. L. and WARD, W. C. 1957. Brazos River Bar: a study in the significance of grain size parameters. *Journ. Sed. Petrol.* 27, 3-26.

FRIEDMAN, G. M. 1961. Distinction between dune, beach and river sand from textural characteristics. *Journ. Sed. Petrol.* 31, 514-529.

FULLER, A. O. 1962. Systematic fractionation of sand in the shallow marine and beach environment off the South African coast. *Journ. Sed. Petrol.* 32, 602-606.

GODWIN, H., WALKER, D. and WILLIS, E. H. 1957. Radiocarbon dating and post-glacial vegetation history. Scaleby Moss. *Proc. Roy. Soc.* B, 147, 353-366.

GODWIN, H. 1960. Radio-carbon dating and Quaternary history in Britain. *Proc. Roy. Soc.* B, 153, 287-320.

GODWIN, H. 1962. Radio-carbon dating. *Nature* 195 (4845), 943-945.

GUILCHER, A. and KING, C. A. M. 1961. Spits, tombolos and tidal marshes in Connemara and West Kerry, Ireland. *Proc. Roy. Irish Acad.* 61 B, 17, 283-338.

HARRIS, S. A. 1959. The mechanical composition of some intertidal sands *Journ. Sed. Petrol.* 29, 414-424.

INMAN, D. L. 1952. Measures for describing the size distribution of sediments. *Journ. Sed. Petrol.* 22, 125-145.

KAISER, R. F. 1962. Composition and origin of glacial till, Mexico and Kosoag Quadrangles, New York. *Journ. Sed. Petrol.* 32, 502-513.

KUENEN, P. H. 1963. Pivotability studies of sand in a shape-sorter, in *Development in Sedimentology*, vol. I, ed. van Straaten, 207-215.

LAPINSKY, W. J., REVELL, R. S. and WINTERS, S. S. 1958. Sedimentary analysis of terrace deposits in Panhandle, Florida. *Journ. Sed. Petrol.* 28, 75-82.

MCCAMMON, R. B. 1962. Efficiencies of percentile measures for describing the mean size and sorting of sedimentary particles. *Journ. Geol.* 70, 453-465.

MASON, C. C. and FOLK, R. L. 1958. Differences of beach, dune and aeolian flat environments by size analysis. Mustang Island, Texas. *Journ. Sed. Petrol.* 28, 211-226.

NOSSIN, J. J. 1959. Geomorphological aspects of the Pisuerga drainage area in the Cantabrian Mountains. *Leidse. Geol. Medelingen.* 24, 283-406.

POOLE, D. M. 1957. Size analysis of sand by a sedimentation technique. *Journ. Sed. Petrol.* 27, 460-468.

POOLE, D. M. 1958. Heavy mineral variation in San Antonia and Mesquita Bays of the central Texas coast. *Journ. Sed. Petrol.* 28, 65-74.

SHEPARD, F. P. and YOUNG, R. 1961. Distinguishing between beach and dune sands. *Journ. Sed. Petrol.* 31, 196-214.

SIMONETT, D. S. 1950. On the grading of dune sand near Castlereagh, N.S.W. *Journ. and Proc. Roy. Soc. N.S.W.* 84, 71-79.

STERNBERG, R. W. and CREAGER, J. S. 1961. Comparative efficiencies of size analysis by hydrometer and pipette methods. *Journ. Sed. Petrol.* 31, 96-100.

TONNARD, V. 1963. Critères de sensibilité appliqués aux indices de formes des grains de sable, in *Developments in Sedimentology* vol. I, ed. van Straaten, 410-416.

TRASK, P. D. 1952. Sources of beach sands at Santa Barbara, California, as indicated by mineral grain studies. B.E.B. *Tech. Memo.* 28, Washington.

TRICART, J. and SCHAEFFER, R. L'indice d'émoussé des galets. Moyen d'étude des systèmes d'érosion. *Rev. de Geomorph. Dyn.* 1, 151-179.

WADELL, H. 1935. Volume, shape and roundness of quartz particles. *Journ. Geol.* 43, 250-280.

WASKOM, J. D. 1958. Roundness as an indicator of environment along the coast of Panhandle Florida. *Journ. Sed. Petrol.* 28, 351-360.

WATERS, R. S. 1960. The bearing of superficial deposits on the age and origin of the Upland Plain of east Devon, west Dorset and south Somerset. *Inst. Brit. Geog.* 28, 89-97.

WRIGHT, A. E. 1957. Three dimensional shape analysis of fine-grained sediments. *Journ. Sed. Petrol.* 27, 306-312.

7   *STATISTICAL ANALYSIS*

In this chapter some of the ways in which the methods of statistical analysis can be applied to geomorphological problems will be mentioned. Some of the methods that have already been discussed are occasionally referred to loosely as statistical techniques, although they are not strictly statistical in character, for example the plotting of altimetric and hypsographic curves. Some of the statistical methods have, however, already been referred to in other connections, for example in the discussion dealing with the analysis of size distribution in sediment. The concept of the mean, median and mode, as a measure of central tendency, is frequently used in statistics to describe the character of a sample, and the use of the standard deviation in describing the sorting co-efficient is again normal statistical practice. The meaning of these terms has, therefore, already been given in this geomorphological context. The mean and standard deviation were also mentioned in connection with altimetric analysis. In this instance the standard deviation could give some indication of the variability of the heights; this variability is partly the result of subsequent dissection and, therefore, in some measure, the standard deviation is a reflection of this factor in the landscape. In describing sediment size the value of the standard deviation and other statistical methods used for this purpose help to assess the processes operating to give the sediment its characteristics, as has already been discussed in the last chapter. This illustrates, however, how statistical methods of analysis may help to understand more fully the genesis of certain landforms in terms of the processes which give them their specific characteristics.

In attempting to put geomorphological research on to a sounder basis various other statistical methods have been used by different workers. The use of such techniques depends upon the quantitative approach to the various problems that can be analysed in this way, because statistics can best be applied where numerical data are available. The statistical method in geomorphology is rarely the main feature of a study, but it is one of the means by which the final goal of a complete understanding of the processes involved in the production of the landforms under consideration can often best be approached. Thus relationships may be established by statistical means, but until the factors on which the relationships depend have been fully elucidated the problem cannot be said to be solved. Nevertheless statistical methods can often establish relationships which were not previously considered as valid, and this may be an important stage in the formulation of a satisfactory theory, while statistical testing may well help to prove the validity of the theory once it has been set up. Thus statistics play an important part, both in the establishment of relationships and in the testing of hypotheses. They are the means of analysis and not its end.

Probability plays a large part in statistical analysis, and this method of approach is relevant to several geomorphological problems; for example, the probable frequency of occurrence of the bank-full stage of a river, or the probability of occurrence of a storm surge of a particular height, can be calculated statistically. Even if the events predicted are very rare, geological time is long, and there is a strong likelihood that the statistical frequency of occurrence of any event over the long period of geological time will be reasonably accurate. This aspect has already been mentioned briefly in chapter 3 in discussing fluvial processes.

The three main aspects of statistical analysis that are relevant to geomorphology are, firstly, sampling and the testing of the validity of the sample against an assumed hypothesis; for example, the hypothesis that the sample is significantly representative of the population from which it is derived may be set up and tested. Secondly, testing for significance of the data collected is important, the hypothesis may be set up that the data are random and do not show any significant trend, tests may then be applied to accept or reject the hypothesis. Correlation between variables is the third method by which statistical analysis can be used to bring more precision into geomorphological studies. These methods all help with the ultimate aim of geomorphological interpretation.

I. SAMPLING

It is frequently necessary to collect samples for analysis; these may consist of sediment samples from different environments, samples of hill-side slopes or many other features. Strahler (1954) has discussed the problems and methods of geomorphological sampling, and he has pointed out that although there is a generic similarity between sets of geomorphological features, each one is an individual example and rarely are two exactly similar. It is useful, therefore, to be able to assess the degree of homogeneity of a sample and to show whether it is representative of the group of which it is an example. The sample can then be used as a basis for examining the processes operating on it and the population of which it is representative.

In some geomorphological features, such as drumlins for example, the form of the feature is diagnostic of its character, and it has already been shown that subtle differences in the form of individual drumlins may have important bearing on the processes within the ice mass that was forming them. The small variations are significant in this instance, although there is a general limit of dimensions and character that determines whether the feature is a drumlin or not. Thus sampling of the characteristics of drumlins can set the limits of the characteristics of the features within which all drumlins must be found. On the other hand one group of drumlins may differ significantly from another and a study of such divergence may provide useful evidence concerning the processes forming the features.

Another landscape form, dealt with by Strahler, is the hill-side slope. These fall into a rather different category from drumlins as they are not defined generically and are an universal attribute of the subaerial and indeed submarine landscape. In this instance it is necessary to define an area in which the study is to be carried out; this may be defined for example by the outcrop of a certain rock type, or the distribution of a particular vegetation association, or possibly within a region where the stream order is of a particular number. Alternatively, the area chosen for the sampling may be a particular rectangle. It is clearly impossible to measure all the slopes over the whole area, and so an estimate of the slope must be obtained by sampling. This can be done by two methods; samples may be taken at even intervals on a square grid pattern, or they may be taken randomly over the area. Random samples can be located by using a set of random numbers for locating the points by reference to the co-ordinates of a grid over the area. The greater the number of random points chosen, the closer the figures approximate to an even distribution over the area. Once the random points have been chosen on the area to be covered the slope can be measured at these points over a uniform vertical interval.

The results can best be analysed by making a frequency distribution of the data from the sample. The figures for the slope are expressed as the sine of the angle of slope and the numbers within appropriate class boundaries are counted, so that the total gives the total number of items in the sample, which may be 100 for ease of calculation, the results being directly in percentage values. These figures provide the data on which the statistical analysis can be based. From the data the modal class can be readily identified as that in which the frequency is highest, but the more significant arithmetic mean can be easily obtained by summing the values and dividing by the number in the sample.

It is important in a study of this type that the sample be identified with the whole population, which in this instance is all the slopes in the area, so that the validity of the sample as a true sample of these slopes must be established. It is also necessary to establish the variability within the sample, and this can be done by calculating the standard deviation; this is the square root of the sum of the squares of the deviation of each slope from the sample mean slope, divided by the number in the sample. The square of the standard deviation is called the variance. It is often not possible to obtain more than a limited number of observations in the field, so that it is important that the characteristics of these should be assessed statistically.

It is required to test the validity of the sample against the character of the whole population from which the sample was derived, and this can be done by statistical formulae that relate the sample mean and standard deviation to those of the whole population. The standard deviation of the sample is denoted by σ and this will tend to be smaller than the standard deviation of the whole population, which is denoted by s. The value of s can be found from

$$s = \sqrt{\Sigma \frac{(x - \bar{x})^2}{N - 1}},$$

᳚re x is the individual value, $\bar{x}$ is the mean of all values of x, and N is the ᳚mber in the sample. This will clearly give a result such that s is greater than σ, but as the size of the sample increases the difference diminishes, which indicates, as we might expect, that a small sample is less accurate than a large one in assessing the total range of slopes or other features. The assessment of the sample means in relation to the sample as a whole is important; it is found that, if a large number of different samples were taken from a population, the means of the individual samples would themselves fall on a normal curve. The mean of the means would coincide with the population mean, but the standard deviation of the means would be very much smaller than that of the population; the curve for the means would be much more peaked than that of the population. This holds even if the population itself is not exactly normally distributed. The estimated standard deviation of the sample means can be obtained by using the formula

$$s_{\bar{x}} = \frac{s}{\sqrt{N}};$$

$s_{\bar{x}}$ is the estimated standard deviation of the means or the standard error of the means, s is the estimated standard deviation of the population and N is the number of variates in the sample. It is possible to calculate the size of the sample that is required to obtain a particular degree of accuracy in the result.

Smith's (1958) work on the slopes of badlands illustrates how this method can be applied to assess whether the values of the degree of slope of two sets of samples are significantly different. The mean angles of the two samples of slopes were 56·07 degrees and 49·53 degrees, with the standard deviations of the samples being respectively 4·75 and 5·67 degrees. The test of significance of the difference between the means that was applied is given by the formula

$$t = \frac{\bar{x}_1 - \bar{x}_2}{S_p \sqrt{1/N_1 + 1/N_2}},$$

where S_p is the pooled estimate of variance, and is the average of the estimated standard deviations, s, of each sample. The result of the test gave a value of $t = 6·82$ and the number of degrees of freedom, which are the total number of observations minus 2, were 151. Using the value of t and the degrees of freedom, that can be considered infinite if the figure exceeds 120, tables can be used to give the probability that this difference of about $5\frac{1}{2}$ degrees could have occurred by chance selection of the slopes measured in each sample. The resulting value of p, the probability, is less than 0·001, meaning that the likelihood that this difference would occur by chance is less than 1 in 1000. The difference may, therefore, be taken as geomorphologically significant and due to some other variable, such as the rock type or vegetation. In this particular instance the rock type was the same in both samples, but their aspect varied, and this was the significant variable.

To take another example of the application of this type of statistical test, Schumm's observations of slopes at Perth Amboy were compared with those made by Strahler. The latter measured a series of slopes in 1948 and the observations of 154 values gave a mean of 49·1 degrees and the standard deviation was 3·6 degrees, Shummm repeated the observations of the same slopes in the badland area in 1952, using the same instruments and methods. His results showed that in a sample of 149 slopes the mean slope was 48·8 degrees and the standard deviation was 3·5 degrees. Statistical tests were applied to ascertain whether the 0·3 degree difference in the means was significant or not by using the same test. The result was as follows:

$$ t = \frac{49 \cdot 1 - 48 \cdot 9}{4 \cdot 64 \ / \ (1/154) - (1/149)} = 0 \cdot 561. $$

In checking with the tables for the value of t, given with the degrees of freedom at 301 or infinity, the probability that this result would occur by chance was nearly 50%, indicating that there is no justification in assuming that the slopes had been weathered back to a lower angle during the period between surveys—an assumption which could have been made if the figures had been taken at their face value and considered to be exactly representative of the landscape at the two dates.

These tests are based on the difference in the values of the variance for the different samples. Some samples have almost identical means, but different variance or standard deviation; this point has already been noted in the last chapter in dealing with the significant difference of parameters used to describe sediment sizes, when the sorting co-efficient, which is the standard deviation, sometimes shows significant variations in different types of sediment. Another example of the use of this method of analysis is the study of slopes on different lithologies. A hundred observations were made of slope steepness in two different formations, one consisting of shale, the other of sandstones and shales interbedded. The shale samples showed a mean value of 31·82 degrees and an estimated standard deviation of 4·42 degrees, the figures for the second formation were a mean value of 33·12 degrees and an estimated standard deviation of the sample of 5·78 degrees. The range of slopes represented was thus greater on the second formation, including sandstone and shale. In order to test the validity of this difference the standard deviations must be treated in the same way as the means. The hypothesis that the variances are equal is set up. A value for F is computed, where F is the ratio of the variances or squared estimated standard deviations of the two samples; thus in the example cited

$$ F = \frac{(5 \cdot 78)^2}{(4 \cdot 42)^2} = 33 \cdot 41 / 19 \cdot 54 = 1 \cdot 71. $$

This value of F may then be checked in tables and it can be shown that the probability of this value occurring by chance is rather less than 1%. The difference between the two figures for the estimated standard deviation is therefore significant and the hypothesis set up is rejected. The reason for the greater variation of slope on the two formations can be sought in the rock type; where shale is the only rock the slopes are much more uniform, whereas on the mixed rock type greater variation in slope character would be expected.

Observations of many natural phenomena have shown that the type of distribution that individuals in a sample frequently show is the so-called normal distribution. This distribution produces a bell-shaped curve on a frequency distribution graph, but a rapid and easy method of testing for normality of distribution is available by graphical means. This is by using arithmetic probability paper, as described in the last chapter, on which a normal cumulative frequency distribution produces a straight line. There are also more rigorous methods of fitting normal curves to statistical data and testing their significance, using the chi-square test; in this way the normality of distribution of a sample can be tested.

Another example of the use of statistics in sampling is the work of Krumbein and Slack (1956) on the sampling of beach environments for the analysis of sediment characteristics, which has already been referred to in connection with field work on beaches. Work of this type can indicate the number of samples necessary to provide a reasonable picture of the sediment characteristics of the area.

There is a relatively simple, non-parametric method of testing whether two samples could belong to the same population; this is called the Kolmogorov-Smirnov statistic. As an example this test is applied to the data on altimetric analysis of the Howgill Fells, carried out by the two different methods of counting closed contours and highest points in grid squares respectively; the data are shown on figure 5.7, p. 241. There is no reason to suppose that the results are normally distributed, so that this non-parametric test, which does not assume normality, is a good one to use. The purpose is to test whether the two methods produce results that could belong statistically to the same cumulative frequency distribution. The hypothesis tested is that the two samples have been drawn from populations having the same cumulative frequency distribution. A graph is given by Miller and Kahn (1962) that can be used to provide a graphic solution. First the maximum difference d_n in the two percentage frequency diagrams is found by working out the cumulative height frequency from the plotted data. This value was found to be 29.5%. The graph is then entered for N, which is given by $n_1 n_2 \,/\, (n_1 + n_2)$, where n_1 and n_2 are the number of observations in each sample, in this instance $n_1 = n_2 = 81$, so that $N = 40.5$. For this value of N the graph gives a figure of 21% at the 95% confidence level, or 25.5 at the 99% confidence level. Both these are less than 29.5%, so there is no reason to consider that the two results could have belonged to the same population; therefore the two methods of working out altimetric frequency curves do not give statistically comparable results.

2. SIGNIFICANCE OF RESULTS

In order to establish the validity of sampling and other techniques in geomorphology it is often necessary to test the significance of the results; this is done on the basis of probability theory, the conclusion being stated in terms that the recorded result is not likely to have occurred by chance, as some previous examples made clear. The probability is given at various confidence levels, such as the 95% level, for example, which implies that the recorded result would be espected to occur 19 out of 20 times, or 99% when the chance that the result is not genuine is only one in 100. This type of testing is necessary to establish whether the results obtained from two different areas could be due to chance differences or whether the results indicate a true difference between the two samples from the different areas.

It has already been determined what are the chances that the sample of each area is a true representative of the population that it was derived from, and then it is necessary to test whether the two samples are significantly different or not. It is easy to see that two sample means are different, but much less easy to assess the significance of their difference unless statistical methods are adopted, such as those already mentioned in connection with sampling and the significance of the differences between samples.

Analysis of the type already mentioned can proceed a stage further by comparing the means of several different samples, rather than just two, which have been considered so far. An example of this type of analysis is discussed by Strahler; the study included the measurement of stream lengths and the relationship between these and the dip of the rocks in the area. Four areas were selected having respectively low dip, medium to low dip, medium, and steep dips, and observations were made both on the dip and the scarp side of the valleys. It might be expected that the dip slope streams would be longer where the dip was low, but scarp slope streams would not be expected to show this relationship. The values for the dip streams for the four classes from low to steep dip were mean values of 0·255, 0·309, 0·301 and 0·129, showing that the steep dip streams had half the value of the low dip ones. The figures for the scarp streams were 0·207, 0·196, 0·229 and 0·217 respectively from low to steep dips. It is required to test whether there is any significant difference between the values of the scarp streams amongst themselves, and similarly of the dip streams. This can be done by testing by analysis of variance. In this example the result is simplified; there is only one variable, the dip of the strata. From the data it is possible to calculate the value of F, where F is the variance of the sample means divided by the average variance within the samples. The results of the calculation show that F for the dip stream observations was 11·24, giving a probability of much less than 0·005. This means that there is less than one chance in 200 of obtaining the results given by chance. The mean differences are, therefore, significant and a geomorphological reason for this difference can then be sought; in this instance it is fairly obvious, but this is not always true. In dealing with the scarp slope streams in the same way, the conclusion was reached that F is such that the probability is well over 0·05, thus the observed differences between the means was most likely due to chance.

Another very useful test can be applied in many examples to ascertain the difference between the observed and expected frequency of any value. This is the chi-square test, which may be stated as

$$\chi^2 = \frac{\Sigma(O - E)^2}{E},$$

where O is the observed value of the variable and E is the expected value. In order to apply the test the expected value must be ascertained, and when this has been done the observed frequencies are compared with the expected on the assumption that they are related to one another. An example of the use of the chi-square test is that of Andrews (1963) on measurements made of the orientation of stones in till. The observations were made by measurement of the direction and dip of the long axis of 50 or more often 100 pebbles in pits dug in the till. They refer to the long or a axis of the pebble when this was at least twice the length of the next longer axis; the average size of the pebbles measured was 25 mm, ranging from 8 to 100 mm. The results were plotted on polar diagrams using a 5-degree scale for each group of orientation measurements, while the dip was shown outwards with vertical pebbles at the centre and horizontal ones at the edge. In applying the chi-square test it was assumed that the expected distribution would be evenly spaced with regard to both the orientation and the dip of the pebbles. Thus 5·5 pebbles would be expected to occur in each 20-degree sector of the circle for 100 pebbles. For the dips it was assumed that the expected frequency dipping up or down was the total number of pebbles less those lying horizontally divided by two, i.e. that an equal number dipped up and down in a 180-degree range at right angles to the mean preferred orientation. The results of the chi-square test on orientation varied from 20 to 156. For the first pit chi-square had a value of 156 and the axis of orientation showed a strong difference from the expected value, which was significant at the 0·1% level. The preferred orientation was shown to be significantly at right angles to the long axis of the moraine from which the sample was dug, and was nearly parallel to the last ice movement. The dip of the pebbles also showed significant trends; 60 of the pebbles dipped up-glacier, and chi-square testing showed that there was a significant difference between the angle of dip of the pebbles and the angle of slope of the surface, this value being significant at the 0·1% level. Other samples taken in the moraine area revealed other significant relationships between the orientation and dip of the particles and relevant variables, such as the slope, the direction of ice movement and the alignment of the long and cross axes of the moraines.

It is important that these relationships should be shown to be statistically valid at a suitable confidence level if the results of the field measurements are going to be used to check the theories formulated to explain the origin of the moraines. The fact that the maximum orientation of the till pebbles on the side adjacent to the ice sheet is up-glacier and at right angles to the moraine crest is consistent with the view that the moraines were formed by squeezing water-soaked ground moraine into basal crevasses behind the ice front or at the ice front, when the till was unfrozen. The results of the statistical analysis give confidence in using the field measurements to support the theoretical arguments.

It is at times useful to be able to assess whether some feature that increases and decreases in size is doing so in a random or a systematic way. An example of the type of problem that can be solved by this method is the variation in thickness of varves. It is required to test the hypothesis that the varves vary in a random way and hence due to a random process. This can be done by the random turning point method. The expected number of turning points which are defined as points immediately preceded and followed by points both of which are higher or lower, is $\frac{2}{3}(n-2)$ and the variance of this value is $\frac{16n-29}{90}$, where n is the number of observations. The 95% confidence limits are found by multiplying the variance by $1\cdot96$. This gives the confidence bands within which the number could occur by random processes. If for example there were 100 observations on a graph of varve measurements, as recorded by J. T. Andrews on a series of varves in north-west Baffin Island, then the expected number of turning points would be $\frac{2}{3}\times98=65\cdot3$, and the variance would be $\frac{100\times16-29}{90}=17\cdot5$. Thus the confidence band for 95% confidence would be $65\cdot3\pm17\cdot5$. Therefore if the recorded value fell within the range 48 to 83 then the result could be random, and only if the observed range was less than 48 or more than 83 would the result be significant at this level. In the example measured in the field the number of turning points was 57; so this suggests a random variation in size.

The sign test provides a very useful non-parametric, rapid method of estimating the significance between two means in paired data. This test can be used in a population whose distribution is not normal, but the results are not so rigorous as those obtained by more exact methods. For each pair the sign of D, where D is the difference between X and Y is listed. If the two populations were equal the plus signs should equal the minus signs, disregarding the values $D=0$. This test should not be applied if n, the number of pairs, is less than 15. The results are found by calculating Z, where $Z=\frac{S-0\cdot5-m}{\sigma}$, where S is the number of plus signs and $m=n\,p=$ number of pairs divided by 2, and $\sigma=\sqrt{n\,p\,q}$, where $p=q=0\cdot5$. Then P can be found from Z, which is the area under the normal curve, and if P is less than $0\cdot05$, then the result can be considered significant, at the 95% confidence level.

The various statistical methods that can be used to test the significance of observations are of great value and give a quantitative method of assessing the probability that any set of results has occurred purely by chance; when this probability is low, then the confidence in the results is high, and they can be assumed to illustrate a genuine physical difference between the observations.

TG L

3. CORRELATION

The methods that have been referred to so far have been concerned with the quality of the samples as representative of the populations from which they were drawn, and the significance of the values indicated by a study of the samples. Another field in which statistics can be of use to geomorphological analysis is in the correlation of two or more variables together and in assessing the degree to which they depend on each other. In this way cause and effect can be studied quantitatively, the cause being the independent variable and the effect being the dependent variable.

The simplest method of dealing with correlations of this type is to plot the two variables against each other on a graph, and if the result shows that the two factors are associated in a straight line relationship then an equation can be fitted to the dots to give the line from which the sum of the squares of the distances of the points is at a minimum; hence the method is often called the least square method of fitting a straight line to the data, and the resulting line is known as a regression line. Sometimes it is quite clear from the graph that the dots are related linearly, but at other times they show a wide scatter and visual inspection of the dots is not adequate to assess their degree of association. It is under these conditions that the statistical method of regression analysis and testing for significance of the results is particularly valuable. The simple method of straight line fitting works well with linear relationships, but if the relation between the two variables is not linear a close correlation by this method of analysis would not be expected to occur. This problem can sometimes be overcome if the relationship is logarithmic, by plotting one of the variables on a logarithmic scale and using these values in the calculation of the regression equations.

There are two stages in the process of calculating a correlation of this type; first, the co-efficient of correlation must be calculated. This value, r, varies from -1 for a perfect negative correlation, in which one of the factors increases as the other decreases, to $+1$ for a perfect positive correlation, in which both factors increase together; while the value zero indicates no correlation at all between the variables. Having calculated the correlation co-efficient it must be decided whether the correlation is significant, and this can be done by reference to tables which give the probability that this particular co-efficient could have occurred by chance for various levels of confidence, such as the 95%, the 99% or 99·9% level. The degree of confidence depends both upon the number of pairs in the sample and on the value of the correlation co-efficient; the co-efficient can be lower if the number of pairs is greater, the table being entered for the number of pairs minus two.

To measure the correlation co-efficient the data are set out in two columns for the X and Y variables, the means, $\bar{X}$ and $\bar{Y}$, of the two sets are found, and two columns are used to list the differences of the members of each set from its mean, giving x and y, so that $x = \bar{X} - X$ and $y = \bar{Y} - Y$. The values for x and y are then squared and summed, and the values are also multiplied to give xy, and the sum of all xy values is found. From these values the correlation co-efficient can then be found by using the formula

$$r = \frac{\Sigma \, x \, y}{\sqrt{\Sigma \, x^2 \, \Sigma \, y^2}}.$$

Having found the degree of correlation it is useful to show this diagrammatically on the graph of the distribution of the variables. This can be done by inserting the regression lines on the graph; there are two lines, one showing the regression of x, the unknown, on y, the known, in the form $x = a \, y + b$, the other the regression of y, the unknown, on x, the known, in the form $y = a' \, x + b'$. The values of a and b and a' and b' can easily be calculated from the data set out to calculate r, the co-efficient of correlation. In some types of problem the two variables are both interdependent and then two regression lines can be inserted on the graph. The size of the angle between the two lines is a measure of the closeness of the correlation; when the angle is very small the correlation is very close.

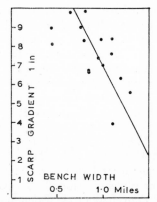

FIGURE 7.1. Correlation of scarp gradient and scarp-foot bench width for the Chalk scarp facing north on the northern edge of the Yorkshire Wolds, overlooking the Vale of Pickering.

In some problems one of the variables is independent of the other and in this type only one regression line is really meaningful; this is the one where the unknown variable is calculated from the known one, which is the one that cannot be affected by the other. An example of this second type may be considered. There appeared to be a relationship between the gradient of the chalk scarp overlooking the Vale of Pickering in Yorkshire and the width of the bench, formed of chalk rubble under periglacial conditions, at its foot. These two variables were, therefore, measured and plotted against each other, as shown in figure 7.1. The gradient of the scarp was measured between the 200-feet and 500-feet contours on the 1 in 25,000 map, and the width of the bench was measured on the geological map. The points for measurement were taken where the 100-feet contour cut each 1-km grid line, thus giving an objective and evenly spaced set of values. There were 16 sets of values and the result of the calculation of r, the co-efficient of correlation, gave

$r=$ 0·775. Checking this value for probability it can be seen that this correlation would be expected to occur less than once in a hundred times by chance; the probability that such a result should occur by chance 1 in 100 times for 16 sets of values is $r=$0·62.

The amount by which the independent variable 'explains' the value of the dependent variable is given by the percentage reduction of the sum of squares in the best fit regression relationship. This value is found by multiplying the square of the correlation co-efficient by 100; so with $r=-0·775$ the percentage reduction would be 60% and thus 60% of the variability of the width of the bench is accounted for by variation in the steepness of the scarp behind it.

Thus there seems to be a genuine negative correlation between the gradient of the scarp and the width of the bench beneath it, where the gradient is expressed as the distance apart of the two contours on the map; thus a smaller value indicates a steeper slope and the steeper slope is associated with a wider bench, giving the negative correlation. In drawing the regression lines on the graph it can be seen that the regression line is $Y=-0·573\,X+8·266$. When the gradient is taken as the unknown or dependent variable, the regression line is almost horizontal. This regression line is clearly not meaningful as the width of the bench cannot affect the gradient of the slope above it. When the other regression line is considered, however, which is $X=-0·105\,Y+1·714$, where the bench width is the dependent variable or unknown value and is calculated from a known value of Y, the gradient, then the regression line gives the best fit line for relating the two factors; the gradient of 1 in 10 is associated with a bench 0·65 miles wide, while a gradient of 1 in 4 is associated with a bench width of 1·3 miles. The relatively large value of the regression co-efficient is due to the larger numerical values for Y than those for X. This means that the range of values for Y covers a much higher proportion of the total range than those for X, which has a much smaller range.

Having established the relationship it is then necessary to consider the reason for it. This may be sought in the relationship between the mass-movement of material and the gradient of the slope, greater movement occurring on a steeper slope. It may also be argued that this relationship is shown to apply to the present gradient of the slope and not to the gradient as it was before the formation of the bench, which is presumably the gradient that affected the formation of the bench. As a correlation has been shown to exist between the gradient and the bench width under present conditions it could be argued that the present gradient must reflect the earlier gradient before the formation of the bench, and hence provide some possible evidence of parallel retreat of the slope.

Other types of problems that correlation and regression equations can be used to study include a wide variety of phenomena. But it must be remembered that even if a close correlation is shown to exist between two variables it does not necessarily mean that they are directly causally connected; both could be dependent on a third variable. The common regression equation can be stated as $y=f(x)$, or y is a function of x, where y is the effect and x is the cause, or *y* is the dependent variable and *x* is the independent variable. In correlating the two factors together their degree of association is shown, but they may both have a common cause and may not be causally related to each other. In many instances it is fairly easy to ascertain which is the dependent variable and which is the independent variable, for example a close correlation can be shown between the size of sand at mid-tide level on the foreshore and the gradient of the beach (see figure 7.2); clearly in this in-

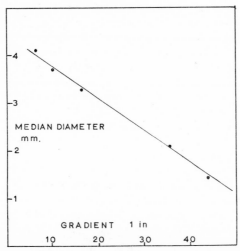

FIGURE 7.2. Correlation of the median diameter of beach sand and beach gradient for beaches in north-west Donegal, Ireland. Regression equations are $X = -14.67\ Y + 65.24$, $Y = -0.068\ X + 4.44$, $r = 0.99867$.

stance it is the size of the sand that determined the beach slope, the coarser sand being associated with the steeper slope because as the sand size increases so its permeability increases and the backwash loses volume relative to the swash and in order to compensate for this the gradient must be increased.

A correlation can also be shown between the sand slope in the swash zone and the length of the waves; in this instance also the length of the waves must be the independent variable and the gradient of the swash slope must depend upon it. For similar reasons to those given above, the volume of the swash relative to the backwash increases as the waves become longer. It is interesting to note that there is a very close correlation between these two variables in model wave tank experiments, where the other factors on which the gradient of the beach depends can be held constant while the wave length is varied. The correlation is almost 1 in this instance. When, however, full-scale prototype values are plotted, as shown for Marsden Bay data in figure 7.3, the scatter is much greater. In fact it appears so great that the validity of the correlation is not immediately apparent, and it is in this type of result that the statistical analysis can help to show whether there is in fact a significant correlation. In the example cited the co-efficient of correlation was found to be −0·56; this value for 40 pairs of observations gives a probability of less than 1 in 100 that this result could occur by chance, or the result is significant at the 99% confidence level.

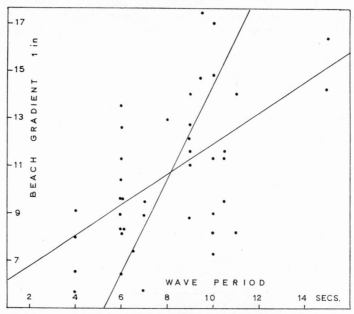

FIGURE 7.3. Correlation of beach gradient and wave period for observations made in Marsden Bay, Co. Durham.

The reason for the greater spread of the results in natural conditions is that other variables, such as wave steepness, which has been shown to influence the beach gradient, could not be controlled as they can in model experiments. Thus the correlation, although shown to be valid, was not so close. Again in this example it is clear that the wave length is the independent variable and the gradient the dependent one.

To take another example, where the causal relationship is not so clear as in those already mentioned, the movement of the position of beach ridges on the Lincolnshire coast can be correlated with time, as shown in figure 7.4. The distance between the seaward face of a sand ridge at an elevation of 7·5 feet O.D. and the fixed datum point for the beach profile was correlated with the time elapsed between successive surveys of the profile. The co-efficient of correlation was found to be 0·9982, which is very highly significant, showing that the landward movement of the ridge was very closely associated with time and is very regular. Clearly it is not time itself which is the causative influence, but some other factor that itself must operate uniformly with time. As the ridges are aligned at a slight angle to the foreshore and the drift of beach material is to the south in the direction of alignment of the ridges, the

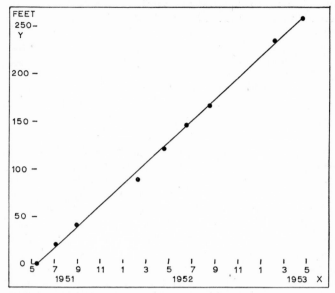

FIGURE 7.4. Correlation of landward movement of beach ridges on the Lincolnshire coast plotted against time.

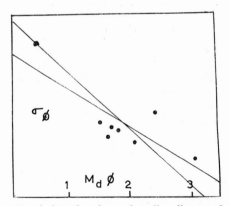

FIGURE 7.5. Correlation of sorting and median diameter for the beach samples from north-west Donegal, Ireland. These results may be compared with those from the offshore zone of south Lincolnshire, shown in figure 6.4.

longshore movement of the ridges causes them to be transferred bodily south-wards; this has the effect of a landward movement on any one profile across the beach. Thus it is the longshore movement of sand that can be inferred to be regular with time and is the real cause of the recorded inland movement of the ridges.

In other instances, however, it is not so easy to assess which is the independent variable. There can be shown to be a close correlation on many beaches between the sorting of the sand and the mean diameter of the sand. The mean and sorting co-efficients were calculated according to Folk and Ward's formula, that has already been discussed. The result of a regression analysis for 9 samples from offshore in Lincolnshire was a highly significant correlation of −0·97, the sorting getting worse as the diameter increased; but as ϕ units were used this is shown as a negative correlation, as the larger particles have the smaller ϕ unit value. Another series of observations, shown in figure 7.5, from beaches in Donegal gave a negative correlation of −0·70 for the same variables, thus accounting for 49% of the variability; both of these values are significant and that for the Lincolnshire beaches is very highly significant. But it is not easy to tell whether the sand size affects the sorting or the other way round; in fact the most likely reason for the relationship is that both variables are affected in the same way by the processes of transport and deposition. The finer particles are selectively moved and deposited together, thus giving both the fine grade and the good sorting. The fine sediment occurred in an environment that was in equilibrium with the forces acting upon it, while the coarser, less well sorted sediment was characteristic of an environment that was undergoing active change and movement.

Another example of correlation that is worth mentioning is from Smith's work on slope measurement in the Badlands of South Dakota. A large number of observations of slope length in feet were plotted against the slope angle in degrees, totalling 134 pairs of observations. When these are plotted the points appear very scattered so that the validity of the correlation is in doubt; however the correlation co-efficient was calculated and found to be 0·485. This seems rather a long way from a perfect correlation of 1, but by testing the significance of the result it can be shown that the result is significant at 0·1% level. This test can be carried out by using the formula for t,

$$t = \frac{r \sqrt{N-m}}{\sqrt{1-r^2}},$$

m is equal to 2, the number of degrees of freedom, the result is $t = 6\cdot4$, which can be looked up in tables for t to give the probability. Thus it may be assumed that the slope angle is associated with an increase in the slope length, but there still remains the problem of accounting for this fact that has been demonstrated statistically.

Not all regression results show that the two variables change together, as work of Schumm has demonstrated. He also worked on slope problems and used statistics to analyse his field results; he fixed 113 rods into the soil along

16 profiles so that they were embedded completely into the straight part of the slope. Then after a period of six weeks the amount of soil eroded during the period of the experiment was measured, and the results varied between 0·4 and 1·6 inches. One of the problems that it was hoped to solve was whether the slope had retreated parallel, had steepened or declined in angle. In order to solve this the depth of erosion must be correlated with the distance down slope. The distance down slope was plotted as a dimensionless figure in the form of the percentage distance from the base to the top of the slope. The results were plotted on a graph, the y axis being the depth of erosion in inches and the x axis the percentage distance along the slope from bottom to top. The regression equation that fitted the points was found to be $Y = 0·92 + 0·00021\ X$, Y being the dependent variable and its value found in terms of X the distance down slope. The regression equation was such that the regression line was almost horizontal, because the regression co-efficient, 0·00021, was very small. The regression would not appear to be significant from the scatter of the dots and the nature of the regression line. The t-test of significance gave a result of 0·80 or 80%, showing that it would be expected that 80 times out of 100 this result could occur through chance alone; thus there is not a significant correlation between the amount of erosion and the distance down slope. The conclusion may be reached from the geomorphological point of view that there is no evidence to suggest that slopes do not retreat parallel to themselves, nor have the hypotheses of decline or steepening been ruled out, but the evidence does not strongly suggest that either type of slope adjustment does in fact occur. Thus although such a test does not provide positive evidence in favour of either view, it does at least provide a definite answer in the negative to the question posed, whether the slope distance influences the degree of erosion. The view that parallel retreat may take place cannot be ruled out.

There are many other possible uses of correlation between two variables, such as Andrews' work on the correlation of moraine numbers with distance, which showed a very high degree of positive correlation. This is another example of the type of correlation where the cause was not apparent, but a second correlation of the number of moraines with the effective stress of the ice showed a good positive correlation also, and the reason for the number of moraines could be associated with the character of the ice-sheet forming them. The significant correlation of sand disturbance depth on beaches with wave height shows clearly a causal relationship, the higher waves being associated with a greater depth of disturbance.

The problems and results of correlation that have been described all referred to two variables, each of which can have a specific value, enabling an accurate regression line and correlation coefficient to be calculated. In some problems the two variables can only be placed in an order of ranking, and not given specific values. For example, mountain summits could be arranged in order of height, even if their precise height is not known, and some attribute of the mountains could also be ranked, such as their position relative to the north or some other significant direction, or their distance from the sea.

This type of information could be of value in an analysis of the slope of a summit surface in a specific direction, but the precise heights and positions would give a spurious idea of accuracy that would not be warranted by the data available. The best method of dealing with this type of correlation is to use Spearman's rank correlation method. The two variables to be correlated are ranked in two columns, the ranks of each variable according to the two criteria being placed alongside each. The difference between the two values is then listed and this difference is squared for each variable and the squared differences are summed. The Spearman rank correlation co-efficient is then given by the formula

$$R = 1 - \frac{6 \Sigma d^2}{n^3 - n},$$

where Σd^2 is the sum of the differences of the ranks squared, and n is the number of pairs in the sample. The co-efficient can vary from $+1$ to -1, indicating both positive and negative correlation, the value o implying no correlation. The significance of the result can be found in the same way and using the t-test table as for other types of correlation tests, but the result is not reliable unless at least 10 pairs of variables are ranked. It has the advantage that it is much more rapid to calculate than the other methods and usually gives a result that is closely comparable.

In problems that deal with a large number of variables, such as Krumbein's study of the Mission beach data, more complex methods of analysis are required, in which many variables are considered by multiple regression analysis methods. In the study of the Mission beach data the variables that were measured included the wave height, the wave period, the angle of approach, the shore current velocity and the co-tangent of the beach slope. The slope was measured at three points along the beach, but preliminary statistical analysis of the data suggested that the variation of slope on the three profiles was not significant, so they were all averaged for subsequent analysis, thus removing one variable from the data. The data were analysed by sequential multiple regression methods.

In this method one dependent variable is studied in terms of the several controlling variables by taking each of these in turn, first one at a time, then two at a time, and finally all together. If two or more of the independent variables are themselves related to each other, then it is redundant to relate both of them in turn to the dependent variable. By multiple regression the effect of two independent variables on the beach slope can be assessed simultaneously. The form of the linear relationship between two variables, such as wave height and period, is in the form

$$S' = a + b\,H + c\,T,$$

where S' is the beach slope, H the wave height and T the wave period, a is the intercept of the y axis and b and c are the linear regression co-efficients. a, b and c change as the different variables are used in the analysis. Up to four or more variables can be analysed simultaneously.

The series of regression analyses carried out consisted of four single variable analyses, six analyses with pairs of variables, four analyses with three variables and one analysis with all four variables, each set being repeated for the five different series of observations with different waves and currents. Such an analysis requires the use of a computer programme for use with a high speed computer.

The results of taking the variables one at a time showed that the noise level, the degree to which the variables interfere with and obscure the effect of each other, was high and the degrees of correlation between the variables and the beach slope were low, although the wave height showed the best correlation. The regression relations on the whole were very weak, showing little correlation between the variables. When the variables were taken two at a time, the pair that gave the best correlation was the pair combining wave height and longshore current velocity. When the variables were taken three at a time the strongest triplet was found to consist of the wave height, angle of approach and the longshore current velocity. The only factor common to the three best correlations was the wave height. When all four independent variables were considered together the resulting correlations for different periods of time showed that the process elements, or independent variables, exerted less effect as their period of action increased. The statistical results showed that only about 63 to 64% of the total variability of the beach was accounted for by the four variables that were used for the analysis. Other factors that could have been taken into account were the tidal variations and the sand size, but errors in the measurement of the variables that were used was probably also important. The problem of the time lag between surveying the profiles and measuring the independent variables also probably accounted for part of the results, as a minimum of 6 hours elapsed between measuring the process elements and the beach profiles. On the other hand, the beach did not respond immediately to changes in wave conditions, and although change was probably most rapid when conditions first changed, it slowed down with time and equilibrium was only reached slowly. It could be shown that it was only the wave conditions of the 24 hours before the beach was surveyed that influenced its gradient. The period of 6 to 12 hours before the survey seemed from the statistical results to be the most significant in accounting for the beach slope. The analysis suggested that wave height was the most important single element in affecting beach slope, when wave period was added to wave height, giving a variable related to wave steepness and energy, the correlation was slightly improved.

Another method of dealing with a number of variables is by multiple correlation analysis; in this method the correlation co-efficient is calculated for each pair of variables, giving in the present examples ten correlation co-efficients. The results were the same, in that the most significant correlation was between beach slope and the wave height. It is interesting to note that wave period was not so strongly correlated with beach slope in the Mission beach data as in the Marsden Bay data already discussed. This may be accounted for perhaps by the fact that relatively few wave conditions were tested for the Mission beach data, so that wave period may not have varied significantly during the observations, whereas the Marsden Bay data covered a wide range of wave periods; but this was the only variable analysed.

Another method of analysis is the trend surface analysis, which can be applied to map data. A variable is treated in terms of its distribution on a map by means of its geographical co-ordinates. The first stage is to prepare a map from field data showing the distribution of any specific variable such as sand size or sorting, by drawing isopleths of equal values of the variable. Then a map of the same variable is constructed using theoretical criteria to calculate the positions of the isopleths for each variable. The observed and theoretical or expected map can then be correlated statistically and the degree of correlation will help to assess the accuracy of the theoretical formulae used to establish the expected isopleths. Miller (1956) and Miller and Zeigler (1958) have applied the method to shore problems and the statistical method of analysis is described by Miller (1956). The method is useful for analysing data that have an areal distribution, such as sediment-size parameters. The trend map from field data can be constructed to give a three-dimensional appearance, the third dimension being used to show the different values of the measured variable. The first step of the analysis is to calculate that plane which has the best fit for the data so that the sum of the squares of the differences is a minimum. The plane is then adjusted to form a surface of best fit by considering the differences between the actual points and the plane; this is the first approximation to the surface of best fit. The values are then further adjusted to give the second approximation of best fit. The method was used to study the shore in the neighbourhood of La Jolla, using observations of sand size and sorting. The preliminary plane showed that size and sorting trend lines were parallel to each other, and at right angles to other variables, such as waves, the axes of the planes being nearly normal to the beach. The curves of the isopleths for the second approximation showed interesting variations, with the sorting being particularly irregular.

The advantage of the method is that it expresses the distributional pattern of the variable used more accurately than simple contouring from the variables especially if the samples are not very frequent in distribution, and local anomalies are eliminated by the construction of the trend surface maps. The correlation of these with the theoretical map carries the analysis a stage further, and is a valuable means of estimating the accuracy of theoretical calculations based on basic physical principles, and of testing such formulae statistically. The methods used are rather complex and require the use of high speed computers, if the problem is large in dimensions and number of observations. The method is still in a fairly early stage of development but should be a very valuable tool in the statistical analysis of complex data on a three-dimensional basis. It also provides a method of relating the effect of two variables simultaneously on any dependent variable. Chorley (1964a) has applied this method to a study of a group of soils in a specific area. The trend surface analysis was applied to two variables of the soil on the Lower Greensand outcrop in east-central England, these were median grain diameter and percentage silt and clay. The outcrop extends over a distance of 50 miles and the aim of the study was one step in the analysis of the reason for the variation in height of the Lower Greensand ridge. The best-fit linear trend surface only accounted for 12% and 22% of the total sums of the squares of the two variables, respectively, and showed an increase of grain size and reduction of silt and clay percentage to the north-west. Using higher levels of generalisation, about 40% of the total sums of the squares could be accounted for. This method is valuable in describing regional soil facies distributions. It also enabled local drift contamination of the soil to be identified and disentangled from the regional trends.

Krumbein (1960) has drawn attention to the types of study that can be dealt with usefully by statistical techniques and he lists five objectives; the first is the estimation of averages from measured data, such as sand size and summit heights. Second is the estimation of the degree of variability, which can also be applied to a study of sediment and altimetric analysis. Third is the degree of correlation between two variables; several examples of the use of this method have been given. Fourth is the study of areal patterns by means of trend analysis, detecting, evaluating and interpreting such patterns of distribution. Last is the detection of significant differences between measurable properties of geomorphological populations. This includes the analysis of variance and the testing for significant differences between average values. Examples of all these methods have been referred to.

REFERENCES

ANDREWS, J. T. 1963. The cross valley moraines of north-central Baffin Island. a quantitative analysis. *Geol. Bull.* 20, 82-129.

CHORLEY, R. J. 1964a. An analysis of the areal distribution of soil facies on the Lower Greensand rocks of east-central England by use of trend surface analysis. *Geol. Mag.* 101, 314-321.

CHORLEY, R. J. 1964b. Geomorphological evaluation of factors controlling shearing resistance of surface rocks in sandstone. *Journ. Geophys. Res.* 69, 1507-1516.

DIXON, W. J. and MASSEY, F. J. 1957. *Introduction to statistical analysis.* McGraw-Hill.

KRUMBEIN, W. C. 1959. The sorting out of geological variables illustrated by regression analysis of factors controlling beach firmness. *Journ. Sed. Petrol.* 29, 575-587.

KRUMBEIN, W. C. 1960. The 'geological population' as a framework for analysing numerical data in geology. *Liv. and Manch. Geol. Journ.* 2, 341-368.

KRUMBEIN, W. C. 1961. The analysis of observational data from natural beaches. B.E.B. *Tech. Memo.* 130. Washington.

KRUMBEIN, W. C. and SLACK, H. A. 1956. Relative efficiency of beach sampling methods. B.E.B. *Tech. Memo.* 90. 43 pp.

MILLER, R. L. 1956. Trend surfaces: their application to analysis and description of environments in sedimentation. *Journ. Geol.* 64, 425-446.

MILLER, R. L. and ZEIGLER, J. M. 1958. A model relating dynamics and sediment pattern in equilibrium in the region of shoaling waves, breaker zone and foreshore. *Journ. Geol.* 66, 417-441.

MILLER, R. L. and KAHN, J. S. 1962. *Statistical analysis in the Geological Sciences.* Wiley, New York.

SCHUMM, S. A. 1956. Evolution of drainage systems and slopes in Badlands at Perth Amboy. New Jersey. *Bull. Geol. Soc. Amer.* 67, 597-646.
SMITH, K. G. 1958. Erosional processes and landforms in Badlands, National Monument, South Dakota, *Bull. Geol. Soc. Amer.* 69, 975-1008.
STRAHLER, A. N. 1950. Equilibrium theory of erosional slopes approached by frequency distribution analysis. *Amer. Journ. Sci.* 248, 673-800.
STRAHLER, A. N. 1954. Statistical analysis in geomorphic research. *Journ. Geol.* 62, 1-25.
STRAHLER, A. N. 1956. Quantitative slope analysis. *Bull. Geol. Soc. Amer.* 67, 571-596.

Geomorphological problems can be approached in many different ways because of the wide variety of landforms to be investigated. The main trend of geomorphological research over the last few decades has been an increase in the quantitative methods of study of all types of problems. An attempt has been made to indicate in table 8.1 the various possible approaches to the study of geomorphology. Four possible methods are suggested. The descriptive approach leading mainly to classification of phenomena on a non-genetic basis may be useful for correlation with other branches of geography. An example is the landform type classification discussed by Wallace (1955), but this method does not lead far in geomorphological interpretation. Some genetic classifications, on the other hand, such as Shepard's classification of coasts, demand a knowledge of the origin of the features classified and cannot be attempted on an empirical basis. This type of classification may only be possible as an end product of a longer and detailed study of the processes, as indicated by the arrow from the response factors in table 8.1

Another possible method of approach is the areal one, or an approach through the study of distribution of phenomena. One or two examples may illustrate the possibilities of this method. Structural patterns, such as that of the mid-oceanic ridges and island arcs, give important clues in the deciphering of world patterns and processes operating to create them. The tetrahedral theory and Vening Meinesz's theory of primaeval convection current cells were both developed out of a recognition of major world patterns of the distribution of land and sea. On a smaller scale the study of drainage patterns can yield important evidence concerning landscape development, particularly when related to structural patterns. The distribution of summit elevations in Scotland, England and Wales was one of the factors that led Linton (1951) to suggest an eastward-flowing original consequent drainage pattern across this area. The distribution of ridge and runnel beaches in relation to tidal and wave conditions and sediment supply again provided important evidence in setting up an hypothesis to account for these features. The study of distribution of individual features may, therefore, provide very useful information concerning the processes responsible for their formation. This approach, therefore, again links with the analysis of processes from the more dynamic point of view, and may be a preliminary stage in this dynamic approach.

The time approach is complementary to the areal approach. Rather than

Table 8.1 (See opposite page)

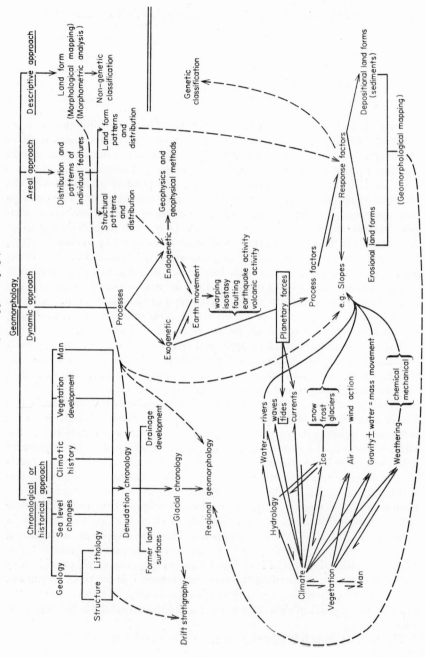

being a preliminary to the dynamic approach and helping in the study of the latter, the time approach is dependent to a considerable extent on the results obtained by the dynamic approach. If the development of the landscape is studied through time, the basis of the study must be an area, so that regional geomorphology can be put in this category, especially when the study is of the denudation chronology of the area. Studies of drift stratigraphy, glacial chronology and recent changes of sea-level all belong to this group, and dating methods can also be included in this category.

Basically the historical approach could be said to include 'structure' in Davis' trilogy, and the time approach also includes the 'stage' element. The remaining element is the essential 'process' factor; this is the dynamic approach, to which so much recent work has been devoted. Processes can be divided into endogenetic and exogenetic forces, the relationship between the two being complex but vital to an understanding of landforms. Penck attempted to relate the two in his study of landforms and their development, and modern work could well pay more attention to this aspect. Some of the landforms most closely dependent on this interconnection are indicated on the table.

In regional chronological studies there have been improvements in the methods of mapping data in the field, such as the development of accurate techniques of morphological mapping. The use of instrumental methods to measure slopes and river profiles and the increasing use of more elaborate methods of studying the deposits of an area have also given greater precision and more reliable results to the analyses of denudation chronology. The detailed study of river terrace deposits has helped to supplement and confirm methods of correlation by altitude of terraces in a valley. On the other hand, there remains the problem of attempting to reconstruct a series of events from inadequate data; when so much of the evidence has been removed by denudation it is inevitable that such studies often cannot come to a definite conclusion, and in some instances the data are so ambiguous that the results are meaningless.

Partly because of the difficulty and uncertainty of the genetic or time approach to regional landscape study, the aim of which often is to establish a

---

TABLE 8.1

The table suggests various possible approaches to the study of geomorphology. The double arrows indicate two factors that interact with each other, the length of each part of the arrow indicating the relative importance of the interaction. The full and dashed lines with arrows indicate various possible approaches to different problems, the dashed indicating a connection between the main approaches.

For example, slopes can be studied by the dynamic approach, by measuring the operative processes and their effect; these are the process factors that are shown on the left and related to the factors of climate and vegetation, etc. which affect them. Slopes can also be studied via the descriptive approach of morphological mapping, while their study can in turn assist in the study of regional geomorphology, as indicated by the dashed line leading from response factors, of which slopes are an example, to regional geomorphology. A genetic classification of slopes could be devised via the response factors, and a nongenetic one via the descriptive approach. A theoretical approach, using slope models and based on assumed effects of process factors, is also possible.

denudation chronology for the area, another method of regional geomorphology has been developed, belonging to the areal method of approach. This morphometric approach is an objective method of establishing fundamental empirical relationships between various attributes of the landscape, usually based on a drainage basin. By this method stream order can be related to stream length, or the slope of the hill-side can be related to the gradient of the stream. This type of analysis is one stage in the development of a theory of landscape development; by itself it cannot explain the significance of the relationships that are set up. However, by showing that the features are related to each other in a systematic way the problem of finding out what does cause the relationship is at least clearly stated. This provides the necessary foundation for the next stage, which is to explore the reason for the relationships set up by morphometric analysis.

A great deal of modern geomorphology is based on the dynamic approach, studying the operation of processes, and many of the techniques that have been developed are used for this purpose. Process was one of Davis' three criteria of landscape development and was the least studied in his time, but is being more and more deeply studied by increasingly complex methods. The steps in the study of process in geomorphology are firstly, the description of the characteristics of the features formed by the process and the study of the actual process in operation; secondly, this should lead to an understanding of the process and its effect on the landscape in terms of landform development, which in turn leads to the third step, that of predicting the effects of the process in the future; finally it may be possible to control the process.

An example of the way in which such a study might be carried out can be considered. A particular coast is suffering from erosion. The nature of the erosion can be studied in the field and from map data or photographic information; this can give the rate of erosion. Then the processes causing erosion can be studied in the field; the waves can be measured, the longshore transport of material can be studied by some of the elaborate techniques that are available for this purpose; changes of sea-level and other relevant factors can be studied, providing a mass of data. This can then be analysed by the statistical methods mentioned and the relationships between significant variables, both dependent and independent, can be set up. The basic physical causes of the relationships can be sought in theory and by model experiments, the results of the field observations can be correlated with the theoretical findings, and the correctness of the latter can be assessed. This will lead to an understanding of the cause of erosion and the factors on which it depends, and the future development of the coast can then be assessed in the light of the results obtained, assuming that the factors on which the development depend will not change. The forecast of future changes should be accurate if it is based on sound observational and theoretical data. Under these circumstances it should be possible to assess the effects of possible controlling measures, both in the immediate vicinity and in adjacent areas. These distant effects have not always been taken into account in the past, with the result that coastal improvements in one area have had an adverse effect elsewhere. An example of this was discussed in connection with the Mersey model study (see pp. 217-221) where the remedial measures in Liverpool Bay were effective, but were shown to have had adverse effects in the upper estuary.

In order to come to sound conclusions when dealing with the very complex problems of natural landscape phenomena, it is necessary to use all the available methods of geomorphological analysis that are relevant to the question. The final analysis should not, however, depend entirely upon the quantitative data, which must be combined with an appreciation of the quality of the problems involved. Quantitative and statistical methods offer no substitute for original thought about the problems, but they do provide a valuable method of guiding the thought and reasoning into profitable channels and in assessing its validity.

In considering the progress of geomorphology a few of the main methods of dealing with geomorphological problems can be summarised. Field methods of investigation have been stressed, as geomorphology is essentially a field science which aims to understand the genesis of a wide variety of landscape forms. In the field, as in other aspects of the study, modern methods are becoming much more quantitative. Equipment for measuring both the static landscape and the operation of processes upon it is becoming more elaborate. For example the use of radio-active and fluorescent tracers for measuring the movement of sand and shingle over the sea-bed is producing more accurate data concerning the important process of longshore movement of material. In other fields of study also elaborate field techniques are being developed; the study of ice movement is carried out with the aid of complex instruments, such as the tools developed to bore holes in glaciers, allowing measurement of movement throughout the thickness of the glacier with inclinometers, and the extraction of cores of ice for subsequent detailed laboratory examination. Accurate field measurements have been made of the mass movement of material under solifluction, with the aid of probes that record this movement. Apparatus is available to study the movement of material in flowing water, whether it be rivers or the sea, and moving sand can be trapped on dunes, while the velocity of the water and wind can be measured in different positions. Even the amount of erosion can be measured in certain localities, such as the badlands where it takes place at a measurable rate. Thus the amount of numerical data concerning the operation of geomorphological processes is increasing very rapidly.

In dealing with all this information, however, it must always be borne in mind that the data can only be partial. The instruments themselves may influence the behaviour of the natural process; sand traps can disturb the flow of the wind that is carrying the sand; the tubes sunk into glaciers have a certain rigidity themselves and may influence the flow in their immediate vicinity, while the presence of a current meter in a river can upset the normal flow. Though the results derived from such measurements must all suffer from this defect to a certain extent, they are nevertheless very much better than no quantitative data.

Another problem must be considered in dealing with quantitative geomorphological data; it is clearly not possible to observe all the phenomena all the time; thus quantitative measurements cover only a very small range of possible conditions, and this must always be taken into account. The example of the study of shingle movement off Orfordness illustrates this point very clearly, see p. 156; it was shown that for the first four weeks of the experiment the shingle moved northwards, which is the opposite direction to the long-term direction of movement, so that there is always the possibility that the observations will not be typical of the phenomenon.

This type of difficulty can be guarded against in obtaining certain field data, for example sediment samples can be collected with careful reference to the methods of statistical sampling. By this means the variability of the environment can be adequately allowed for, but this is rather more difficult where the observations are those of variable processes. Although even in this field it is possible to calculate statistically the probability of the occurrence of any particular value of the phenomenon under consideration. Thus it can be stated, for example, that waves will exceed a given size for some definite percentage of the time, and that the maximum wave is likely to be of a given value and to occur once in a given period of time. This gives the limits within which the particular feature will fall, whether it be wave height, river flood level or some other factor.

It must be remembered that only a minute fraction of geological time can be sampled and there is no guarantee that the rates and characteristics of the action of processes recorded in this period are representative of long-term changes. Some landform processes have a cyclic pattern of operation and the landforms resulting have a cycle of development that may be difficult to recognise from the small time sample available. This is true on a large scale of the cycle of erosion, and on a much shorter time scale of features such as Spurn Head, which G. de Boer has shown to have a cycle of growth and decay lasting about 250 years in the absence of human interference.

Because of the difficulty of controlling and analysing data from natural full-scale observations, scale models have been used to solve some problems. Models are expensive to build and operate and are usually made by organisations rather than individuals. They are often used to solve practical problems, such as specific engineering projects. Nevertheless a great deal of basic geomorphological and physical research has been carried out in models. They are particularly valuable for establishing the basic relationships between the dependent and independent variables, the former being the character of the landscape features and the latter being the processes that operate to shape it. Their main disadvantage is the problem of scale relationships, which have already been considered. The difficulty of maintaining correct scale in all aspects of the model and prototype is readily apparent, but the results of model tests have proved of great value in indicating the best way in which to overcome a particular problem, or at least in demonstrating the cause of the difficulty.

One way in which the problem of scale can be overcome to a certain extent is to make models of different sizes, so that a continuous sequence may be set up. This can be done with rivers, for example, by using small rivers as models of large rivers, and laboratory models then form one end of a sequence of sizes. A similar approach has been made with wave tanks, by building large wave tanks to test the same controlled conditions as those used in smaller tanks. The largest wave tanks that have been designed are over 600 feet long and waves can be generated in them up to 6 feet in height and with the length of natural ocean waves. This type of model is in reality a controlled version of the prototype, as the wave dimensions and other variables are full size and can be directly compared with the natural conditions, while still retaining the controlled conditions that are the major asset of model studies.

Other forms of laboratory work can also help in geomorphological analysis; the detailed study of sediments in the laboratory can yield valuable information for geomorphological analysis, and may require the use of elaborate equipment, for example the electron microscope required for the analysis of silts, although such work is normally carried out by sedimentologists rather than geomorphologists. However, geomorphologists have much to learn from a study of sediment characteristics even if the simpler methods are used to analyse it.

Laboratory methods may also include a study of the nature of the material concerned, such as the study of the physical properties of ice, although again this work is largely carried out by physicists. Other forms of laboratory and field analysis also give valuable data on landscape development, such as the various methods of dating, including pollen analysis, the study of varve clays, tree rings and lichens, and the assessment of age by the more elaborate techniques of fluorine and carbon-14 testing, which require elaborate equipment. Although most geomorphologists cannot be expected to be familiar with the more elaborate of these techniques, they have their place in geomorphological analysis.

The basic theoretical work on the processes of water, ice, wind and gravity in the erosion, transport and deposition of sediment can be facilitated by testing with models, to establish essential constants, and these can then be checked in the field. Such basic work will eventually provide a much sounder foundation for geomorphological analysis. Its use accounts for the inclusion of mathematical formulae in some geomorphological work, because the basic physical laws governing the operation of the processes acting on the landscape can often be best expressed in mathematical terms. Much of the modern geomorphological analysis is based on such mathematical formulae, which can then be tested in model or the field, by experiment and observation, the theoretical model providing the basis for further work. Thus all approaches through theoretical models, scale models and field work are required, and for each stage in an investigation the methods are becoming more elaborate and quantitative.

Increasing use is being made of statistical methods for various stages in the conduct of a geomorphological investigation. In the preliminary stages of the collecting of data, the use of statistical knowledge of sampling techniques is of importance, to ensure that the data sampled are as representative of the whole population of that particular variable as they can be. The use of sampling techniques will ensure that an adequate number of samples is obtained to give a valid representation and also that time is not wasted in obtaining unnecessarily large collections of material. Statistics can also be of use in determining the correlation between two or more variables, but in using this method it must be borne in mind that even if a significant correlation is established between two variables, this does not necessarily imply that the two are directly causally related. The establishment of the relationship by statistical techniques is only the first stage, and a valid physical reason for the relationship must be set up to explain it. This can often be done by experiment or by reference to theoretical results. The method may in fact often proceed the other way, with the theoretical model suggesting that a particular relationship ought to exist and the observation and statistical testing confirming the theoretical results. The use of statistics is also very valuable for testing the significance of data and for analysing the distribution within any particular sample of data. The development of statistical methods for analysing the spread of size distribution in sediment is a good example of the use of these methods of describing sediment and of relating the parameters used, such as sorting and skewness, to the nature of the processes responsible for the transport and deposition of the sediment.

The field of geomorphological study is well defined, but in its methods it makes use of techniques developed by other scientists, and also incorporates the results of other scientists into the geomorphological analysis. The value of the work of the physicist in establishing the basic data concerning the movement of ice, wind and water, and the material that is carried by each moving medium, is greatly appreciated by the geomorphologist, who can apply these basic results to the fuller understanding of the genesis of landscape forms. The work of the geophysicist is of great importance to the geomorphologist, as this throws light on the operation of the endogenetic processes acting within the earth, but whose effects are seen in its external morphology. The isostatic recovery of a land mass, for example, depends on the nature of the crustal rocks, the field of the geophysicist, but the results are visible in the formation of raised beaches and therefore of direct interest to the geomorphologist. The geological study of rock type, stratigraphy, mineralogy and sedimentology are only a few of the relevant fields of geology that interest the geomorphologist. In fact the fields of interest of the geologist and the geomorphologist overlap in many ways, though the aim of the study of each science is rather different. Geomorphologists in America especially belong to geological science in its broad sense. It is, therefore, difficult to separate the two fields of study, and methods used in both fields may be very similar in their region of overlap. Geomorphologists also have much to learn from soil scientists particularly in the study of mass movement and slope formation, the geomorphologist may use the methods and results of the pedologist. In more specialised fields of study the work of the botanist, for example in salt marsh and coastal dune studies or in pollen analysis, can help the geomorphologist. Zoological methods of approach may help in the study of coral islands, and chemical methods of dating and sediment analysis may also be required in some problems. Engineers adopt a practical approach to many of the geomorphological problems that they have to consider; their methods, for example the use of models and their work on river flow and control, have considerable relevance for the geomorphologist.

The wide field of geomorphology and the great variety of problems that geomorphologists study account for the great range of its contacts with other sciences and the many methods of approach and techniques that are used in the attempt to solve its many and intriguing problems.

REFERENCES

BOER, G. de 1964. Spurn Head: its history and evolution. *Inst. Brit. Geog.* 34, 71-89.
SHEPARD, F. P. 1963. *Submarine geology.* 2nd edition. New York.
WALLACE, W. H. 1955. New Zealand landforms. *N.Z.Geog.* 11, 17-27.

INDEX